# MY LIFE IN STALINIST RUSSIA

# MY LIFE IN STALINIST RUSSIA

## AN AMERICAN WOMAN LOOKS BACK

MARY M. LEDER

EDITED BY LAURIE BERNSTEIN,

WITH AN INTRODUCTION BY LAURIE BERNSTEIN

AND ROBERT WEINBERG

**INDIANA UNIVERSITY PRESS**
*Bloomington and Indianapolis*

This book is a publication of

Indiana University Press
601 North Morton Street
Bloomington, IN 47404-3797 USA

http://www.indiana.edu/~iupress

*Telephone orders* 800-842-6796
*Fax orders* 812-855-7931
*Orders by e-mail* iuporder@indiana.edu

The paper used in this publication meets the minimum requirements of American National Standard for Information Sciences—Permanence of Paper for Printed Library Materials, ANSI Z39.48-1984.

Manufactured in the United States of America

**Library of Congress Cataloging-in-Publication Data**

Leder, Mary M.
    My life in Stalinist Russia : an American woman looks back / Mary M. Leder ; edited by Laurie Bernstein ; with an introduction by Laurie Bernstein and Robert Weinberg.
        p.  cm.
    ISBN 0-253-33866-2 (cl : alk. paper) — ISBN 0-253-21442-4 (pa : alk. paper)
    1. Leder, Mary M. 2. Americans—Soviet Union—Biography. 3. Jews—Soviet Union—Biography. 4. Political persecution—Soviet Union. 5. Soviet Union—Politics and government—1936–1953. I. Bernstein, Laurie. II. Title.

DK268.L4 A3 2001
947.084′2′092—dc21
[B]                                                                00-061424

2  3  4  5    06  05  04  03  02  01

To the memory of my friend Dorothy Draper who was among the first to welcome me back to this country; who guided me every step of the way, making my acculturation much easier; who drew my story out of me in long, nightly talks and urged me to write. She missed publication by only a few months.

# CONTENTS

# ACKNOWLEDGMENTS

Over the past fifteen years or so, since I started writing this memoir, many of my friends have read the manuscript at various stages of its development and offered valuable advice and encouragement for which I thank them from the bottom of my heart. I wish to give special thanks to several whose contributions were pivotal in turning the manuscript into a book: Elliot and Morrine Barnett, who after having read the typescript arranged without my knowledge to transfer it to a computer, then presented me with a computer and showed me how to use it, thereby starting me down the road to preparing this memoir for publication; Cerisa Mitchell and Lenore Parker, who were "on call" whenever I needed editorial or technical assistance, as was Eleanore Dinkin, who rescued the manuscript when I had given up on it and whose constant support enabled me to do the work that had to be done; Irene Lowe, who was determined to find a publisher and persisted until she found the right person to help, that person being Robert Weinberg, chairman of the history department at Swarthmore College, who set the ball rolling and who was very generous with his help all along the way.

I was very fortunate to have as my editor Laurie Bernstein. Laurie was a pleasure to work with—understanding, dependable, committed. I could never have done it without her.

And last, but not least, Indiana University Press editor Janet Rabinowitch, who was always accessible and smoothed out the bumps on the road to publication.

Thank you all.

# INTRODUCTION
## LAURIE BERNSTEIN AND ROBERT WEINBERG

ᴄᴏᴏᴏᴏ

At the beginning of 1931, Mary Leder (neé Mackler)[1] was a fifteen-year-old teenager attending high school in Santa Monica, California. By the year's end, she was living in a Moscow commune thousands of miles from her family and learning a trade in a factory. She would spend the next thirty-four years of her life in the Soviet Union, half of them as a dedicated member of the Young Communist League who looked forward to full-fledged membership in the Communist Party. Yet, by the mid-1940s, Mary's loyalty to the USSR would collapse, eroded by the ugly anti-Semitism and xenophobia of postwar Russia. Although the Mary who came to Soviet Russia in 1931 believed in socialism and internationalism, it was a totally disillusioned Mary who finally returned to the United States in 1965.

*My Life in Stalinist Russia* chronicles Mary's experiences from her parents' Depression-era decision to leave the United States for the Soviet Union and her separation from them when she was sixteen, until she returned to America. The narrative focuses primarily on 1931 to 1953, the era when Joseph Stalin wielded supreme power. Through Mary's eyes, we see the Soviet Union during the First Five-Year Plan, Stalin's Great Terror, the German invasion of the USSR and World War II, and the beginning of the Cold War.

Her parents were Jewish left-wing immigrants from Priluki in Ukraine. Her father was a carpenter who frequently moved the family in search of work. She went to "grade school in New Haven, junior high in Albany, and high school in Los Angeles and Santa Monica." Though she was a member of the Young Communist League, when her parents first told her of their intention to move the family to Birobidzhan, the Soviet Union's version of a Jewish socialist homeland, she did not want to go. When they arrived and she discovered Birobidzhan to be a mud-ridden backwater, she insisted on pursuing the socialist dream elsewhere, some five thousand miles west in Moscow, a city to which she had never been, among people who spoke a language she

---

1. Many women in the USSR of Mary's generation retained their maiden name after marriage. In the Soviet Union, Mary was known as Mary Mackler.

did not know, and where her only connection was a step-uncle she had never met. Nevertheless, off she went, leaving behind her family, who apparently shared her father's faith that "nothing bad could happen to you in a socialist country."

Their faith was unwarranted. Her parents would find that the socialist motherland was not what they had expected. They had been willing to bear up under the extreme deprivations and hardships in Birobidzhan; after all, socialism could not be built in a day. Other unexpected obstacles, however, defeated them—corrupt bureaucrats, a system of perquisites for the Party elite, and harassment instead of support for their attempts to set things right. They moved on to Stalingrad, several hundred miles southeast of Moscow, only to find more of the same.

Mary, for her part, survived the train trip to Moscow and found her way to the headquarters of the Communist youth organization, the Komsomol. There, someone assigned her to a bed in a young people's "commune" (really a small apartment with shared expenses, whose other residents had also been placed there by the Komsomol) and to an apprenticeship in a Moscow factory that made engine parts for trolley cars. On her own at sixteen, she struggled to learn Russian and master a trade. At the same time, she found romance and experienced the thrill of being in Moscow at the dawn of Soviet socialism.

In 1933, after their disastrous stint in Stalingrad, her parents decided to return to the United States. But Mary, who had been delighted by the prospect of going home with her family, could not accompany them. Having applied for Soviet citizenship in order to keep her job, she was denied an exit visa to leave when they did. The rest of her family was forced to leave Mary behind, denied even an eleventh-hour bid to extend their visa.

Left entirely on her own, she made the best of a bad situation and assumed—incorrectly as things turned out—that she would at least be able to *visit* her family in the United States. Meanwhile, Mary realized that she was not cut out for manual labor and asked for a new job. This time, she was sent to the Foreign Languages Publishing House, an organization that published Marxist classics in various languages. Her job was reading English-language copy for both editors and proofreaders, most of whom were also foreigners who had come to the Soviet Union to help build socialism. Because Mary was so young and alone, several of her fellow workers essentially adopted her. She made lifelong friends there and maintained her ties with the publishing house throughout her stay in the Soviet Union, even when she pursued other goals: studying at Moscow University, training at the Commissariat of Defense during the Terror of the late 1930s, and working at TASS, the Soviet news bureau. It was at the publishing house that she met her future husband, Abram Leder, a Jew from Rostov-on-the-Don and fellow Komsomol member.

As was true for all citizens of the Soviet Union, the Second World War was a defining experience for Mary. Separated from her husband by the war, Mary gave birth to a daughter named Victoria in honor of the Soviet Union's anticipated victory. Tragically, her baby died when they were evacuated to a remote city as the German army came within a hundred miles of Moscow. A bereft Mary spent the rest of the war years back in Moscow, where she worked as a translator for TASS while Abram remained at the front.

In 1944, she suffered a shock: rejection of her application for membership in the Communist Party. When a Party bureaucrat assured her that her rejection had nothing to do with her being Jewish (an idea that had never occurred to her!), she wondered whether the Soviet Union was living up to its professed commitment to socialist internationalism. Other doubts crept in. Why, in 1944, had all the Moscow University graduates with Jewish surnames been denied admission to graduate school? Why were Jews being denied access to high-level jobs? Adding to her suspicions were Stalin's words upon the Soviet Union's victory in the war when, instead of praising the efforts of *all* Soviet citizens, he singled out only those of *Russian* nationality. And he remained silent about the Nazis' slaughter of the Jews.

In 1946, Mary was allowed to join her husband, who was stationed in Berlin. There, she had a welcome taste of Western culture. But in 1947, as the Cold War heated up, Abram was abruptly decommissioned and told to return to Moscow. Mary considered defecting, but she could not bring herself to turn Abram into someone who would be perceived as a traitor. So they returned to Moscow, only to face new horrors: strident anti-Americanism and increasing anti-Semitic policies thinly veiled as a campaign against "rootless cosmopolitanism." It was at this time that Mary's doubts about Soviet socialism turned into full-blown disillusionment. Dropped from graduate studies, she was left to watch as Abram, branded as the husband of a Cold War enemy, unsuccessfully tried to find work for an entire year. More ominously, a wave of arrests began that hit much closer to home than the purges of the 1930s ever had. Mary even learned from a close friend that the secret police had her under surveillance.

During the next five years, she was in constant danger of being arrested. As a result, she withdrew from most of her friendships and retreated into the cocoon of her marriage. In 1949, the publishing house, where she had again been working since their recall from Berlin, fired her, fearful of having an American on board. She was able to do freelance editing for TASS, but Abram could only find a job far beneath his qualifications. He fell ill in 1956, three years after Stalin's death. Mary nursed him until he died in 1959 and then began her fight to return to the United States. She had lived in the Soviet Union for nearly thirty years, yet she "felt more than ever a stranger in the land. Truly, a rootless cosmopolitan!" Only in 1961, and only because of the intervention of the veteran Bolshevik Elena Stasova, did Mary receive permission to visit her family again. Not until 1965 was she able to return for good.

* * *

We are extremely fortunate to have access to this autobiography, for Mary Leder's story is a microcosm of Soviet history and a window into everyday life, culture, and politics in the Soviet Union. It grants us the rare perspective of someone who was very much on the inside of Stalinist Russia, yet who retained the point of view of an American. Much to her dismay, Mary found that no matter how long she lived and worked among Russians, they always regarded her as an outsider, because of both her Jewish heritage and American background. Her sense of being "once a foreigner, always a foreigner in Russia" enabled Mary to maintain, often to her dismay, a unique distance. Although she lived as a Soviet citizen and subscribed to the standard Communist Party line, Mary nevertheless brought with her the civics lessons from her grade school years in the United States and her father's advice that "the most important thing was to live an honest, decent life."

*My Life in Stalinist Russia* provides a counterpoint to the tragic history of Stalin's Russia. Readers will find themselves drawn into the life of a young woman coming of age in a society that she believed was on the verge of achieving justice for all. Mary's ideological commitment (some would say blinders) may strike some readers as difficult to understand. But Mary was not alone in her faith in the Soviet Union as the beacon of freedom, justice, and progress in the 1930s. Similarly, Mary was not alone in her disappointment and disillusionment as the dreams of 1917 turned into a nightmare. Mary Leder's life, while certainly extraordinary, parallels the journey of many Americans whose commitment to socialism and left-wing politics was reversed as Soviet realities came to light. We have much to learn from their experiences, just as we have much to learn from their dreams of a better world.

☙☙☙

# MY LIFE IN STALINIST RUSSIA

# PROLOGUE

❧

"You will not be allowed to leave this country, no matter how many times you try."

The colonel from the Soviet Ministry of Internal Affairs did not look up at me as he spoke.

With difficulty, I had obtained an appointment to see the head of the department of visas and registration (OVIR) in Moscow. On that day in 1960, I had come to appeal their refusal to let me visit my parents in the United States. My husband had died and I had made up my mind to do everything in my power to return to the land where I was born.

"Why not?" I asked. "What are your reasons?" I stood in front of his desk, not having been asked to be seated.

"We don't have to give you an explanation," he replied. "It is not in our interests to let you go. There is nothing to discuss," he said, dismissing me.

But I was not ready to leave. "Since you will not tell me your reasons and I cannot judge for myself whether they are valid, I will continue to fight, even if I end up going east rather than west."

I had not really expected an explanation. I was merely going through the motions. According to regulations, I could apply again in six months, though I would probably be refused. After that, I could apply again and again, hoping for some twist or turn, a swing of the pendulum. Since the Soviet Union was not ruled by law, anything might happen.

The colonel shrugged. I turned and left the room.

Although I was not surprised, I was bitterly disappointed. This was a period of comparative liberalization known as the "thaw," following Nikita Khrushchev's denunciation of Stalin in 1956. Several of my acquaintances had been permitted to visit family in the United States. A woman I knew had gone in January 1956 and had brought back much-needed medication for my husband, who was already ill with the disease that killed him three years later. I, too, had wanted to apply in 1955, when she did. My husband had not yet fallen ill, but he was afraid to let me go, were I granted permission, and even more afraid that I would get into trouble just for applying. He did not trust the thaw—the machinery for oppression was still in place.

But after his death I had nothing to lose.

This was not my first application for an exit visa since my family had returned to the United States in 1933 after a brief stay in the Soviet Union. I had been left behind. The first two applications, in 1934 and 1935, had not been answered and I stopped applying; the purges had begun then and it had become dangerous even to admit one wanted to go abroad.

I had no family in the Soviet Union. Our only child had died during the war. I had many dear friends whom I would miss if I left. I would probably never see them again, but in my mind I had made the choice—to get out of the country which I had come to hate with every fiber of my being.

Six months later, after I had applied again and was refused again, a friend offered to speak to someone she knew who had been high up in the Communist Party hierarchy and who might be able to help me.

Elena Dmitrievna Stasova came from an illustrious and wealthy family. Stasova, like many young people from the upper classes in tsarist Russia, had joined the revolutionary movement. She had become a member of the Russian Social-Democratic Labor Party when it was founded in 1898, and then had been part of its Bolshevik faction led by Lenin in 1903. She had worked closely with Lenin until his death and was a staunch supporter of Stalin in the ensuing power struggle. Though she had not held a position of power for many years, she still had contacts and was known to have helped victims of the Stalinist Terror. My friend had worked for the magazine *International Literature* from 1937 until 1938, when Stasova was editor-in-chief, and had stayed in touch with her.

Stasova agreed to see me.

The meeting was brief. She already knew my story from my friend. My request was for a visit to the United States and she asked me if I planned to return to Moscow. Yes, I did. She did not promise me anything, but said she would make inquiries. She sent my papers to the appropriate authorities and asked that she be informed about the results. In about a month, I received a notice from OVIR telling me what documents to bring for an exit visa. At OVIR I was issued a passport for travel abroad and was instructed to take it to the American embassy, where I would apply for a visitor's visa for entry into the United States. When I had it, I was to come back for the Soviet exit visa.

I spent six months in the United States in 1961; then, reluctantly, I returned to the USSR. As I told a friend of my parents, I felt as if I had escaped from a cage and now was going back into it, letting the gate slam behind me. Among the several reasons why I went back, the most important was that I did not want to let down the friend who had vouched for me to Stasova. Stasova died two years later at the age of ninety. I applied again for a visitor's visa in 1963, but was refused. Then there was a sudden change of policy and in 1964, I was granted an exit visa.

This time the U.S. Department of State took a very long time processing my papers. My Soviet permission, good for six months, had almost expired when I got an excited call from one of the secretaries at the consulate. I must come right over right away, she said, for the consul himself wished to speak with me. She would not tell me over the phone whether the entry visa had come through.

The American consul met me with words I shall never forget.

"We have determined that you never lost your American citizenship and we have issued you an American passport." I was speechless. "My secretary will stamp our visa in your Soviet passport. You will present it at OVIR, where they will enter the exit visa. After that you will come back here and get your American passport."

The reason for this turn of events was that I had been a minor when I was taken to the Soviet Union. Now, my parents had applied for a permanent residence visa for me, and this had, apparently, prompted a more thorough investigation.

The secretary had my papers ready. It was a Wednesday afternoon. OVIR did not receive Soviet citizens on Thursdays. I said I would go to OVIR on Friday.

"No, no!" the women in the office cried. "You can still make it today! We'll call a cab for you."

To this day I am convinced that the women, who were Soviet employees, wanted me to get to OVIR before they were obliged to report to their KGB handlers that I had been issued an American passport.

I walked out of the American embassy later that week with the American passport in my pocket. I looked around. It was as if I had a new pair of eyes. The familiar sights—the too-wide Sadovaya Kudrinka, where the embassy was, the tall Ministry of Foreign Affairs building a few blocks away, the grim-faced passersby hurrying as usual—were no longer part of my life.

"You think I am one of you!" I exulted to myself. "I'm not. I'm an American. I'm going home and I'll never come back!"

When I left Moscow, I presented my Soviet passport. My American passport was in a concealed pocket of my skirt. Only two of the many friends who had come to see me off knew that this time I would not return. They were very nervous as the female customs official searched my handbag. None of the other passengers was searched. The official removed twenty dollars which I had brought back from my previous U.S. visit, although I had papers for it, and instructed me to call over a friend and give the money to her. I was able to tell my friend that all was well. (She later wrote to me that they had not seen me board the plane and were very worried until I telephoned them from Paris that evening.) I deplaned in Paris and walked right through with the American passport. I arrived in New York in January 1965.

Though I have now lived in the United States longer than in the Soviet Union, the thirty-four years I spent there—my entire young adulthood—were the most significant years of my life, as was the historical period I was compelled to live through. Hence my story.

# 1

## My Family Leaves for the Soviet Union—1931

The Depression hit our family early.

My father, a carpenter, built houses for a living. A slowdown in the building trades was an early signal of worsening conditions despite outward signs of prosperity. Long before the stock market crash in October 1929, he was having difficulty selling the houses he built. By the beginning of 1929, he was heavily in debt to the bank and had several unsold houses on his hands (we lived in one). He tried to support our family of five by doing odd jobs.

We lived in Albany, New York.

Several families from my parents' circle of friends had left Albany for California a few years before. They wrote that life was easier there and that jobs were more available. In the summer of 1929, my father traded in his old Chevy, made a down payment on a new one, and we set out for Los Angeles. I was fourteen, my sister was ten, and my brother was five.

Our route took us to Niagara Falls; to Chicago, where my mother's older brother and his family lived; to St. Louis, where we visited the zoo, one of the largest in America at the time; to Santa Fe and Albuquerque, which were still adobe villages then; to the Grand Canyon; the Painted Desert; the Petrified Forest; and many other wonderful places. We kept expenses down. Cabins with showers and cooking facilities cost one dollar a night. Most of the time we bought groceries along the way and my mother cooked our meals. Roads were not what they are today and some of the going was rough. Somewhere in Arizona, our car was pulled out of the mud by Indians in full regalia who, incidentally, refused any payment. The trip took three weeks. We arrived in California at the beginning of September.

Those days on the road were probably the most carefree weeks in my parents' lives. However, though it may have been easier to live in California, with its mild climate and no need for heavy clothing or winter fuel, jobs were just as scarce. My father barely made a living driving a doughnut delivery truck.

Two years later, we pulled up our stakes again and set sail for the Soviet Union, where it was said there was no unemployment and the workers ruled the land.

This most drastic decision of our lives, which ultimately broke up our family and left me stranded in Moscow at the age of eighteen, was taken almost lightly. Or so it seemed to me, for I had not heard any discussion about these plans. For my parents, however, that decision was not as impetuous as it might have seemed.

My father was born in 1886 in Priluki, a small town in the Ukrainian part of the Russian Empire. His family had a cow, and so were not among the poorest in town, yet he was taken out of school when he was ten years old after five years of *cheder* (traditional Jewish elementary school). At that point, he was apprenticed to a carpenter. Whatever book learning he acquired subsequently came through his reading in Yiddish and in Russian and, later, in English in night school in America. My mother, four years younger, had also been born in Priluki. Her father died when she was very young and her mother remarried a "scholar" widower who studied the Torah all day long and never earned a living. She was twelve years old when she went to work, wrapping candy at a factory. Working at so young an age was illegal, so when an inspector came around, her co-workers would hide her under their long skirts. The little schooling she received was in Yiddish, but she taught herself Russian and took an interest in the banned literature her older brother brought into the house. Her brother and my father were members of the local chapter of the Jewish Social-Democratic Party, known as the Bund.[1]

My father came to the United States in 1907. He was part of the wave of Jews emigrating to escape the repression and pogroms that followed Russia's defeat in the war against Japan and the failed revolution of 1905. He brought with him vague ideas about socialism and strong feelings about social justice and secular Jewishness—language, literature, and tradition. He joined his older brother, also a carpenter, who had settled in Albany the year before. My mother's older brother emigrated at about the same time and settled in Albany as well. My mother and the rest of her family—her mother, younger brother, and two younger half-sisters—joined him in 1910. (The Torah scholar remained in Russia, as did his son by his first marriage, Yevsei Mikhlin, who was in political exile in Siberia at the time.) My mother took a job in a dressmaking shop, which she left when she married my father in 1914. I was born the following year.

In 1918, we moved to New Haven, Connecticut, where I started school. I was often the only Jewish child in the class, sometimes in the entire school. Each morning when we laid our heads on our desks to recite the Lord's

---

1. Founded in 1897 as a result of the rising revolutionary activity among the Jews of Russia's western provinces, the Bund was the party of many socialist Jewish workers.

Prayer, I was silent, not because I was Jewish, but because I was not sure if God existed. To my question, "Is there a God?" my father replied that he did not know, but that it did not matter: The important thing was to live an honest, decent life.

My parents were not observant and I had no religious upbringing at all. This did not mean that we denied our Jewishness. Once a week, from the time that I was nine or ten, my parents sent me to an *Arbeiterring* (Workers' Circle) school in New Haven. There, I learned to read and write Yiddish and I studied some Jewish history, mostly stories adapted from the Old Testament. At home, we had many Yiddish books, and my father would often read aloud to us from Sholom Aleichem and other Yiddish writers. We observed Jewish holidays in a secular manner, as occasions for family and friends to get together, to eat the traditional foods, and to recall some of the traditional rituals. My mother did not keep a kosher home, but, as I realized many years later, she never served the prohibited foods. (When my parents came to visit me in Moscow in 1957 and I served pork or crab meat, she would not touch the food.) Generally, I took being Jewish for granted and did not think about it often. I can recall only two anti-Semitic encounters in my childhood. The first was unintentional. One day, an Italian girl with whom I often walked to school began to talk about "Jew Christ-killers." She was terribly embarrassed when I stopped her and told her I was Jewish. Two or three years later, in a much more affluent part of New Haven, a classmate called me a "dirty Jew." I never spoke to her again, though she apologized the next day.

We moved often, in and out of houses my father had built in various sections of New Haven, and later, Albany, to which we moved back when I was in the eighth grade. As a result, we often lived in lovely residential neighborhoods that would ordinarily have been above our means and in which, especially in New Haven, our family and my uncle's were the only Jewish ones in the community. Social life in these neighborhoods centered around the church and the country club; naturally, our families were not a part of it. I made friends easily, but none of my school friendships were lasting. My more stable friendships were among the children of my parents' friends. Considering the milieu and how frequently we moved, this was not surprising. I seldom attended the same school for two consecutive years, and each time I changed schools, I found myself ahead in some subjects and behind in others. I went to grade school in New Haven, junior high in Albany, and high school in Los Angeles and Santa Monica, California.

My parents had always been connected with Yiddish left-wing circles. They belonged to the socialist-oriented *Arbeiterring*, which was primarily a social club and mutual aid organization whose political activities consisted chiefly of impassioned discussions about current issues, especially about revolutionary developments in the old country. When the *Arbeiterring* split in the mid-1920s, my parents kept their allegiances with the faction that sympathized with the Bolsheviks. We eleven- and twelve-year-olds had a club of our own, which we called the Young Pioneers. The Communist organization for children had the same name, but in New Haven and Albany it had no official guidance or affiliation. Until we moved to California, my general ideas about socialism did not impinge on my feelings of patriotism derived from American history classes and from the books I read. I had no difficulty reconciling the ideas that came from my parents with those that came from outside.

On the whole, my recollections are of a happy childhood. Except for following some basic rules requiring me to be home by a certain hour and to do my homework before going out, I pursued my own interests without much interference.

In all our moves, my one constant friend was the public library. Wherever we lived, there was a public library within walking distance. What a joy it was to wander among the shelves, leafing through books from the school reading list or picking books at random from the shelves. During my years in the Soviet Union, I often thought of American public libraries and their accessibility—such a contrast to the restrictive rules of Moscow libraries.

California in 1929 was a big change for me and I loved it—the mild, sunny days and cool nights, the fragrant orange groves, the snow-capped mountains in the distance, the wide, sandy beaches and huge ocean waves, the feeling of spaciousness.

The left wing in Los Angeles was much broader than anything we had known on the east coast. Through their friends, my parents made contacts with individuals on the fringes of the Communist Party, though they themselves never actually joined. Those were years of rising unemployment, soup kitchens and bread lines, of Communist-led demonstrations and hunger marches.

The first friend I made was the daughter of one of the families who had come from Albany, but whom I had hardly known. Miriam Brooks was exactly my age, a lovely-looking, unassuming girl with luminous grey eyes set far apart, curly, dark hair, and a ready smile. We became close friends (she is the only friend I have retained from my early teens).

When I was fourteen, I accompanied Miriam to a demonstration. The Los Angeles police department had a particularly vicious anti-Communist "Red Squad," and violence was expected. We promised our parents that we would be careful and would stay on the sidelines. But I was horrified as I watched policemen with clubs literally breaking heads open. Until then, I had been reluctant to commit myself to the Communist youth organization, as I was determined to concentrate on my education. On that day, I made up my mind. I joined the

Communist youth group at Roosevelt High School—comprised of about twenty or twenty-five students—and became an active member.

We were chiefly a study group. We read Marxist literature, usually under the guidance of older comrades. We also carried out assignments such as distributing leaflets and speaking at public meetings. Distributing leaflets and participating in demonstrations do not seem like much today, but in those days they were dangerous activities. Arrests and beatings were commonplace. In a short time, I became more militant than my parents had ever been.

Nevertheless, I was dismayed when my parents informed me in the spring of 1931 that they were making arrangements for the family to go to Birobidzhan in the Soviet Union.

Birobidzhan was an area in the Soviet Far East that the Soviet government had designated as a Jewish homeland. OZET (the Russian acronym for "Organization for Agricultural Resettlement of Jewish Working People") had the task of persuading Jews, both inside and outside Russia, to settle in Birobidzhan. In the United States, a pro-Soviet organization called ICOR (the Russian acronym for "Association for Jewish Colonization in the Soviet Union"), operating under the direction of OZET, sent speakers to Jewish leftist groups to urge American Jews to help colonize Birobidzhan. Jews were asked to contribute their skills and to help fund modern farm machinery. Some of the speakers were very persuasive. One of the most effective was a beautiful, dark-eyed woman named Gina Meddam who became friendly with my parents.

To my father, Birobidzhan seemed the answer to a dream I did not know he had, a dream of a Jewish homeland, with socialism, too.

My first reaction was "I'm not going!" I had just completed my junior year at Santa Monica High School. I was planning to go to college and to have a career in journalism. Though interested in the Soviet Union and wholly supportive of its goals, I felt that my place was here, in America, and that any fight I might wage should be in my own country. The Russians could take care of themselves. Besides, I was not the least bit interested in a Jewish homeland.

However, my refusal to go along was unrealistic. I had no way of supporting myself. The family had no resources and there was no one with whom I could live. I revised my statement: "I'll go, but I'm coming back in a couple of years no matter what you decide to do."

Before we left, I applied to the Los Angeles branch of the Young Communist League (YCL) for a transfer to the Komsomol, the Soviet equivalent of the youth group. My request was refused on the grounds that I was not worthy of membership in the Soviet youth organization. I had had several conflicts with the California district YCL and the Communist Party leadership. For example, I had opposed missing school to participate in demonstrations, arguing that the impact of a few fourteen- and fifteen-year-olds was not worth the trouble it would cause us. Nevertheless, I had followed orders and, as a result, was suspended from the Los Angeles school system, whereupon the YCL officials ordered me to stay out of school and get a job and join the ranks of the proletariat (at fifteen!). Instead, my parents moved to Santa Monica so that I could continue my schooling. The refusal of the YCL leaders to allow my transfer was retaliation for that incident as well as for other occasions when I annoyed them with my unsolicited opinions.

We left California in August 1931, aboard a Japanese freighter bound for Yokohama. From Yokohama, we planned to go on to Vladivostok and Birobidzhan.

Birobidzhan, with an area of about 22,000 square miles, is bounded on the south by the Amur, a mighty river some 1,800 miles long that forms the border between Russia and Manchuria for 300 miles; the river then turns northward at Khabarovsk. It is named after the Bira and Bidzhan rivers that join in this area to become the Amur. In the fall of 1931, 5,125 Jews lived in Birobidzhan, where the total population of 44,574 consisted mostly of Russian and Ukrainian peasants.

The enterprise was doomed from the start. The area was remote and had no historical meaning for Jews. The climate was harsh and the land difficult to cultivate—it had very cold winters; hot summers plagued by gnats, mosquitoes and ticks; hilly terrain; swamps; and virgin forests. The Jews were aliens in the land and the local peasants were not welcoming. (In 1995, people identified as Jews on their passport comprised around 5.4 percent of the population of about 220,000.)

But in the early 1930s, a pioneering spirit and enthusiasm brought many young Soviet Jews and a significant number of Jews from foreign countries to Birobidzhan. My family was among them.

\* \* \*

A group of friends gathered at the pier in San Pedro to see us off— intrepid pioneers in pursuit of a socialist dream.

I did not feel like an intrepid pioneer. As the ship receded, I stood on the deck holding on to one end of a ribbon while Miriam held the other end on the pier. The ribbon snapped and I turned away. The break seemed final. I knew there was no money in the bank to assure a possible return. All our worldly goods—several cardboard suitcases of assorted sizes, three or four heavy leather valises, and bundles of bedding and household articles—were right there on deck. What lay ahead? I have no idea what my parents felt, but I felt very sad.

That evening, I started writing in the green, leather-bound diary with lock and key that had been a farewell gift from my friends.

The ship was a veritable "slow boat to China." No one could tell us precisely how long it would take to cross the Pacific Ocean. The weather was generally good during the crossing. No one except my mother was seasick, and she was so ill that she hardly emerged from the cabin. I resisted the queasiness I felt the first day or two and felt fine afterwards.

Once en route, I was caught up in the excitement of the adventure. I spent a good deal of time on deck, mesmerized by the changing colors of the sea and sky, thrilled by the spectacular sunsets, watching for signs of life in and above the ocean. For the first few days, screaming gulls followed the ship, but later, there were days when the sea was as smooth as glass and the silence absolute. Once in a while, a school of porpoises would appear, following their food channel. Very rarely, we sighted another ship, and that was an event, but most of the time, we were alone in the vast ocean.

It took eighteen days to get to Yokohama. The trip was far from luxurious, but it was comfortable enough. We had two cabins with bunks. I don't remember the food at all, but I do remember the Japanese waiter with his constant gold-toothed smile and his "yes, yes" to everything we said, whether he understood us or not.

The only other passengers were two Germans in their late twenties, Gerhard, an architect "temporarily unemployed," and Hanli, who taught school in a small New England town. Both young men were going home for a visit after an absence of five or six years and were making this a round-the-world journey, having started from the East Coast and driven cross country. They were charming to everyone and graciously included me in their conversations. To my sixteen-year-old self, they seemed terribly sophisticated. Much of their talk was above my head; they discussed art and architecture and the political situation in Europe and in Asia. "Get out of Japan as quickly as you can," they said to my father. They questioned him about his plans and shook their heads without comment when he told them about his hopes. Gerhard was the livelier of the two, tall, good-looking, with a square jaw, light brown hair and blue eyes. I was smitten for the duration, but no one seemed to notice. We parted company in Yokohama. They went on to China. We planned to stay in Japan only as long as it would take to make arrangements for continuing on to Vladivostok.

At that time, the United States did not have diplomatic relations with the Soviet Union. Official correspondence had to go directly to Moscow. Thus, my father had written directly to the Soviet authorities in the spring, asking for a visa. Week after week had gone by without a reply. Our travel arrangements had been made, so as the departure date approached, my father decided to go ahead without a visa, confident that he would not have any trouble when he, a true proletarian, appeared on the Soviet doorstep.

He was right. The Soviet embassy in Tokyo had been informed of our plans. On the day we arrived, a representative came to see us at the hotel that Gina Meddam had recommended. The man told us that a Soviet ship would be leaving for Vladivostok from Tsuruga in about a week, but that there were formalities to be attended to before we could board it. He was reassuring and we settled down to wait. Our main concern was making our money last.

The small, family-owned hotel in Yokohama was spotless. We were asked to remove our shoes on entering and were given slippers to wear indoors. The floors were covered with thick rugs. We slept on straw mats placed on the rugs and had wooden headrests for pillows. Sliding screens served as walls and could be adjusted to change the size of the rooms. There were no chairs, only low stools and tables. The owners knew little English, but we got along very well with smiles and gestures.

Within an hour of our arrival at the hotel, a gold-toothed young man appeared, offering his services as a guide. My parents tried to put him off until after we had settled in, but he was very persistent and they finally agreed to hire him for just one day of sightseeing in Tokyo. Our hotel owners would let him know which day. Nevertheless, he turned up the next morning and stuck to us during our entire stay in Yokohama, smiling and saying "yes, yes," like the waiter on the ship. He would arrive at the hotel early in the morning and accompany us wherever we went, though my father had paid him for only one day. I ignored him, but I learned later that he had asked my sister a lot of questions: Who were we? What were we doing in Japan? Where were we going and why? and so on. It was obvious that he had been sent by the Japanese government to spy on us, but I don't think we realized it at the time.

Yokohama, a gateway to Tokyo and the rest of Japan, was a busy seaport where most ships from foreign countries docked. The streets of Yokohama and Tokyo were very colorful. The women wore kimonos, some of them very striking. Many of them wore their hair piled high in elaborate coiffures which, I was told, they did not let down for weeks. The prevailing dress among men was a white kimono-like garment or shapeless overblouse and what looked like pajamas or underwear held up by a drawstring. There was a celebration taking place in Yokohama at the time. Streamers waved from buildings and telegraph poles. We saw processions every day, with marchers, floats, paper dragons, cardboard or papier-mâché figures that were obviously caricatures, and placards inscribed with thick, black Japanese characters that seemed to bristle with anger.

It was September 1931. In a few months, Japan would invade China and set up the puppet state of Manchukuo in Manchuria. The militarism and jingoism were palpable. I doubt that we knew what we were in the middle of, but we could not miss the warlike atmosphere and it made us feel uneasy.

The narrow streets of Yokohama contrasted with the bright colors, the military music, and the hustle and bustle of the celebration. Scenes of wretchedness remain etched in my memory: emaciated, wizened men and women, literally skin and bones, huddled against walls of buildings or lay in alleyways, too weak to beg. I remember ragged children with swollen bellies and, most horrifying of all, women half lying, half sitting on the ground, with infants sucking at flat, empty breasts. Militarism and despair—those are my strongest impressions of the Japan we saw nearly seventy years ago.

We took the one-hour trip to Tokyo several times to sightsee and to conduct our business at the Soviet embassy.

Tokyo was a city of more than two million people, with low buildings and rather wide streets; it seemed very new and clean. It had been rebuilt after a devastating earthquake in 1923 and had been designed to withstand further shocks. The railroad connecting Yokohama with Tokyo was clean and comfortable. There were very few women passengers on the train. The men behaved rather casually, often stretching out on the long seats and sleeping, or sitting slumped over with their legs sticking out in the aisles. There were not many European travelers in Japan in those days and our little group attracted attention, but no one attempted to strike up a conversation with us.

On one of our trips into Tokyo, a fat, puffy-faced young man entered our car a few stations after we had gotten on. He remained standing by the doors and was not aware that as they closed, the end of his flowing white overblouse got caught between the doors. I don't know what prompted me to do what I did next. Perhaps it was the pompous expression on his face, or my impression that he was staring at us. There was an empty space beside me. I returned his look, lowered my eyes, and moved over as if to make room for him. He took a step forward and could not move. At that time, I thought this was very funny. He got off at the next stop. My mother, who had observed this episode, was shocked and she rebuked me. I still feel embarrassment when I recall how unthinkingly I humiliated that stranger.

We wandered rather aimlessly in Tokyo with our not-very-useful guide in tow. By early evening, we'd be back in our hotel in Yokohama. I felt frustrated, certain that we were missing a great deal and itching to get away from my family.

An opportunity presented itself.

We were standing on a sidewalk in Tokyo one afternoon, discussing what to do next, when we caught sight of a tall, handsome, brown-skinned man walking on the other side of the street. Surely he was an American Negro! I assumed that he was someone who spoke English who might be able to tell us what to do in Tokyo! In a split second, I was across the street. He stopped when he saw me running towards him. I stuck out my hand.

"You're an American, aren't you? I'm an American, too."

"No," he replied, "I am Indian, from India. But I've been to the States."

I was taken aback. No matter, he spoke English and we could communicate. I told him we were spending a few days in Japan on our way to Russia and we had no idea about what to see and do here. Could he give us some advice? Did he know Tokyo and Yokohama?

Yes, he knew Tokyo and Yokohama very well indeed. As a matter of fact, he knew Moscow, too, and Paris and London and Rome. I was impressed. We talked a bit. He made some suggestions and at the end of the conversation, he remarked that he was free that evening and would be happy to show me Tokyo by night. He told me his name, which I have forgotten, and offered to call for me at my hotel or to meet me somewhere.

All this time, the others were watching from across the street. No one had made a move to join us.

I asked my new acquaintance to wait for a minute while I talked to my parents. I hurried back across the street and exclaimed breathlessly,

"He's not an American. He's Indian. He speaks English and is going to take me out tonight and show me the city."

Silence. Then:

"Go back and tell him that you cannot go. We have other plans." my father said.

"Plans? What plans? We never have plans!"

"Go back and tell him whatever you like. You are not going off with a complete stranger."

I could not believe my ears. I had always done pretty much as I pleased, and was proud that my parents trusted me. But my father was adamant. Slowly, I went back and explained that we had other plans for the evening and thanked him. He smiled, said he was sorry, and we parted. I was angry and upset.

My father was probably right, though very likely the stranger had been an honorable man and I would not have ended up a white slave in an Asian house of prostitution.

A few days later, we got the go-ahead from the Soviet embassy and left for Tsuruga by rail. We had to change trains in Kobe. We arrived in Kobe in the evening and spent the night in the railroad station, sleeping as best we could on the hard benches, more like refugees than travelers from America! Our funds were running low.

We arrived in Tsuruga two days before the boat was to leave. I have absolutely no memories of Tsuruga, but my father filled them in for me more than fifty years later. There were no hotels in Tsuruga, he said. A Russian family took us in, fed and lodged us, and refused to accept payment.

# 2
## Birobidzhan—1931

Watching from the deck as the ship sailed into Vladivostok harbor, we saw a group of people on shore waving and smiling. We were pleasantly surprised to discover that they were members of the local Komsomol who were delegated to welcome us. They helped unload our baggage and, to our amazement, cautioned us not to leave any of our belongings unattended. Then they formed a circle around our baggage and guarded it while my father went to the customs office.

Customs did not take long. The official asked my father a few questions and told him to get our papers validated by the local authorities as soon as we were settled in our hotel. Our baggage was not examined.

The hotel to which our greeters took us was nearby, up a cobblestone hill and around the corner. They loaded our baggage onto a horse-drawn cart and we walked alongside it. There was something peculiar about the horse; I realized what it was—it was yoked and not wearing blinders. The occasional horses still seen on the streets at home in America—drawing the milkman's or iceman's wagon—always wore blinders, and I had never seen a wooden yoke before. I called my father's attention to this and he said, yes, farm horses in the old country were always yoked. They did not need blinders, as there was no motor traffic to speak of in the streets. The recent night that I had spent sleeping on benches in the Kobe railroad station, and now, walking alongside a horse and cart like a European peasant, made me feel as if I had been thrown back a few centuries, to a previous life perhaps? It seemed unnatural.

At the hotel, we were given one large room. My father set out at once for the local government office, and I went with him.

A sandy-haired man with fair skin and blue eyes, wearing the khaki tunic, breeches, and high leather boots that I later found to be a semi-uniform worn by virtually all Communist Party and government officials, received us cordially. He introduced himself and told us that he was Jewish. It did not seem strange that he mentioned being Jewish at the outset of the conversation. This information established a bond and impressed my father, who told me afterwards that in the Russia of his youth, no Jew could have held what was clearly an important government position. The meeting gave my father immediate confirmation of his feelings about the new world he had come to help build.

The conversation was in Russian and my father gave me the gist of it. The "commissar" had said that it was unusual to admit people who arrived as we had, not in an organized group and without proper entry documents, but since my father was a worker and had arrived in a workers' state, an exception would be made for him. He charged us a nominal fee for the visas and suggested that we exchange the money we had left—about $250—for rubles. The transaction took place on the spot, at the official rate of exchange. My father was given a receipt that entitled him to exchange the small number of rubles he now had for certificates. These could be redeemed at the Torgsin hard currency shops, a retail network established in 1930 that sold food and manufactured goods for foreign currencies. The shops also issued scrip in exchange for gold, silver, or other precious metals and valuables.

The Soviet state was badly in need of hard currency for foreign exchange, as the ruble was worthless outside the country. Accordingly, the government had issued a decree obligating all citizens to turn in their valuables and establishing harsh penalties for noncompliance. Enforcement was accompanied by search and seizure, usually carried out in response to tips by informers. Along with a stick, the government offered a carrot, the Torgsin network to extract bits and pieces from less affluent citizens—a gold wedding ring, a silver spoon, a pearl necklace, for example. The Torgsin shops were also used by foreigners residing in the Soviet Union (Torgsin was abolished in 1936, by which time the population did not have many valuables left to trade in).

Exchanging our dollars for rubles was a terrible mistake. There wasn't a Torgsin shop for miles around. Besides, the rate of exchange for dollars at the Torgsin shops was much higher than the official rate. The pleasant-spoken commissar must have known this.

The commissar spoke at length about the aspirations of the Soviet state, assuring us that the hardships we might encounter were temporary. He wished us luck and said he would arrange for us to purchase train tickets to Tikhonkaya, the capital of Birobidzhan.[1] As we took our leave, he said that a family living in the hotel had a daughter about my own age who spoke English; he was sure that she would be happy to show me around and practice her English.

Early the next morning, a girl of about fifteen knocked on our door. She spoke serviceable English which she said she had learned at school. She told us that her father was an important official and that most of the rooms in the hotel were occupied by permanent residents, all high Party or government

---

1. Tikhonkaya's name was later changed to Birobidzhan. (Ed.)

officials. Hotels were not available to the general public, only to persons with official business in the city. She seemed very self-assured. Noticing the initialed gold ring and gold locket I was wearing, she declared disdainfully that it was "petty bourgeois" to wear jewelry. I removed my ring and locket at once, and left them in the dresser drawer before we went out to walk about the town. The next day when we were packing to leave, I could not find them anywhere. The thought that they may have been stolen was unbearable. I told myself that they must have fallen through a crack or been mislaid, but deep down I knew that they had been stolen.

Among the passengers on the Vladivostok–Moscow express that took us to Tikhonkaya was a group of students who were intrigued by the foreigners in their midst. When they discovered that my parents spoke Russian, they crowded around them, plying them with questions. At one point, my father turned to me and said, "You cannot imagine what this means to your mother and me: Russians speaking with Jews as with equals and treating them with respect. This could not have happened in the old days."

The train stopped at Tikhonkaya for two minutes. We were the only passengers getting off and there was a frantic rush to unload our baggage. The students were a great help. Then they stood on the steps, waving to us as the train pulled out.

I looked around me. There were signs of a recent heavy rainfall, but now the air was crisp and dry and the sun was shining. Beyond the wooden platform, the mud was knee-deep, as I could tell from the figures plodding through it. It was difficult, even at a short distance, to tell whether those figures in their padded jackets, heavy boots, and visored caps were male or female, old or young. Wooden planks led to a nearby two- or three-story building and to another a little farther away. In the distance, I could see a cluster of squat, low houses. It was late September 1931, and this was where our journey from California had ended, on a wooden platform in the middle of nowhere, on an island in a sea of mud. I turned to my parents and said, "If you think I am going to live here, you are very much mistaken. I'm going to Moscow."

My poor parents. As if they did not have enough to deal with!

There was no one to meet us. I stood guard over our baggage while my parents went to look for the authorities. They soon returned, accompanied by a youngish man carrying a briefcase who got some men to help us. They escorted us to the nearby building, which served as a station house and transit hostel. The room we were given on the second floor contained single bedsteads with lumpy mattresses on narrow boards. My dismay increased when I discovered that there were no bathrooms and no running water, just a backyard privy reached by planks laid over the mud. We got our water from a tin washstand nailed to a wall on the ground floor, a tin cup and tin basin on a stool underneath the washstand, and an empty bucket to be filled at a pump outdoors. We were given vouchers for three meals and afternoon tea in the dining room.

It was tea time—all the boiling green liquid you wanted, one lump of sugar hacked off a huge loaf, and one roll that had the consistency of stone. You had to dunk the roll in the hot liquid in order to bite into it.

The dining hall rang with an animated mixture of Yiddish and Russian. This was where all transients and some of the local residents took their meals. There were bare wooden tables, each seating from four to six persons, and posters on the walls. A waitress collected our vouchers and plunked down five rolls and five lumps of sugar in front of us. The tea was in a kettle on the table, and we poured it into glass tumblers. People came over to greet us. They urged us to come to the clubhouse that evening where there would be music, a film, perhaps a local dance group performance. Later that day, right after supper, several young people came over to our table and carried me off for the evening.

We spent a week in Tikhonkaya while our papers were being processed and my parents tried to decide where to settle. I was taken over by the young people, many of whom had arrived recently and were on their way to jobs in various communities. Most were in their early twenties, some younger, and many had come from teacher training schools in Ukraine and Byelorussia. They were a happy, lively group. In the daytime, they were busy arranging their affairs, conferring with officials, attending meetings, and filling out forms, but they would all gather in the dining room for supper. I was always invited to sit with one or another group, and I listened, fascinated, as they talked about what they had done during the day, who had said what to whom, who had received assignments to go where, and how they felt about their assignments. After supper we'd go to the clubhouse where there was always an accordion and sometimes a film or concert. I enjoyed it all. This was my first taste of being the center of attention merely because I was a foreigner, an exotic—it was fun.

One young man at the hostel was not Jewish and did not have any business to attend to in Tikhonkaya. He was a geologist from Leningrad, on his way to join an expedition in the Far East. He had met the Birobidzhan group on a train and got off with them because he had time to spare. He was twenty-eight years old, tall, lanky, and wore a pince-nez. And he was extremely curious about America. The weather was beautiful. The mud had dried, so we took long walks and shouted with laughter as we tried to understand each other. He spoke French, of which I had a smattering from high school, and he knew a few English words. Reinforcing our vocabularies with gestures, we managed quite well. We talked about ourselves, we joked. He had many specific questions about America. I enjoyed his company and was sorry to see him go a few days before we ourselves left Tikhonkaya. He was different from the others and, in some ways, more interesting. I did not realize then that he was one of a disappearing breed of old Russian intelligentsia, a type that was to become very rare as time went by.

With the others, I communicated in Yiddish, which I understood quite well, though I had hardly spoken it for years. As in many immigrant families, my parents spoke to me in Yiddish and I replied in English. Now I had to speak, and it wasn't long before I was fluent enough to get along. I have always found Yiddish to be a very useful language, not only that first year in the Soviet Union before I knew any Russian, but also in recent years, during travels to Europe and South America. Someone has always known how to speak Yiddish, even in the most out-of-the-way places.

Among my new acquaintances was a girl who was especially warm and friendly—plump, rosy-cheeked, dark-eyed Feigele, nineteen years old, who had come from Ukraine to teach school in Birobidzhan. Feigele had arrived in Birobidzhan with her sweetheart, a quiet, sensitive-looking young man, and they were hoping to get assigned to the same community. Despite her youth, Feigele was a member of the Communist Party. She talked for hours to my parents and me about the new socialist society under construction that had improved the situation of the Jews in Russia. Consequently, she maintained, it was the Jews' duty to become part of the working and peasant classes. She described the difficulties of teaching people new attitudes, and praised the dedication and political consciousness of the proletarian vanguard. Feigele spoke reverentially of the leaders of the Soviet Union, especially Stalin, and pointed out all they were doing for the formerly disenfranchised masses.

The enthusiasm of my new acquaintances was contagious. Gradually, my mood changed. So what if there was no plumbing and the food consisted mainly of watery cabbage soup, cooked millet, and tea with jaw-breaking rolls? These were the difficulties of growth. Someday soon, a new, modern, just society would arise from the backward heritage of the tsars in Birobidzhan and all over the country.

Nevertheless, I was determined to leave Birobidzhan. I was not interested in a Jewish homeland. Besides, there was no place for me to finish school in Birobidzhan. I could have gone to school in Khabarovsk, a major city even then, three to four hours away by train, but my mind was set on Moscow. I went to see the local Party secretary to enlist his support. He conceded that Birobidzhan had nothing to offer me and agreed to help. He said I would need a paper from the local authorities, identifying me and stating my purpose in going to Moscow. I would also need assistance in purchasing a train ticket, as long-distance train tickets were almost impossible to obtain without official intervention. Finally, I would also need some financial assistance. He did not know how long it would take to arrange these matters, so he advised me to stay with the rest of the family, but only for the time being.

Why no one attempted to discourage me I will never know. Khabarovsk had secondary schools and universities, and I could have remained in close contact with my family. It is useless now to speculate on what might have been, but it is human nature to do so. As I look back, I cannot help thinking how different our lives might have been had we all stayed together.

My parents made inquiries about various communities. We could have stayed in Tikhonkaya, which had a furniture factory where my father could have worked, but the prevailing opinion was that food was more readily available in the countryside, at an agricultural commune. This seemed to make sense, so my parents finally decided to settle in the ICOR Commune where there was another American family from New York City.

The trip to Volochayevka, which was the town that had a railroad station closest to our destination, was extremely uncomfortable. Though Volocha-yevka was only about fifty miles away, the trip took nearly six hours in an airless, crowded boxcar without seats. Men, women and children sprawled on the floor beside their bundles. The stench was unbearable and there were no amenities of any kind. Other passengers took advantage of the frequent and prolonged stops to go off into the bushes or fields, but we could not bring ourselves to do this. In contrast to everyone else we had met so far, no one showed curiosity about us and no one spoke to us.

But we had one piece of luck. A commune tractor-trailer happened to be at the station when we arrived and we were able to hitch a ride to the village, fifteen miles away. Otherwise we might have been stranded at the station for days, as there was no direct telephone connection with the commune.

When we reached a wooden barrack, the driver stopped and announced that we had arrived. We unloaded and he drove off. Some children and a few grown-ups gathered to greet us. We had been expected, but no one had known when we would arrive.

Quarters had been set aside for us. They consisted of one bare room in a barrack with a naked light bulb suspended from the ceiling. The first thing my parents did was unpack and set up the canvas army-type cots we had brought from the United States. After Tikhonkaya, I was prepared for the absence of plumbing. The privy was quite a ways off, reached in the same way, via a path of wooden planks over mud.

Exhausted, we went to bed at sundown.

I woke up suddenly. It was pitch dark. Something was biting me and I did not know what to do. The others were stirring in their cots, too. Some-one, my mother or my father, turned on the light. Insects the size and shape of ladybugs were swarming over us, crawling out of cracks in the walls! Bedbugs. I had never seen a bedbug, but my parents knew what they were. We moved the cots away from the walls, but this did not do much good. The bugs just crawled along the ceiling and dropped onto the cots. We left the lights on for the rest of the night. That first night was a horror, and the following nights were not much better. We fought the bedbugs with boiling water and kerosene and plugged the cracks as best we could, but it was a losing battle. The only way to get some sleep was to cover ourselves from head to foot, leaving no spot exposed.

The next day, we went to the bathhouse in a nearby village. It had been heated especially for us.

It was a basic Russian village bathhouse, variations of which were found in every town and village in the land. This one was built of logs and consisted of two sections: an anteroom where you left your clothes and the main room. The bathhouse was heated by steam produced from cold water that was poured onto red-hot stones in a fireplace. The structure was equipped with wooden benches at several levels—the higher the level, the hotter the steamy air. You took two tin basins, one for your feet and the other for the rest of you, and you washed the basins thoroughly, rinsing them with boiling water. Next, you filled them from buckets of hot and cold water, using dippers or tin cups. We had the bathhouse to ourselves that day, so it was a real treat. Generally, the bathhouse served several communities and was heated on specific days for each community once a week, with separate times for men and women.

At the commune, my mother was assigned to a kitchen job, my father to a carpentry repair team. My father's first job was to re-hang all the doors so that they fit properly.

Since it was acknowledged that I would be leaving soon, I was not assigned any duties and was free to do as I pleased. But I was considered not ladylike because I wore blue denim overalls and whistled. I also met disapproval in the village because I went bareheaded. So I avoided the villages and spent my time roaming among the hills, known as *"sopki."* I learned later that there had been fierce fighting here against Japanese and White Russian forces in February 1922. As a result, the *sopki* and the countryside around Volochayevka were celebrated in song and poetry.

About three weeks later, Feigele arrived alone. She had been assigned to teach in a Yiddish school here at the ICOR Commune. Her fiancé, also a Party member, had been sent to another community.

"Don't you mind, Feigele?" I asked.

"Of course, I mind, but the Party needs us in different places. That is more important than our personal wishes."

"If you married, would you have been sent to the same place?"

"Not necessarily. Maybe."

The reason given for separating them was the need to strengthen the Party groups in the various communities. A popular song of the period was about a young Komsomol couple going off on assignment, "he in one direction, she in another."

Feigele brought word that my travel papers were ready and that tickets for the Vladivostok–Moscow express had been reserved for the following week for me and for Mikhail Bengelsdorf, an Argentinean from the ICOR Commune who had been admitted to the Yiddish Theater school in Moscow. We had met Bengelsdorf briefly after arriving at the commune, just before he left for Tikhonkaya to settle his affairs. My parents had asked him to try to arrange for me to travel with him; they were now relieved that I would not have to make the trip all by myself.

The rest of the Birobidzhan saga is not my story. I heard it from my parents when I saw them a year later. I questioned them again after I returned to America, but the events of forty years before had dimmed and their memories were so painful that I could not press them for details. Briefly, this is what they told me:

Basic foods—sugar, flour, cooking oil, grain, bread and meat—were rationed. However, salmon were running in the river and fish was plentiful. The situation deteriorated in the winter. Food proved to be scarcer in the countryside than in the cities. A tax-in-kind imposed on the peasants to feed the urban proletariat was so burdensome that there was very little left over for the collective farms. Peasants who had their own subsistence gardens, some poultry or a pig, managed to get by, but when that resource was not available, people went hungry.

The commune was part of a cluster of three *tochki*, or sections. One was an old established village of about forty-five households founded before Soviet times by peasants from Ukraine who had come there attracted by offers of land under the tsarist government. It was known as the "Ukrainian" village and had been quite prosperous before it was coerced into becoming an agricultural commune. It had a windmill, a bakery, a hog farm, and, even as a commune, was run efficiently. It was able to supply bread to all three sections. The second section was a newer resettlement village that had also been settled by Ukrainians and by some Russians. The third, where my parents lived, was known as the "foreigners'" section and had the fancy-sounding name "Red Army Socialist Riverfront Settlement." It consisted of wooden barracks which housed several families of Polish Jews from Argentina, several families of Russian Jews (most of whom were in the administration), the other family from New York, and my family. Meals were cooked in a communal kitchen and served in a dining room. This section represented the Jewish core of the commune and was intended to be a model for attracting other Jewish settlers to Birobidzhan.

Only a small minority of the commune members were card-carrying Communists, among them the couple from New York. He was the director of the section, a position that he had apparently arranged for prior to his departure from the United States. His wife was in charge of the kitchen.

They ran the section with the help of a board consisting of a bookkeeper, a work team leader,[2] and the other Party members in the administration. None had any previous farming or management experience.

The Jewish section of the commune failed completely. It was unable to produce enough food for itself and it became a burden to the other two sections. It is not surprising that the "Ukrainians" (as they were called, though not all were Ukrainians) were hostile to the "foreigners" (who were not all foreigners either).

The gross inefficiency was compounded by deception and corruption. The Communist cell was a privileged caste. Supplies received for the entire section were divided unfairly, but any criticism of this practice was labeled a "remnant of bourgeois attitudes." The figures presented to the regional authorities in Khabarovsk were falsified; accordingly, it took a long time to get to the bottom of what was really going on. Worst of all, the director and board members took extra food for themselves, which they consumed stealthily in their own rooms. My mother, who was in charge of meals for the children, was especially distressed by the thievery and the underallotment of supplies. She protested, first locally and later, when that did no good, by writing to higher authorities. But her letters were returned to the very people whom the letters sought to expose. This only made things worse, leaving my parents subject to ugly harassment.

Few dared to speak up at open meetings. Feigele, who had been very fond of our family, joined the pack, speaking set pieces against my parents at meetings and severing all personal contacts with them. In 1934, I met Feigele by accident in Moscow. She had married her sweetheart and they were both students at Moscow University, living in the Ostankino "student town," a huge complex of dorms for students from many Moscow colleges where I, too, lived at the time. She told me she thought of my parents often and was ashamed of the role she had played in their conflict with the commune administration. But it would have been unthinkable, she admitted, for her to have supported non-Party people against Party members.

My parents were miserable. Worst of all was their frustration at their inability to fight the petty and dishonest bureaucrats on the spot (eventually, however, the director and his flunkies were exposed and dismissed). After nine months, they left Birobidzhan. It was not easy for them to get away. By then, there was a new administration and the new director did not want to let them go. He put all kinds of obstacles in their way. Finally, when my

2. The members of collective farms were divided into teams called "brigades." The team leader (brigadier) assigned the jobs, allocated credit for jobs done, and had quite a lot of power.

father refused to take no for an answer, the director gave him a paper stating that he had quit his job without permission to do so. My father did not realize the seriousness of that kind of black mark against him and took it lightly until he had to present the document when applying for another job.

My mother's brother and his family had gone to Stalingrad from Chicago at about the same time that we had left for Birobidzhan. He urged my parents to join them, writing that there was a good market for jobs requiring my father's skills. They arrived in Stalingrad in May 1932.

None of the negative undercurrents were apparent to us over the few weeks I spent in Birobidzhan. My parents were concerned about the harsh conditions, but they believed that the situation would improve through the efforts of the people who lived there.

\* \* \*

A local train stopped at Volochayevka once a day, but there was no telling when that would be, as trains ran erratically. I would have to get to the station very early in the morning and be prepared to wait there all day. I worried about boarding the train. The local trains were so crowded that passengers rode on the steps, on the platforms between cars, and even on roofs. They clung to any protuberance they could grab.

We left at daybreak, my father driving the horse and cart. I was to meet my travel companion in Tikhonkaya. My mother, very upset, gave me some parting advice, the only piece of which I remember was never to use newsprint for toilet paper. I often thought of her admonition with amusement. For the next twenty years or so, no other toilet paper was available. In all toilets, indoors and out, if there was any paper at all, it was a square of newspaper of suitable size, spiked on a nail.

As we drove into the station, we heard the sound of a train in the distance. The station master told us we needn't hurry—it was the Moscow express and it would not stop. But what was happening? The train was slowing down! Incredibly, it came to a full stop! My father snatched up my two suitcases from the back of the cart and, calling to me to follow, ran toward a first-class car. Before the astonished conductor could object, he flung the suitcases onto the platform and pushed me up after them.

"This is a foreign child," he said to the conductor. "She was left behind accidentally. She doesn't speak Russian. Please see that she gets off at Tikhonkaya."

The train started moving—it had stopped to take on water for an overheated engine. My father waved to me, and I was off. No embrace, no parting words, nothing.

I stood in the corridor, looking out of the window all the way to Tikhonkaya, which was only one hour away on this train. Now and then, someone would emerge from a compartment and stand in the corridor smoking. No one spoke to me. The passengers were all men wearing either military uniforms or the semi-uniform of Party and government officials. Most were heavy-set and looked well-fed, a different breed from the people I had met so far.

Did I have any misgivings about leaving my family the way I did? About going off alone to a city thousands of miles away where I did not know a single soul, didn't know the language, didn't know where I would lay my head? True, my parents had been assured by the Party secretary in Tikhon-kaya and reassured by Feigele that the Moscow authorities and the Komsomol would help me. Besides, my mother's stepbrother Yevsei, the Torah scholar's son who had been exiled before the revolution, lived in Moscow and my parents hoped I'd be able to locate him (though he had not replied to the letters they had written to him from Birobidzhan). As soon as I had my train ticket, I wired him the date and time of my arrival with a prepaid reply, but there was no answer to that either, so I was not counting on him. Still, I do not recall any agonizing doubts. It never seems to have occurred to me that I might not see my family for a very long time, perhaps years, that there might be danger along the way, that I might not find help everywhere I went, that I might not be able to make it on my own. No one tried to discourage or frighten me. Was it because of a lack of imagination? Naïveté? Ignorance? Many years later, when I asked my father how they could have let me go off like that, he replied, "We thought nothing bad could happen to you in a socialist country."

Clearly, it was faith.

# 3
## Settling in Moscow—1931 to 1932

My ticket and the official papers I needed were waiting for me in Tikhonkaya. Three days later, Mikhail Bengelsdorf and I boarded the Trans-Siberian express, destination Moscow, for an eleven-day ride across endless plains and wide rivers, past dense forests and deep lakes. Sometimes we came to a standstill for no apparent reason; other times we traveled continuously for several days. At regularly scheduled stops, peasants—mostly women and children—lined up on the platform and on the side of the tracks with their wares. The women wore kerchiefs on their heads and long skirts of dark colors. So did the little girls. The boys, many with quilted jackets to protect them against the cold October weather, wore long pants and caps. Vendors walked through the cars or came up to the windows, offering hard-boiled eggs; scrawny boiled chickens; fresh, sour, or baked milk in thick glass tumblers; pot cheese; pickles; and sometimes berries or small green apples. They emptied the purchases into the buyers' containers—cups, pots, kerchiefs, hats, whatever. At each station, usually at the end of the platform, was a large sign that read *kipyatok*, which means "boiling water." Underneath the sign was a huge, samovar-like container called a *titan*. The moment the train stopped, and often even while it was still slowing down, passengers carrying teakettles, pots, pans, or mugs jumped off the steps and ran toward the sign. Others headed for food vendors, and still others ventured into the station to see what was available at the buffet. At some stations, hot meals were sold right on the platform. Three gongs at one-minute intervals would announce that the train was about to leave. At the third gong, the train would start slowly and people would come running from all directions, jumping on wherever they could. For a long while afterwards, the coaches were a-bustle with passengers moving through to their own seats.

Despite the urging and reassurances of my fellow passengers, I was too fearful of being left behind to leave the train. I had brought two weeks' worth of food with me—bread, sugar, roasted chicken, hard-boiled eggs— and I supplemented these rations by buying from the vendors who came through the cars or up to the open window. In Tikhonkaya, I had been given a lump sum of money to carry me through the month. The boiling water for tea was brought by others and, of course, by Bengelsdorf, who kept his promise to my parents to look after me.

Mikhail Bengelsdorf was a tall, handsome man of around thirty who had been an actor in Argentina. I was startled when other passengers took us for a couple. He seemed far too old for me to consider him romantically. When I was getting acquainted with other passengers, I was invariably asked my age and whether I was married—a preposterous question. At sixteen, marriage was the farthest thing from my mind, but apparently in overwhelmingly peasant Russia, sixteen was a marriageable age.

There were four classes on the train, and we traveled "hard, reserved." First class was called "international": it had a compartment for one, upholstered berths for sitting and sleeping, and bedding. It shared a washroom with an adjoining compartment. Second class, called "soft," had compartments for two people, with upper and lower upholstered (soft) berths, bedding available for a fee, and a common washroom at each end of the car. The compartment doors locked. The conductor would unlock them for passengers who had to pass through, but the hoi polloi were not allowed to loiter. "International" and "soft" were not available to the general public, and could only be purchased by special vouchers issued to privileged travelers.

As a matter of fact, it was difficult for ordinary travelers to purchase tickets even for the "hard, reserved" section. We had had to obtain our tickets through official connections. "Hard, reserved" consisted of compartments for four, with three tiers of bare wooden shelves on each side, the lower and middle shelves for sleeping and sitting, and the top shelf for luggage. There were "side" shelves in the corridor between the windows. Passengers had to bring their own bedding. Bengelsdorf and I had a lower and middle shelf, that is, the entire side of one compartment, which was the best combination under the circumstances, as we could take turns sleeping or resting on the middle shelf during the day. Then there was "hard, general" class, exactly like ours, but the places were not reserved. Often, six or eight passengers squeezed into compartments for four, with the lucky ones occupying the middle and top shelves and two or more passengers sharing the bottom shelf. The doors between the hard-class coaches were not locked and sometimes we got the overflow from the unreserved sections. One could not very well refuse to share a seat for a few hours.

Many women and children rode in the unreserved cars, chiefly local peasants on short trips. But in our car and in all the other coaches, the overwhelming majority of passengers were men traveling long distances, many all the way to Moscow. The group of strangers in the moving iron box separated from the outside world became friends for the duration. They visited back and forth, played cards or dominos, exchanged life stories, read or studied. I studied my Russian grammar book and read. I had brought five books with me from America, for no special reason except that I happened to own them: H. G. Wells's *Outline of World History,* Will Durant's *Story of Philosophy,* John Galsworthy's *Forsyte Saga* (the first three volumes), Oscar Wilde's *Ballad of Reading Gaol,* and the Edward Fitzgerald version of *The Rubaiyat of Omar Khayyam.*

Many of the passengers were students on their way to schools and universities in the larger cities along the Trans-Siberian route. Everyone was friendly, but my limited Russian frustrated me. I had picked up some everyday Russian, but it was far from adequate for serious conversation. Bengelsdorf's Russian was not great, but it was much better than mine. He spent most evenings socializing in other compartments. I was always invited, but seldom went, for I felt shy about slowing down the conversation and trying to understand and reply to questions. It was easier to communicate one-on-one. I did, however, become friendly with a few of the students, especially a small group of *natsmeny* (national minorities). They were Evenks and Yakuts from the Far East who were surprised that I had never heard of their tribes. They were on their way to a special school in Leningrad, the University of the Peoples of the North. There, they would be trained in various fields and sent back to help their people enter the modern world. They had all been to secondary school in Vladivostok or Khabarovsk.

One of the pleasures of the long train journey was to gaze out of the window, the best position for which was lying face down on the middle shelf, eye level with the top half of the window. For long stretches, the terrain was practically unchanging. First came the grassy hills and the woods of the Far Eastern region, then the dark green Siberian taiga, then the flat steppe. In late autumn, the predominant colors were dull yellows and quiet browns. It looked tranquil out there in those vast spaces with hardly a sign of human habitation for hours, sometimes days, on end. The villages we passed all looked alike: houses built of logs unpainted or plastered over; white-washed, dirt roads; small girls wearing kerchiefs on their heads and small boys in long trousers, waving as the train went by. On our third or fourth day, the train started climbing and the terrain became mountainous. We were approaching Irkutsk, one of the larger towns en route, but before arriving, we passed a section of Lake Baikal. Set in the midst of the primeval taiga, Baikal had an otherworldly mystery and beauty that left me with an unforgettable memory. The train moved slowly, perilously close to the water's edge. I could hardly tear myself away from the window for nearly two whole days. Baikal is one of the most remarkable lakes in the world. It has an area of over 12,000 square miles and a maximum depth of more than 5,300 feet (our Lake Superior, for example, takes up nearly three times the area, but is not nearly as deep). It supports forms of life found nowhere else. Today, judging from reports in the press, there are paper mills on its shores, the forest is being depleted, and the water and the air are polluted. But when I saw it from a train window in 1931, it was practically untouched, and was a paradise for hunters, trappers, and woodsmen.

Stops in cities were events. Chita was the first sizable town en route, then came Irkutsk, Barnaul, Omsk, and Tomsk. As we passed through Omsk, I caught sight of a trolley car, the first I'd seen in the Soviet Union.

As the journey neared its end, I grew increasingly anxious. Now I was finally facing the reality of what I had done. Over the remaining few days I was so silent and preoccupied that my fellow passengers wondered if I was ill. I was worried. What would I do when I arrived in Moscow? Where would I go? Had my mother's stepbrother received my telegram? Would anyone meet me? I had little hope of that. If worse came to worst, I could go with Bengelsdorf to the theater school until I knew what to do next. But I hated the idea of saddling him any further with my problems. We were on good terms, but had not become friends and I knew he was eager to get on with his own life. The *natsmen* students, especially Yura, a Yakut, said I shouldn't worry. They were spending time in Moscow before going to Leningrad and I could stay wherever they stayed. In fact, they proposed, why didn't I go on to Leningrad with them?

The train emptied slowly, amidst a din of greetings and exclamations. Suddenly, I heard my name. A short, stout, middle-aged woman was pushing her way against the current, calling out in Yiddish and in Russian, "Is Mary Mackler here? Does anyone know Mary Mackler?"

This turned out to be my step-uncle's wife. She was very businesslike—no embraces, no welcoming smiles. She told me to call her "Liza" and asked where my luggage was. Then she summoned a porter, issued instructions to him, gave her address to Bengelsdorf and the students who had waited with me, and we hurried away. I saw Bengelsdorf once after that.[1] Yura came to see me several times, but after he left for Leningrad, we too lost touch.

We followed the porter out of the Kazan railroad station onto a huge cobblestone square. This was Kalanchevskaya (a.k.a. Komsomolskaya) Square, where three of Moscow's eleven railroad stations are located. Coachmen stood nearby, singly or in groups, calling out to prospective fares. After bargaining with several of them, Liza hired one and suggested that I climb up in front with the driver so as to get a better view while she got into the back with my suitcases.

---

1. In 1971, six years after my return to the United States, I was reading an article about Birobidzhan in the *American Jewish Yearbook* and was astonished to come across the name Mikhail Bengelsdorf, the seventy-year-old director of a theater company in the town of Birobidzhan. It was a voice from the past. He must have returned to Birobidzhan after finishing the Yiddish Theater school in Moscow and been there ever since—survived the purges, the war, the postwar political terror, everything. On a visit to Moscow in 1973, I wrote to him, providing a friend's return address in Moscow, but he did not reply.

There I was, riding into Moscow, perched high beside the black-bearded driver of a strange, low-slung, one-horse carriage. For a moment, I felt like a character in a story that I must have made up.

My first impression that day was of flat-roofed, one- and two-story yellow or pink stucco houses, low wooden buildings badly in need of paint, five-story brick apartment buildings, and a few beautiful stone mansions with ornate doors and uniformed guards on some of the side streets. And hustle and bustle. The wide main streets were crowded with people in a hurry. This was a good way to enter Moscow, far more interesting than had we taken one of the few taxis in the square.

The Mikhlins lived a short distance away, in the heart of the city. They occupied an apartment of their own on the third floor of a fairly new five-story walk-up. The apartment consisted of one large square room with a balcony overlooking a courtyard, one long, narrow room overlooking an alleyway, a small kitchen with a gas stove, a sink, and a table at which two could sit comfortably (though four could squeeze in). A small open alcove off the kitchen contained a washstand and a bathtub. Hot water was supplied once a week from a central boiler in the cellar. There was a "cold closet" or cooler under the kitchen sink, as well as a dumb waiter, the first I had ever seen. A string bag with perishable foods hung outside a transom window called a *fortochka,* which could be opened separately at the top of double French windows, standard in all Moscow buildings. The toilet was in the small entry hall. The household consisted of my step-uncle and his wife, their two small daughters aged eight and ten, and his wife's two unmarried sisters. My step-uncle was away at a clinic in the Caucasus.

The two little girls met us at the door, their eyes sparkling with excitement. One of Liza's sisters was at home. She was a tall, thin woman with reddish hair, probably in her thirties, but seeming much older to me. The other sister was away visiting relatives.

After I had washed and been fed, Liza sat down opposite me at the kitchen table and said, "Let's talk."

The others left the room. The conversation was in Yiddish. Liza's Yiddish was different from my parents' and I had to strain to follow it, but what she had to say was perfectly clear: Life was hard. Food was rationed. As for housing, it was inadequate and for new arrivals, practically impossible to obtain.

"What in the world were your parents thinking, sending a child off just like that, without making arrangements with anyone?"

I had nothing to say. My mother's letter from Birobidzhan had been received, but since her husband was away, Liza had not replied. The telegram announcing that I was on my way had been a complete surprise to her.

"Until Yevseiushka comes home you will stay here," she told me (my step-uncle's name was Yevsei, but she always used the affectionate "Yevseiushka").

"You must not tell anyone that you have a place to stay, even temporarily. Don't tell anyone that you have relatives in Moscow. If you do, you will never get a place of your own and you cannot live with us."

Subsequently, once she and her husband realized that I expected nothing from them, we became good friends, and she was especially very kind to me in the early years when I was frequently ill and always a little hungry. But I never forgot how I felt that first day in Moscow with the rebuff I had received. The rejection had felt all the more cutting as I had had no intention of foisting myself on anyone. From the beginning, I had planned to go my own way.

My mother's stepbrother had been arrested in 1907 for his involvement in a political disturbance while he was serving in the tsarist army. In Siberian exile, he had received an education of sorts—he improved his Russian (his earlier education had been in Yiddish) and he learned much from other exiles, the majority of whom belonged to the intelligentsia. In exile, he met Emelyan Yaroslavsky, a leading Bolshevik who took him under his wing and whom he continued to see from time to time in Moscow. However, my step-uncle was not involved in the politics of the exiled revolutionaries, and he had never joined any faction before or after the revolution. After the February Revolution of 1917, he was set free, at which time he went back to Ukraine, where he met and married his wife. A few years later, the family moved to Moscow.

As a former political prisoner, he had special status that made life quite a bit easier for him than for the average citizen. The building in which he lived was a residential cooperative that had been built by the Society of Former Political Prisoners and Penal Exiles, of which he was a member. All the residents had their own separate apartments, which was very unusual in Moscow at that time. He had a "personal" pension, that is, a stipend awarded for his services to the revolution, along with which went special privileges such as better rations, access to food and clothing stores not open to the general public, more than the normally permitted "living space," discounts on fares and rent, and access to the Society's own clinics, hospitals, and so forth.

My arrival coincided with the week before November 7th, the fourteenth anniversary of the Bolshevik Revolution and the country's most important holiday. The seventh and eight of November and the first and second of May were the only two-day national holidays in the entire year, and everybody looked forward to them. The city buzzed with preparations. Posters were mounted, streamers and banners hung, and electric bulbs strung for the "illumination," or light display.

My step-uncle was due back for the holiday. Meanwhile, Liza introduced me to the Atlases, a family who lived in the same building and had a teen-age daughter and son.

Anya was my age, and her brother Dodya two years older. Their father had died the year before and they lived with their mother, Rivekka Matveyevna, in a three-room (plus a large kitchen and full bathroom) apartment that for many years seemed the pinnacle of luxury in my eyes. A cousin, who was a few years older, lived with them, as did a domestic (*dom rabotnitsa,* "domestic worker"—the word *servant* was frowned upon) who slept on a cot in the kitchen. Dodya was a first-year chemistry student at Moscow University. Anya attended a factory training school (FZU) where she was completing her secondary education and learning a trade at the same time. Their mother had a personal pension in a higher category than my step-uncle's (hence, with more privileges) and also held a part-time job. The cousin worked in a factory and contributed to the household expenses.

The Atlases had lived in the southwestern Siberian city of Barnaul until a few years before. They were Jewish, but they had little in common with the Jews I had met so far, the majority of whom had come from small towns in the former tsarist Pale of Settlement.[2] Culturally, the Atlases were Russian. They did not speak Yiddish, which made communication difficult for us, but with the Russian I had by then picked up, a dictionary, and help from some of their friends who spoke English, French, or German, we managed to make ourselves understood. Their father had been a well-known revolutionary and the family maintained close ties with his former comrades-in-arms, many of whom were important government officials who often had business in Moscow. Among their friends were government and Party officials from Siberia and Buryat-Mongolia. Theirs was a hospitable, open house, constantly filled with the chatter and laughter of Anya's and Dodya's friends and the conversation of their mother's guests.

They made me feel very welcome. They were my first friends in Moscow, and Anya remained one of my dearest friends for many years. Full of merriment, with black eyes, black hair worn in a Dutch-boy cut, ivory-white skin, and dimples, she was always surrounded by beaux, whom she ordered about mercilessly. She dressed in the fashion of the day—a knee-length narrow black skirt, short black bolero jacket, and a black beret set rakishly over one eye. When we went out, she'd laughingly point to other girls dressed in exactly the same way.

Early on the morning of November 7th, the adult inhabitants of the two households left for their respective places of work or school to form marching columns in the mass demonstration that followed the military parade. "Demonstration" is actually a misnomer, for the event was actually a civilian

---

2. From the time of Catherine the Great until 1917, Jews in Russia were confined to the western regions of the Empire. This area was known as the "Pale of Settlement." (Ed.)

parade in which every working member of society, unless disabled, ill, or a privileged guest on the bleachers next to the reviewing stand overlooking Red Square, was expected to participate. (For the most part, they participated willingly, but pressure was exerted on the unwilling, as I discovered when I had a job myself.) In later years, the main event of the day was the review of the armed forces and military technology, and the "demonstration," a token march of "representatives" of the working people. In those early days and in the remaining years before the Second World War, however, columns of civilians eight or ten abreast, many with small children on their shoulders, streamed across Red Square from noon until dusk, holding posters and placards, and shouting slogans while straining to see the Soviet leaders on the reviewing stand. Most of all, they were eager to catch a glimpse of Stalin. The columns came from all directions to merge, first with other columns from the same district (Moscow was divided into administrative districts) and then to converge at the foot of the hill that led to Red Square.[3] Usually the pace was brisk, but at times the marchers stood around singing, dancing, and running up and down the sides of the columns to greet friends and look at the displays. In addition to the mandatory portraits of Marx, Engels, Lenin, Stalin, and the members of the Politburo carried at the head of every column, each district and large factory group carried portraits of its leading workers, posters illustrating production achievements, caricatures of bureaucrats, drunkards, idlers, and malingerers. Displays lampooned capitalist exploiters and those who served them (the pot-bellied, fat-faced capitalist with a cigar in his mouth, the bourgeois journalist holding a huge pen dripping with blood, the black-robed priest leering unctuously) and current political figures in the West.

My impression that day was that all available talent had been pressed into service. There were tableaux of cardboard figures, grotesque puppets on sticks, posters with striking futuristic art, and models or pictures of the various factories' wares. Delegations from the national republics marched in native costume. The procession was colorful and festive. I learned that demonstrations and parades such as Moscow's took place all over the Soviet Union on different scales.

The columns broke up on the other side of the square and the hassle to get home began. There would be no public transportation until late in the evening. The entire center of the city was cordoned off. Militiamen (as Soviet police were called) channeled human traffic out of the center beyond the cordon; only those who could prove residence within the cordoned area were allowed through. For those who lived far away, it was a dreary trek

---

3. Red Square (*Krasnaya ploshchad'*) was not named in honor of the Bolshevik Revolution. *Krasnaya* means "beautiful" as well as "red," and the name goes back to the seventeenth century.

home—anyone who could, stayed at the home of friends who lived nearby. To reach such homes, one had to get through the cordon, and many techniques and ruses were devised to do so. For many years, my place of refuge would be the Atlases' apartment, where friends and acquaintances would straggle in all afternoon and sit around drinking tea and comparing notes until the streetcars started running again (their most exciting topics of conversation concerned who saw whom on the reviewing stand. Those who claimed to have seen Stalin were the envy of the rest). Everybody had an amusing incident to report or an especially interesting piece of extravaganza to describe. One May Day, everyone talked about a huge wheel with spokes of beautiful girls with perfect figures clad in bathing suits at the head of the Institute of Physical Culture column. And, of course, there were many stories of how we fooled the militia or rushed their lines.

That November 7, 1931, I was among the spectators who lined the sidewalks. In the evening when it grew dark, Anya and her friends took me around the city to see the illumination, which was spectacular. The city was ablaze with lights: Every building had, at the very least, portraits of Lenin and Stalin and five-pointed stars outlined in electric lights. Entire scenes from the Russian revolution or the history of the Soviet Communist Party were displayed in electric lights on the bridges and squares, of which Moscow has so many. There were fireworks in the parks and music in the streets. The struggling young Soviet republic spared no expense to celebrate its triumphs.

The next day, Anya and her friends decided that I ought to visit Lenin's tomb. To embalm a corpse and build a shrine for it struck me as weird, but I could not offend them by refusing to go. When we arrived at Red Square and I saw the queue stretching down the hill into the park outside the Kremlin wall, I urged my companions to postpone the visit for another day, but they would not hear of it. Though we stood in line for over two hours in the cold November drizzle, they did not seem to mind at all.

Most of the people waiting in line were out-of-towners, many clad in the national costumes of the Central Asian republics, the Caucasus, and other parts of the Soviet Union. Two soldiers with rifles stood at attention at the entrance to the red granite mausoleum. The queue straightened into single file and moved solemnly past Lenin's casket. Lingering was not permitted. I must admit that I was profoundly moved as I looked down upon the legendary figure. He looked very much like his pictures, quite lifelike, only smaller. He had been dead almost eight years. In the thirty-four years I lived in Moscow, I never again went to the Lenin mausoleum.

When my step-uncle returned to Moscow, he looked nothing like the pictures of the dashing young man my mother had shown me. Though he had recently lost weight (I was told), he was still a very fat man who looked flushed and puffed when he walked. He was fifty years old and, because of a heart ailment, could not hold a regular job. He greeted me warmly, asked about my mother, recalling that she had sent him packages when he had been in Siberian exile, and about his half-sisters, my aunts in Albany whom he had not seen since they were young children. He also asked about my father, who had been a friend of his youth.

Now that the holiday was past, it was time to deal with my affairs. The idea of going to school (which had been my reason for leaving Birobidzhan) was dropped immediately. For one thing, I had not mastered enough Russian. (There was an Anglo-American school in Moscow where instruction was in English, but I did not know about it. Besides, I believe it was an elementary school.) More important, however, was the fact that I needed a place to live and, according to my step-uncle, the only and quickest way to get one was through a job with an organization that could provide its employees with housing. I needed ration cards, and I had to support myself. My parents were in no position to help me, and even if they had been, I would not have wanted them to know that I needed their help. My step-uncle mapped out a simple and what proved to be an effective strategy: I was to go alone to the Central Committee of the Komsomol and tell them my story. But I was to say that I was staying temporarily with someone I had met on the train and that I was being pressed to leave and had no place to go.

The offices of the Central Committee were located on Staraya Ploshchad (Old Square), a fifteen-minute walk from my cousins' apartment. In those days, neither a pass nor an appointment was required to get into the building. When I showed the soldier in the entrance booth my papers from Birobidzhan, he made a phone call and directed me upstairs to the international department. My step-uncle had assured me that there would be someone there who spoke Yiddish—and he was right.

I had to go to these offices several times before my affairs were settled. Each time, the same words preceded me upstairs: "The *Amerikanka*[4] is here. Get Venya" (or Misha, or Riva, or Izzya)! And Venya (or Misha, or Riva, or Izzya) would come running to greet me with a broad smile. We would speak in a Yiddish mixed with Russian and some English.

Toward the end of November, one of the girls met me with the words, "I have good news for you. Dinamo has room for you in their Komsomol commune. You'll be hired as an apprentice and learn a factory trade. What would you like to be? A *slesar'* or *tokar'* are the best."

Slesar? Tokar? I looked up the words in the Russian-English dictionary I carried with me, but neither "fitter" nor "turner" meant anything to me.

---

4. American woman.

"All right, " the girl said, "you'll be a slesar. That's settled." I was to be a fitter.

She told me I was to start my apprenticeship on December 1st. Meanwhile, I was to go to the personnel department of the Dinamo factory as soon as possible to fill out forms and be issued ration cards for December. I was then to go to the Komsomol committee where I would be given a housing order. I could move into the commune dormitory whenever I was ready. They had been informed and were expecting me.

# 4

# The Factory and the Commune—
# The Winter of 1931/1932

The very next day, I set out for the Dinamo (pronounced Dee-NA-mo) Factory. It was located in the working-class outskirts of Moscow, the Proletarsky district, and it was one of a group of pre-Soviet factories that included the Moscow Automobile Association Plant (AMO) and a ball-bearing plant (Sharikopodshipnik). Dinamo, formerly owned by Westinghouse but nationalized and given a new name during World War I, manufactured electric motors for trolley cars.

My step-uncle accompanied me. We boarded a trolley car on Chistiye Prudi, not far from his apartment building, and it took us all the way to the factory, a forty-five-minute ride. After making sure that I was in the right place and that I knew my way back, he went home. I gave my name to the guard at the gate and he gave me a pass to the personnel department. I found my way by showing the pass to people I met and having them point in the right direction. I was asked to wait at the front desk in the personnel section. A few minutes later, a man walked in, held out his hand, and said in English: "My name is Paul Lifshitz. I am an engineer here and I have been delegated by the Party Committee to look after the needs of the foreign workers at the plant. Welcome!"

He had a strong accent which at the time I could not place. It was German.

Paul took me into the personnel director's office and interpreted for us. He helped me fill out the forms (which were minimal), accompanied me to the office where ration cards were issued, and warned me to be very careful not to lose them, as they would not be replaced. Then he took me to the Komsomol committee where I got my housing order.

A few days later, my step-uncle called a taxicab and I left his home, with my baggage. He went upstairs with me when we arrived at my new address. Apparently, it didn't really matter any more if it became known that I had relatives in Moscow.

Tyufelev Lane (Proezd)[1] number sixteen was one of a group of five-story apartment buildings about a ten-minute walk from the factory. The

---

1. Tyufelev Lane, renamed Avtozavodskaya in 1950, was originally named after the village of Tukholya on the site of Tyufelevo woods.

building was owned by Dinamo; the other buildings in the complex belonged to AMO. A three-room (plus kitchen)[2] apartment on the third floor had been allocated to the Dinamo Komsomol committee to be used as it saw fit.

The brick building of three- and four-room apartments was typical of the housing constructed in the early 1930s. All rooms opened onto a central vestibule so that each room could be occupied by a separate family. There was central heating, electricity, indoor plumbing, but no bath or gas stove and no hot water. This was a great improvement on the one- and two-story wooden houses with wood-burning Dutch stoves for heating the barracks in which the majority of the factory workers lived.

I rang the bell. The door was opened by a fat girl with wavy, black shoulder-length hair, dark brown eyes, and a welcoming smile. She invited us in and introduced herself as "Valya." She took our coats and hung them up in the vestibule and showed us into a small room that contained four narrow iron beds neatly covered with white piqué bedspreads, four night tables with one top drawer and a storage compartment underneath, four chairs, and an oak wardrobe against one wall. She indicated the bed that was to be mine (farthest from the window, nearest to the door) and suggested that I put my suitcase under it for the time being. There was space in the wardrobe for my clothes. Outer clothing was to be hung on hooks in the vestibule.

Seven narrow iron beds lined the walls of the slightly larger room she took us into next. The beds were made in the same way as in the smaller room: white piqué bedspreads with a fold down the middle. Next to each bed was a night table.[3] There was a large oak wardrobe at one end of the room and a square table with chairs in the middle.

Two youths sitting at the table looked up from their books and smiled. This was the boys' room, but it also served as the commune's dining room and social area. Both rooms were neat and looked clean. There was a loudspeaker attached to the wall in the larger room. These megaphone-shaped speakers were everywhere—in the hotel in Birobidzhan, in my step-uncle's and the Atlases' apartments, and in public places. They were outlets for the state central broadcasting system, a relay system that served as radio for the general public.

The commune occupied these two rooms. The third room of the apartment—the largest—was occupied by a young Party official and his wife who were there supposedly to keep an eye on the communards and help them

2. The kitchen was not counted as living space. Further mention of apartment size will assume "plus kitchen."

3. Night tables such as these were a feature of every dormitory I lived in in the Soviet Union, and so were the white piqué bedspreads with a fold down the middle. That fold gave me a lot of trouble!

out. But by the time I arrived, the official had been promoted out of the factory and was not in the least interested in his young neighbors.

The kitchen contained two work tables, one for the commune, the other for the couple in the other room. A Primus stove and two kerosene stoves stood on each table. The toilet was at the end of a hall between the kitchen and the vestibule onto which each of the three rooms opened. But there was no bathroom or washroom, and the small kitchen sink had just one cold-water faucet. Every inch of space in the vestibule was occupied by trunks, large wicker chests, boxes, and bundles. Each resident was assigned a specific amount of floor and wall space. Naked bulbs hung from the ceilings.

Valya, who spoke Yiddish, assured my step-uncle that I would be fine. He left. I was now on my own.

It happened to be Valya's day off and she helped me through that first day in the commune. We went back into the girls' room and she pointed out her bed and told me about the other two occupants, Zina, a member of the commune, and Vassiona, the domestic. Vassiona was out marketing and would be back soon. Zina was at work and would come home in due course, as would the boys.

Vassiona came in soon afterwards. Her face was pock-marked, her mouse-colored hair pulled back in a tight bun. I could not tell her age. She was dressed like the peasants I had seen along the train route, in a padded jacket which she hung in the vestibule, a full, dark-colored skirt, a blouse, and a kerchief on her head. She nodded to me and went into the kitchen.

After a while, Zina came home, a very pretty girl of eighteen, with short black hair cut like a boy's, slightly slanting deep-set brown eyes, and high cheekbones. Valya had told me that Zina was a Chuvash and had an older brother who was an important official in Cheboksary, the capital of Chuvashia.[4] Zina's greeting was reserved, cool.

All the communards gathered for supper that evening. (I was to discover that this was unusual, as they worked different shifts and had different days off. There were no set mealtimes.) Valya had told me a little about them. All were skilled workers in the tool-making trades, some very highly skilled, though none was more than nineteen or twenty years old. Valya, in fact, was the oldest at twenty-one. She and Zina worked in the factory tool shop as lathe operators (*tokars*). Shura, Vanya, and Yura had been *besprizorny;* that is, they had been among the millions of children made homeless in the aftermath of revolution and civil war. Large numbers of these "wild"

---

4. The Chuvash people were descended from Finno-Ugric and Turkish-speaking tribes that lived along the Volga River and chose to be incorporated into the Russian Empire in the sixteenth century. A Chuvashian Autonomous Soviet Socialist Republic had been formed in 1925. (Ed.)

children roamed the country, sleeping wherever they could and living by their wits. As in Nikolai Ekk's classic film, *Road to Life,* which appeared in 1931 (and was shown widely in the United States), these boys had been picked off the streets and sent to "colonies," actually reform schools for juvenile delinquents, where they had received an education and vocational training. Now they had gone to work at the Dinamo factory and to live in the commune. Shura and Vanya, one dark, one fair, were steady peasant types of few words, yet they were quietly friendly. Yura was bright-faced and full of curiosity. He was the only one who had attempted to impress his individuality on his "corner" of the room by placing a small picture of a landscape over his bed and a vase on his night table. The Levitin brothers, Boris and Yefim, worked in the factory and planned to go on to college. They were acquiring proletarian status so as not to be rejected when they applied. It was whispered that their parents were *lishentsi*—that is, persons deprived of their civil rights because of "bourgeois class origin." They spent little time in the apartment and generally kept to themselves. There was also an absent communard whose bed was being kept unoccupied for him. This was Volodya, who had gone to work as a volunteer at Magnitogorsk, a major construction project of the First Five-Year Plan, and was due back in a few months.

The seventh bed was occupied by an outsider, Haitin. (He was always addressed by his surname.) He had been expelled from the commune for disruptive behavior, the nature of which I was never able to ascertain. He did not share in the commune's expenses and had a special arrangement with Vassiona for her services. Haitin was employed at AMO as an electrician. Attempts had been made to evict him, but in vain. Eviction was a complicated process involving the factory administration and the trade union, as well as the district housing authorities, and he had succeeded in blocking the process with the help of AMO organizations. Haitin was tall, broad-shouldered, with straight black hair, black eyes set close together, and a habitual expression of amusement on his face. He seemed older than his nineteen years. He spoke Yiddish fluently.

This was my first experience in dormitory living. I had never gone to camp as a child and, except when cousins visited us, had never shared a room with anyone but my younger sister (and a very large room that was, with walk-in closets!). However, by now I knew what crowded conditions people lived in and I accepted my lot without a murmur. I had no choice.

The commune had been established three or four years earlier, one of several Komsomol communes in the Proletarsky district. It represented a vanguard attempt to live by the communist principle: From each according to his ability, to each according to his needs. Members turned over their earnings and ration cards to a common treasury. Ration cards were "attached" to specific shops where some unrationed food and other necessities were also available. Some of the commune's money was set aside for house-keeping, Vassiona's salary, and other regular expenses. Each communard received pocket money for transportation, for the very inexpensive meals at the factory canteen, for "culture" (entertainment, books, sporting goods), and for small extras.

Our commune was not a voluntary organization in the sense that a group of congenial people decided to live together. Applications for membership were submitted to the district Komsomol committee with a recommendation from the applicant's place of work, in this case, the Dinamo factory. The applicant had to have a good work record and had to be active in Komsomol affairs. For young people from out of town who had no place to live, a communal residence was preferable to a cot in a factory dormitory, where they would often share a room with ten or fifteen others in a wooden barrack with no basic conveniences. Given housing conditions in Moscow, I was considered lucky to have been admitted to the commune. It was the intervention of the Komsomol Central Committee that did it.

Many of the members of the Dinamo commune had been living in it from its inception, though there had been some turnover. The first chairman had left. He had made the young girl who was their domestic at the time pregnant and the factory finally gave the young couple a room of their own somewhere else. He used to visit us once in a while, never with his wife. No one had been chosen to succeed him as chairman. Vassiona, whom I came to detest for her vulgarity, filthiness, and sly, troublemaking ways, made all the decisions regarding meals and practical matters, sometimes consulting with one or another of the communards. Meetings to discuss other matters were called by anyone who wished to take the initiative.

It was bitter cold at 7:45 A.M. on December 1, 1931, when I set out for the factory. My American sheepskin-lined leather jacket was warm enough as far as it went, but it only reached the top of my knees. I wore a visored cap, thin gloves, lisle stockings, and plain oxfords. Valya, who had taken me under her wing, was worried. "You'll freeze," she said. "We must get you *valenkie,* warm gloves, and a hat. I'll see if I can get you orders for them."

*Valenkie*—standard winter equipment—were felt boots, not quite knee-high. Major items of clothing, such as *valenkie,* shoes, suits, coats, and household goods were usually purchased by order. If an order was given to the commune, the members decided at a meeting to whom it should go and allotted money for the purchase. If it was given to an individual communard, the commune paid for the article. Orders were usually issued by the factory trade union committee or administration, sometimes to individuals for good work, but more often for communes and collectives to distribute.

It was a very cold winter. It was not unusual for the temperature to fall to twenty degrees below freezing and on some days, it was even colder.

Valya, true to her word, got orders for me. I bought a hat with ear flaps and mittens, but had to wait several weeks for *valenkie* as they did not have my size in stock. However, my knees froze even after I got them. I would practically run the short distance to and from the factory. Those first weeks, I never saw daylight except on my days off. It was dark when I left in the morning and dark by the time I got into the house a little after three o'clock in the afternoon. Days off were on a sliding schedule—every fifth day. There were three shifts—the factory never closed.

Six of us formed the team of apprentices to which I was assigned: four boys and two girls. Apprentices worked only the morning shift. I was the only one under eighteen and was required to work only six hours a day (the others worked eight), beginning at eight with an hour for lunch (actually, dinner—*obyed*). The first step involved learning to file a block of metal held in a vise to a smooth, even surface. Try as I might, I could not do it. I filed and filed the whole day long until I was ready to drop. The block of metal would look perfectly smooth to me, but the instructor would run his finger over it and shake his head—not smooth enough. A longtime factory worker and Party member, our instructor was a gentle, patient man. He never reproached me, never said a harsh word to me. He must have been a competent teacher because the other apprentices went from step to step within the prescribed time limits. I, however, never mastered the first step.

As I walked through the factory and observed the bright, alert, young faces bent intently over machines, the workers stripped to the waist in the foundry shop tending the roaring furnaces, the many women in the tool shops and quality control, young girls and middle-aged mothers of families wearing bright red or flowered print cotton kerchiefs on their heads, splashes of color against the otherwise drab background, my spirits were high. These workers did not resemble the proletarians as I imagined them to be under capitalism. They were the revolutionary vanguard of Russia and of the international working class, honored in songs, poems, and the press, urged to take pride in their status, constantly told how fortunate they were to be the first unexploited working class in history. The Soviet state was their state and everything the government did was supposed to be in their interests. Many were recent peasants who had close ties with the countryside. There was a core of men and women from urban, working-class backgrounds, but they were in the minority. On the one hand, war, revolution, and civil war had decimated their ranks: on the other hand, many had moved up the ladder to administrative posts in the Party and the government.

To have come from a working-class family was an enormous asset. This background opened doors to swift advancement for anyone with ambition and intelligence. I learned the magical significance of being from "worker origins." "Worker origins" made you trustworthy. Not only your loyalty, but your instincts could be relied upon. "Worker origins" automatically made you capable of understanding (and supporting) the Party's policies. Poor peasant origins were good too, but not as good. They did not automatically confer political insight. This attitude was based on the assumption that the interests of the proletariat were identical with those of the Party, whereas the peasants had acquisitive instincts that could lead them away from the path to socialism and along the road to small-scale capitalism.

I was proud of my worker origins—after all, my father was a carpenter. It puzzled the communards that someone of worker background should be so unsuited to proletarian ways, but they made allowances for the influences of the capitalist society I had lived in.

Jews had been affected more widely than the general population by this class approach. Because of residential, professional, educational, and other restrictions under the tsarist regime, a large percentage of the Jewish population had been small-scale artisans, merchants, or businessmen. Though most barely eked out a living, they were classified as "petty bourgeoisie." Even the poorest craftsmen—shoemakers, tailors, roofers—had often been self-employed and, as such, came under that heading. Many of the more prosperous citizens, Jews among them, had been deprived of their civil rights and branded *lishentsi*. Even though restrictions against Jews had been abolished and anti-Semitism was punishable under the law, many Jewish young people with suspect class backgrounds could not or were afraid they would not gain admittance to higher schools. As a result, young Jews from the former Pale of Settlement headed for industrial cities to find jobs in factories and at construction sites. After two or three years as workers, the majority went on to higher schools, mostly engineering, because engineering was the most popular profession in that period of industrialization. The influx of young Jews into Birobidzhan in the early 1930s was one result of that "rehabilitation" process.

The class approach applied to intellectuals and professionals as well, regardless of ethnic origin. Thus, the work force at Dinamo and other factories included quite a few young people from families of engineers, physicians, professors, and other professionals. These untypical workers were especially receptive to appeals to proletarian pride and class consciousness. They worked with enthusiasm, participated in all extracurricular factory activities, and added a gloss to factory life that it probably never had before or since. Intensifying the sense of excitement was the widespread striving for education, especially among the young. Many workers came to their jobs carrying books, and were prepared to hurry off to night school or college preparation courses after their shifts. Factory workers who were students enjoyed special privileges, such as time off with pay to study for annual and semi-annual exams and adjustments of work shifts to accommodate their school schedules.

Those were my first impressions, and they proved to be valid. However, as time went by, I became aware of some serious problems at the factory and of other attitudes among workers. Though I was not involved in production, I heard a good deal of talk about it, about fulfillment of the plan, criticism and self-criticism, socialist competition, *udarniki* ("shock workers" who set the pace for others), absenteeism, and mismanagement. Much of this talk took place around the commune's dining table. The factory production rhythm was uneven. At the beginning of the month, workers often had nothing to do (at half-pay): Parts had not been delivered, machines were out of order, raw materials had run out. Toward the end of the month, everyone had to work overtime to fulfill the plan. Absenteeism, usually connected with drunkenness and worst right after payday, was also a major problem. I often found myself zigzagging down the street as if I were drunk myself, crossing to the other side each time I saw a drunk weaving towards me. It was years before I lost my fear of them. Most drunks were foul-mouthed, but harmless, except when they got into brawls with other drunks.

Every free moment at the factory was used for *vospitaniye*. *Vospitaniye* was an important word in the Soviet vocabulary. It could mean "upbringing," "education," "enlightenment," "indoctrination," or just teaching someone good manners. During the lunch hour and between shifts, workers were expected to attend current affairs groups at which newspapers were read aloud and the news discussed and explained. And the workers did attend. Perhaps they were really interested. At the time, I thought they were. (If they were not, they concealed their feelings. Non-attendance was noticed and it was not advisable for people who wished to maintain or improve their position to be labeled politically immature, philistine, individualistic or, worse still, discontented.) There were compulsory weekly political classes for Komsomol and Party members. There were meetings nearly every day at some level—shop, team, section, department, factory. There were production meetings to discuss progress and plan fulfillment, trade union meetings (everyone was a member of the trade union), Komsomol and Party meetings (some restricted to members, others open to all). Of course, there were delinquents who did not give a hoot and avoided these activities whenever they could. Some of these were alcoholics and low-life types. Many were married women who rushed off after work to stand in line at food shops, pick up their children at day care centers, go home and cook, clean house, scrub floors, wash and mend clothes late into the night, only to begin all over again at daybreak.

When a general meeting of special importance was scheduled, the factory gates were locked so that no one could leave without a special pass. I did not find out about this practice for a long time, as I finished my shift before most of the others and usually went straight home. When I did find out, I was shocked. I believed (and said so) that our cause should stand on its own merits and that compulsion had no place in *vospitaniye*. My peculiar views were attributed to my bourgeois *vospitaniye*.

At the factory Komsomol committee, I was issued a membership card without ado. They could not have cared less whether I had a transfer from the United States. They took my word that I had been a member there, so I started out with two years of membership to my credit.

My participation in factory affairs was minimal, especially that first winter. There was no point in my attending meetings, as I did not know enough Russian to understand what was going on. My life centered around the commune and the few friends I had outside it.

The commune was in the throes of an ideological conflict that I understood only vaguely. The question was whether to change status from "commune" to "collective." In a commune, the members would contribute all of their earnings and would be given equal shares of spending money. In a collective, the operating principle was "from each according to his ability, to each according to his work." In a collective, each would contribute a percentage of his or her earnings to the common fund and keep the rest. When the commune started, the members had all been at approximately the same earning level. Now there were high earners and low earners. (I was the lowest, with an apprentice's stipend of forty-five rubles a month. The others earned from eighty to one hundred rubles a month.) The theoretical grounds for the proposed change were two recent speeches by Stalin, titled "Dizzy with Success" and "Problems of Agrarian Policy in the USSR," better known as the "six conditions" speech. The communards were astonished that I had never heard of the speeches, and that I knew little about Stalin and practically nothing about the history of the Party. Valya was delegated to explain everything to me. Apparently, the gist of the speeches, which dealt mainly with collectivization and the countryside, was that communes had been formed too hastily. Conditions were not ripe for them. At the present stage of economic and social development in the Soviet Union, collectives were a more stable form of organization.

The lively discussions culminated several weeks after my arrival in a decision to change from commune to collective, though we continued to be known as the Dinamo Komsomol Commune. The change did not affect me. I earned so little that what I had left over for myself did not matter. And it made little difference in our way of life. Vassiona continued to shop, cook one meal a day, and clean after a fashion.

Breakfast was standard: tea, bread and butter, or more often margarine, hard cheese or sausage if the ration had not been used up, leftovers from the day before. The person on duty for the week rose before the others in the morning, lit the kerosene or the Primus stove, and put the kettle on for tea. We had one meal at the factory. For those working the morning shift, this was the noon meal; for those on the night shift or swing shift, it was the evening meal. The meal in the factory canteen was the main meal of the day. Dinamo was a heavy industry enterprise and therefore in the highest supply category. Meat was served several times a week. What was for dinner at the factory was a daily topic of conversation among those coming from and going to work. Communards in the evening shift had a meal at home, usually around three o'clock. The morning-shift people came home shortly after four, but were frequently detained by meetings or classes, so that until late in the evening there was usually someone eating supper at the table in the bigger room. Often, there were several of us at the supper table, talking, laughing, and joking.

Vassiona was not expected to serve us. Someone, usually the person on duty if he or she was not at work, heated a large pot of whatever soup Vassiona had made that day, stuck a ladle into the pot, and set it down in the middle of the table. We helped ourselves to the food. What we ate depended on what Vassiona had managed to procure that day in the store or at the open market. At the so-called "collective farm market," peasants stood at long wooden tables with little piles of this and that, mostly vegetables (cabbage, sometimes onions, carrots, potatoes) and dairy products. Money was not important. Barter was the prevalent means of exchange. We all had "worker" category rations, so there was more than enough bread and sufficient cooking oil in supply. Vassiona exchanged bread, cooking oil, sugar, and soap for milk, butter, pot cheese, and whatever else we needed that was available. Frequently, the soup was cabbage soup, with or without pieces of meat in it. Potatoes fried in sunflower seed oil were standard fare. Millet porridge was often served with meat or eaten with milk. For dessert, there was a kind of pudding called *kisel'*, made with potato starch and milk or, later in the year, cranberries or red currants.

Frequently, no one was at home when I returned from work. That hour or so when I was alone was precious to me. I could shut the kitchen door, heat water in the kettle or in a big pot, and wash myself at the sink. In the morning, I hardly had time to splash cold water on my face and hands, grab something to eat, and run. But in the afternoon, I could read, write letters, or write in my diary. I could sit still in an empty room.

An empty room! A room of my own, where I could close the door and shut out the world—I was obsessed by this dream. It was a fantasy I dreamed of nearly all the years I lived in the Soviet Union. (By the time I finally got a room of my own, it hardly mattered anymore.)

Valya, Zina, and I managed to keep our room tolerably clean, no thanks to Vassiona. Vassiona willingly picked up after the boys, dusting and washing the floor in their room, but she did ours only when we made a fuss. Females could do their own cleaning. She seldom bathed or changed her clothes. Our room was stuffy, but I could not persuade the others to keep a window—not even the *fortochka*—open. The double windows were sealed for the winter. It was too cold, they said. Besides, the night air was bad for you.

I remember how my first day at the commune, I woke up in the middle of the night. Something was biting me. I switched on the light. More bedbugs! The girls laughed at me the next morning (the light had not awakened them). "Fresh meat," they said. "You'll get used to them. Don't squash them, they'll stink up the room if you do."

I had no intention of getting used to them. I kept at Zina and Valya until they agreed to help me do something about the bugs, and they made Vassiona help, much against her will. We turned all four mattresses and poured boiling water into the springs. By repeating this procedure every once in a while, we managed to keep the bedbugs under control.

Not so the cockroaches. When I turned on the light in the kitchen late at night, swarms of black insects the size of large beetles scurried off in all directions. The first time I saw them, I quickly turned the light off, ran into the boys' room, and pulled Yura after me into the kitchen. "*Tarakany,*" he said, and shrugged his shoulders.

My Russian-English dictionary told me the meaning of *tarakany*. I had never seen cockroaches this size. When I told Valya about the cockroaches, she showed me a packet of yellow powder called pyrethrum, kept on a kitchen shelf, and said it sometimes helped. I sprinkled it in all corners, but it did not do much good.

My efforts to improve hygiene, especially in the "places of common usage"—to get everyone to flush the toilet after using, to do something about the roaches and bedbugs, to get them to open windows more often— were not taken seriously. I composed signs with the help of the dictionary, often using the wrong word to everyone's amusement, and tacked them up. No one corrected the signs and no one paid attention to their exhortations.

On the other hand, they found some of my habits not *kul'turno*. The Russian word *kul'turno* has a multitude of meanings, the least of which is "cultured." It may refer to, among other choices, hygiene, cleanliness, manners, erudition, or forms of recreation. Its emphasis changed over the years. In those days it was a potent word, expressing a goal toward which the Soviet people in general and the proletariat in particular were striving. *Nye kul'turno*—not cultured—conveyed strong disapproval. I did not use a fork to spear a slice of bread from the bread basket on the table, as they did. That was *nye kul'turno*. I'd forget myself and start whistling (though I was not very good at it). Whistling indoors was bad manners for males as well as females. ("You're not in the middle of a field!") I'd come in from the street and throw my coat down on the bed instead of hanging it up in the hall. This was shockingly *nye kul'turno*. (This last had a sound basis. You never knew what you might bring in on your collar from the factory cloakroom or a crowded streetcar. I got into the habit of inspecting my outer clothing carefully when I came in from outside and hanging it on a hook in the hall.)

Was this all really happening to me? Surely I'd wake up and find that it was a dream! Half nightmare, half fantasy.

No, California was the dream. Four months and 10,000 miles away. California was as remote as if it were in another galaxy. And so it was. And so was the sheltered adolescent who used to be me, with her visions of college, a career, independence, and hope for a better world. Here I was, on my own with a vengeance, plunged into an alien world, living with and among strangers, learning new ways and a new language, earning my living (such as it was) for the first time. I was so busy coping with my daily life and absorbing the hailstorm of new impressions beating down upon my head that I had neither the time nor the energy to brood about the past. Besides, the difficulties I was having had not shaken my faith in the socialist cause, my belief that the Soviet Union was on the right path and would eventually achieve socialism. Russia had been a very backward country. It was not the ideal place for the socialist revolution to have taken place, but having occurred, it would be carried through. These were my beliefs, not conclusions based on facts or knowledge. They were feelings, and they derived in part from conversations with my new acquaintances. Anya and her brother, Valya and the other communards, and Feigele in Birobidzhan were all fervent believers in their country's special mission to become the first socialist state in the world.

In any case, there was nothing I could do about my plight. I could not rejoin my family. Life was much harder in Birobidzhan. My letters to my parents were unfailingly cheerful. Why worry them? What was the point of telling them that acquiring clothing had become a problem? I had not been properly equipped in the first place. My supply of stockings ran out almost immediately—the felt boots tore them mercilessly—and new stockings were hard to come by. Every day after work, I darned stockings, either to wear the same evening or for the next day. "Darn" is not the correct word. I used to sew the holes together. I had never darned a stocking before. In fact, I had never done any of the things I had to do now, such as make my bed, light a Primus stove, even, as I realized to my horror, cut up the meat on my plate. (When I told my mother this twenty-five years later, she did not believe me.)

❧❧❧

# 5

# A Teenager in Moscow—Spring 1932

Despite the aggravations and frustrations of trying to master the details of daily life, I was not unhappy, at least not entirely unhappy. My mood fluctuated between despair at my incompetence, especially on the job, and elation at the exciting newness of my life. And although I was not conscious of it, I realize now that I enjoyed the feeling of being special and the attention, even affection, with which I was surrounded.

Little by little, I got to know my fellow communards. At first, I gravitated towards those with whom I could communicate best—Valya, Haitin, and Yura.

Haitin was very attentive to me from the start. More and more often, he was already at home when I came from work. He'd light the Primus stove, put on the kettle to heat water so that I could wash, and keep anyone who turned up out of the kitchen until I was finished. He also kept Vassiona in line. Vassiona never talked back to him as she did to the rest of us, and she did what he told her to do. He must have paid her well. He always seemed to have plenty of money and plenty of time.

Yura was attending night school, preparing to take college-entrance exams. He spent every spare moment studying, but was always happy to put his books aside to talk to me. Literature was his love. Had I read Mayne Reid[1]? No, I had never heard of Mayne Reid. Yes, I had read Cooper (James Fenimore) and did not like him much. And Upton Sinclair and Mark Twain, whom I did like. Those were the English-language writers most widely read in Russia. And I had read the Russian novelists, too, in English translation. This surprised him. Between the ages of thirteen and sixteen, I had read Tolstoy's *Anna Karenina, The Kreutzer Sonata,* and *Resurrection,* but not *War and Peace.* In my local public library I had also discovered Turgenev's *Fathers and Sons,* Kuprin's *The Pit,* and Dostoevsky's *The Idiot.* When I read them again in Russian decades later, I realized how

---

1. Mayne Reid (Thomas Mayne Reid), 1818–1883, an English writer of adventure stories, was very popular in Russia.

little I had understood, but I had found them absorbing nevertheless. I had never heard of Pushkin or Lermontov. Yura, on the other hand, had never heard of the Brontës or George Eliot (neither had any of my other Russian friends). Yura and I became friends and our friendship lasted for several years after both of us left the commune.

The Levitin brothers were inseparable. They would come home to eat and soon run off again. They, too, were studying, but they did this elsewhere and were also active in Komsomol affairs—chalking up credit for the future. While they were pleasant and polite, they never took part in discussions in the commune. Though they spoke Yiddish, they showed no interest in talking with me. This attitude puzzled me at the time, but I realized later as I recall that their family background had probably made them very cautious and that they were acting on the principle that they would be safer with less involvement. Shura and Vanya seldom initiated conversations, but were happy to listen and they radiated warmth and concern.

Zina was seldom at home. She did not even turn up for meals most of the time. She'd come home to sleep and go off right after breakfast. We hardly spoke to one another.

The winter evenings were long. If we went out, it was usually as a group to see a movie or attend a concert (a *kontsert* was variety entertainment) at the factory clubhouse or at the Proletarsky district "house of culture." Ekk's *Road to Life* and Sergei Yutkevich's *Golden Hills* were two of the popular Soviet films of the era. An American movie starring the comedian Harold Lloyd was playing, with the Russian title *Harry, the Physical Culturist*. The audiences loved it. Theater tickets were available at a discount from the factory trade union committee. I saw my first opera and my first ballet that winter—*Rigoletto* and *The Red Poppy*, both at the Bolshoi Theater. Barsova and Maksakova were the reigning sopranos, Kozlovsky and Lemeshev the tenors of the day, for years to come. Teen-age girls mobbed them for autographs, jumping and screaming outside the stage entrance, just like the bobby soxers at home.

Other times, especially when blizzards hit or on very cold days (twenty-five to thirty degrees below freezing was considered cold), we spent the evenings at home, sitting round the table. Visitors dropped in frequently.

Among the most frequent were Haitin's friends, Senya and Boris. Senya was older, twenty-four or twenty-five, pale and intense with hollow cheeks and bags under his eyes. Valya told me that Senya had been a member of the Party and had taken part in the opposition to Stalin. As a result, he had been expelled from the Party and demoted to a lowly factory job. Boris, curly-headed, red-cheeked, looking younger than his twenty-one years, reminded me of the boys I had known at home. He had a cared-for look that none of the others had, though he, too, lived in a factory dormitory. I became very fond of Senya and Boris and was always pleased to see them. Another frequent visitor was Pasha, who was part of a Komsomol commune at the Ball Bearing Factory. Pasha took me to his commune one day to meet another American—Harry Eisman. The name was familiar to me. Harry Eisman had been a *cause célèbre* in the United States (at least, in my circles) a few years earlier. He had been deported to Russia (where he had been born) for some silly prank during a Communist-led demonstration in New York. The Russians made a great fuss about him. Harry and his older brother had a room of their own in the commune. They showed me a collection of newspaper clippings and talked about the important people Harry had met.[2]

I was picking up Russian quickly and incorrectly, and the communards and their friends had a lot of fun at my expense. I had a hard time telling when they were teasing and when they were serious.

"Meri,[3] do you have birch trees in America?'

"Of course."

"And sparrows?"

"Yes, sparrows, too, and cats and dogs. By the way, I haven't seen a single cat or dog in Moscow."

"They've all been eaten." Shocked silence followed Senya's remark. Me, because of the import of the statement, the others, because of Senya's bluntness.

"Meri, do people walk on their heads in America?" Now I knew they were teasing.

They howled when I mispronounced words in such a way that they acquired different meanings from those I intended. My dictionary often misled me.

"Don't go, Meri, it's early."

"I have letters to write." But the word for "write," *pisat'*, with the accent pronounced on the first syllable, means "to pee."

I didn't mind their teasing, except when it got me into trouble. Not only didn't they correct me, but they frequently deliberately led me astray.

I complained that my felt boots were tearing my stockings.

"Why don't you get a pair of these?" Yura said, indicating the foot rags they wrapped around their feet before putting on their *valenkie*. "They have them in the factory store—unrationed."

"What are they called?"

---

2. I did not see Harry again until long after the war, but I heard about him from time to time. He spent several years in Siberian exile in the 1950s because of an earlier association with Anna Louise Strong, an American journalist in Moscow who was accused of espionage and expelled from the country (yet remained a loyal Stalinist to the end of her life). He visited family in the United States in the 1970s, but died in Moscow.

3. This is how Russians pronounced my name.

My friend told me to ask for "portki."

I should have known better. The sales clerk, an older woman, was not amused when I asked for men's underpants (instead of *portyanki*—foot rags). I tried to explain, pointing to my feet, but it did no good. She called me a hussy.

I cut my finger at the factory one day. They bandaged it at the first aid station and put a rubber finger over it to protect it. When I got home that afternoon, the boys looked at me strangely.

"What's that, Meri? Where did you get it?"

"At the first aid station. I cut my finger."

"Ah." (The Russian equivalent of "Oh.")

Others came home, stared, but said nothing. Valya came home and was immediately taken aside for a whispered conversation. I began to wonder what was wrong.

Valya: "Meri, what's that on your finger?"

I explained.

"Don't you know what that is?" she continued. "It's a 'preservative'."

"What's a 'preservative'?"

"How ignorant can you be?" And she proceeded to enlighten me. A 'preservative' was a condom, she said, sold over the counter in pharmacies. I blushed and pulled the rubber off my finger. It was quite some time before I discovered that they were fooling me.

It was customary to go the bathhouse once a week, usually in the evening before your day off. Valya and Zina took me the first few times. Basically, the public baths were a city version of the village bathhouse I'd known in Birobidzhan. After a short wait in line, we bought our tickets and entered an anteroom with wooden benches against the walls. Here we took off our clothes, put them in our little satchels that also contained our clean clothes, and checked the satchels with the cloakroom attendant. Then, stark naked except for the cloakroom checks on a string around our necks and a piece of soap in our hands, we entered a huge room with tiled floors and walls, marble benches, and faucets with hot and cold running water. The girls showed me where to find the tin basins most likely not to have been used that day. They taught me to slosh the bench with boiling water before sitting on it. Adjoining this room was a smaller steam room with wooden benches at different levels. The higher it was, the hotter.

I disliked the entire procedure: the soapy water on the tile floor, the mass of naked bodies bumping into one another, the stares, the comments, ribald remarks. But there was no other way to keep clean. The only people I knew who had private baths were my step-uncle and the Atlases, but their hot water supply was limited and I rarely happened to arrive at the right time to take a bath. Moscow also had two luxury bathhouses from pre-Soviet times: the Central Baths and the Sandunovsky Baths, where one could get a private room (for one or more persons), but they were far from where I lived and beyond my means.

Most people with whom I came into contact were helpful and kind, but now and then I encountered hostility. Vassiona had her ups and downs—times for ranting and scolding—but she was like that with everyone (though I reacted more angrily than the others when she shouted at me). Much more disturbing was Zina's hostility. She had a quick temper and we sometimes quarreled openly, once or twice to a point where the commune held a meeting to discuss our relations. I cannot remember specifically what provoked our quarrels. They may have arisen from having conflicting personalities in such close quarters, touched off, no doubt, by Zina's contempt for my clumsiness in practical matters and her resentment of the attention I was getting and the allowances being made for me. Valya tried to keep the peace between us. She made excuses for Zina. Zina was unhappy. She was in love with the Dinamo Komsomol secretary, who was married. Zina was under another kind of strain, too, though I did not know about it until later. Her brother was in trouble in Chuvashia where several high-ranking officials had been expelled from the Party and arrests were taking place. Eventually, he was arrested and Zina left the commune and the factory (about six months before I did). She could not face this disgrace and expected to be turned out of the commune and evicted from her "living space." If left to themselves, the communards would not have expelled her, but they would certainly have been ordered to do so by the Komsomol committee. I heard about Zina from time to time over the years from Galya, a close friend of hers who also became my friend.

Galya was a lathe operator at the same tool shop where Valya and Zina worked. On my first day at the factory, she came to my workplace to make my acquaintance. Galya Babushkin belonged to one of the most privileged sections of Soviet society. Her parents had been professional revolutionaries and members of the Bolsheviks since the faction's inception in 1903. They had supported Stalin unwaveringly in all factional fights after Lenin's death. Galya was born in 1911 in Siberia, where her parents had been exiled by the tsarist regime. As a young child, she had spent a few years in Persia, where her father was in the Soviet diplomatic service and where she learned French. Her father had died some years earlier and she and her mother lived in the Metropol Hotel. With her background, Galya could have gone to the university straight from secondary school, but she chose to go to a factory training school and then to a factory job to acquire the "proletarian mentality." At nineteen, she was already a member of the Communist Party. Tall and slim, with grey eyes and a grave expression on her rather plain face, she seemed earnest beyond her years. Galya was a frequent visitor at the commune. She had come there originally as Zina's friend, but now had friends of her own among us.

The Metropol is an old hotel in the center of Moscow. Some of the staff had been there since the days of the tsar. The shabby luxury of the carpeted lobby, the ornate brass carvings, the red plush and gilded furniture, and the gold-braided uniforms of the reception personnel contrasted sharply with the world outside. The Babushkins' windows looked out upon Theater Square, home of the Bolshoi and Maly Theaters; Revolution Square with the Museum of the Revolution and the Grand Hotel; and the approaches to Red Square. On holidays, when a parade and demonstration were scheduled, residents had to obtain special permission well in advance if they wished to invite guests. Several times in later years, I watched the parade from those windows—the closest I ever came to viewing it from the Red Square bleachers, which was something I wanted very badly to do. The first time Galya brought me to her home, she made a point of introducing me to the hotel administrator, the desk clerk, and the elevator man, telling them that I would be coming again. The desk clerk had a list of visitors expected each day. If the visitor's name was not on the list, he or she had to call upstairs from the house phone and wait for the call back to the front desk. After the staff got to know me, I was allowed to pass without the rigmarole, except on holidays. The staff never seemed to change. For ten, fifteen, twenty years the same elevator operator took me up to the top floor where the Babushkins lived. For all I know, he is still there. Or did they all look alike?

A small vestibule with double doors led into the very large room which Galya and her mother shared. The room was at least three times the size of the commune's bigger room. Beautiful Persian rugs hung on the walls and were spread over the three couches. A small table and chairs were placed at one end of the room near the window, with a larger table in the middle of the room. They had an electric hot plate, but shared other facilities with the apartment's residents: a huge kitchen with eight or nine work tables; two stoves and sinks; and two spacious bathrooms, one at each end of the wide corridor, with hot water boilers that could be heated whenever required. The top floor was inhabited by permanent residents, all of them old revolutionaries or their survivors—widows, children, relatives, and several former retainers.

Lydia Sergeyevna, Galya's mother, was a tall, stately woman with a mass of thick, white hair that she often wore in a braid around her head. Galya did not resemble her in the least. Her mother could not have been old—probably in her forties—but I could not judge. She greeted me warmly.

The dining table was laden with delicacies—white bread, butter, smoked salmon, sturgeon, caviar, sliced sausage. I was urged to help myself freely. As a member of the Society of Old Bolsheviks,[4] Lydia Sergeyevna used the

---

4. The Society of Old Bolsheviks was an elite organization, restricted at that time to Communist Party members who traced their membership back to the formation of Lenin's faction within the Russian Social Democratic Labor Party (RSDLP).

same general retail network as the Atlases and my step-uncle, but she received the highest category of rations within that system. They had reached the highest rung in the ladder of privilege, except for the high government and Party officials.

The Society of Former Political Prisoners and Penal Exiles was several rungs below. Its members had been jailed or exiled by the tsarist regime for political activities, but they came from every branch of the Russian revolutionary movement. Among them were non–Party members, as well as persons who had joined the Bolshevik Party after the revolution—former Mensheviks, Socialist-Revolutionaries, and anarchists. Until January 1927, they had published a journal of their own called *Katorga i ssylka* (*Penal Servitude and Exile*). They enjoyed numerous material benefits, but were looked down upon and distrusted by the Old Bolsheviks. Both societies had offices in old Moscow mansions where they held meetings and official gatherings. The main business of the staffs of both societies, however, was to distribute ration cards, arrange health resort accommodations, supervise medical facilities, and so forth. They also had one central dining room where members and their families could have meals or take meals home. Lydia Sergeyevna never cooked. She or Galya would go every few days to bring cooked food home in special containers—three aluminum pots in one with a handle—and warm up the food as needed.

The intricate system of privilege for acquiring the basic necessities—food, clothing, shelter, and medical services—was beyond my comprehension. I noted it, but did not question it. Foreigners who had made contractual arrangements before coming to the Soviet Union (engineers and skilled workers, mostly) as well as others in important positions had access to a special retail network called *Insnab* (acronym for *Inostrannoye snabzheniye*—foreign supply). The Germans at Dinamo and the Americans at AMO had Insnab. Food rationing was abolished in 1935, but the caste system continued with special privileges for the elite. (I remember how incredulous I was when British Communists I met in Moscow after the war told me that everyone had had the same rations in wartime England.)

At my first visit, Lydia Sergeyevna questioned me during supper about my background, my parents, what had brought us to Russia, how I was getting on in the factory and in the commune, and what plans I had for the future. I found it natural to be questioned in this manner, both because I still felt like a child and because I was a stranger in the land. Being a stranger, I also found it natural that many of the people I was meeting, even my contemporaries, were eager to explain things to me. I assumed that all Soviet people were idealists. It did not surprise me that they could always justify everything that occurred in their country and their society.

Among the idealists, however, the Babushkins stood out. Lydia Sergeyevna felt a real responsibility for everything that happened within her range of vision. She was a gadfly. Whenever she saw something she thought was wrong, she immediately set about putting it right or bringing the "perpetrators" to justice. Her target might have been someone who dirtied the communal kitchen, or a drunk shouting obscenities in the street, or a lazy co-worker. Nevertheless, she was constantly approached for help, often by people who disliked her, and she gave help freely whenever she could. She had a keen sense of noblesse oblige and this, in part, was the reason she took an interest in my well-being. Galya had the same sense of responsibility. Consequently, she was concerned that I interpret events correctly (that is, in accordance with the Party line) and that I come under the right influences. For many years, the Babushkin residence was a refuge for me in times of difficulty, unhappiness, and doubt.

My friendship with Haitin was becoming a dominant factor in my life. I'd come home from work, tired and dispirited because I was doing so poorly at my apprenticeship, and he would be there to greet me with concern and words of sympathy. I wondered why he had so much free time. He explained that he was an electrician on call servicing the factory residential units and so had a great deal of leeway in arranging his hours. It was obvious that he took no part in the extracurricular activities in which everyone else seemed involved. He did not talk in clichés and did not try to "educate" me. I enjoyed his company. He was extremely curious, had a quick sense of the ridiculous, and seemed to understand my reactions to my surroundings better than anyone else. He told me he had come from the south of Russia and that both his parents had died when he was twelve. He had lived on the street for some time and when things got very hard, usually in the winter, he stayed with his married brother. When his brother moved to Moscow, he followed and then went the usual route—to factory training school and a factory job. His first job was at Dinamo—hence his connection with the commune. He brushed off my questions as to why he had been expelled from the commune, declaring that he had wanted to leave it anyway and implying that he had deliberately provoked his expulsion. Why should he, who was more skilled and earned more money than the others, turn over all his earnings for the benefit of the less capable communards? He was planning to become an electrical engineer and was not worried about passing the entrance exams as, he said, he knew as much and more than most engineers at the plant.

The communards watched our developing romance with disapproval and alarm. At first, they tried to use persuasion. That Haitin was very smart and would go far they did not doubt, but they said he was undisciplined and refused to obey the rules of the collective. They reminded me how he had been thrown out of the commune for disruptive behavior. They said he was putting on a show for me. They also said that he had so much time and money because he falsified his work reports and did favors for the foreman, and was too clever to get caught. Valya went further. She told me that he had been living with a girl who worked at AMO and that the girl claimed he had promised to marry her. She said he was sexually experienced beyond his years, that I was naïve and gullible, and she urged me to break off the relationship before I got hurt.

Their remonstrances fell on deaf ears. I attributed them all to envy.

Rumors about us reached the Dinamo Komsomol committee, probably through Zina and Galya. The secretary sent for me. I had met him once before, briefly, a pleasant young man of about twenty-eight. His greeting was cordial. He said he had been keeping an eye on me from a distance, making sure that I was being treated well, and now he felt, reluctantly, that he must talk to me about my relationship with Haitin. Haitin was politically unreliable, he said. I demanded proof. Well, he had politically unreliable friends. He was undisciplined, he drank, he was an individualist who ignored the needs of the collective. I departed, outraged at this interference in my personal affairs. I did not regard the Komsomol in loco parentis, though, in fact it *had* been so since I had left my family. Furthermore, by this time I was so strongly attracted to Haitin that no warnings would have made any difference to me.

Senya and Boris (Haitin's "unreliable" friends) would drop in several nights a week. Senya had a sardonic attitude toward life and a sharp tongue. I noticed that the communards felt uncomfortable around him. Sometimes he turned up with the smell of liquor on his breath and a bottle in his pocket. Haitin would quickly hustle him out of the apartment for fear, I realize now, that his tongue might run away with him. As a rule, Senya did not discuss politics in general conversation, except to make an occasional remark. But he did talk to me alone at times, and some of the things he said have remained in my mind. One was a statement that in the recently published second edition of Lenin's *Collected Works,* passages had been omitted or altered to suit the aims of those presently in power. Another concerned the role of the controlled press in fitting people's minds into a single mold. I listened and said nothing, filing away in my mind what I probably regarded as a quirky opinion.

I did not know then how incautious it was of Senya to speak to me as he did. Not that I might have deliberately informed someone in authority, but that I might have in my political naïveté repeated his remarks in search of confirmation or denial. But I don't think Senya cared what happened to him. He was bitter and disillusioned. And even though I was a staunch member of the Komsomol, I knew instinctively that what he said was not to be repeated or attributed. In retrospect, I see that for me, so soon after my arrival in the Soviet Union, this was a test, the first of many to come, when the dogma I believed in came into conflict with my instincts.

Many things troubled me, and I spoke of them freely. The adulation of Stalin repelled me. The reverence with which Lenin was regarded was a different matter. He was dead. But Stalin was alive. The continuous outpouring of praise over the ubiquitous loudspeakers, the extravagant expressions of gratitude to Stalin for everything big and small, the children in their red bandannas reciting poems thanking Stalin for a "good life," Stalin's portrait on every building, in every office, in practically every house, Stalin's words quoted as if they were received truth—all this went against my grain. The communards and my other friends were ready with an explanation: The worship of Stalin was not meant for him as an individual, but as a symbol of Soviet power and leader of the revolutionary workers and peasants all over the world.

But, in many ways I was happy. So many things were new, and I had someone with whom I could share my feelings. Aggravations were less aggravating, discomforts easier to bear. Haitin and I roamed the city together. We went to the theater, to concerts, and to films. We smiled at strangers in the street and they smiled back. Sometimes he accompanied me to the Mikhlins, impressing my step-aunt and uncle favorably as a serious young man. I introduced him to the Atlases, but we did not join their company. We did not need anyone but each other.

We talked about applying for a room together. Marriage was not discussed. If a couple set up housekeeping together, they were considered to be married—in the eyes of the law as well as society. Formalization of the relationship was not important. What was important was to find a place to live. Meanwhile, we took advantage of every opportunity to be alone together because privacy was hard to come by. Like courting couples all over the city, we would embrace in dimly lit doorways of the building before going upstairs, jumping apart when we heard footsteps. We snatched moments when there was no one home in the apartment or when we thought (or hoped) everyone else was sound asleep.

I lived from day to day, not thinking very far ahead. My conversational Russian had become fluent, but it would be a long time before I knew the language well enough to take the college entrance exams. I should have been studying the language formally with a teacher, but I did not get around to this and continued to increase my vocabulary without regard for gender or case endings.

One morning, I woke up and the girls cried out in horror when they saw me. I had turned yellow. I went to the local clinic and the doctor assigned to our building, a woman (as so many doctors were), diagnosed my condition as yellow jaundice ("zheltukha"—I looked it up). She put me on a special diet and gave me a chit entitling me to three meals a day at the factory's special diet canteen, but she did not give me sick leave. Eventually, I recovered (though the after-effects showed up some ten years later).

On my days off from work, I liked to get away from the "worker out-skirts" where I lived, away from the dust, the dirt, and the mud, away from the drunks sprawled on the sidewalks or, if standing on their own two feet, shouting obscenities or singing at the top of their voices. I never heard spontaneous singing by sober people, neither in the street nor in homes.

In 1932, the working-class sections of Moscow looked very much as they had in pre-Soviet times. The big factories, built in the latter part of the nineteenth century, had arisen on the banks of rivers that wound around the outskirts of the city. In Moscow, these were the 300-mile long Moskva, which flowed through the city and most of the Moscow region, and its tribu-tary, the Yauza River. Dinamo and AMO were on the Yauza. The workers lived in low wooden houses or barracks. The five-story walk-ups, such as the one I lived in, had been built more recently, and the factories were build-ing more of them, though not nearly fast enough to keep up with the influx of workers from surrounding villages.

Luckily, Tyufelev Passage was at the end of a streetcar line, the other end of which was in the center of the city about four miles away. The forty-five-minute ride was an easy one, even though public transportation was generally woefully inadequate. As with housing, it had been unable to keep up with the growth of the city. There were very few buses. The chief means of transportation was trolley cars, usually consisting of a head car with a motorman and two attached cars with conductors, and they were always crowded. In order to get out at your stop, you had to start pushing through, using your elbows, almost as soon as you boarded. Rush hours were the worst, with passengers clinging to anything they could grab. Sometimes it looked as if people were pasted to the sides like flies on the wall. Accidents were frequent, and pickpockets plied a lively trade.

The center of the city had charm, despite the dilapidated appearance of many of the buildings. The oldest part of the city was within the Kremlin wall, an area to which the general population had no access. (It was not until several years after Stalin's death that the public was allowed inside the Kremlin.) This was the original site of the citadel that had arisen on the Moskva River in the twelfth century. The crenellated wall with its three gates and its towers had been built in the fifteenth to seventeenth centuries. Now the towers were topped with small, ruby-red, five-pointed stars that sparkled in the sunlight and shone in the dark. The clock on the main Spassky tower chimed the Internationale at midnight.

The Spassky gate opened onto Red Square. To the left was Lenin's tomb of red marble and granite, blending with the red brick of the Kremlin wall. (The wall was white when first built, but by 1931 it was red.) To the right was the Cathedral of Vassili Blazhenny (St. Basil's), its Byzantine cupolas dimmed and dirty. Farther left was the red brick History Museum. Taking up nearly a whole side of the square was a three-storied grey stone building with galleries and passages, formerly a shopping arcade but now partly converted to offices. (After the war, the shopping arcade was restored and became Moscow's main department store, known as GUM, pronounced "Goom," an acronym in Russian for "State General Store".) Along the northwest wall of the Kremlin was Alexandrovsky Garden, a lovely little park in the heart of the city.

The next-oldest part of the city adjoined the Kremlin on the east, composing a maze of narrow, crooked lanes that had been settled in the fourteenth century. This section, called *Kitai-gorod* (Chinatown)[5] was still standing when I came to Moscow and, together with the Kremlin, presented a medieval look.

Moscow spread radially from the Kremlin and, as it spread, especially in the sixteenth century, protective walls went up around the settlements of merchants and artisans. Walls had once surrounded areas that were now the inner and outer rings, known as the A and B rings after the streetcars that circled them. My step-uncle and the Atlases lived between the A and B rings, walking distance from the Kremlin. The Metropol, where Galya lived, was just outside the Kitai-gorod wall.

Moscow had been known as a city of a thousand-and-one churches. Many had been torn down, while some had been converted to other uses— schools, offices, warehouses. I'm not aware of any that were functioning at the time. The streets were always filled with animated crowds, among them a large number of transients. The wide variety of types, especially the Asiatic peoples in their colorful dress, was striking. The look of the Moscow crowds changed greatly over the next years, with fewer visitors from the national republics and fewer still in national costume, so that the general impression became of a grey monotone, except on special occasions, such as meetings of the Supreme Soviet and the yearly ten-day festival of national cultures that required the presence of citizens in national dress.

Most people I met were curious about the United States. I was impressed by the expressions of friendliness towards the American people, and I found this friendliness to be prevalent among ordinary Russians throughout the years I lived in the Soviet Union. "American know-how combined with Bolshevik scope will lead to Communism" was a popular slogan of the day. I was asked detailed questions: What kind of houses did American workers live in? What did they eat? How much did they earn? Did everybody have a bicycle? Some of the questions gave me pause: Was it really true that there

---

5. Though dubbed "Chinatown," this part of Moscow probably derived its name from another historical connection. It was (and remains) nothing like the Asian-dominated Chinatowns of American and Canadian cities.

were large numbers of unemployed in America, that there were hunger marches, that people rummaged in garbage cans in search of food? (This was during the Depression, known in Russia as the "economic crisis of capitalism.") Was it true that Negroes were lynched in America? They read about these things in the press, and though they tended to believe what they read, they wanted confirmation.

The preoccupation with nationality struck me very soon after my arrival. "Is he Russian?" "No, he is a Jew." "But," I protested, "he was born and raised in Russia, and he doesn't know the Jewish language or anything about Judaism. He is Russian." "It doesn't make a difference. He is not a Russian."

Or: "What is your nationality?" (on hearing my accent). "American." "American? That's not a nationality. Are you Jewish?" "Yes, but Jews are not a nation and Jewish is not a nationality." I had learned this from Stalin's essay "On the National Question." "You should know that," I would add. "Comrade Stalin said so. America is a nation and American is a nationality." I never met a Russian who did not regard the Jews as a nationality and America as a conglomerate of nationalities, despite having been taught what Lenin and Stalin had written on the subject.

This preoccupation applied to all nationalities. "Do you know the Armenian who lives on the second floor?" "the Tatar in the foundry?" "the Assyrian shoeshine man?" "the Georgian schoolteacher?" and so forth. I did not at that time detect any condescension or chauvinism in this overriding concern with ethnic identity.

One sunny afternoon in March as I approached the house, I saw a boy of about twelve begging. His clothes were in tatters, his hair was matted, his face streaked with dirt. I was horrified. With difficulty, I persuaded him to come upstairs with me. I made him wash and gave him something to eat. Vassiona was disgusted. Haitin came home and questioned the child, but it was impossible to get a coherent story out of him. His eyes darted back and forth like those of a trapped animal. When Yura and Shura arrived, they suggested we take him to the militia, where there was a special department that dealt with homeless children. They tried to assure him that he would be better off in a colony where he would be fed and clothed and taught a trade, but he set up such a howl that they desisted and let him go. After he left, I was warned never to do such a thing again—he might have stolen something, he might have had a contagious disease, he might have had a knife. I had better leave such matters to the militia.

The extent of these matters was becoming apparent to me. With the onset of milder weather, an increasing number of beggars were appearing in our part of Moscow. Many of them were women with infants at shriveled breasts and small children clinging to their ragged skirts. The militia cleared them out periodically from the areas near the railroad stations and from the center of town where the hotels, Party and government offices, and foreign missions were located. They were more lenient, or less concerned, in our proletarian quarter. Old men, women, and children sat on the curbstone or stood in front of bakeries, pleading for the *doveski* (the small pieces of bread placed on the scales to make the exact weight) and begged from door to door and in suburban trains. I did not know what to make of this. It was not until much later that I learned there had been a devastating famine in the south of Russia, a region that possessed some of the richest farmland in the world. How was I to know? No mention of it was made on the radio, in the newspapers, or at the current events class that I was attending. In reply to my persistent questions, Galya and her mother told me that these were peasants who refused to work in the collective farms and who were moving about the country without residence permits or ration cards. What I knew about collectivization came from official pronouncements. The *kulak* (prosperous peasant) was the class enemy who had to be destroyed—a hard-fisted exploiter, out to enrich himself at the expense of others, he would never be an ally of the proletariat in the struggle to build socialism. I did not know that the regime's method of collectivizing agriculture had destroyed the most productive, industrious section of the peasantry and that this was one of the major causes of the famine, on top of the disruption of war, revolution, and civil war. Haitin must have cautioned Senya to hold his tongue or he would surely have had something to say to me on the subject.

The large number of cripples in the streets also upset me. Though I realized that this was a consequence of the many years of upheaval, I recoiled from the harsh scenes before me. In America I had seldom seen a lame, legless, or armless person.

Thievery was widespread. The line between honesty and dishonesty was blurred. On my first day in the factory, I left a Parker pen and pencil set in the pocket of my coat when I checked into the shop cloakroom. They were gone when I collected my coat after work. The attendant merely shrugged her shoulders when I complained. My one suitcase at the commune (I had left the other at my step-uncle's at his suggestion) did not have a lock. I did not miss any clothes, but in the course of a few months my ice-skates, tennis racquet, and a few other items disappeared. (Taking a tennis racquet to the Soviet Union is an indication of how unrealistic my idea of the country had been.) I never suspected any of the communards, but I thought Vassiona might have taken some things to sell or exchange at the market, and I did suspect our neighbor of having taken the skates and the racquet. It was a disaster when my handbag containing my ration cards for the month was snatched as I boarded a crowded streetcar. After a while, I learned to take better care of my belongings and to hold onto my handbag tightly.

To an urban resident in America today, these measures might not seem so unusual, but when I was growing up we did not lock our doors, not even in a comparatively large city such as Los Angeles. We were not at all concerned about petty thievery. To me, this state of affairs was shocking. Whether it was due to the years of shortages since the revolution or was a Russian phenomenon, I cannot tell, though the numerous Russian proverbs on the subject ("no deception, no sale," "what's fallen off the wagon is gone," "badly placed," meaning the article is visible and therefore a temptation) seem to indicate that thievery was not a problem produced solely by the Soviet system.

A few weeks after I started my apprenticeship at the factory, I was summoned to personnel and asked for my "documents," that is, my identification papers. All I had was the paper from Birobidzhan, but this was not what they wanted. Where was my passport? I explained that I did not have a passport of my own, and that as a minor I was included in the family passport which was in Birobidzhan. A week or two passed and I was summoned again. This time Paul Lifshitz was present. He told me that I must produce a passport and advised me to write to my parents, asking them to mail the family passport to me. After personnel had seen it and copied the relevant information, I could then mail it back to them. I wrote to my parents. My father took the U.S. passport and posted it registered mail at the local post office in Volochayevka. Weeks went by, then months, but the passport did not arrive. Paul kept checking with me periodically. Finally, he told me I could not go on working in the factory and living in Moscow without a valid document. I did not know what to do. The nearest American embassy was in Riga, Latvia, not a Soviet republic at the time. I could not travel outside the Soviet Union without a passport, even if I could have raised the money. There must have been an embassy that looked after the interests of American citizens, but it did not occur to me or to anyone I knew that I could get help from some other embassy in Moscow.

My father's efforts to get the passport traced were fruitless. Now, the whole family was without a passport. All they had was a postal receipt. Paul continued to press me. Finally, he suggested that since I did not have an American passport, I should apply for a Soviet one. He told me where to go and what to do. So in May 1932—I had just turned seventeen—Haitin and I went to the passport office on Samotechnaya Square on the B line where I filled out an application for Soviet citizenship. I was given an official paper stating that my application was under consideration. I showed it to personnel and they stopped bothering me.

Several years after I left Dinamo, in 1936 or 1937 as I recall, I heard that Paul Lifshitz had been arrested and denounced at factory meetings as an "enemy of the people and a German spy." Many Germans, especially

German Communists, were among the victims of the Terror. As far as I know, he never turned up again. He was probably shot or died in a prison camp. Like thousands of loyal and dedicated Communists who perished during Stalin's lifetime, he was undoubtedly innocent of the charges brought against him. It may be that the only "crime" he ever committed was to persuade an ignorant seventeen-year-old to take a step, the consequences of which she was incapable of assessing.

I had a cough that kept getting worse, a harsh bronchial cough at times so bad that it kept my roommates awake at night. The same doctor who had treated me for jaundice prescribed cough medicine but, again, would not give me sick leave as I was not running a temperature. To stay home from work without official leave was against the law.

I remember that doctor well. At that time, to qualify for a medical degree all that was necessary was to graduate from a six-year medical college. Bureaucratic doctors at the local clinic level were among the most unpleasant characters I encountered, then and for quite a number of years thereafter. She was typical of them. Her manner was brusque and her expression stern. The patient was an adversary, very likely a malingerer, to be exposed by her vigilance. Not only was the general criterion for sick leave an elevated temperature, but the number of sick leaves granted was monitored by a commission consisting of the clinic's head doctor, the administrator, and the Party Secretary (usually a doctor). Unduly long sick leaves were reviewed and had to be approved by the commission. The system sucked the doctor in, and most doctors preferred to go along with it rather than worry about the patient.

Here, too, privilege came into play. Those with access to special clinics received very different treatment. Their doctors were better paid, more highly qualified, and happy to receive favors from patients. Galya and Anya, though factory workers like the rest of us, never had to use the services of the neighborhood clinics.

One morning, I felt so bad that I could hardly drag myself to work. That night I was delirious. The next thing I knew, I woke up in a hospital bed with white-clad figures bending over me. They smiled when I opened my eyes. It turned out that I had been unconscious for several days and was suffering from double pneumonia, a very serious illness in those days. There was little that could be done for the patient, except to wait and see. My bed was curtained off at the end of a long corridor. A few days later, I was moved to a ward. I remained at the Yauza Hospital for several weeks. My principal recollections are of eating farina every day and of having difficulties communicating with the doctors and nurses. The vocabulary was new to me, but everyone was very kind.

The hospital discharged me with a paper saying that I must go to a sanatorium to convalesce before returning to work. My sick leave was extended indefinitely by the same watchdog doctor who had sent me to work with bronchitis. She was all sweetness now. The responsibility was no longer hers.

In the hospital, my hair had started coming out in handfuls, a condition caused by the high fever, the nurses said. They urged me to shave my head. I resisted, but when the condition persisted after I left the hospital, I was finally persuaded. I wept as the barber shaved off my thick, curly, chestnut hair.

The communards told me what a fright I had given them. The night I became delirious, Valya and Zina got dressed and ran to the clinic to press the doctor on duty to come back with them. They were hysterical. A doctor came and said I must go to the hospital at once, but he would have to put me on a waiting list because there were no beds available. Hospitals were terribly overcrowded and sometimes a patient had to wait for days for a bed. Early the next morning, the girls went to Galya who, luckily, was working the day shift. Galya dropped everything and hurried over to her mother's office. Lydia Sergeyevna used her influence to get me into the Yauza Hospital that very afternoon. If I had had to wait my turn like everybody else, the outcome might have been different and this story never told.

While I waited for sanatorium accommodations to become available, I attended a "day sanatorium" about twenty minutes away by streetcar. I went there in the morning, had three "reinforced" meals a day, was given quartz lamp treatments and other therapy, and went home to sleep. Haitin came every day and we strolled in the lovely old park in which the converted mansion stood. It was spring. The leaves of the birch trees and the aspen were a delicate green, the flower buds were about to burst, the severe winter was over. It was wonderful just to be alive.

At last, I was notified that there was a place for me at the sanatorium. Most Soviet rest homes and sanatoriums were organized vacation centers, the former for persons in good health, the latter for persons recovering from serious illness or suffering from chronic illnesses. Mine was to be a sanatorium for young people with lung diseases.

Early in May, Haitin saw me off at the railroad station where I joined several other young people due at the sanatorium on the same date. It was a three-hour ride on the train. A horse and cart would meet us for the twelve-mile ride from the station. I was to stay two months. Haitin promised to visit me at least once and write often.

The sanatorium was situated in a beautiful pine and birch wood, typical of the countryside around Moscow. There were about seventy or eighty boys and girls between the ages of sixteen and eighteen there. Each room contained fifteen to twenty beds, with girls and boys in separate quarters. Treatment consisted mainly of fresh air, plenty of food, especially dairy products, and quartz lamp therapy. Otherwise, we were left pretty much to ourselves. It was noisy, with a great deal of coming and going during the night. There was much pairing off, changing of partners, gossip, and sexual rivalry. The room I slept in buzzed with whispers and giggles far into the night. A strong sexuality pervaded the atmosphere, a feverish absorption with the physical—no talk, no interest in anything but the opposite sex. The young people who had seen us at the station spread the word that I had a boyfriend, so none of the boys bothered me. The girls, however, quickly discovered that I hated to be touched and, thinking it was a great joke, proceeded to make my life miserable. I dreaded undressing for the night and, after a couple of times in the bathhouse, I obtained permission from the head doctor to take sponge baths alone in one of the therapy rooms. The girls were amused by my limited Russian and insisted on teaching me the basic obscenities, demonstrating their meaning. During the day, I could get away and would roam the woods or walk to the nearby village. There, I first heard the peasant songs about unrequited love, called *stradaniya* (from *stradat'*, "to suffer"), which the village girls sang, their clear, soprano voices carrying for miles in the stillness of the night.

To add to my unhappiness, I had not heard one word from Haitin. I wrote nearly every day, but there was nothing in return. I received several short notes from Valya, but she did not mention his name. I worried and racked my brain for an explanation, and yet nothing prepared me for what was coming.

After one month, I decided I could not stand it any longer and told the head doctor that I'd like to leave before my time was up. He did not raise any objections and arranged for me to go the next time the sanatorium horse and cart went to the station. I asked him to send a telegram to the commune, which he did. I left at six o'clock in the morning, but I missed the one regularly scheduled passenger train. The stationmaster put several people who had gathered there on a freight train that moved so slowly and stopped so often, that it took nine or ten hours to get to Moscow. It was a dismal trip. It was a hot day in June. There was no drinking water and the box lunch I had with me was not sufficient for a whole day.

It was a dismal homecoming, too.

The sight of Senya waiting for me at the station alarmed me. Where was Haitin? Was anything wrong? Senya was evasive. Haitin was fine. He'd met the morning train, but I was not on it. He'd learned that a freight train with some passengers was due in the evening, but he could not get away. Senya took me home and left. Vassiona was uncharacteristically solicitous. Was I hungry? She'd made something special. As Valya and Zina and the boys came home, they welcomed me, said I looked well and healthy again, and exclaimed how much my hair had grown.

Late that night when I finally went to bed after everyone else, Haitin still had not come home. Nor did I see him at breakfast. No one was talking except to assure me that he was alive and well and that nothing had happened to him. They treated me like an invalid. The next afternoon, I heard the key turn in the lock of the outside door. It was he. I knew his step well. I was absolutely still in my room, but he did not come in. Half an hour later, I heard him leave. When I saw him the next morning, he greeted me politely and asked how I was, behaving as if there had never been anything between us. I was stunned and unbelieving.

Yet that was how it ended. He never offered to talk about it, and I never asked. He was seldom home. Boris had left for a better job in Leningrad, but Senya came to see me often during that period. Several weeks later, when it must have seemed to him that I had gotten over my unhappiness, he offered his view: The relationship with me had been an aberration for Haitin, who always had tight control of his emotions and whose philosophy in life was to take the maximum and give the minimum. He had begun to worry about where his romance with me was leading and had concluded even before I went away that he had involved himself in something too emotionally demanding. My background and upbringing were too different and my plans for the future too complex to fit into his life, so he had decided to make a clean break. No doubt he was right, if not strangely calculating for a twenty-year-old. But it was a cruel thing to do and a cruel way to do it.

The others tried hard to divert me. Even Zina was considerate, and no one said "I told you so," though it was obvious that they thought Haitin had merely reverted to his true nature. My pain was deep and despairing, but my pride compelled me to try to conceal my feelings. If I had had a place to go, I would have moved out of the apartment at once. But I had nowhere to go.

For months, I could not believe the relationship was over. I kept expecting a miracle that would set everything right. But no miracle came. It wasn't until I left the commune in the fall of 1933 that I was able to put my heartbreak truly behind me.

In later years, I rarely thought of that first period of my life in the Soviet Union—that time not only of my first experiences of love, sex, and pain, but also the entire inauguration into life on my own. When I did, and as I recall it now, it is as if this were not a story about me at all, but about a young girl I once knew. Then I am appalled at the thought of what might have happened to her and I marvel that she came through intact.

Aunt Liza was very wise. She asked no questions when I stopped coming around with Haitin. She managed to convey, without actually saying it, that pain was part of life and one gets over it, though the young may find that hard to believe. It must have been at this point that she told me the story of her marriage. She was betrothed at the age of eighteen to a man she hardly knew. All the wedding arrangements had been made according to Jewish Orthodox custom. The day before the wedding she refused to go through with it. She was single for twelve years after that until she met and married my step-uncle. Liza believed in destiny.

# 6

## My Parents Leave—Summer of 1932 to Summer of 1933

In the spring of 1932 I had a wonderful surprise. My friend Miriam wrote from Los Angeles that she had been chosen to accompany Tom Mooney's mother on a trip to Moscow. Mother Mooney's trip was part of a world-wide campaign to free her son who had been incarcerated in a California prison since 1916, framed, it was claimed, because of his activities in the International Workers of the World (IWW—a radical labor organization known as the Wobblies).

They arrived when I returned to Moscow from the sanitarium. A tentative understanding existed that Stalin would see Mother Mooney, so we were all excited at the prospect. Several times during her stay, arrangements were supposedly made for an interview, but each time something interfered. She met with a few officials and that was all. She was a frail old woman, rather bewildered, who seldom left her hotel. For much of the time, Miriam was free to do as she pleased. I was still on sick leave and stayed in their hotel suite, enjoying the unaccustomed luxury, especially the hot baths. The young man assigned to look after the American guests outdid himself in his eagerness to show them a good time. He fell madly in love with Miriam and begged her to remain in Moscow. He was quite despondent when she left, and so was I.

Meanwhile, my parents left Birobidzhan in May 1932 for Stalingrad, where my uncle from Chicago and his wife and three children, aged fourteen, nineteen, and twenty-one, had been living for the past year. My uncle, who was a tinsmith, had come to the Soviet Union through regular channels, with a group and a contract, so he enjoyed the privileges accorded "foreign specialists"—an apartment for the family on arrival, the right to shop in Insnab stores, and special wage rates. He helped my father get a job at the tractor plant where he worked. Surprisingly, personnel accepted my father's explanation as to why he did not have a passport. When he presented the postal receipt, the authorities checked with Volochayevka and said that his status was all right. The passport had been mailed to me four months earlier and my father hoped that it might still arrive.

It is perfectly clear to me now that, had the passport really been lost in the mail, the Soviet authorities would not have accepted my father's explanation so readily. There is no doubt in my mind that the passport was stolen on official instructions; genuine American passports were valuable commodities. The postal officials in Volochayevka must have informed the local authorities that they had one in their possession and then turned it over to them.

My father's job did not entitle him to any special privileges. His wages and rations were the same as those of ordinary Soviet workers. He was put on a waiting list for housing, but for the next six or seven months, the family lived with my uncle and his wife and three children in a three-room apartment very much like the one in which I lived in Moscow. Not only were they crowded, but they had different rations categories. It is a tribute to them all, especially to my mother and her sister-in-law, that relations between the two families did not sour.

Compared to Birobidzhan, Stalingrad was a stone's throw from Moscow, only forty-eight hours by train, and I could go for a visit. My sick leave was extended when I reported to the hospital after my return from the sanatorium, for I had what they diagnosed as "dry" pleurisy. The medical commission did not object to my going away for a month, so in July I took the train to Stalingrad, having been assisted by the trade union committee in obtaining the ticket. I had not written my parents that I had been ill and did not tell them when I saw them. I explained my "boyish bob" as a whimsical act.

It was less than a year since we had seen each other, but it seemed like a decade. So much had happened to them and to me. They described their experiences in Birobidzhan. My mother was bitter, especially about the way Feigele had behaved. Still, none of us had drawn any general conclusions. We all attributed the stupidity and corruption to dishonest individuals and the frailties of human nature. However, by now we realized that the road to socialism was neither as straight nor as smooth as it had been depicted by enthusiasts.

The Tractor Plant in Stalingrad (changed from Tsaritsyn in 1925; now called Volgograd) was one of the major projects of the First Five-Year Plan (1928–1932). The Soviet government had proclaimed with great fanfare that alone, without help from outside and surrounded by enemies, it would industrialize the country, a necessary prerequisite for the victory of socialism. Tractors from Stalingrad, trucks from Gorky (now Nizhni-Novgorod), electric power from Dnieprostroi, and steel from Magnitogorsk would transform Russia. Sacrifices would have to be made, but the goal was worth it. Philistines might grumble, but their opinions did not matter. The future was in the hands of the idealists.

This was the first large-scale experiment in socialist planning, and the world was watching. In other countries, the armies of the unemployed were swelling. But in the Soviet Union, there was a labor shortage. Skilled workers came from Moscow and Leningrad and other old industrial cities to help. Peasants flocked from famine-stricken villages. The Party and the Komsomol sent contingents to assist in the developments. Newspaper and radio correspondents reported from the projects as if from the battlefield, with stories of sacrifice and heroism and miracles. And, indeed, there *was* heroism. Men and women working under appalling conditions showed courage, stamina, and resourcefulness. They were inspired by their conviction that they were blazing a trail for the workers of the world. If there were doubters, they were not heard in public. Enthusiasm ran high.

The word went out to foreign countries that skilled workers were welcome, and foreign workers and engineers came, some for ideological reasons and many simply for jobs. All of the First Five-Year Plan projects employed some foreign workers and engineers, mostly Germans and Americans. There was a large English-speaking colony in Stalingrad, many of whom were of Polish or Hungarian descent and had been employees of the Ford Motor Company in Detroit.

Stalingrad was a pleasant interlude for me. I was overjoyed to see my family again, as well as to be with my aunt and uncle and cousins. I appreciated the homelike touches—the glass of milk and cookie or piece of cake left for me on the kitchen table when I came in late at night. It was good to be home and it was a pleasure to speak English again.

But on my first visit to Stalingrad in the summer of 1932, I found that at times I had to grope for English words. This was disquieting. I had not spoken the language at all for nearly a year and had not read much English either. The few books I had with me I knew by heart and the only other English reading matter around was the English-language *Moscow News*, which I obtained only occasionally. My English came back to me quickly, but I was suddenly aware that I could forget my native language and that, if I did, I might never know *any* language properly.

A day or two after my arrival in Stalingrad, a young man named Izzy Lapitsky came to call. Izzy was a dedicated Communist who had been drafted by the Komsomol to do a stint as an interpreter for English-speaking foreigners at the tractor plant. He was a likable young man with an easy smile, a friendly manner, and a fluent knowledge of English. He knew everybody and everybody knew him. Through him, I was immediately introduced into a circle of young Americans, most of whom worked in the factory. I spent a lot of time with Izzy that month. I talked with him about matters that I did not discuss with my parents: my job, the way I lived, my bouts with illness, my desire to get out of the factory and into something more interesting and worthwhile until I could go to school again. He told me about himself. He had lived in England for five years as a child with his parents and older sister. His mother was a trained midwife who lived and worked in a clinic in a small town near Moscow. His sister was a student at the Institute of Transportation Engineers in Moscow. He himself planned to enter a school of journalism as soon as he could get a release from his present job. We continued our friendship by letter after I left.

The month in Stalingrad passed very quickly. I was not eager to return to Moscow, but neither did I consider remaining in Stalingrad. I did not like the artificial atmosphere of the foreign colony there. Besides, everybody wanted to go to Moscow, not leave it. My step-uncle met me at the station and took me to his place. He was eager to hear about my parents and my uncle. My Chicago uncle and his family had stayed with him for a few days en route to Stalingrad from the United States, but he had not seen my parents since his Siberian exile.

I reported back to the factory for a new assignment. I had not worked for about four months. The team of apprentices had long since completed the training program and been disbanded. And it was obvious that I would never become a skilled machinist. I was transferred to a less physically demanding job: archivist in the factory blueprints library. It was my duty to file and cata- logue foreign-language blueprints (mostly in English and German) for ninety rubles a month, twice as much as I had been earning as an apprentice. It was clean and quiet in the library. My co-workers were three women, none of whom were members of the Party or the Komsomol. Here were ordinary people with ordinary concerns, better known in my circle as *meshchane,* an- other widely used word with several shades of meaning. Like *kul'turno,* it had broader implications than its dictionary translation, "philistine." In my first encounter with the word, it seemed to mean someone who was more inter- ested in personal and private affairs than in the good of the collective, the Soviet state, or the condition of the world. For me, it was somewhat of a relief to descend from the high plane of constant discussion of the general welfare.

Soon after I returned from Stalingrad, I received a postcard from Loren Miller, a young Black journalist I had met in California at a meeting in defense of the Scottsboro boys.[1] Miriam, whom he had met quite by acci- dent on the street in Moscow just before she left, had given him my address. He was in Moscow at the Grand Hotel and asked me to come to see him. I hurried off to the hotel my next day off. Loren told me that he had heard that there was a "Negro" boy living in the Bolshevo colony for homeless children outside Moscow.[2] His repeated efforts to arrange a trip there had come up against a stone wall. We decided to go to Bolshevo—about an hour's ride from Moscow—on our own.

---

1. The Scottsboro boys were nine young Black males who were accused in 1931 of having raped two white women. The youths were convicted and sentenced to life in prison. The case attracted worldwide attention because of the evident racial bias during the trial and sentencing.

2. The Bolshevo colony for homeless boys was the model for the one depicted in a popular Soviet film, *The Road to Life.*

We had no trouble getting directions when we got off the train in Bol-shevo. Everybody knew where the colony was. We caused something of a flurry when we walked into the administration's office—a tall, handsome, dark-skinned man and a young white girl who spoke Russian incorrectly, with an accent. But they welcomed us warmly. Yes, indeed, there was an eleven-year-old *negritanskii* (Negro) boy in the colony. No, he did not speak English and they did not know where he was at the moment. They would send someone to look for him. Too bad we had not let them know we were coming. They would have arranged everything. After a short while, the grounds attendant returned with a report that he had found the boy, but that the child had refused to talk to the strangers. They suggested that we take a walk on the grounds; perhaps the child would change his mind. It was a beautiful day and we spent several hours in Bolshevo. We actually got a few glimpses of the boy peering at us from behind bushes or a tree, but when we called or tried to approach him, he ran away.

Many years later, I had occasion to recall that visit to Bolshevo. It was during the war. My husband described his retreat from Riga, where the outbreak of the war had caught him. He and a fellow officer had been given a car and a driver. The driver was a nineteen-year-old Black male who spoke perfect Russian and no English. He did not remember his parents, but he had been told that they had been American entertainers who had died in a typhus epidemic in the south of Russia. The three men would drive all day until late at night, when one of the officers would knock at the door of a village house to ask permission to sleep somewhere, usually in the barn. In the morning, the peasant woman would come to wake them and, at the sight of a dark face, would invariably throw up her hands and scream. The driver said he was used to this type of reception and did not mind. If the child in Bolshevo had been eleven in 1932, he would have been nineteen in 1941. It could have been the same person.

Langston Hughes, whom I greatly admired, was in Moscow, and one day when I'd come to see Loren, he took me along to Hughes's room, where some of his friends had gathered. I had read *Not Without Laughter* and was thrilled at the prospect of meeting the author. He opened the door for us, a slightly built man, rather short, with a very lively, expressive face. There were seven or eight young men and women in the room, all of them Black Americans. They greeted me politely and went on with their conversation about their recent sojourn in Europe en route to Moscow. They talked about how they had felt in France and Germany, about Jim Crow experiences at home, and about the pros and cons of settling in Europe as opposed to returning to the United States. No one paid any attention to me. I listened spellbound. (Since my return to the United States, I have read Langston Hughes's autobiographical *I Wonder As I Wander* and learned from it that in 1932, a group of Blacks had been invited to make a film in Moscow about racial oppression in the United States. The project fell through and most of the company soon returned home, but Hughes spent a year traveling in the Soviet Union.)

At this time, life in our commune was deteriorating. Nothing was holding us together anymore. Zina had left. Now Valya, Vassiona, and I shared a room. Valya's older sister who lived in Ukraine came to visit several times and stayed longer each time. Volodya, a good-looking young man of twenty-two or twenty-three, blond and blue-eyed, had returned from Magnitogorsk and he and Valya had resumed an affair that they had apparently been having before he had gone away. Volodya made several approaches to me, but I repulsed him sharply. I was not so naïve at this point as not to realize that because Volodya had been told about my relationship with Haitin, he could see no reason why he should not enjoy the same favors. As a result, my relations with him and Valya became strained.

Galya and Anya remained my closest friends. I got them together once, but they took an instant dislike to one another. Galya thought Anya flighty. Anya could not stand what she termed Galya's sanctimoniousness. So I kept my friends separate.

I used to visit my step-uncle's family about once a week (where I'd be fed) and then spend the evening at the Atlases. Most of the young people who came to their home were university or engineering students. Vladimir, whom Anya subsequently married, was studying forestry. One friend of theirs had recently graduated from the Mining Institute in Moscow and worked in a Siberian gold field. On his visits to Moscow, he would take us to restaurants and drive us around in taxis. I enjoyed the fun, the gaiety, the flirting, and the conversation, which was often serious in a light way: We described major conflicts at school or at work with laughter, and we talked about future plans and current events and politics. These young people were active members of the Komsomol, loyal to the Party and the regime and dedicated to the goals of socialism and Communism, but they were not deadly serious all the time.

Galya and her mother were still my mentors. They had answers to all my questions. They were also very good friends, genuinely concerned about my well-being, both physical and ideological. They urged me to study Russian more intensively and to prepare to continue my education. Whenever I needed a reference—and references were required at every step of the way: to get into school, for a new job, and so forth—I could always count on Lydia Sergeyevna, whose references carried weight.

I made inquiries and discovered the Foreign Language Library on Stepan Razin Street near Red Square, and started borrowing books regularly. Having English books to read again was a joy. I enrolled in a course two evenings a week at the Proletarsky district school of journalism, mainly to see if I could handle the subject. Comprehension was manageable, as the vocabulary was limited and familiar, but my written work was poor. Once in a while, I attended activities arranged for foreign workers at the AMO plant.

At one meeting arranged by the *Moscow News* at AMO, members of the newspaper's staff urged us to regard the paper as our own and to offer suggestions and criticism. I took those declarations seriously. I saw the occasion as an opportunity to put what I was learning in journalism school into practice. Who knows, they might even offer me a job! So I sat down and wrote a long letter of criticism and mailed it. A week or two later, I went down to the newspaper office to follow up in person.

The editor-in-chief was Mikhail Borodin (of China fame).[3] I was ushered into his office. Borodin, an imposing-looking man with a luxuriant, reddish mustache and a leonine head of reddish brown hair, received me affably, though briefly, and thanked me for my interest in the paper. He asked if I could type (I could not) and turned me over to his managing editor, Comrade Stolar.[4] When Stolar connected my name with the letter of criticism I had written, he literally threw me out of his office. Who was I, an ignorant schoolgirl, to have the audacity to tell him, an experienced journalist, how to run a newspaper? I was stunned at this reception. No matter how inappropriate my letter may have been, he was certainly overreacting. He was, after all, a professional old enough to be my father. I never went back to the *Moscow News* and ceased to read it, even occasionally. The incident was a lesson: not to take people at their word, especially when they asked for criticism.

In April 1933, engineers from Britain and the Soviet Union were put on trial, allegedly for sabotaging the USSR's electrical industry. The proceeding became known as the "Metro-Vickers trial." There had been other trials of this nature before, but this was the first that attracted my serious attention, partly because I could read the Russian newspapers now and, of course, because of the British engineers involved. It never occurred to me to question the truth or the charges of sabotage brought against them. Nor did I know anyone who expressed any doubts. We had been told over and over

---

3. Mikhail Borodin (Gruzenberg) had been a Bolshevik since 1903. He was a professional revolutionary who traveled to many countries on assignments for the Party, both before and after the revolution. On and off from 1906 to 1918, he lived in the United States. Best known for his role as head of the Soviet mission to China and his attempts to reconcile the Kuomintang and the Communists, he returned to Moscow in 1927 and was appointed editor of the newly established English-language newspaper in 1928. Borodin was arrested in 1949; he died in detention in 1951. Posthumously, he was cleared of the charges against him.

4. Stolar was an American Communist who had brought his family to the Soviet Union in 1931. He was arrested in 1937 and died in prison. He was the father of Abe Stolar, a well-known refusenik who, after more than fifteen years of trying, was allowed to leave the Soviet Union with his family in 1989.

again that the Soviet Union was surrounded by enemies who would naturally do all in their power to prevent it from achieving its goal.

When vacation time came around in June, I returned to Stalingrad. My parents were awaiting my arrival anxiously because they had an important matter to discuss with me. My uncle had decided not to renew his contract and had already obtained exit visas for his family. They would be leaving for the United States and Chicago shortly. My parents were thinking of leaving too, but they wanted to make sure that I would go back with them.

Stalingrad had proved disappointing to them. As in Birobidzhan, my father's advanced house-building skills were not applicable. As a general repairman at the tractor plant, he noticed many flaws in the utilization of labor and in the quality of the materials. But his numerous suggestions for improving efficiency were regarded as a nuisance. He was an outsider and not a privileged one, and therefore was barely tolerated. His wages were low, his rations insufficient, and even under the best of circumstances, it was difficult for one wage-earner to support a family of four. It was unlike my father to take things to heart, but now he looked downcast and dejected. My mother was haggard. Whatever the far-off future may have held, the immediate future was bleak and their spirit broken. We talked the situation over thoroughly that month. I had no difficulty making up my mind. The opportunity to go home brought to the surface feelings that I had been un-consciously suppressing. I would go, gladly. My parents were relieved. They had not known what to expect. They had been worried about my friendship with Izzy, and had an exaggerated notion of its importance to me. My Stalingrad romance had progressed, but I was not deeply involved emotionally. Izzy stayed out of the discussion and would not even talk with me privately about it. He did not wish to influence me. It was decided that my father would apply for exit visas for the family immediately. Before I left for Moscow, my father filled out the necessary forms (which he already had) and mailed them.

The reply, when it finally came several weeks later, was a thunderbolt—exit visas with three weeks to get out of the country for all the family except me! An official letter stated that Mary Mackler, eighteen years old, had been granted Soviet citizenship and if she wished to leave, she would have to apply for permission on the same terms as any other Soviet national.

More than a year had passed since I filled out the application in the office on Samotechnaya. I had received no word, despite having made several inquiries. My parents knew about my application for citizenship (after the fact), but we assumed that since the process had not been completed, the details did not matter.

This turn of events completely unnerved my parents. My father left for Moscow at once to see what he could do. My mother stayed behind to do all the packing for the return trip and would join him as soon as she could at her stepbrother's. Her brother and his family had already left Stalingrad.

The first thing my father did upon arrival in Moscow was to try to get his exit deadline postponed so that there would be time to appeal my case. But it was to no avail. At the People's Commissariat for Foreign Affairs, he was told that the family would have to leave by the specified date and that his daughter could apply for an exit visa afterwards. Then my father made a desperate attempt to arrange for the whole family to remain in the Soviet Union, even at the price of forfeiting their American citizenship.[5] He went to OZET and asked for help to resettle in a Jewish collective farm in the Crimea. At first, he was welcomed and promised help. However, when he returned the next day, he was told that OZET could do nothing for him. Obviously, they had received instructions.

When my mother arrived from Stalingrad and learned that nothing had been accomplished, she was devastated. I tried to calm her down, assuring her that we would see each other again soon. Neither my parents nor I dreamed that I would not be able to leave. I don't know what we would have done had we known.

Whether more vigorous or more sophisticated action would have made any difference will never be known. We had no idea what to do next, nor where to turn. My step-uncle shook his head and said it was "madness" to leave a child behind, but he did not lift a finger to help, though he could have tried, as I realized much later. Emelyan Yaroslavsky, the Bolshevik leader to whom he had easy access, was very influential then and a word from him might have settled the matter. But Yevsei was afraid of getting involved. He must have been keeping his true feelings to himself if he realized so early on that involvement in this kind of matter could mar his record and jeopardize his family some day.

Looking back, the whole episode seems incredible, illogical. Why did the authorities permit my parents to leave? A postal receipt is no substitute for a passport. Why were they in such a hurry to get rid of them? If they knew where our passport was, shouldn't they have preferred having the rightful owners where they could keep an eye on them? And if they were eager to get rid of them, why didn't they let me go, too? Was it mere chance? Was our plight occurring simply because a particular official in a particular mood happened to open the envelope that day? We would never know.

My feelings were mixed. First, I felt shock. I had inquired about my application for Soviet citizenship less than a month before I went to Stalingrad and

---

5. At that time there was a law in effect that naturalized citizens who returned to their native land and stayed away more than two years forfeited their U.S. citizenship.

had been told that there was no decision yet. I was distressed by the refusal to grant me an exit permit, but accepted this as a formality and believed that all I had to do was apply on my own when I was ready to leave. I rationalized: Since this was the way events had turned out, we'd make the best of it. Let the family go back and get settled. The economic situation was still bad in America and their future uncertain. I would go to college as planned and would visit them during my summer vacation. We were still staunch believers and we regarded the hardships of the Soviet people as part of the struggle to build socialism in one country. That we had found it hard to adjust to this way of life did not make the goal any less desirable or less attainable.

I do not recall discussing the matter with any of my friends. Except for Izzy, none of them knew about our decision to leave. I did not want them to know how I felt and did not want to face their probable disapproval.

Today, I can see how incredibly naïve, even stupid, our attitude must seem. In justification, I have to point out that these were the feelings of a great many neither naïve nor stupid people in those years.

In spite of my feelings of astonishment, I was not in favor of the whole family remaining and was relieved when nothing came of the Crimean proposition. I did not analyze my attitude, but just wanted the rest of the family out of the way in a safe place.

At any rate, it was lucky that they got out when they did. I do not believe any of the family would have survived the purges, the war, and the postwar Terror that lay ahead.

I saw them off at the railroad station. They were going to Riga, where the closest American embassy was located and where they would obtain new passports. There were no hysterics, no wailing. Hardly a tear was shed. That was not our way. We assured each other that the parting was only until the following summer. The train pulled out. It was September 1933. The next time I saw my parents was twenty-four years later, in 1957.

෴

# 7

## Americans and Other Foreigners in Moscow—1933 to 1934

In novels and stories about Jewish life in the "old country" and about Jewish immigrants in America, the characters are not noted for "keeping a stiff upper lip." Rather, emotions are expressed loudly and clearly. The stereotype of the Jewish family is not one of people who practiced self-restraint, especially among the lower economic classes. Would tears, shouts, hysterics in front of high officials have done any good? Who knows? Possibly. I know of one family of homeless Americans in Moscow who obtained an apartment by making such a scene in the early 1930s.

But the "ranting and raving" possibility surely did not occur to my parents. Our family had always been subdued, both in good times and in bad. There were the usual ups and downs of family life—anxiety when there was sickness or when my father was out of work, petty irritations, scoldings, reproaches, the pleasures of friendships, encouragement and praise when we did well in school—yet all of this was carried out in a low-key manner. We talked about many things, but never about our feelings. I did not confide in my parents and, as much as possible, we kept our troubles to ourselves. Expressions of affection were rare. As I grew older, hugs and kisses were reserved for parting. I accepted this as a matter of course. When I wrote to my parents, both before and after they left the Soviet Union, I tried to avoid upsetting them and gave them bad news only when the telling was unavoidable. The result of my consistently cheerful letters over the years was that they got a distorted picture of what my life was really like.

Does suppression of feelings atrophy one's emotional capacity? Lead to insensitivity? Certainly, it creates a shell, perhaps a protective shell. The fact is that at this turning point in my life, I was outwardly calm (perhaps inwardly, as well). I remember the words of a comparative stranger, a seamstress who was working for my aunt shortly after my parents had left. Having heard my story, she shook her head sadly and said to me that the pain of separation would get worse, not better, with the passage of time, and that it would not dull. She was right. The passage of time deepened my sense of loss, especially when I finally had to face the fact that I might never see my family again. However, at that time I brushed aside the doomsaying.

My immediate plan was to look for a new job and then to continue my schooling. My friends encouraged me, most of all Izzy, who wrote often and was trying to get released from his job in Stalingrad.

One day, not long after my parents' departure, I went to the Moscow Central Committee of the Komsomol. I had letters from my factory's Komsomol committee and from the administration stating that they had no objection to my leaving the factory. Such a statement was routine procedure: anyone quitting a job in the Soviet Union had to be released by the administration and, if the worker were a member of the Komsomol or Party, by those organizations as well.

The Moscow committee was located in the center of town. Admittance was still as simple as it had been at the Central Committee two years before—no pass or appointment was necessary. The guard directed me to the "instructors'" department where a young man greeted me, questioned me briefly, and asked me to wait in the anteroom while he consulted his colleagues and made a few calls. This did not take him long. When he summoned me back into his office, he had a letter ready for me to take to the Foreign Languages Publishing House (of which I had not heard). He suggested I go straight there: the head of the English section was expecting me.

The publishing house was nearby, in an old walk-up on Nikolskaya Street near Red Square. A tall woman with reddish blond hair who spoke English with a heavy accent ushered me into the room adjoining hers. She introduced me to a pleasant-looking man with dark eyes and the sensitive features one sees in portraits of Jewish intellectuals. This was Comrade Talmy, head of the English section. He looked middle-aged to me, but he must have been no more than in his early thirties. He spoke English with a slight accent.

The interview was brief. Talmy was pleasant, but impersonal. He asked me for details about my education and where I lived, and offered me a job as a copyholder, a position that I accepted without hesitation. There were formalities: a long application form to fill out and written references from Party members to be submitted. Ordinarily, three references were required, but since I had a letter from the Komsomol, I needed only two and could submit them even after I started my job. Galya's mother supplied me with one reference and someone from the factory gave me the other. I asked for time to put my affairs in order and we agreed that I would start the job in three weeks.

Leon Talmy, as I discovered later, was an American Communist who had emigrated from Russia before the revolution and had been a writer for the Yiddish-language Communist press in New York. He was very well-known in American-Jewish literary circles, and had been appointed to his present position by the Soviet Communist Party, of which he was now a member.

I did not need three weeks to obtain my release from Dinamo, but I was determined to find another place to live before I started my new job.

The commune had fallen apart. Vassiona had been dismissed and had gone back to her village. With Zina gone as well, Valya and I had the room to ourselves, a very good housing situation, except that Valya's domineering older sister was practically a permanent fixture. All the AMO and Dinamo buildings had been transferred to the local housing authority and the people living in them were no longer tied to the factory. I had every right to stay, but I hated the place and wanted desperately to get away. Now, two years later, I felt even more like an outsider than I had when I had first arrived. I did not feel close to anyone, and unhappy memories were still sharp in my mind. So I did what no native would have done: I walked away from "living space." In the end, Valya got married (not to Volodya) and left, and her sister gained possession of a room to which she had no right at all. She and Valya had undoubtedly planned this from the start.

The publishing house had plans to build an apartment house for its employees. It even had a site. But that was to be in the future. Like other institutions that did not supply housing, it received a housing allotment from the city to be distributed to needy employees. Only the most valuable or influential employees could hope to be considered, and I was neither. My only recourse was to rent from someone who had "extra" space and wanted additional income. And very few people had an extra room. Besides, I could not have afforded a separate room even if I had found one. So I looked for a "corner," a part of a room to share. This was perfectly legal so long as the room was larger than the minimum required size (nine-and-a-half square meters per person) and the renter was a registered resident of Moscow. "For rent" notices were posted along with other notices of various kinds on glass-covered bulletin boards at information booths around the city. A set fee was charged for a notice, depending on its length and the amount of time it was to remain posted.

I finally rented a curtained-off corner of a rather large room in a communal apartment, located about a third of the way closer to my new job. My "landlady" was a slightly lame young woman with straight blond hair and thin lips, a "divorcee," she said. I moved in with the suitcase I had had at the commune and a large cardboard case my parents had left me. I filled the case with clothes I would need on a daily basis. The woman was friendly at first, but she became less so when she saw that I had nothing special to offer her— no extra rations, no worthwhile gifts. She also thought I must be crazy or stupid to have exchanged America for Moscow. After awhile, she started bringing men home, something she had apparently been doing before I came, to supplement her meager salary as a clerical employee in a nearby office. If I happened to be home, I'd be pressed to take part in the preliminary drinking and was resented when I refused, which I did consistently.

Verily, I had jumped from the frying pan into the fire. I dreaded going home, so I often spent the night at the home of friends. To find another place to live was not easy, but six months later, I rented space in a solid old building much closer to my office and within walking distance of my step-uncle's and the Atlases. I moved out one day when my "landlady" was at work, taking one suitcase with me and leaving a note saying that I would come back for the other. When I went back a few days afterwards, I found that the lock had been changed and I could not get in. I always intended going back some evening accompanied by a friend or friends, but I kept putting off the distasteful errand and never did go back, abandoning the large case with clothing and odds and ends. The by-now shabby little suits and dresses I left behind were irreplaceable. Clothing of any kind was hard to come by, so this was more of a disaster than it might have seemed. That I didn't have the nerve to go back bothered me for a long time. I was more distressed about my inability to take action than I was about the loss of my possessions. Even now when I think of it, I get a sick feeling, even though I have long since forgotten what was in that cardboard suitcase.

The room I now shared belonged to an illiterate old woman who had been a servant in the household of the former tenant. Her former employers had left for parts unknown and their very large apartment had been divided up among as many families as there were rooms, all sharing one kitchen, toilet, and (separate) bathroom (which I never used). By then, I was going to school in the evenings and came to the apartment only to sleep, so I did not get involved in the messy kitchen gossip and quarrels. When I happened to come home earlier than usual, my landlady would talk to me about the old days. She had mixed feelings about her former life—while she felt a malicious glee about her former employer's come-down, she also felt nostalgia for a time when she was better fed and clothed. She lived on a tiny old-age pension and had the lowest category of ration cards so that my small contribution was important to her. We had an easy relationship. She didn't bother me and I didn't bother her. I lived there for about eight months.

I started my new job in October 1933. One year later, I left it to enter Moscow University. During that one year, I made many good friends, and formed several lifelong ties. Through my friends, occasional freelance work, and two returns to regular employment over the years, I maintained my connection with the publishing house for the next fifteen years.

The Foreign Languages Publishing House, state-owned like all Soviet institutions, was affiliated with the Comintern.[1] It published translations of Marxist

---

1. Comintern—Communist International, policy-making headquarters of the international Communist movement, established in 1919, officially dissolved in 1943.

literature into many languages. Most of the original works were in Russian, but there were also translations from the German, as well as reissues of works by Marx and Engels written in English. It also put out brochures about various aspects of Soviet life, so-called popularization literature, selected or written by the Russian staff, as well as translations of current Russian fiction and new translations of some of the Russian classics. The publishing house had a printshop and a technical staff, among whom were several experienced printers and layout workers from the United States, Austria, and Germany. It was organized along linguistic lines, with editorial sections arranged by language or groups of languages. The largest sections were the English and the German (which included Hungarian and Serbo-Croatian), and the Romance languages (French, Spanish, Italian, and Romanian). There was also a Chinese section. A small number of books were published in Urdu and Hindi.

The majority of foreigners employed in the language departments were Communists or Communist sympathizers, although a few had come to the Soviet Union because their spouses or they themselves were unemployed and they wanted to wait out the "world economic crisis." Most of the Germans, Austrians, Hungarians, Italians and, probably, Chinese had come to escape persecution in their countries. They had the status of "political emigré," which gave them special privileges for housing and rations. There were no political emigrés in the English section.

Employees of the Russian section stood in greater command, acting as supervisors, censors, and liaisons to the Comintern and the Party Central Committee. Consisting of the publishing house administration and an editorial staff, the Russian section was responsible for acquisitions and selection. One of its important functions was to see that the flock of foreign workers (Communist or not) did not make or overlook "political mistakes." Vigilance was the watchword—issued from the top and relayed down to the lowliest employee.

Working hours were five days in a row, from nine to four with an hour for lunch, and the sixth day off. (The five-day week, with four days of work and the fifth off, which had been in effect when I arrived in the Soviet Union, had been changed to a six-day week with Sundays off for most people. With the earlier system, family members had often had different schedules and rarely saw one another.) As in all Soviet organizations, there was a trade union, a Communist Party, and a Komsomol organization. Also, as with all other Soviet institutions, a threesome ("troika")—consisting of the Party secretary, the director, and the head of the trade union—made all but the most important decisions concerning day-to-day operations.

This was a different world, but one in which I felt much more at ease than I had at the factory. It had ties to the world from which I came, not in the sense of supplying material goods, but psychologically. Its inhabitants were familiar to me: They knew the milieu I came from and I knew theirs.

I arrived early for my first day on the job. Anna Sareyeva, the woman I had met at my interview, showed me into a large room with eight or nine desks. She told me that for the first few days I would be working with Sophie. Another woman looked up from her desk and smiled:

"I'm Betty Pollak," she said. "You must be the new copyholder, Mary, right?"

I nodded.

Betty was a plain, pleasant-looking woman in her early thirties. When she got up from her desk, I saw that she was shorter than she had seemed when seated—long-waisted, short-legged. She had a lovely, rich speaking voice and had, I learned later, sung professionally in the United States. She came from New York and was divorced from an artist well-known in Leftist circles for his contributions to the *New Masses*.[2]

As the others drifted in, the room filled with animated chatter, much of it, I gathered, about an important meeting the day before. At nine o'clock sharp, a bell rang. Sophie had come in a few minutes before the bell and now she asked me to pull up a chair so that I could read to her from a typescript in a low voice while she checked the galleys. Other pairs had gone to work in the same manner. This was the proofreaders' room.

I don't suppose that Sophie was deliberately chosen to help me through the first few days, but I could not have had a better guide. She was patient, correcting me gently when I stumbled over unfamiliar words, and seemingly pleased to have me working with her.

It was my job to read aloud to the proofreaders or editors as they checked for errors at every stage of production. We would review the manuscripts, galleys, page proofs, and the final "signal" copy before publication. I found the subject matter of the copy that I read in the course of my work very interesting—such works as Lenin's *What Is to Be Done?* and *One Step Forward, Two Steps Back*, Marx's *The Eighteenth Brumaire*, Engels's *The Origin of the Family, Private Property and the State*. Skewed as the list may have been, it opened up linguistic and intellectual vistas to me. That year restored my English and expanded my vocabulary, for the people I worked with were older and better educated than I was, many of them having gone to college. From that time on, through all the years I lived in the Soviet Union, I was never again without friends who spoke native English.

The English section had a staff of about twenty to twenty-five workers. At the top of the hierarchy were the senior translator-editors and editors of Marxist literature. The former knew Russian well and had the ultimate

---

2. *New Masses*, literary magazine of Communist and Communist sympathizer intellectuals, published from 1926–1948.

responsibility for the finished product; the latter edited the translations of others and reviewed the reissues of works that had originally been written in English. "Control editors" checked every word of every manuscript to see that the Russian was rendered precisely in translation. Noisy arguments frequently erupted between control editors and translators. After the control editors came second-rank editor-translators, followed by assistant editors whose job it was to perform the research on manuscripts and see them through the various stages of production and, generally, to smooth the translator-editors' way. The proofreaders and typists were on lower rungs of the ladder, and the copyholders were at the very bottom. Some of the proofreaders were junior assistant editors. Everyone, from assistant editors down, read proof and took turns holding copy for the others. I was a welcome addition to the staff as I was the only "straight" copyholder. The administration consisted of Talmy and Sareyeva. Sareyeva was a screamer. Hardly a day passed that you did not hear her yelling at someone.

The members of the Communist Party of the Soviet Union (CPSU) in the English section formed the political guidance core, at least in their eyes and in those of the overall Party committee who, supposedly, trusted them more than they trusted the other "foreigners." (Once a foreigner, always a foreigner in Russia, whether you became a citizen or not and no matter how long you lived there.)

The political authority of the CPSU members was not taken very seriously by the rest of the English section. Daily shouting matches occurred as editors, control editors, and even a lowly proofreader now and then argued the subtleties of political meanings of texts and how they were to be rendered in translation. The staff, especially those who had been card-carrying Communists in the United States, did not accept the premise that Soviet Communists were ideologically superior. Politically, they were, if anything, more zealous than the people I had lived among for the past two years. Hadn't they come to Moscow by choice and didn't they regard themselves as the vanguard of world revolution, engaged in the important work of spreading the Communist gospel to the workers of the world?

We worked steadily, with no break until lunchtime. Sophie invited me to join her and several others at the publishing house canteen in the same building. Now they had time to ask me questions: Where had I lived in the United States? How much schooling had I had and where? How old was I? (I was short and small-boned and looked several years younger than I was.) Everyone was very cordial. When they found out that I had no family in Moscow and lived in a rented "corner," the women's maternal or at least sisterly instincts were aroused. Before long, I was being invited to their homes for meals and often overnight. All were better off than I was. Their husbands or parents had *Insnab* or other special privileges, whereas my situation had worsened now that I was no longer employed in heavy industry. Having reached the age of eighteen, I was no longer even entitled to special rations for working minors.

Sophie was the first to invite me to her home.

Sophie Oken was a native New Yorker, about thirty years old. Her husband, Jimmy Tevan, had been born in Hungary and had come to the United States as a young man. He was a skilled auto mechanic, and the factory where he worked had provided him with housing and *Insnab*. Their one-room apartment on Novinsky Boulevard was in a building well-known in Moscow for its avant-garde architecture. It was built to look like a ship and had been designed for communal living. (My first sight of the Guggenheim Museum in New York years later brought that building to mind.) The apartments opened up onto a long corridor and had no kitchens. It had been assumed that the residents would have their meals in a communal dining room with adjoining kitchen on the ground floor, but this idea fell apart very quickly. The communal dining room was remodeled and the residents did their cooking on primitive ceramic electric plates or on kerosene stoves in the small halls of their apartments. The bathrooms and toilets were shared—one per four or five apartments. Though this arrangement was not as good as having a self-contained separate apartment, it was much better than the average living conditions. Many were the meals I had in their home and many the times I stayed there when they were away. Sophie and Jimmy were very kind and generous to me and I was sorry to see them go back to New York in 1938, when many foreigners living in Moscow were given the choice of becoming Soviet citizens or leaving the country.

The prima donnas of the English section were the Feinberg brothers, Joe and Bram, who had come from England—Joe, soon after the revolution, and Bram, some years later. Both were members of the Soviet Communist Party and were senior translator-editors. Joe was Party secretary of the English section and a member of the overall publishing house Party committee. They were tyrannical, demanding, and impatient—especially Bram, who was better educated than his older brother and more openly arrogant. Joe had a more friendly manner; as Party secretary, he had the obligation to respond to people's needs and to boost morale. Both brothers were married and had young families, but both also had an eye for pretty girls. Neither brother had looks or charm and I used to wonder what the bright, articulate assistant editor who was rumored to be Joe's girlfriend, and the attractive, efficient typist who was Bram's inamorata, saw in them.

Lasker, a senior editor, came from Philadelphia, where he had practiced law and espoused left-wing causes. He had been transferred from the Communist Party of the United States (CPUSA) to the CPSU in the nick of time. A Party purge (*chistka*) had been announced in January 1933 and admission to the Soviet Party had been suspended for the duration.

The declared aim of the purge was to cleanse the Party of "chance," "immature," and "alien" elements. In fact, the purge was the culmination of the inner-Party fight of the 1920s and the consolidation of the victory of Stalin's supporters. Quite a few foreign Communists living in the Soviet Union were caught in the hiatus. Though all the members of foreign Communist Parties who were employed in the publishing house and the Comintern were required to go through the purge process and were promised eventual transfers to the CPSU, very few were ever transferred, even when this was recommended by the purge commissions.

Purge proceedings were conducted at open Party meetings presided over by a commission, in this case appointed by the Central Committee of the CPSU. I attended the meetings with the rest of the staff.

The large hall would be filled to capacity. Extra chairs would be put in the aisles and in the back of the room. People would keep coming in and pushing through to friends who had saved seats for them. The members of the commission would come in and take their seats on the raised platform. Everyone would fall silent and I could feel the tension in the hall. After the "defendant" was examined in great detail with emphasis on positions taken during past struggles within the Party, theoretical knowledge, and personal history, the audience would be invited to participate, to ask questions, and to express their opinions. Anyone who had doubts about the "purgee" would be urged to come forward.

And come forward they did! What an opportunity to settle scores, to exhibit one's superior knowledge, to capture the attention of people in high places! There was much petty criticism and backbiting, but also some praise. Certainly, many of those who spoke, perhaps the majority, sincerely believed that they were ferreting out enemies, strengthening the Party, and serving the revolution. The commission took note of everything that was said. Its decisions, however—retention of Party membership, demotion to provisional—that is, candidate, status, expulsion, or, in the case of foreign Communists, transfer or no transfer to the CPSU—were made public weeks later and were often unexpected. The purges and the long waits were nerve-racking experiences for the principals and their friends. "Performances" were assessed, decisions anticipated, and discussions continued as the recommendations were anxiously awaited.

During my first few days on the job, the office was a-buzz with the recent "performance" of one of the Americans, Liz Goldman. She had, everyone agreed, come through with flying colors.

Liz, a twenty-six-year-old member of the national committee of the Young Communist League and an active member of the CPUSA, had come from

Boston. She was far removed from the stereotype of a fiery young revolutionary. Just over five feet and slim, with straight brown hair, hazel eyes, and freckles, she was soft-spoken and rather mousy looking except on the rare occasions when a smile lit up her face. She had come to Moscow with her Russian-born husband, a talented engineer who had grown up in China and whom she had met in Boston when he was a student at the Massachusetts Institute of Technology. His dream had been to go back to now-revolutionary Russia to help build socialism. Reluctantly, because she believed that Communists should remain in their own countries and fight the good fight there, Liz had agreed to this move before they were married.

Liz was an assistant editor, soon promoted to full editor. From the talk in the office, it was clear that no one doubted that she would be admitted to the Soviet Communist Party as soon as the doors reopened, and, indeed, that was the commission's recommendation. However, the doors were never reopened to Liz or to most of the foreign Communists. Though Liz lived the rest of her life in the Soviet Union, she never became a member of the CPSU. She was not transferred and refused to apply as a new member.

Preparations for the celebrations of November 7, 1933 were underway. The newspapers were filled with declarations of fulfillment and overfulfillment of production plans and paeans to Stalin. As usual, streamers, posters, and banners were going up all over the city. Party and Komsomol members were given special assignments in connection with the forthcoming demonstrations and with the holiday meetings and entertainments at various institutions. Our publishing house had a special relationship with a large factory on the outskirts of the city. These ties were part of a nationwide system of *shefstvo*, a word usually translated as "patronage," whereby one organization "adopted" another and assisted it in various ways. A factory might "adopt" a collective farm, for example, and, among other things, send workers to help with the spring planting or the fall harvesting and receive in return some of the farm's after-tax produce. An important component of such relationships was ideological, with the more "advanced" organization providing speakers on special occasions, conducting political classes, and so forth.

The Komsomol committee decided that I should make a speech at the "adopted" factory, bringing greetings from the American Young Communist League and working youth. I protested: My Russian was not good enough. I did not know what to say. I was not representative of American young workers as I had never held a job in America. But my protests were in vain. They'd tell me what to say and someone would interpret for me, if necessary, to help me through the proceedings.

A co-worker was assigned to accompany me.

I had hardly more than exchanged greetings with Mussia, a dumpy, awkward girl with straight black hair cut short, but I knew her reputation—

she was a topnotch assistant editor and proofreader, bilingual in Russian and English and fluent in German. Nothing escaped her eagle eye. Though she was the youngest staff member in the English section and possibly in the publishing house—two years my junior—many of her older colleagues stood in awe of her, especially the lower ranks, partly because of her unpredictable moods. One day she would come into the office looking as threatening as a thundercloud, and everyone would try to keep out of her way. On other days she would be warm and friendly, helping anyone who needed her assistance. She had been born in London and had attended a private school there. That was all I knew when we set out. As our journey progressed, Mussia began to worry about what I might say at the meeting. She was afraid I might depart from the prepared speech and say something "erroneous." By the time we reached our destination an hour later, she had easily persuaded me not to give my speech at all. She would give it herself as I sat on the platform, a symbolic delegate from American youth.

After our expedition to the factory on that bungled Komsomol assignment, she was filled with remorse, certain she had offended me by her lack of trust. No matter how vigorously I assured her that I had not been offended (rather, I had been relieved not to have had to speak in public), she kept apologizing until I begged her to desist.

We had many a laugh over this incident in later years. Though we treated it as a humorous episode, it was by no means insignificant. As I got to know Mussia better, I saw that anxiety clouded her every move. The causes of this were deep and stemmed from a confused and insecure childhood, followed by tragedy and disasters. Mussia was not a happy person, yet she had an enormous capacity for enjoyment. The simplest pleasures would lift her spirits: an evening at the theater, an afternoon in the country, a kind word from someone she admired, the successful purchase of an article in short supply. Mussia Jochel became one of my closest friends, however it was years before I knew all the facts and still longer before I acquired the maturity to understand how they could affect a person's emotional and mental make-up for an entire life.

She lived with her mother and stepfather, a professor of Latin at Moscow University, in a communal apartment in which they had two small, connecting rooms. Her mother was a petite blond, beautifully dressed and self-assured. Mussia adored her mother, but wanted desperately to get a place of her own. About a year after I met her, she rented a room privately and moved out. She visited her mother regularly on specific days and sometimes I went with her.

It took me until the 1980s to learn her whole story. Her father had been a member of the Lithuanian Bund. He had left Russia before the war and had gone to England, where he had relatives. Her mother came from Warsaw and had a teaching job in London; they met and were married in 1917. Mussia was born in London in February 1918. The family returned to Russia later that year and her father went to work as a journalist for the Soviet news agency ROSTA, the predecessor of TASS (the Telegraph Agency of the Soviet Union). Her mother was secretary to Georgi Chicherin, the first Soviet foreign minister (People's Commissar for Foreign Affairs) for a short time. Soon afterwards, her father's job took them to Germany, where her mother was employed as a code clerk at the Soviet embassy in Berlin. In 1925, they went to China. After two years, he was recalled and he took Mussia back to Moscow with him. The marriage had been breaking up and her mother remained behind to be with the man with whom she was involved and whom she later married. (Mussia's stepfather was my Latin teacher in the university a few years later.) Mussia's father arranged for her to attend the Isadora Duncan School for dance, an academy established by Duncan herself in 1921 and the only available boarding school in Moscow. A year later, she was sent to England to live with an aunt. In 1929, her father was arrested on charges of Trotskyism and he was imprisoned. Released after several months, he subsequently committed suicide. Mussia did not know any of this for a long time. She learned of her father's death only from one of his close friends, who had come to London from Moscow. Mussia completed secondary school there but then returned to Moscow. She had come to work at the publishing house only a few months before I had.

My services as a copyholder were much in demand and I got to work with most of the staff at one time or another. Working with the British English gave me some trouble at first, but after a short while, I got used to their accents. In addition to the Feinbergs, there were three other staff members who had come from England.

Eve Manning, an assistant editor, seemed to me the very image of English womanhood—fresh-faced with pink cheeks, violet eyes, dark wavy hair, and a cheery manner. Despite her friendliness, we knew little about her. It was rumored that she came from an upper-class family and that her father was a member of Parliament. John Evans, a slightly built man of medium height, had come to Moscow in search of a job, and John Scott, a tall, lanky redhead, had wandered into the Soviet Union in the course of a walking trip through Europe and had decided to remain for a while. Scott was twenty-eight, Evans a year or two younger. Both were talented editors. Eve Manning eventually married someone from the Soviet Republic of Georgia, had two sons, and lived in Moscow where she was a leading translator from Russian. Scott went to Spain during the Spanish Civil War and was killed in action. Evans stayed in Moscow through the war, becoming an accredited foreign correspondent, then returned to England where, we heard, he died a few years later. I do not recall Evans, Scott, or

Manning expressing any political opinions. Their interest in the work seemed to be chiefly literary.

Americans made up the majority of the staff. Chaika Wattenberg, an assistant editor, was a friend of Talmy's and came from the same Jewish literary circles. Her husband, an economist, was employed in one of the commissariats. A most valuable member of the staff and one of the few true professionals was technical editor Harry Cantor, a skilled printer who had come from Chicago with his wife and children. Tall, mustachioed Harry spent most of his work time at the printshop, but when he did drop in at our office, he livened it up with his good-natured banter. A longtime member of the CPUSA, he devoted much of his free time to working with young people at the foreign workers' club in Moscow and was well-known and liked by the younger set of Moscow's so-called Anglo-American colony.

An American who did not fit into the pattern was Elsa Dobo, a typist whose father was a wealthy Japanese importer in New York and whose mother was of Swedish descent. She had been completely uninterested in politics until she met her husband, a Hungarian Communist journalist. Another who did not fit the pattern was Edmund Stevens, the only "WASP" among us, who came on staff a few months before I left the publishing house to go to university. Stevens was an official of the National Student League, an organization thoroughly infiltrated by Communists, but he himself was not a Communist and was possibly unaware of the Communist influence.

Though I made many friends that year, I felt closest to Mussia, the Laskers, and to two other Komsomol members, Helen, and Naomi. Naomi Lerner[3] was an assistant editor and, at twenty-one, already married. She and her husband Bill had been high school sweethearts. Naomi was a strikingly pretty girl with curly dark blond hair and a charming, dimpled smile. Bill was tall, blond, good-looking, and together they made a very attractive couple. Bill worked in a factory and went to engineering school in the evening. When I met them, they lived in two rooms of a three-room apartment that belonged to a relative in a cooperative occupied mostly by foreigners. They had acquired these quarters after more than a year of living in crowded communal apartments.

Naomi was close enough to me in age to be my confidante; at the same time, as an experienced married woman, she was also my mentor. She was outgoing, easy to talk to, not judgmental in personal relations, and kind and generous to her friends. She played a part in knitting together a cohesive, friendly group of young people in the publishing house. She and Bill gave many parties—small parties for intimate friends, holiday parties for

3. Naomi Lerner is a pseudonym.

coworkers. These parties were lots of fun, with dancing to American phono-
graph records, joking, and flirting. How lighthearted we were that year!

The Laskers lived in the same cooperative building as Naomi and since
I often worked with Lasker, sometimes at his home, I became friendly with
him and his wife. They were a childless couple, much older than I, without
any family in Russia, and they seemed to have adopted me. Lasker was a
big, fat man with a round face and a quick, childlike smile. His wife Reba
was fat and round like him. When I saw them together for the first time, I
almost laughed out loud—they reminded me of Tweedledum and Tweedle-
dee. Where her husband was concerned, Reba was a tigress, defending her
young. Lasker, with his stodgy, lawyerly language, was a frequent target of
attacks by overzealous colleagues for what they considered to be an inappropriate translation style. Reba was much more bitter toward those colleagues
than he was. Generally a jolly, hospitable person, she never forgave anyone
who criticized her husband. Reba had been a pharmacist in Philadelphia.
Now she taught English in a specialized secondary school (technicum) for
foreign languages, where Mikhail Borodin's wife was the director.

Helen Altshuler, twenty years old, had come on staff as an assistant
editor only a few months before I was hired. She had recently graduated
from Hunter College in New York, then a college for women, where she had
majored in mathematics. She knew Russian quite well, as she had spoken it
at home. Before long, she was promoted to a translator's position.

Helen did not make friends easily. She seldom initiated a conversation.
She responded to overtures with a shy smile and replied to direct questions
in monosyllables whenever possible. This was especially noticeable in social
situations, and people soon gave up trying to draw her out. She was intelligent and an excellent worker, well-liked by her colleagues, but close to no
one. And that was the way it remained, with one exception—myself.

It was Helen's mother, rather than Helen, who told me something about
the family's history. Unlike Helen, she was outgoing, sociable, at ease with
people. She greeted me warmly the first time I came to their home, clearly
pleased that Helen had made a friend. She was introduced to me as "Vera
Pavlovna." Helen's Aunt Katya, her father's sister, lived with them.

Helen's parents had come from the south of Russia and had met in
Nikolayev, where they as well as Katya and her other brother had belonged
to a revolutionary student group. After the failed revolution of 1905 and the
pogroms that followed, the group broke up. Helen's parents emigrated to the
United States and settled in Perth Amboy, New Jersey, where their daughter
Lydia was born in 1908 and Helen was born in 1913. Katya and the other
brother had gone to Germany.

The Russian Revolutions of February and October 1917 galvanized
Russian emigré circles abroad. Many politically involved emigrés returned

to Russia at that point. Katya and her brother went back in the late 1920s and settled in Moscow. Several years later, Helen's father decided to go on an exploratory trip to Russia and, if satisfied, he planned to send for his family. In Moscow he met and started living with a woman whom he had known in his younger days and who now held an important position in the Soviet Communist Party. He wrote to his wife, asking for a divorce. Vera Pavlovna agreed to the divorce, but made it a condition that he bring the family to Moscow first and help them get settled. Helen and her mother then left for Moscow. Lydia, who was married, was going to follow with her husband, but something went wrong and she did not come, which was a constant source of pain to her mother, who spoke of her often. (Lydia came to visit her mother in Moscow for the first time in the early 1960s.) Vera Pavlovna never spoke to me of her ex-husband, except to remark once that Helen took after him in personality, as I could see on the few occasions I met him in their home.

Their two-room apartment had been obtained for them through the combined efforts of Helen's father's new wife and of her uncle, who became a well-known literary critic in Moscow and wrote under the name of Lezhnev. Katya lived in the smaller room. Helen and her mother shared the larger room, which also served as a dining and living room. The pride of the kitchen was a General Electric Frigidaire that Vera Pavlovna had brought from America over everybody's objections. It was now the envy of relatives and friends.

I never really understood what part ideology had played in their decision to move to the Soviet Union. Helen had been a member of the YCL, but she certainly was not an activist. That was not her nature. Her mother did not seem particularly interested in politics. Yet in all the years I knew them, they were staunch supporters of the regime. Helen became a fine translator of Russian literature and one of the very few ex-Americans to be admitted into the Union of Soviet Writers. Although Vera Pavlovna enjoyed talking about their life in America and described Perth Amboy to me in great detail, she never expressed regret at having left. One of the reasons was that she was convinced that Helen would not have done as well in a competitive society.

Getting used to my new job, making friends, being involved in after-work activities—some of which were onerous but some of which were fun—left me with little time to think about my situation, which was not very good and which would have been much worse if not for the tactful concern of my now numerous friends. Not only was my rations category low, but I had no place to cook meals, even if I had known how to cook. Yet I never went hungry in those days. Wherever I went, I was fed, and fed well by Moscow standards. Even the people whom I seldom saw outside the office showed concern for me. I have never forgotten the time an editor who had gone to Paris to renew her passport presented me with two lemons on her return: "for your bronchitis," she said.

The publishing house was a lively, interesting place. Most of the people who worked there were young; the "oldsters" were in their forties, and thirty was practically middle-aged. The intermingling of many people from different countries and cultures was exhilarating. And, yes, that all these so different people believed in the same ideals and goals—at the very least in social justice and the possibility of achieving it—established a special bond among us. No one seemed to have any doubts about the importance of the work. The bonds were further strengthened by the peculiar situation of so many of the foreigners, particularly those who could not or did not plan to return home. They were cut off from their families and did not have a circle of old friends in Moscow. Consequently, the publishing house became a surrogate family. Often office events that, in other Soviet institutions, might have been official functions from which people hurried home as fast as they could get away turned into parties and social occasions.

My contacts with other sections of the organization were mainly by way of the Komsomol. Through Mussia, who was as much at home in the German section as in the English, I got to know some of the Germans. There was Hilda Angarova, an attractive young woman of about twenty-eight from a well-to-do, assimilated German-Jewish family, who had married a Soviet trade official she had met in Germany. The marriage broke up soon afterwards. She lived with her five-year-old daughter in the spacious apartment she retained after the divorce.

Maria Rivkin, twenty-one, was the youngest of four daughters of a struggling Jewish tailor in Leipzig. She had been active in the Communist youth movement at a time of rising fascism and had fled Germany to avoid arrest. Very soon after I met her, she married a co-worker, a Russian who had lived in Germany and gone to school there. I did not get to know her very well that year, but later she became one of my closest friends.

Naomi's cousin Eda Litvakova was an editor in the Russian section. Eda was the daughter of one of Naomi's father's brothers who had not emigrated from Russia. Another brother, Moisei Litvakov, who also had not emigrated, was now a leading writer and the editor of the Soviet Yiddish-language newspaper *Der Emes* (*The Truth*).[4]

Meanwhile, major changes were taking place in Soviet-American relations that autumn, but I was so absorbed in my own life that I hardly noticed them. One harbinger of the improving climate was the aviator Charles Lindbergh's visit to Moscow in September 1933. In October, negotiations began for American recognition of the Soviet Union. On November 18th,

---

4. Moisei Litvakov was accused of treason and executed along with other Jewish writers during the postwar Stalinist Terror.

normal diplomatic relations were established between the two countries and on November 21st, the former Menshevik Alexander Troyanovsky was appointed as the Soviet Union's ambassador to the United States.

In November, I attended my first English section's production meeting. Everybody without exception was expected to attend these monthly meetings, the purpose of which was to discuss works in progress, production plans, translations, and editorial problems. That meeting and every other meeting I attended that year was a free-for-all, the main purpose of which seemed to be to expose and humiliate anyone who had had the misfortune to have made or overlooked a mistake at any stage of the publishing process. There might have been a typo overlooked by a proofreader, a misspelled word, an omission, or a mistranslation. People pounced on their colleagues with malicious glee. The "discoverer" of a mistake was self-righteous and smug; the "perpetrator" was abject. Woe to anyone responsible for an error that had crept into the printed edition! Official reprimands, salary deductions, and demotion were the penalties. Criticism was offered in the spirit of devotion to the cause and concern for quality. Questions of translation and style were debated heatedly and discussions frequently turned acrimonious.

Not everyone took part in the attacks with equal fervor—and this had little to do with rank. There were predators and prey at every level. Most active were a clique of two or three top editors and two or three assistant editors who considered themselves more talented and politically knowledgeable than the others and therefore more entitled to instruct. They seemed oblivious or unconcerned about the pain and bitterness their scorn aroused.

Despite the anxieties and apprehension of many of the staff, the meetings were often exciting and challenging. They usually lasted late into the evening; afterwards, a group would repair to the nearby Hotel Metropol for a late-night snack, as if after the theater (which the meetings often resembled). The size of the group depended on how many husbands joined their wives and how the victors and vanquished felt after the fray.

When I came back to work at the publishing house in 1938 after an absence of four years, the atmosphere had changed considerably. The Terror was at its height and people were much more subdued and less inclined to throw stones at one another.

At the factory, I had not gone to many meetings. But at the publishing house, I had my full share. Hardly a week passed without several after-work meetings of one kind or another. There were trade union meetings at the section level, joint meetings with other language sections, and general meetings of the entire organization. There were Party meetings open to the public (and the public was expected to attend). There were Party-Komsomol meetings and Komsomol meetings at various levels. In addition to the meetings, there was after-hours "volunteer" work (*obshchestvennaya rabota*, usually translated as "social work," but actually meaning community service). Everyone had some kind of after-work assignment: It might have been to visit a sick coworker or to help put out the wall newspaper[5] or to maintain contacts with the "adopted" factory or any one of innumerable tasks. It was the same all over the Soviet Union, and it was taken as a sign that working people were running the country. My coworkers performed these duties cheerfully, convinced that what they were doing was needed and important.

Except for the few of us who did not have living quarters of our own or special food rations, my coworkers had a much easier life than the ordinary people of Moscow. They lived in a world of their own inside and outside the office, and they knew very little about that other life. Several of the spouses worked alongside Russians, but they hardly saw them socially. Expatriates, they formed new friendships within their own group with persons of similar background and interests. For those who ultimately stayed in the Soviet Union, many of these friendships lasted all their lives. By contrast, those Americans who returned to the United States usually scattered and lost contact.

Sometime in this period, I received a notice from the local precinct to come and get my new Soviet passport (internal identity card). The captain asked me to sit down while he filled out the forms. "Name?" "Address?" "Date of birth?" "Place of birth?" "Nationality?"

To "nationality," I replied "American."

He looked up, pen in hand, poised to write down my answer.

"American? There's no such nationality. Aren't you Jewish?"

"Yes, I am Jewish, but Jewish is not a nationality."

"What do you mean, Jewish is not a nationality? American is not a nationality! It is a conglomeration of nationalities."

I argued with him. I quoted Lenin and Stalin on the nationality question. The Jews were not a nation: They did not have a common language, a common territory, a common culture, or a common economy. The captain was not convinced, but he wrote down "American" as I requested.

Izzy's reaction when I told him about the argument surprised me. He interpreted my attitude as an attempt to deny my Jewishness. I protested hotly, referring him also to essays on the national question. He said I had not understood, that nation and nationality were not the same thing, and, anyway, Jews were Jews whatever the theories. He did not convince me, but I recalled his words on more than one occasion in the future.

---

5. A feature of every organization, the wall newspaper was a current newspaper or journal that was posted onto the wall for the benefit and edification of workers, students, and passersby.

One of the most riveting events of 1933–1934, at least to us, was the Leipzig trial of Communists accused of having set fire to the Reichstag (German Parliament). Fire had gutted the Reichstag in Berlin on February 27, 1933. The next day, one hundred Communist members of the Reichstag were arrested. The general assumption (since disproven) was that the Nazis had engineered the fire in order to discredit the Communists and assure their own victory in the forthcoming elections. On March 23, 1933, the Reichstag voted Hitler dictatorial powers. Eventually, five people were charged, among them the Bulgarian Communist leader Georgi Dimitrov. Dimitrov's brilliant defense turned the trial, held in Leipzig in the latter part of 1933, into high drama. Dimitrov and the two other Bulgarians on trial with him were acquitted. They received a hero's welcome when they arrived in Moscow in February 1934.

The first American ambassador to the Soviet Union, William Bullitt, arrived in Moscow in March 1934. Now there was hope for a better relationship between our two countries.

# 8

## A Biology Student at Moscow University— 1934 to 1935

I had begun to look into opportunities to continue my education.

I was admitted to the Institute of Foreign Languages without having to take entrance exams. I attended a few evening classes and met several Americans who were studying there, among them Bernie Koten and his sister Nora, who both were enthusiastic supporters of the Soviet people's struggle for socialism. I was invited to the Koten home a number of times. The father was a veterinary doctor in the meat-packing industry and was working on a contract. They were well-off and generous to their friends. I remember Bernie's reaction when I told him that my parents had gone back to the United States and that I had stayed behind. Instead of praising me as I had expected him to do, he was horrified and urged me to follow them at once. He returned to the United States with his family soon afterwards and became an active supporter of Soviet-American ties. When I met him again in New York some thirty years later and reminded him of the incident, he had absolutely no recollection of it. Bernie was well known in the field of Slavic studies and ended up at New York University, in charge of the Slavic Department's library.

I did not remain at the Institute for very long. It could not offer me a dormitory and its stipend was not enough to live on. Besides, it was not what I wanted. I wanted to study history at Moscow University. But first I had to be admitted. To this end, I took advantage of the system of college preparatory courses.

Preparatory courses for college entrance examinations were offered at most institutions of higher education to help applicants who had been away from school for several years or who had gaps in their schooling. Preference was given to applicants who had work experience, preferably in blue-collar fields, or who had been in the army. The Soviet educational system was quite unstable and uneven, and Russian language and literature suffered the most. The old gymnasiums had been eliminated, though in some schools the traditions of excellence persisted. Science and mathematics were the fields most likely to have maintained high standards.

A whole generation of Soviet youth thus received a spotty education. Many of the reorganized and newly opened schools had conducted radical experiments of various kinds, such as the "brigade system" under which teams were formed and each member was responsible for everyone else's performance. At the same time, encouraged by the government policy of bringing education to the masses, thousands—perhaps hundreds of thousands—of illiterate and semi-literate workers and peasants flocked to special courses that had been established for them. Most important among these were the *rabfaks* (acronym for *rabochiye fakul'tety*, or "workers' faculties") set up in 1919 all over the country to enable "workers and toiling peasants" to complete secondary schooling and go on to higher education if they wished. The *rabfaks* played a crucial role in education until the late 1930s, when they were phased out as the school system stabilized.

In the 1920s and early 1930s, students in colleges and universities were older than their counterparts had been in former years and than they would be in years to come. Students at this point did not necessarily attend the institutes and universities straight from secondary school. No longer were the institutions of higher learning the exclusive abode of the elite and the affluent. Many young people with scanty educational backgrounds managed to earn college degrees and rise through the ranks of their professions in those early years. A large number were talented; others succeeded by sheer determination.

In January 1934, I enrolled in a six-month preparatory course at the biology department of Moscow University. I chose biology because there were fewer applicants than for the other disciplines, particularly history. In the sciences, the departments of math and physics, geology, and chemistry were competitive because engineers were needed to help rebuild and industrialize the country. Biology, however, was at the bottom of the list. That is not to say that the biology department attracted the least talented students. Many of the students were very bright, and most were genuinely interested in the field, but the level of prestige was not high. This was reflected in the size of the stipends available.

History was what I really wanted, but the competition was fierce, especially that year because Moscow University had not had a separate history department since 1919 (when its History and Philology Faculty and its Juridical Faculty were merged to form Social Sciences). In 1922, that faculty was divided into the Russian Association of Research Institutes, where research would be conducted, and the Faculty of Law and Ethnology at Moscow University, where history would be taught.[1] But in May 1934, the

---

1. The Research Institutes went through several reorganizations, reflecting the turmoil in historical scholarship, and finally expired in 1936. In 1931, the section at Moscow University was divided into the Moscow Institute of Philosophy and Literature (IFLI) and was placed directly under the People's Commissariat of Education, where it remained until 1941 when it was incorporated in the university. From 1931 to 1934, social science instruction at the university was conducted in all departments, chiefly as courses in the history of the CPSU, Leninism, and political economy.

CPSU Central Committee issued a decree establishing a history faculty at Moscow University and appointing a commission to implement the decision. The first class was admitted in September 1934. There were 700 applicants; 164 undergraduates and 20 graduate students were admitted.

To be admitted to the preparatory course for studies in biology, I had to submit my school records, indicating the subjects I had taken and my grades. I wrote to the principal of Santa Monica High School and, to my surprise and relief, received a prompt reply with a copy of my entire school record from Santa Monica, Los Angeles, and Albany. I was admitted without further ado.

Founded in 1755, Moscow University consisted of two buildings on Mokhovaya Street on opposite corners of Herzen Street, across from Alexandrovsky Park and the Kremlin. The biology department was in number eleven, then known as the "old building," as it was on the site of the original structure that had been destroyed in the great fire during the Napoleonic War of 1812. It was a lovely building in the classic style of so many of Moscow's nineteenth-century structures. Both the original and the later buildings had been designed by leading architects of the day.

It was exciting to be at school again, at the university, even if I was not yet an official student. My classmates were excited, too. They chattered, laughed aloud, and asked each other questions to get acquainted. I held back, knowing that as soon as I opened my mouth, I would become an object of curiosity. But I was in for a surprise. One of the livelier girls who had been talking a blue streak nearby whirled around as I was replying to someone's question and stared. Then, in perfect American English, she said:

"You're an American, too? I'm from New York."

"I'm from California."

California! To a New Yorker, it must have sounded nearly as exotic as Moscow.

"My name is Miriam Katz. When did you come to Moscow?"

The wonder of it! Here, at the other end of the earth, in an ordinary situation, a school and not a place where foreigners gathered, I was meeting a compatriot—one who was even my age!

Mira (her name in Russian) turned to the students who had clustered around us and, in perfect Russian, translated our conversation for them.

Now, Mira too was an object of curiosity. She had come to Moscow with her family eight years earlier, when she had been eleven, and had been placed in the fourth grade of a Russian school. After some hard going, she learned Russian and now spoke it like a native. From the seventh grade on, she had gone to a factory training school (like the one Anya attended), where she had completed her secondary education and learned to be an electrician. She had worked as a factory electrician for two years and had recently quit her job to prepare to enter the university full time.

Lectures were held in the large amphitheater-like auditoriums, with semi-circular rows of wooden benches and writing shelves that had been polished by generations of restless students. The professor spoke from a raised platform with a podium and a blackboard. Classes were held four times a week from six to nine P.M. The freshman class was divided into groups of twenty or twenty-five students for seminars and lab work. Our preparatory course class had been kept as a unit, and we were delighted to see one another when school officially began. Of the approximately twenty of us, all but three were female.

Our group presented a motley picture. Some of the girls came from "good" families. Their parents were teachers, journalists, scientists, and personal pensioners. They had completed secondary school and had gone to work for a year or two to better their chances of being admitted to college. They would spend the next six months reviewing material. In reality, they did not need the preparatory course, but applicants from the university's preparatory courses were given preference. Others came from families of bookkeepers, low-paid clerical employees, and factory workers, and had gone to work out of necessity as much as to gain college entrance advantages. Several came from out of town. Most were between nineteen and twenty-one, though a few were older, and one pink-cheeked, matronly looking young woman, all of twenty-four, was married and had two young children. Her husband was in his last year at the university's math and physics department. Some of the girls had gone to school or worked together, but the majority were strangers to one another. Of the few males in the program, one had already completed his army service. He was Russian, and the other two men were from Central Asia. The group knit together very quickly, with the better-prepared students willingly helping the laggards. The genuine camaraderie that I felt in that group was rare in my experience, both before I met them and after I left.

The majority were better prepared than I was. The secondary school curriculum was the same for the entire Soviet Union, though the quality of the schools differed and the students from small towns and rural areas were at a disadvantage compared with the Muscovites. The curriculum for Soviet schools required both chemistry and physics, intermediate algebra, solid geometry, and trigonometry. A great deal of the material was completely new to me. I had studied no physics at all in high school, having elected to take chemistry instead, and in math I had chosen not to continue beyond the required plane geometry and elementary algebra. The purpose of the course was to review the material, not to explain new material, and this made the situation even harder for me. I crammed and memorized. Helen Altshuler, my friend from the publishing house, was a great help. She tutored me in math and physics, and I did much of my studying at her home.

The first-year biology program was very demanding, with its required subjects including physical culture and military training. Physical culture was like gym back in high school—climbing ropes, running, jumping, marching drill—except that we went skiing in the winter. All I remember about military training is learning to fire a rifle at a target. Surprisingly, I did not do badly, in spite of being nearsighted and unwilling to wear glasses. Male students were required to take four years of military training and were commissioned as officers upon completion. Women had to take one year.

My attitude that year was to enjoy the subjects I liked and that were easy for me. I tried to ignore the rest of the program, for I planned to transfer to the history department at the first opportunity. Among the subjects I found most interesting were geology and anatomy. We had an excellent teacher of anatomy, a female physician, and we went to class in the university's anatomy theater. I vividly recall a cadaver we worked on, a boy of about ten who had a big hole in the side of his head. He was probably one of the homeless children who roamed the country in those days. In her lecture on medical ethics, the professor made a statement I had occasion to recall years later. She said that every medical professional, even a veterinarian, must know how to perform a tracheotomy to save the life of a child with croup.

The Russian class I attended met in the other building and was comprised of students from several departments. It was taught by a gruff, no-nonsense teacher of the old school, who had taught in a gymnasium before the revolution. He singled me out after the first few days, having noticed that the mistakes I made in dictation and composition differed from those the other students made. One day, he asked me to stay after class.

"You are wasting your time here," he said. "I have arranged for you to be excused from this class. My advice to you is to read. Read Leskov. Leskov will teach you Russian."[2] He shook my hand and wished me well. That was the end of my formal instruction in Russian. As for Leskov, he was far beyond me. It was years before I could enjoy reading him.

Surprisingly, my three years of Latin in high school helped me in my study of Russian. I grasped the grammar easily—more easily than many of my classmates—and I remembered the rules. I had a hard time applying the rules, however, as I could not determine gender, which Russians do instinctively. The gender for a large group of nouns in Russian can only be memorized, rather than gleaned from the words themselves. But no one had told me that! Instead, I was told: Ask the question "which" or "what." The ending of those words or any other modifier would tell me the gender. But I did not know the gender of the modifiers either, so the advice was of no use.

---

2. Nikolai Semenovich Leskov was a nineteenth-century Russian writer.

I saw a lot of Mira outside of class. I was often invited for meals or to stay overnight with her family. She lived with her mother and younger brother in two rooms of a large three-room cooperative apartment in a four-story walk-up, similar to the building I had lived in on Tyufelev Lane. Like that building, it was one of a complex of apartment houses built by a nearby factory for its employees, though Mira's family had no connection with the factory that owned the building. Her father, who was prominent in Jewish left-wing circles, had been able to buy the apartment through his connection with the Central Committee of the CPSU. When I met Mira, her father had recently gone back to New York, temporarily, it was believed, to resume editorship of the *Freiheit,* the Yiddish-language Communist daily newspaper. Mira's mother, a tall, handsome woman with long, black hair and strong features, informed me immediately that she was no ordinary housewife, but an intellectual and a poet whose works had been published in the Yiddish press.

Mira did not resemble her mother in looks or in temperament. She had very expressive, mobile features, shiny brown eyes with beckoning lights in them, and a lively, open personality, trusting to the point of vulnerability. She possessed a madcap spirit, was always ready for an adventure, and was inclined to ask outrageous questions and make outrageous statements. Her boyfriend, a young worker from the factory where she had been employed, would often meet her after school and go home with her. Her mother did not approve, but neither did she interfere.

College entrance exams were standard and were held all over the Soviet Union in August. Subjects included written and oral Russian, mathematics, physics, social studies, and one's subject of specialization, in my case, general biology. Exams were spread out over, give or take, ten days, with two or three days between them. Our classes ended on August 1st. I was entitled to a month off with pay to study and I had my annual vacation of one month coming to me, so I took off time from my job in July and August. (I had been attending classes after work.)

The examination procedures were in the pre-revolutionary and European tradition, very different from what I had known at home. I was accustomed to a set of written questions, the same for everyone, with a limited choice of questions to answer and ample time to write. Here, however, you drew lots—slips of paper with three or four questions from the course material—to which you replied orally after a short time for preparation. The examiners, usually three, might let you go after you had answered the questions you had drawn, or might test you on any other part of the course. Under these circumstances, it was easy for the examiner to guide the questioning in such a manner as to fail a good student or pass a poor one, as the occasion might require. I felt this to be unfair. Too much depended on luck and personalities.

My worst fears were about the math and physics exams. Thanks to Helen's tutoring, I passed, but just barely. In the Russian language tests, I did well in the dictation and oral exam, which was mainly on grammar, but failed the composition. I was not alone. Quite a few native Russians and most of the ethnic students did poorly. If the results of the other exams were satisfactory, they were admitted conditionally but were required to attend special Russian classes and re-take the exam at the end of the school year. The two Central Asian students in my class and I were admitted conditionally.

Helen was also admitted to Moscow University. Our coworkers at the publishing house were very pleased for us. I tried to persuade Mussia to apply, too, and did not doubt that she could pass the exams without preliminary preparation. But she refused and was evasive when I pressed her for her reasons. I did not know then how much she feared rejection because of the political skeletons in her closet.

* * *

Moscow had two huge "student towns"—Stromynka and Ostankino, where dormitory space was allotted to students from towns and villages beyond commuting distance. Few students were in my peculiar position—residents of Moscow with no living quarters of their own.

I had visited Izzy's sister Eva at Stromynka. The buildings of grey stone or brick were comparatively new. The rooms varied in size, but most were large—for six to twelve persons. The much-coveted smaller rooms went to privileged students, for example, Party and Komsomol officials and activists, graduate students, and some married students who were completing their last two years of school. Eva and her husband had recently been given one of these rooms. Each building had clean, adequate toilets and washrooms with running water, and separate facilities for men and women. A bathhouse was on the grounds, as was a library, an all-night reading room, and a canteen (*stolovaya*).

I asked for a place at Stromynka, but was given an "order" for Ostankino, which had fewer amenities and was farther away from the university.

Ostankino was at the end of the line. As the trolley car jangled along past brick factories, five-story apartment houses, and ramshackle wooden houses, I found myself once again in a working-class section of the city, this time on its northern outskirts (Dinamo was to the south). On one side of the street was the entrance to the Ostankino museum and park; on the other side were rows of two-story wooden, barrack-like buildings separated by dirt walks covered with wooden planks. I was directed to the administration building where a clerk put a house and row number on my chit and said I could go at once to select a room. The building had been set aside for first-year students and was still practically unoccupied, as the out-of-towners had not yet arrived.

The rooms were of different sizes, each containing two, three, or four beds. I chose a first-floor room with two iron bedsteads in it, two night tables, a table, two chairs, and nails on the wall and on the door for clothes. The beds had springs and thin mattresses. Bed linen and towels would be supplied. There was no indoor plumbing; water was hauled from strategically placed pumps. The washing facilities were similar to those in Birobidzhan—a bucket under a container of water with a device that could be pushed up to release a stream of water. There was a canteen, a library, and a reading room on the premises. A public bathhouse was located a few blocks away. The only amenity was electricity.

There were some advantages to living in Ostankino. For one, the rooms were smaller; this meant fewer roommates. The neighborhood's location at the end of the streetcar line meant that I usually could get a seat and could read or study all the way to school. There was a beautiful park across the street where students studied in good weather. The Ostankino museum and park had been one of the country estates of the Sheremetyevs, an aristocratic family whose beginnings went back to the era before Peter the Great. The chapel had been built in the seventeenth century, while the palace and the landscaped park were completed in the late eighteenth. The estate was famous for its wooden theater commissioned by Count Sheremetyev to honor the serf actress Zhemchugova. It had been designed by serf architects, built and decorated by serf craftsmen, and had served as the permanent residence of a remarkable serf theater company. In 1917, the Provisional Government, which ruled after the tsar's abdication, designated the Ostankino estate a national treasure to be maintained as a museum of theater and decorative arts, free and open to the public. The landmark was continued as such by the Soviet and post-Soviet government.

My roommate, Zhenya, a seventeen-year-old student from Smolensk, turned up a few days before classes began. She was a thin, fair-skinned girl with reddish hair and freckles, accompanied by her father, an army colonel, who had come from their home in Smolensk to help her settle in. Zhenya had entered the university straight from secondary school and was an ideal roommate—quiet, considerate, friendly, but not inquisitive. We actually did not see each other much, as we were in different groups at school and I seldom spent my free time at the dorm. We got along well, but were not close. I was, therefore, surprised to receive a letter from her mother inviting me to spend the three-day November holiday with them. I was hesitant, but Zhenya was persuasive and I accepted the invitation.

As I look back, I realize that this act of inviting a classmate home for the holidays, so normal in other countries, was very unusual. It was not the practice in Moscow at all. Possibly this was due to the difficult economic conditions experienced by most households. The invitation was surely a throwback to earlier traditions.

Smolensk is an old Russian town about 225 miles from Moscow. It would have been very difficult for us to obtain railroad tickets in the ordinary way. The trains were crowded, the demand for tickets far greater than the supply. People used to stand in line for hours, sometimes days, at the ticket offices. But Zhenya's father sent us the tickets—reserved, hard class, express. He met us at the station with a car and driver.

Zhenya's parents and younger brothers went out of their way to make me feel welcome. They lived in a single-family wooden house, one of many in Smolensk. They were curious, of course, and asked many questions—I was an unusual guest—but they were tactful. They seemed unusual to me, too. Here was an intact family with a mother who was a full-time housewife with what I remembered as normal, everyday concerns. Also, they were an army family, members of a privileged caste with which I had had no previous contact. Despite their privileged position, they were simple people, representative, I should think, of the middle strata of provincial Russia. In later years, when privilege became more entrenched and social differentiation more pronounced, it would have been hard to find an officer's wife so modest and unassuming. Needless to say, these thoughts did not enter my mind at the time. I enjoyed my stay—the domestic atmosphere, the good food, the plays and concerts to which we were taken.

Soon after my return from Smolensk, I had a piece of luck. A friend's father offered me his room to stay in while he was away on a work assignment for several months. For the first time in three years, I had a place where I could shut the door behind me and be alone.

This was not exactly legal, as I could not be registered there, but the legal tenant had connections and assured me that as long as I kept a low profile and did not have much company, no one would bother me. A law had been enacted in December 1932, strengthening the regulations that required all urban residents to register with the local militia and to carry an identification document, the so-called internal passport, at all times (it was probably in anticipation of this law that the authorities at Dinamo had become so insistent that I provide them with proper documents).

The room was in a two-room communal apartment, a wonder apartment by Moscow standards. The other room was occupied by a childless couple who were away at work the whole day and whose free days did not coincide with mine. The apartment had all the basic conveniences: a large kitchen with a gas stove and a sink with running water, a bathroom with a hot water boiler, a separate toilet, and a foyer.

The building was one of a group of apartment houses on Koptelsky Lane, owned by several research institutes. Some American and other foreign families lived there as well. Liz Goldman lived in the next building with her mother and husband in two connecting rooms of a four-room communal apartment provided by the institute where her engineer husband was employed. The location was very convenient. I could board the Number Ten streetcar on the corner and be at the university in twenty minutes (instead of forty or more from Ostankino). The Number Ten started out at Sokolniki Park, a few stops beyond Stromynka, and was always filled with students.

My stay there is associated with popular films of that period. One neighbor used to hum the theme songs incessantly. Lyubov Orlova was the leading film star of the day and her husband, Georgi Alexandrov, was a prominent director. In one of the films, *Circus,* the blond, blue-eyed Orlova played an American circus performer who gave birth to a Black baby and was hounded out of the United States, only to find refuge in the Soviet Union. In the final scene, the baby was passed from hand to hand in an audience of Russians as they sang a song about equality, internationalism, and love. I disliked the picture, finding it silly, simplistic, and sentimental, but my Russian friends loved it. I did like the other films, all of which were very patriotic. Among them were *Chapayev,* about a civil war hero; *Happy-Go-Lucky Guys,* about a postmistress who did her job no matter how difficult the circumstances; and *Counter Plan,* about the dedication of factory workers.

This part of my life was also closely linked with Izzy. We had a few months of privacy when I had the room on Koptelsky Lane, but we had to be discreet so as not to get the legal tenant into trouble. It was bad enough that I was not registered there, but Izzy was not even registered to live in Moscow.

When Izzy had learned I had stayed in the Soviet Union after the rest of my family had left, he managed to get released from his job in Stalingrad. After he arrived in Moscow, we started seeing each other regularly. He shared a room with his mother and aunt in a communal apartment in a small town about twenty miles from Moscow. We did not have much free time. I was attending evening preparatory courses and, later, the university. He worked irregular hours and went to journalism school in the evening. Neither one of us had a telephone, though I could phone him at his office. We met whenever we could. He would meet me after school and sometimes we'd go to a movie or to the theater. Other times, we walked the streets or sat on park benches. But, aside from using Sophie's apartment on occasion, we had no place to meet privately until I moved into the temporary quarters. Many a time, the guard at Alexandrovsky Park chased us out at ten P.M., closing time.

Izzy would often come for a hurried meeting just to help me out with food or money so that I could buy my rations. Because my stipend from the biology department was so small, it was not easy to make ends meet, even though food and residential costs were low. Most students got help from their families. Either they lived at home or received money and parcels from home. After my parents got settled, they started sending me parcels once a year for my birthday, and that was a great help. But that was later.

My relationship with Izzy lasted until 1938. If either one of us had had a permanent room, we probably would have married. My parents certainly assumed that this was where we were heading, but they were mistaken. I was fond of Izzy, yet my feelings for him were not intense. I did not feel the way I had felt about Haitin, my first love. After the first flush of our romance, tensions crept into our meetings. No doubt, much of this was due to the frustrations in our lives. More significant was the way our personalities clashed. We often parted in anger. Izzy used to say that when he was with me he was miserable, but that when we were apart, he longed to see me. Perhaps if we had been able to get married, we would have worked things out, but I doubt it.

Izzy's mother was not happy with our romance. Even in those early days, and more as time went on, she felt that a foreign-born wife with ongoing foreign connections would hinder her son's career. She did not interfere, but I sensed her disapproval.

It was during a visit to Izzy's place in the summer that I had my first experience with a typical Russian drunken party.

We arrived in the afternoon to find that his neighbors were having a celebration. The party had been in progress for some time and they insisted that we join them. We joined them reluctantly, for we had looked forward to a quiet evening by ourselves since Izzy's mother and aunt were at work. I did not want to join, not even for a short while, but Izzy insisted, saying that they would be offended—they would assume we were "too good for them, eh"—and this would make things difficult for his mother. We were welcomed noisily and places were set for us. The table was laden with food— boiled potatoes, herring, pickled beets, sauerkraut, hard-boiled eggs, bread, and a bottle of vodka. The hosts and their guests—buxom women and red-faced men—were already quite tipsy. Tumblers were set before us, filled to the brim with vodka, and we were urged to "catch up." "Bottoms up," they yelled. I tried to refuse. The entire company insisted; a few became truculent. I was furious at Izzy for getting us into this. Annoyed, I downed the whole tumbler in one gulp to the others' applause. And that was not the end of it. Toast after toast was proposed and it was not possible to avoid drinking with the rest.

That was a memorable occasion, especially memorable because I did not get drunk. When Izzy referred to it later, it was always with awe. My anger must have done something to my metabolism so that the vodka did not take effect.

The evening was ruined and it was a long time before I went there again.

Subsequently, I encountered social occasions of this kind many times, and not only among uneducated types. Every guest was expected to drink every toast and to drain the glass (not usually a tumbler) each time. The drunker the host, the greater the offense taken at a refusal. I learned to handle such situations when I could not avoid them: 100 grams of butter eaten about half an hour in advance did the trick.

\* \* \*

The newspapers in 1934 had been filled with accounts of turbulent events inside and outside the Soviet Union. The domestic scene produced daily reports of the Party purges. "Class enemies, saboteurs, and double-dealers" were uncovered all over the country. We were told of the vigilance of loyal citizens, and of crimes committed for political reasons. An item in the Soviet newspaper *Pravda* in November reported the murder of teen-age girls in a remote rural area. The girls had been Young Pioneers, killed by "kulak" elements. A sophisticated reader might have perceived in the lurid account a non-political crime of rape and murder, but in the atmosphere of the time, every crime was reported as politically motivated.

Genrikh Yagoda was the head of the political police, known as the newly created NKVD (People's Commissariat of Internal Affairs).

The doom and gloom of the reports on sabotage and violent crime were mitigated by news of achievements of workers and peasants—plan fulfillment, overfulfillment, pledges to do even better, and so forth. A note of cheer was provided by the announcement in November that the rationing of bread, flour, cereals, and some other food products would end on January 1, 1935, and that stable retail prices would be established for the various "supply zones" (the country was divided into supply zones, depending on the degree of industrialization and role in the Five-Year Plan). Today, it occurs to me that this was part of a plan to soften up the population in preparation for the wave of terror that would come in the very near future.

The news from Europe confirmed our view of a worldwide class struggle. We believed that the struggle would lead to a world revolution, even though for the present the right wing had the upper hand, particularly in Italy and Germany.

Then came December 1, 1934.

When I boarded the streetcar on the morning of December 2nd (a Sunday, but a school day), I found the din much greater than usual. I soon saw someone I knew.

"What's going on? Why is everyone so excited?"

"Haven't you heard? Kirov has been killed."

"Kirov? Who's Kirov?"

He looked at me in disbelief.

"Kirov is the First Secretary of the Leningrad Party."

"How was he killed?" (There is no word for assassination in Russian.)

"He was shot. Shot in the back. It's in today's newspapers."

That day changed our lives. Perhaps that is not quite the way to express it, now that we know so much more about the event. Today we know that December 1, 1934 was not just a day that changed our lives, but a logical continuation of Stalin's ruthless consolidation of power and the beginning of the next stage in the evolution of the Soviet regime. The Great Terror that followed was not a reaction to Kirov's assassination; instead, Kirov's assassination had been engineered by Stalin in order to get rid of a popular figure and potential rival. The assassination was then used as an excuse for outright terror.

I learned who Sergei Mironovich Kirov was. He was not just the head of the Leningrad Party organization but was a member of the Central Committee of the CPSU and the Politburo, and had been an unwavering supporter of Stalin throughout the inner Party struggle. The Party had sent him to Leningrad in 1925 to combat the influence of the opposition there, and he had become a very popular figure in Leningrad and throughout the Party.

Classes at the university were canceled. There was to be a meeting of the entire department later in the day. Students stood around in small groups, talking in low voices, or reading the newspapers posted on the walls.

The usually lively audience was subdued as it gathered in the auditorium long before the speakers were due to appear. The stillness was eerie. The meeting was addressed by the dean of the faculty, the Party secretary, the Komsomol secretary, some professors, and student activists. We were told that Sergei Kirov had been murdered in his Leningrad office the day before by a Party member and former official, Leonid Nikolayev, on direct orders from enemies of the Soviet people and the Soviet state who pretended to be loyal Communists. We were informed that these camouflaged enemies were a gang of spies and saboteurs in the employ of foreign intelligence, and that the enemy was all around us, fighting with the desperation of a dying beast. We were to be vigilant. We were to watch for the slightest sign of enemy activity. We should take a new look at family and friends and trust no one.

That first meeting was followed by others, every time a new revelation appeared in the press. Calls for vigilance rang out at meetings all over the country, at every level. Newspapers were filled with accounts of Kirov's life and descriptions of his lying-in-state and funeral. Editors printed hundreds of letters from "ordinary people" and from celebrities—well-known writers, aviators, scientists, foreign Communists. Trials already in progress were linked to the Kirov assassination, as, for example, a trial of railroad workers in Omsk who were accused of sabotage.

Grigori Zinoviev was arrested on December 16th, but his arrest was not made public until December 21st, when it was officially stated that the Kirov murder had been organized by a "Leningrad center" consisting of former members of the Zinoviev opposition. A list of those arrested, published the following day, included Zinoviev and Lev Kamenev.

I did not have to be told who Zinoviev and Kamenev were. Anyone who had the slightest familiarity with the history of the Russian revolution knew that Zinoviev and Kamenev had been comrades-in-arms of Lenin, old revolutionaries, prominent figures in the Bolshevik party before and after it had come to power.

The official indictment in the Kirov assassination was published on December 27th. On December 29th, it was announced that Nikolayev and fourteen conspirators had been sentenced to death and executed. There was no open trial. At that time, Zinoviev and Kamenev were not directly linked to the plot, but they were brought to trial in January 1935, at which time Zinoviev conceded that he was responsible for having created an atmosphere that had stimulated his followers' criminal activities. He was sentenced to ten years and Kamenev to five years' imprisonment, mild sentences in light of future reprisals but sensational for such eminent Bolsheviks.

Gradually, but steadily, controls over the population tightened.

An April 1935 decree entitled "On Measures of Struggle against Juvenile Delinquency" ruled that children older than twelve who committed serious crimes would be tried in the adult criminal courts. It also made them liable to adult penalties, including the death sentence. That was a shocker, but, as usual, my friends were able to explain it away as a "temporary measure" needed for dealing with juvenile crime. The following month, another decree, "On the Liquidation of Child Homelessness and Neglect," established parental responsibility for their children's delinquency and called for better children's homes (orphanages) and work colonies (reform schools). Carrying a knife was made illegal, punishable by five years' imprisonment. In June, flight abroad (illegal crossing of the border as well as not returning from foreign missions) was declared to be treason, punishable by death. Family members were subject to exile, whether or not they had advance knowledge of the "traitor's" intentions.

Any breakdown in the system was blamed on sabotage.

Wholesale arrests were made among the tens of thousands of former oppositionists and their families, friends, and acquaintances. In May and June, the societies of Old Bolsheviks and Former Political Prisoners and Penal Exiles were disbanded. Actually, they were reorganized as clubs, with surviving members retaining their consumer privileges; however, their newspapers were closed down and political activities were forbidden. Residential complexes where members of those organizations lived, such as the one where my step-uncle and the Atlases lived, were hit by arrests nightly.

My step-uncle had never been politically active. His arrest and exile in pre-revolutionary Russia had occurred by pure chance. As a matter of fact, he was treated with condescension by other members of the Society. I even recall hearing Anya's mother making disparaging remarks about his non-involvement. He had less to worry about than others, for there were plenty of bigger fish in the pond. The Atlases' circle, which included prominent figures among Siberian and Far Eastern revolutionaries, was very vulnerable. Neither my step-uncle nor Anya's mother talked to me about how they felt, except to mouth a rote phrase that was uttered by many in all the succeeding waves of terror: What did they—the exposed "enemies"—want? They had everything!

The extent of the sweep and suffering was not apparent to me, for arrests were made public only selectively. Solid information was scarce. The names of most of the principals were abstractions, and I did not know anyone who had been arrested. None of my friends or acquaintances had been affected. Galya and her mother were staunch Stalinists. Lydia Sergeyevna was proud that she had always been on the "correct" side in the inner-Party fights. She was not a bit worried and was very much in favor of the "housecleaning." It wasn't until I read Robert Conquest's *The Great Terror* after my return to the United States in the 1960s, long after I had lost all my illusions, that I learned many details I had not even suspected. I did not know, for example, that there had been an organized resistance in Leningrad, that the Komsomol oppositionists had refused to capitulate, and that Nikolayev had refused to implicate Zinoviev and Kamenev in the Kirov assassination. When the arrests occurred, I was more interested than horrified, and accepted the assertions that revolutions were not made in a day and that the events represented the continuation of the class struggle. To have been able to read between the lines so as to analyze the available information without access to any other points of view, either in the press or privately, would have required more political acumen and common sense experience than I had at the time.

There must have been many who did not believe everything they read and who were critical of what was happening, perhaps even among my friends and acquaintances. But people were very careful about opening up to persons who did not already share their views.

∽◐◑∼

# 9

## A History Student at Moscow University— 1935 to 1936

I passed most of that fateful winter in the room on Koptelsky. But in the spring of 1935, I was back in Ostankino.

I had inquired about obtaining permission to visit my family in the United States. I was given an application and told to submit it about three months before I wished to go. Consent of the Komsomol organization was required. I got authorization without difficulty and handed in my application in time to go for the summer.

Around the same time, I took steps to transfer to the history department. With the help of the secretary of the KIM (Communist Youth International), whom I knew from my previous connection with the publishing house, I was able to obtain a recommendation signed by the secretary of the executive committee of the Comintern and of the Central Committee of the CPSU. My transfer was approved and I entered in 1935 as a first-year student, but without having to retake the entrance exams. I was also able to arrange for a transfer from Ostankino to the Stromynka dormitory. I wanted everything to be in order so that I could leave without delay when my visa came through.

It never arrived. I waited on tenterhooks all summer. By August, I knew I couldn't make it for the summer vacation, but I still hoped for an answer of some kind. There was none.

My situation at Stromynka was better in some ways and worse in others than it had been at Ostankino. It was certainly an improvement to have indoor plumbing and running water. The library, study rooms, and dining facilities were superior. But I was assigned to a room for eight girls, and it felt as if I were living in a hospital ward or an army barrack, especially with all the rules and regulations. There was constant snooping by committees. I had trouble with the inspections and problems with my roommates similar to the ones I had had in the commune. We were required to make our beds in a particular way, with a fold down the middle of the bedspread—I could never get this right! I also had a hard time following rules about where to place belongings. I wanted the windows open at night. My roommates did not. I wanted lights out at eleven in keeping with the dormitory rules. Others insisted on reading or studying late into the night, even though they had access to an all-night reading room. Nevertheless, overall, we got along tolerably well.

I remember three of my roommates very clearly—Raya, Tussia, and Lera. Raya, like Feigele in Birobidzhan and Valya in the commune, came from a small town in the Pale of Settlement, and she reminded me of them. Like them, she was pink-cheeked, chunky, with dark hair and dark eyes, and like them, she had a didactic bent and bubbled over with political enthusiasm. Tussia and Lera were tall, blond, blue-eyed beauties, but very different in temperament and looks. Tussia wore her hair short. Slim, she walked like a dancer and sparkled with the joy of life. Lera was a languid, candy-box cover type with shoulder-length hair. She was slow moving, slow of speech, and "delicate." In my mind's eye, I can see her lying in bed with a compress on her forehead and her devoted young man seated on the edge of the bed, holding her hand and gazing into her eyes. Tussia's sweetheart Mahomet was a tall, handsome Chechen, the image of a Circassian prince. He was an honor student in the math department and a member of the university Komsomol committee. Together, they made an extraordinarily striking couple.

Most of the girls had boyfriends and, now and then, one would stay overnight. (There was no public transportation in Moscow after one A.M.) Girls would double up so the boy could have one of the beds. There was no boy-girl sharing of a bed when anyone else was at home, but the girls would sometimes accommodate each other by arranging to be out at a specified time. All of us had the same problem—lack of privacy—and each couple handled the situation the best it could. Sex there was, but it was not promiscuous.

A restraining factor in sexual relations, both pre- and postmarital, was fear of pregnancy. Condoms were easily available over the counter, but like most Soviet consumer goods, they were of poor quality and unreliable. Abortion, legal until 1936, was by far the most widespread method of birth control. It was widely believed, however, that to abort the first pregnancy would ruin a woman's health and possibly make her sterile. The other alternative was interrupted coitus, but this was considered "bad for the nerves."

Tussia, Lera, and Raya, whose boyfriends were students, hoped to be given private rooms eventually. But neither Izzy nor I could hope for a room of our own in the foreseeable future. Izzy did not intend to remain at his factory newspaper job and could not apply for a room there and I could not qualify for a room of my own in the dorm.

The history department was much more to my liking than biology had been. In some ways, the studies were also easier. My American education had prepared me better for the humanities than for the sciences. I was more familiar than my fellow students with the introductory material in the general studies courses—ancient history, mythology, medieval European history. I was way ahead in Latin, though the pronunciation that was taught was different from that which I had learned in high school. Marxist subjects were taught in greater detail than they had been in the biology department. A great deal of the source materials on which our courses on Marxism-Leninism were based was available in the publishing house, but now I did not merely read it. I studied it with great interest, impressed by the logic and the structure of the theory.

Our lecturers were distinguished historians, many of them gifted orators. I recall the fascinating lectures of professors Nikolsky on ancient societies, Reisner on the Middle East, Skazkin on the Middle Ages, and Trachtenberg on political economy. The auditoriums were filled to overflowing at their lectures. Seminars, too, were conducted by luminaries. In the first year we were required to select two seminars, one in eighteenth-century Russian history and the other in ancient civilizations. For the former, I chose the early exploration of Kamchatka (attracted by Kamchatka's proximity to Alaska, no doubt) conducted by Professor Bakhrushin. Bakhrushin, a big, burly man, was an object of some curiosity. A non-Party member, former "bourgeois" historian, he had been arrested in 1930 or 1931 and had spent several years in prison. Upon his release, he had been allowed to return to the university.[1] His seminar was interesting, but I had a hard time understanding his rather old-fashioned Russian. I remember well his comment when he returned my paper to me at the end of the year. "Matushka,"[2] he said, "learn Russian."

The other seminar, on primitive communist societies, was with Professor Kosven. I recall it not so much for the material, which was standard, but for the instructor's approach to scholarship. He stressed that the important thing to learn in one's university years was not facts and dates, but where to look for information, how to use books and references in search of the truth (which is a never-ending process), and how to judge which books and papers were worth spending time on and which should be skimmed. This may not seem special to students in American universities, but in the Soviet Union's secondary schools, and, perhaps in the old gymnasiums as well, this was unusual advice. By contrast, the Soviet system stressed memorization. Over the years, I observed how my step-uncle's two daughters and children of friends in secondary schools were expected to reply to questions and write compositions in the words of their textbooks or their teachers' lectures.

---

1. Ultimately, Bakhrushin fared better than many of his colleagues who were Marxists and Party members. He died a natural death in 1950.
2. Matushka—a very old-fashioned mode of addressing a woman.

Relations between professors and students were very formal. I can recall very few teachers who talked with us outside the classroom. Kosven was one, and I remember him fondly.

The atmosphere in the department was politically charged. Soviet historians were still sorting out their concepts of the historical process, especially their attitudes toward the controversy surrounding the teachings of Professor Mikhail Pokrovsky, who had until then been the leading Marxist historian in the Soviet Union. I shall not try to describe in detail the often savage conflicts, because I was only vaguely aware of the issues at the time. Briefly, Pokrovsky, an Old Bolshevik who had already been an established scholar before the revolution, had led the way in applying to history Lenin's principle of *"partiinost'"* in intellectual pursuits—that is, the requirement that all historical study be politically relevant and that it serve the interests of the Communist Party and the Soviet state. In Pokrovsky's interpretation, the tsarist epoch had caused unrelieved oppression for the masses and disaster for Russia. Those who ventured to disagree with this interpretation or even to criticize it mildly were accused of promoting bourgeois ideology.

In 1930–31, all non-Marxist historians had been ousted from the Academy of Sciences and some had been arrested. But Pokrovsky had Stalin's complete support. He died in April 1932, and was given an impressive funeral. Stalin, Viacheslav Molotov (then premier of the USSR), and Valerian Kuibyshev (then chief of Gosplan) delivered funeral orations.

The teaching staff of Moscow University's history department included many who had been Pokrovsky's most devoted disciples, such as Professor Anna Pankratova, head of the Russian history chair; Lev Fridland, dean of the faculty when I was a student; and Militsa Nechkina, a rising star in the field of Russian history. But times were changing, and even before Pokrovsky's death, some criticism of his views had begun to surface and he himself "admitted some mistakes."[3]

There were also those who had criticized his views and been harassed for it. Feelings ran high. There were frequent Party meetings, sometimes for students and teachers together, other times separately; sometimes with the Komsomol, sometimes without. Nearly half of the teaching staff of thirty-two professors and thirty-six assistant professors were members of the Party. The student Party organization was the biggest in the university and practically every student who was not in the Party was in the Komsomol. No one disputed the need for *partiinost'* in history and the need to root out non-Marxist

3. Subsequent denigration declared Pokrovsky a "vulgarizer" of Marxism and culminated in a Central Committee decree in January 1936 pointing out Pokrovsky's mistakes and calling upon Soviet historians to root out the anti-Marxist views of his school.

know. He did say that the appointment was confidential and I was not to speak to anyone about it. My first thought was that it had something to do with my visa application.

My guess was both right and wrong.

I don't remember with whom I talked at the Central Committee, but it was probably an instructor in the international section. At first, the conversation was general—how was I doing? did I like my studies? was I in touch with my parents? Then he told me that there had been no reply to my visa application for the time being, but that the visa department had sent my papers to the Central Committee, which in turn had arranged for me to be interviewed in another organization. I was given an address and an appointment and told that there would be a pass for me at the guard's booth. Neither the name of the organization nor of the person I was supposed to see was mentioned. And once again, the instructor emphasized that this issue was confidential and that I was not to tell anyone about it (I did, however, tell Izzy).

The address was in central Moscow in the vicinity of the Arbat, on a side street lined with faceless stucco walls. There was no name on the building. I showed the guard my identification and he told me where to go.

Most of the people I met in the halls were in military uniform. I was ushered into the office of a grey-haired man who wore the uniform of a colonel. I happen to remember his name—Stiga, a Latvian name. His friendly manner put me at ease at once. He said that we were having a get-acquainted talk, and for ten or fifteen minutes he asked me general questions about my background and my present circumstances, the answers to which he undoubtedly knew. At one point, he asked me whether I knew where I was. I said that I did not. I really did not know, but he may have thought that I was just being discreet. Finally, he came to the point. The Komsomol, he said, had recommended me for a special job. He asked whether I would be willing to take a break in my studies for this assignment.

I did not ask what the assignment was or how long it would take. I replied that I was honored by the trust placed in me and would do my best to justify it. Even more than the others before him, he stressed the confidentiality of our meeting. He told me to go back to school and go on with my studies as usual until I was contacted. Before I left the building, I was to go to the financial department where, to my amazement, I was handed 700 rubles, a huge sum of money for me.

No mention had been made of my application for an exit visa except indirectly, when I said in the course of our conversation that I wanted very much to visit my family in America.

I had much to think about. It was clear that I was not going to be granted permission to visit my parents at this time, and I was disappointed. Nonetheless, I was excited by the prospect of change and also of relief from the hand-to-mouth existence I had led since arriving in the Soviet Union. Izzy guessed immediately that the assignment had something to do with intelligence. He was vehemently opposed to my accepting any proposition that might be made to me, but I paid him no mind.

Nothing happened for a long time.

Meanwhile, a nationwide discussion began on a proposal to ban abortions. The official reason given for the proposed ban was concern for women's health. The press carried letters from readers, and those in favor of the ban outnumbered those who were against it. It was obvious even to the most gullible that the press was practicing selective manipulation. The "population" was indeed interested in the issue and there were lively discussions wherever people gathered, especially among young people at school and in my circle of friends. Everyone I knew was opposed to the ban. Yet no one was surprised when a government decree was published in June banning abortions "at the request of the population and in order to protect the health of women."

None of us believed the official reason. Some of my friends said openly that the purpose of the ban was to replace the enormous population losses that had been suffered in the years of war, revolution, and civil war. In the eyes of some—Galya and her mother, for example—this factor justified the ban. The abortion issue was never one of morality, neither when it was prohibited nor when it was eventually permitted again. It was solely an issue of expediency, of what was good for the state.

Some women I knew had undergone five, sometimes ten, legal abortions. Though it was true that numerous abortions could endanger a woman's health, self-induced and illegal abortions were even more injurious. The ban ushered in a nineteen-year period of rampant illegal abortions, sometimes leading to permanent injury and death due to infection. No statistics were available and the practice was never acknowledged, but nearly every woman I knew had one or more illegal abortions, either self-induced or (for large sums of money) by doctors or midwives. Discovery meant oppression for the woman and jail for the doctor, but women nevertheless found ways to end their pregnancies.

With the summer vacation coming and no reason for me to stay in Moscow, I applied for a *putyovka* to the university rest home in Gelendzhik, on the Black Sea coast in the Caucasus.

*Putyovkas*, rest homes, and sanatoriums were very much a part of Soviet life. A *putyovka* was a voucher or pass for a subsidized stay in one of the numerous rest homes or sanatoriums in various parts of the country. Many of them were in mountain or seaside resort areas. Some vouchers were provided free of charge, but in the later Soviet period, most were paid for but heavily discounted. Rest homes were general vacation guesthouses that provided meals, lodging, and minimal medical or other kinds of supervision.

Sanatoriums provided close medical supervision and spa facilities, in addition to meals and lodging. Some sanatoriums were specialized—with facilities for patients with lung ailments, intestinal, bone diseases, and so forth—but most were vacation guesthouses. Though all were under the jurisdiction of the Ministry of Health (Commissariat in those days), most large institutions had their own vacation homes for their employees. There was a great demand for vacation vouchers. They were awarded by the trade union committees on the basis of merit and also of need. In the university, qualifiers had to show excellence in studies and participation in extracurricular activities. My grades were average and I was not much of an activist, but I had been ill a great deal during the winter with chronic bronchitis and, for a short time, I had had acute anemia (for which I was given green iron pills and recovered quickly). The university clinic gave me a letter stating that it was necessary for me to spend a month in the south. On this basis, I was given a voucher for the month of August.

The moment I boarded the train for the two-day journey to Novorossiisk, the nearest railroad station to Gelendzhik, I left my cares behind me. I bathed in the Black Sea (not nearly as salty as the waters of the Long Island Sound or the Pacific Ocean, but much warmer), basked in the sun on rocky beaches, and went on organized hikes in the mountains. I had more fresh fruit that month than in all the years I had been in the Soviet Union combined. My cough and tiredness vanished, and I think some of my fellow students wondered if I had really been sick at all. It was a month full of fun, including an innocuous summer romance, and I enjoyed every minute. In September, I returned to the university and to the Stromynka dormitory.

Back at school, arrests were rampant. One of the first to go was Tussia's sweetheart. Lively, fun-loving Tussia changed overnight. We all felt terrible and assured her that it was a mistake, that Mahomet would be released soon. Tussia continued at the university, but withdrew into herself. I met her in the street one day, long after we had both left the university. She was pretty again, married, had a child, but she told me that she had never forgotten Mahomet and had never fully recovered from the blow. She also told me what I had already guessed—Mahomet had been executed.

Students started disappearing from the history department. Sonia Tsal—the woman who had spent time in a Polish prison—was arrested, and was denounced at a general meeting at which her pals, all activists, joined in the chorus and blamed themselves for "blunted vigilance." That was the usual pattern.

In November, I was summoned to the university Komsomol committee and told to be prepared to leave the dormitory any day. Again, I was cautioned not to say anything to anyone. The secretary shook my hand and wished me luck.

# 10

## At the Commissariat of Defense—
## November 1936 to March 1938

Few students were around in the afternoon when a car called for me at Stromynka.

The driver headed out of Moscow. The first snow had already fallen and the fields and villages gleamed under a white blanket. Night falls early in November, so by the time we arrived at a military post some forty minutes later, it was dark. A soldier waved us on and in a few minutes, we drove through the gate of a high fence and stopped in front of a two-story frame house. The door was opened by a middle-aged woman who turned out to be the housekeeper. She showed me to a room on the second floor and said that supper would be served downstairs in the dining room in an hour. The driver brought up my luggage and left.

The room contained one bed—did that mean I would have a room to myself? There was a wardrobe, a table, a few chairs, and a rug on the floor. One door opened onto the corridor. Another apparently led to a connecting room, but it was locked. I looked out of the window—I always do that when I arrive at a new place. A broad expanse of snow-covered grass lay before me, and in the distance, I saw trees. I felt elated, ready for a new adventure.

There were two other diners that evening, a young man and woman.

"Kostya," the man said, stretching out his hand. "And this is my wife, Katya."

Katya stuck out her hand, holding it stiffly, like a board.

They appeared to be in their late twenties, both tall, Kostya—slim and dark-haired, Katya—a Junoesque blond with a pretty but ordinary face. Kostya wore an army uniform with the insignia of a lieutenant and had an air of authority about him. He informed me that he was the *starosta,* the senior person among the students at the school.

For this was a school.

It was a school in the Moscow suburb of Khimki, and it was run by the People's Commissariat of Defense to train military intelligence personnel for work in foreign countries. It was only when the head of the school summoned me to his office the next morning that this was spelled out for me.

It was not what I had anticipated. Of course, I had known that I was getting involved in some kind of secret work, but I had assumed that it was connected with the Comintern. I knew that the Comintern trained people for political work in their own countries, and this was exactly what I had expected—the opportunity to go home and carry on the fight there. However, I realized at once that there was no turning back. Whatever would be, would be.

The head of the school was a Captain Averikhin—we addressed him as "Comrade Captain" or "Comrade Chief"—a portly man with jet-black hair, very white skin, and a handlebar mustache. He was, I was told later, thirty-two years old, but he looked older because of his corpulence. The Captain told me there would be another female student who would have the room adjoining mine. Room and board were free and I would receive a stipend. I don't remember how much the stipend was, but it was more money than I had ever had. He described the school regimen to me and spoke of the rules and regulations, those that were posted and those that were not. One of the most important rules was not to ask anyone personal questions and not to give anyone personal information—we were to reveal nothing about family background, how and where recruited, real name, and so forth. I was told to choose a name to be known by and I chose my mother's maiden name. Later, I learned that others had done the same. It was as if one were reluctant to surrender one's identity entirely. I was also told to submit a list of the people I would continue to see outside the school. I would have most weekends and holidays free, and could travel then to Moscow by local train from the Khimki station, a twenty-minute walk away. If I planned to return late at night, I was to inform the housekeeper and someone would meet me at the station. There was a telephone in the office, but it was to be used only in an emergency or to communicate with Averikhin.

A brief written report was required after each trip out of the school—I was to note where I had gone and whom I had seen.

My list consisted of Izzy, the Mikhlins, the Atlases, Naomi and Bill, the Laskers, Galya and her mother, Helen and her family, and Marussia. My cover story to all except Izzy was that I was teaching conversational English in a special army school. To Izzy, I told the truth.

All our mail went through the central office via a post office box number and was hand delivered. We assumed it was read. I continued to receive my mail from the United States at my step-uncle's address for a short while, and when he got nervous about this, I had it sent in care of Helen.

Each day, there were new faces at the supper table—young men in military uniform, a lieutenant or junior lieutenant. After everybody had arrived, a tailor came to measure us for civilian clothes, which were then worn most of the time. Their ages ranged from nineteen to twenty-eight and, by the following week, there were about fifteen students in all. The other woman was among the last to arrive.

Some of us were gathered in the parlor-library adjoining the dining room, reading or talking in low voices when she came in.

"Came in" are not the right words. She made an entrance, a slim young woman, rather tall and seemingly taller because of the way she carried herself.

"What an interesting face," I thought as I looked up—olive skin, high cheekbones tinged with pink, brilliant black eyes, jet black hair pulled back tightly over her head and worn in two braids tied together low on her long neck. Pocahontas!

She greeted the company politely, but coolly, and sat down with a book. No one approached her or asked any questions. It was obvious she expected to be left alone.

At supper, she unbent. She introduced herself—"Ksena"—and we introduced ourselves to her: "Petya," "Shura," "Vassya," "Volodya," "Misha," and so on. When it came to me, she smiled and said:

"I know—Mary. I have the room next to yours."

Ksena was not an ordinary student. She was also a part-time teacher of English, which she spoke with an accent, but quite well. She had a room to herself, which is why I had a room as well; all the others were males who doubled up.

Most of the instructional staff lived elsewhere. The Captain was driven in each weekday morning, sometimes accompanied by a teacher. Teachers were driven in on the days they had classes, which for the language teachers was almost every day. The only other residents of the main building besides the students were one of the German teachers, Hans Baumann, and his wife, who was the housekeeper. They kept an eye on things in the Captain's absence. Baumann had a wooden leg; it was rumored that he had lost his leg in the line of duty as a Soviet agent. Some of the service staff had quarters in a smaller building in the back of the main building, but most came from nearby villages. There was a vegetable garden and some small livestock. Beyond the fence were woods and fields.

Now that everyone had arrived, classes started. The heaviest concentration was on foreign languages—English, German, and French. I had had two years of German at the university and was only required to attend conversation lessons with Hans Baumann a few hours each week.

There were two English teachers and one French teacher. The English teachers were both Americans and they were addressed as Nina Davydovna and Anna Isaakovna. Nina was a petite, stylishly dressed woman on the plump side with a pretty, heart-shaped face and a supercilious manner. Her sense of superiority derived from her special relationship with Colonel

Smirnov, who was responsible for the school and to whom Captain Averikhin reported. Anna was a friendly soul, a pleasant-looking woman in her
late twenties or early thirties.

The practical subjects were introduced gradually. The first, and apparently the most important, were short wave radio operation and microphotography. We learned the Morse Code for transmission and reception. It
turned out that I had an aptitude for reception—surprising, as I have no ear
for music. As I became more advanced, I was able to hear and understand
ham operators in distant lands. That was fun, though it was never a two-
way contact. I was hopeless at microphotography and was allowed to drop
the subject after a while. Later, we took up topography and cryptography,
two areas that gave me no difficulty. However, I was turned down for para-
chute jumping and driving because I was nearsighted. In those days, you could
not get a driver's license in the Soviet Union if you were nearsighted, even if
you wore corrective eyeglasses. Besides, you had to know the structure of the
internal combustion engine and be able to do minor repairs yourself.

Political subjects were the mandatory history of the Soviet Communist
Party—I had studied it three times already—the history of the Red Army,
the history of the Russian and foreign intelligence services, and a weekly
current events class led by the Captain, mainly to keep us abreast of what
was in the newspapers. There was not much discussion. Captain Averikhin
did not encourage jingoist speeches. It was taken for granted that we were
loyal, patriotic citizens. The important task was for us to get ahead with
our training.

In this sense, we were insulated from the jolts that were shaking the
country almost daily. We did not arrive at work in the morning to find
coworkers missing, arrested during the night. We did not have to participate
in meetings denouncing the victims or to witness the public breast-beating
by their friends and relatives. We did not have to listen to speeches calling
for the stiffest sentences before and after trials and convictions. I knew what
was in the newspapers, but was protected as if by a thick, glass wall through
which I could see, but not feel. How the others felt I had no idea, for we did
not talk about such things outside the current events class.

The great wave of arrests, now known as the Great Terror, had begun in
the fall of 1936. In September, while I was still at the university, the head
of the secret police, Genrikh Yagoda, was arrested and replaced by Nikolai
Yezhov. Yezhov presided over the NKVD through the most violent period—
all of 1937 and part of 1938. Party leaders Yuri Pyatakov, Grigori Sokolnikov,
Leonid Serebryakov, and Karl Radek were arrested in the fall and tried in
January 1937 on charges that they had formed an "anti-Soviet Trotskyite
center." These were big names: Pyatakov and Sokolnikov were members of
the Central Committee of the Communist Party, and Radek was one of the

most widely read journalists in the country, noted for his acerbic wit and penetrating analyses of world affairs. Because he sang Stalin's praises in every article he wrote, his arrest was deeply shocking. They were all convicted and sentenced—Pyatakov and Serebryakov to death, Sokolnikov and Radek to ten years "deprivation of freedom."[1]

The death in February 1937 of Sergo Ordzhonikidze, People's Commissar of Heavy Industry and a very popular figure, was also a tremendous blow. The official announcement said that he had died of a heart attack, but rumors (which have since been confirmed by the historical record) circulated that he committed suicide, shocked by the trials and convictions of his friends and colleagues.

Among the foreigners, the first to be stricken were the Germans. Ironically, many of the Germans were anti-fascists who had come to the Soviet Union to escape persecution. Others were specialists or highly skilled workers. After the Germans, hardest hit were the Poles, Hungarians, and other East Europeans.

The Laskers had a Bulgarian neighbor occupying the other room of their apartment. He worked in the Comintern. Lasker was away on an undisclosed mission and I sometimes stayed overnight with his wife on weekends. One night while Lasker was away, we were awakened in the middle of the night to the sound of banging on the outside door. We did not stir. Finally, the door was opened. We heard the commotion, the slamming of the door. When it was quiet again, we got up. There was a seal on the man's door. This was an unsettling experience. Why were we so sure it was not meant for one of us when the banging began?[2]

Another night, when I was delayed in town, I decided to stay over at the Mikhlins. I turned up there unannounced at about midnight. My step-uncle answered the doorbell. His usually ruddy face was ashen. He let me in and for a few moments did not say a word. Then:

"How could you drop in like this, without warning? In the middle of the night!"

His wife joined us.

"You know that Yevseiushka has a bad heart," she said reproachfully.

"But why?" I exclaimed. "You never go to bed until after midnight. Were you asleep?"

"Asleep? Who sleeps these nights?"

The next morning, we talked about the arrests for the first time.

---

1. Both Sokolnikov and Radek survived only until 1939. (Ed.)

2. The Bulgarian was released a few weeks later, thanks to the intervention of the Bulgarian Communist leader, Georgi Dimitrov.

"Someone is arrested in this house almost every night," he said. "We stay awake, listening for the sound of a car, waiting to hear at which entrance it will stop. Everybody has a bag packed."

"You, too?"

"Of course, me, too."

"But what are you afraid of? You never did anything wrong."

He did not reply. What was the use of talking to me . . .?

Not very long after that incident, Marussia sent me a message saying that she had to see me urgently. We met the next time I went into town.

"Mary," she said, "you were denounced at a Komsomol meeting. Everybody thinks you have been arrested. I couldn't speak up or I would have had to explain. They are pressing me to make a public statement confessing to lack of vigilance and are threatening me with a Party reprimand or worse."

I was appalled and very, very angry. I marched into Averikhin's office the next morning.

"What is the matter?" he asked. "You look as if you are spoiling for a fight."

I was. I repeated Marussia's story and demanded that something be done about it immediately. Why hadn't my situation been taken care of when I left the university?

"All right, all right, don't worry. I'll see to it. This has to be done carefully," he said.

It took several weeks, during which Marussia continued to have a hard time. Finally, the Captain told me that everything was in order.

The agency had acted through the Central Committee of the Komsomol, which had relayed its word to the university committee, which, in turn, had informed the history department's Party secretary. They stopped harassing Marussia—that is how we knew for certain that matters had been straightened out. However, the membership was not informed that it had been a mistake to denounce me. When I returned to the university several years later, I was congratulated by some of my fellow students on having been released from prison!

The admonition not to ask personal questions leant an air of mystery to my new life. How do young people get to know each other without talking about themselves? For the first time since I came to the Soviet Union, I was not plied with questions from new acquaintances. Of course, the other students knew that I came from America. Ksena had been told in advance that she would have the opportunity to speak English with an American girl there. The two English teachers spotted my American English at once, but did not ask questions. And some of the students who were having difficulty with English came to me for help.

One way or another, friendships were formed and kindred spirits found each other. I had taken a liking to Ksena from the first time I saw her and we became friends. We spent many a long evening talking, usually in her room, which was larger and had more comfortable chairs than mine. Nevertheless, all I knew about her was that she had a degree in English language and had taught in a secondary school. She probably knew more about me, but not from me. I did tell her that I had been a student at Moscow University and she indicated that I may have made a mistake by dropping out. Despite taboo subjects, we always had a great deal to talk about, on mundane topics such as the books we had read or were reading, points of grammar, and our philosophies of life, attitudes, politics. With her original mind and unconventional ideas, Ksena was a very stimulating companion. Sometimes we were joined by Volodya, a bright nineteen-year-old from one of the Central Asian republics who was smitten by her. Ksena enjoyed Volodya's devotion, but made it clear that she was otherwise engaged. Every once in a while, she would go to town in the middle of the week and return in the evening or early the next morning. I assumed that this had something to do with a mysterious stranger in her life.

My studies did not require much time or effort on my part. I spent hours curled up with a book in front of the fireplace in the common room. There were lots of books to read, many of them English detective and spy stories, including Agatha Christie paperbacks. These books were not available to the general public. In fact, most were "classified"! Since many of the books were about foreign and Russian intelligence operations, they were considered part of our training and I could read to my heart's content without any guilty feelings about wasting time. But we were not allowed to remove them from the premises, not even to read in the train.

An atmosphere of friendliness and camaraderie prevailed. The Captain was liked and respected and got along well with the young officers. As the only unattached females, Ksena and I received a lot of attention. Once in a while, other young men would join us in Ksena's room. Most often we were joined by Misha, one of the more cultivated officers, who was interested in music, art, and literature. Misha was irreverent about the secrecy rules. He told me his real name and that he was a Jew from Odessa. He had been serving in the army and was having an affair with a superior officer's wife. Misha thought that he had been recommended for this assignment so that he would be out of the way. He was quite cynical about the morals of career officers and their bored wives.

Completely different from the other persons I had befriended was Leonid, a Senior Lieutenant, twenty-eight or twenty-nine years old. He was a hard drinker, a great dancer at our frequent parties, and aggressive in his attentions to me. First, he asked me to help him with his English. He was not a good student. Foreign languages were the most important element in our training and the inability to master one could lead to dismissal from the school. I began to tutor him on a daily basis. It was obvious from the start that he would never learn English or any other language. His teacher, Nina Davydovna, had given up on him and told me that I was wasting my time.

I may have been wasting my time trying to teach him English, perhaps, but not in other ways. One thing led to another and, before long, English was the least important part of our tutoring sessions.

Romance between students was strictly forbidden and we knew it. But he was out for a conquest and I was strongly attracted. I knew all along that this was an infatuation on my part, strictly chemistry, and that it was not serious on his, but he was much more experienced than anyone I had known and I did not resist very hard. Finally, as was inevitable, news about our affair came to the Captain's ears. He sent for me. He started from afar.

"Have you been seeing much of Izzy lately?"

"As much as usual. Perhaps a bit less."

"Does he know what is going on between you and Leonid?"

"No."

"Why not?"

"Because it's not serious."

"Not serious?! Yet you break rules here and jeopardize a serious relationship for a fling with a Casanova!"

Averikhin suggested that perhaps I ought to marry him. The implication was that if I wanted to, it could be arranged. But I did not want anything of the sort. Though I was by no means over my infatuation, the thought of spending my life with a man with whom I had nothing in common was far from my mind.

"You should both be thrown out," the Captain fumed. "How do you expect me to get you out of this mess?" and he dismissed me. A few days later, Leonid left the school, bag and baggage, without telling me or anyone else where he was going. For several weeks, I waited for the axe to fall until the Captain told me to stop moping. Leonid had not been fired. He had been transferred to the central office and, before long, became the new boss's adjutant. Ksena, who knew about the affair and may have been the one to tell the Captain, surmised that Leonid was probably transferred as unsuited for training since he could not learn a foreign language. I was not penalized, she believed, because I was valuable to the program.

I had not told Izzy about the affair, but he sensed that all was not well between us. One day, he confronted me.

"I'm not getting any younger," he said (he was all of twenty-three), "and I want to settle down. TASS has promised me a room as soon as its new apartment building is finished. We could get married. Either that, or we should stop seeing each other."

I told him the whole story about Leonid and how I felt—it was an episode and all over. I would marry him if that was what he wanted.

Izzy was terribly upset. He said he needed a few days to think it over. The next time we met, he said he could not ignore what I had told him, that he had felt for a long time that I was not really in love with him. It would be best for both of us, he thought, to stop seeing each other.

So now it was over. It had lasted four years.

Although my plans for the future had, indeed, not included Izzy, I suddenly felt very lonely. It was spring and beautiful in Khimki. I took long walks by myself, trying to deal with my feelings. I tried not to think beyond the immediate future. I would cross the next bridge when I came to it. I also started to wish that I had studied Spanish. Then, perhaps, I could have asked to be sent to Spain.

The Spanish Civil War had been raging for nearly a year. The vivid reportage by Soviet journalists like Ilya Ehrenburg and Mikhail Koltsov brought the horror of the war and the agonies of the Spanish people into every Soviet home. Thousands of young people volunteered to go to fight in Spain. As far as I knew, only those with special skills were chosen, among them several Spanish speakers I had known in the publishing house. Lasker had been sent to Spain, though I did not know where he had been until he returned—and he never spoke of what he did there. He did not know Spanish and did not have a military background, so I assume that he translated from English for Russian advisors.

The reportage was political as well as descriptive. "Our side," the Loyalists, were having a hard time opposing the well-armed supporters of Francisco Franco who was heavily aided by Fascist Italian and Nazi German air and land power. France, Britain, and the United States not only did not help the legitimate Spanish government, but even refused to sell arms to it on the pretext of neutrality. The Soviet government was the only government helping the elected government of Spain.

The year 1937 was definitely the year of Spain for many of us. Our spirits rose with each victory and fell with each defeat. Our hearts ached as it became increasingly clear that the Loyalist cause was lost. We were as bitter about the role of Britain and France as we were about that of Germany and Italy. That bitterness would make it easier two years later to accept the unofficial Soviet explanation of the 1939 pact with Nazi Germany: England could not be depended upon.

We knew very little about the dissension in the ranks of the republican leadership, the disunity, and the role of the Soviet advisors. We were told that the Trotskyite POUM (United Marxist Workers' Party) and anarchists were disrupting the struggle for victory. The first inkling I had that all had not been as depicted came in the 1950s when I happened to get hold of a copy of Hemingway's *For Whom the Bell Tolls*. That novel was not translated into Russian or published in the Soviet Union until the death of Dolores Ibarurri, Spanish Communist leader and heroine, who was known as La Passionara and was greatly admired in the Soviet Union. (After the defeat of the Loyalists, Ibarurri found asylum in the USSR.)

One side effect of the Spanish Civil War, though, was an abundance of oranges from Valencia in Moscow.

The year 1937 was a memorable year in many ways. The Terror was mounting. For us in our sheltered little enclave, the most shattering events that June were the arrests among the military. First, there was the suicide of Yan Gamarnik, chief of the political administration of the Red Army and First Deputy Defense Commissar.[3] I remember the meeting held the day the news appeared in the press early in June. Averikhin read the announcement to us, made a very short speech, and we dispersed. No one spoke.

Greater shocks followed. On June 11th, a leading article on the front page of *Pravda* described a wide-ranging conspiracy in the army. A decree printed on the second page stated that a plenary meeting of the Central Committee of the CPSU had expelled Mikhail Tukhachevsky, Ion Yakir, B. M. Feldman, I. P. Uborevich, and others, all distinguished military leaders whose names were inseparable from the history of the revolution and of the Red Army. They had been charged with high treason. The very next day it was announced that they had been tried, convicted, and executed.

They were the flower of the army. What did it mean?

Colonel Smirnov came to run the meeting, but neither he nor anyone else could enlighten us. He told us what we already knew from the newspapers and the radio and urged us to work harder and be vigilant. In private conversations, some of us wondered what effect these events could have on our future.

There was also some good news in June. Prices on manufactured goods were lowered. This produced a flood of letters of appreciation to Stalin and the Party for their concern for ordinary people. That summer, too, saw the non-stop flights to America over the North Pole by two Soviet aviators. These were exciting events on both sides of the ocean.

One day, Ksena said to me suddenly:

"Mary, let's go for a walk."

This was unusual. Ksena was not a great one for fresh air or for walks. When we were outside, she said:

"There's something I've wanted to say to you for a long time, but I did not know how to put it or how you would react. Anyway, here it is: Be careful what you say and to whom you say it."

---

3. His death occurred in the midst of Stalin's purge of the Red Army leadership. Gamarnik shot himself when the NKVD arrived at his apartment to arrest him. (Ed.)

"What do you mean?"

"Exactly what I said. Be careful. Don't just say what's on your mind to anyone. You cannot know who is reporting everything you say or do."

"Reporting? To whom? What for? To Averikhin? What in the world are you talking about?"

Gently, Ksena tried to explain to me that anyone could be an informer, especially in a place like this where responsible officials have to know how stable, loyal, and trustworthy we were.

"Well," I said, "I am stable, loyal, and trustworthy, so it doesn't matter what I say and to whom I say it."

Ksena shrugged her shoulders. "Words can be misunderstood or misconstrued. Please pay attention to what I have just said. And do not repeat our conversation to anyone."

At that time, it did not occur to me that Ksena herself may have been an informer and was warning me because she knew there had to be others who might not be as circumspect as she probably was. In hindsight and with a better knowledge of the informer system, I am pretty sure that she was, indeed, reporting to the authorities.

The Terror was striking in all directions. On June 4th, *Pravda* printed a letter from students of Moscow University's history department denouncing "camouflaged Trotskyites who had been in charge of the faculty from the beginning." They labeled dean Fridland and the Party secretary, both Jewish, "Gestapo agents" and declared that they were using graduate students as "tools" and "accomplices." The two were arrested. I had had dealings with both and could not believe the accusations. For the first time, I believe, the seeds of doubt entered my head. Happily, I was not a student at the university any longer, for I might have been swept up in the wave of arrests, but that, too, is hindsight, for I was not thinking along those lines at all at the time.

The horrors mounted, but we did not dwell on the most recent accusations and revelations for long. The semester ended in June and we scattered. The officers went to training camps for one month. Katya left with her husband. Ksena left on the day after classes were over, saying she would see me in September. A few days later, I left for the Crimea. Captain Averikhin had arranged for me to spend six weeks at a resort run by the Red Army Chief Administration. The sanatorium in Gursuf was much more luxurious than the university rest home in Gelendzhik. The majority of guests were officers, with or without their wives; officers' wives without their husbands; and some sons and daughters and retainers. The atmosphere was calculatedly flirtatious. Territories were staked out, with each new arrival appraised and evaluated. My two roommates, young married women, were perfectly open about looking for men to pair off with. A few days after my arrival, an officer who was being very attentive asked me if I was married. When I said I was not, he did not mince words:

"Sorry, I would have liked to have gotten to know you better, but I have no time to waste on a virgin." And off he went to play the field. It did not take him long to find a new partner.

I was amused, especially at his assumption. Obviously, most of the men and many of the women were looking for temporary, painless liaisons without complications.

I returned to Moscow in the middle of August. Because I was not due back in Khimki until September, I spent the remaining time at the Mikhlins. There were just the two of us, Liza and myself. The girls were away at summer camp, my step-uncle was at a spa in Kislovodsk, and Liza's two sisters were visiting relatives in the Ukraine. Liza was a fantastic cook and a talented raconteur. I never tired of listening to her tell of her girlhood in Ukraine, her marriage, the pogroms, all of which she described in vivid detail. In her philosophy of life, marriage, and politics, she put her husband first; her family, including her unmarried sisters, second; and the rest after them. In politics, she supported the regime and blamed its shortcomings on underlings who did not tell Stalin the truth. This was an attitude I encountered frequently and it seems to have been a traditional one, a continuation of the attitude that if the tsar knew, he'd take steps to correct whatever was wrong. Yet Liza was neither stupid nor naïve, and her commonsense attitude to everyday existence worked very well for her.

One day in late August or early September, I bumped into a former coworker and fellow Komsomol from the publishing house. Lina's family had come from Argentina and she and her father had worked in the Spanish section. I was less surprised to see her than she was to see me, for I knew that she had gone to Spain and was probably connected with the military. But what she had to tell me did surprise me. She had met and married a Soviet general in Spain and was expecting a baby. The name she mentioned rang a bell: It was a rather unusual name I had heard Ksena mention in an unguarded moment. It was not a Russian name, more like one of the national minorities. Could this have been Ksena's romantic connection? Subsequent events convinced me that it was.

Back in Khimki in mid-September, I found to my great disappointment that Ksena had not returned. I did not ask and was not told why or where she was. Meanwhile, the wave of arrests had reached our agency. We were told at a meeting that Colonels Stiga and Smirnov, our immediate superiors, had been arrested. Nina Davydovna, the American English teacher, did not reappear. I learned several years later that she had been arrested at the time of Smirnov's arrest. Our sheltered existence was no longer sheltered, as the ring of arrests closed in around us.

Nevertheless, classes met as usual. One day, the Captain announced that we were in for a treat. An experienced agent who had recently returned from abroad would give a talk about the lives of Soviet agents in foreign countries, about how to behave and how to deal with commonplace situations.

The man who arrived with the Captain the next morning was introduced as "Alyosha." He wore a well-cut civilian suit, was on the short side, and was slight in build. His thick, black hair was grey at the temples, and he looked to be about forty. He won over his audience at once with his sense of humor that had a sharp edge to it. He talked about clothes, manners, local customs in Germany, Scandinavia and the United States, about how to recognize and shake a "tail," and what pitfalls to watch out for. He combined serious information with amusing anecdotes, and charmed us all. This was Alex Ulanovsky, the Soviet intelligence agent who recruited Whittaker Chambers and was referred to as "Ulanov," "Ulrich," or "Walter" in the book *Witness*.[4] Of course, I did not know that at the time. I did not know anything about his past, nor did I know who Whittaker Chambers was. I read the Chambers book when I got back to the United States; by then I had known the Ulanovskys for some twenty years.

On one of my regular visits to the Mikhlins in November 1937, they had shocking news for me: Anya's brother Dodya Atlas had been arrested. What? How? When? A few nights ago, in the usual manner, a car had stopped in front of their entrance at around two A.M. A couple of men and the janitor had banged on the door of their apartment (the janitor was always taken along as a "witness" to verify that proper procedure had been followed). As he was being led away by one of the men, Dodya had said to his mother what so many of the arrested used to say:

"Don't worry, it's a mistake. I'll be back home in a few days."

One of the men stayed behind to search the apartment.

Against my step-uncle's advice, I went right over to the Atlases. Anya, her mother Rivekka Matveyevna, her future husband Volodya, and Volodya's parents were there, and so was Anya's closest friend who lived in the building and whose family would soon suffer the same fate. Anya's mother hugged me and thanked me for coming. She had made inquiries, but had been unable to learn anything. Surely, I said, they'd soon find out that Dodya was innocent of any wrongdoing and release him. No one responded.

Dodya was charged along with other students in a "group case" of conspiracy to assassinate Soviet leaders. He did not return, not until long after the war.

---

4. Chambers, an editor for *Time* magazine, testified in 1948 to the House Committee on Un-American Activities (HUAC) that he had spied on behalf of the Communists in the 1920s and 1930s. See Whittaker Chambers, *Witness* (New York: Random House, 1952).

This was the closest the arrests had gotten to me. Dodya was a personal friend. I knew him well. We had had many talks on all kinds of subjects. I never for a moment believed that he was guilty of a crime. His cousin Misha rationalized the situation to me with these words:

"When you are cutting down trees, chips will fall."

I was to hear that Russian proverb often. It implied that when big shots are guilty, innocent people will become victims as well. Misha did not seem terribly unhappy about his cousin's arrest. He now had a room of his own in the apartment and did not have to fear being asked to move out. Rivekka Matveyevna needed the bit of money he contributed to the household and she would have lost Dodya's room if Misha had not moved into it.

I reported the arrest to the Captain, as was my duty.

"What was your relationship to him?" the Captain wanted to know.

"I've known the family ever since I arrived in Moscow. His sister is one of my closest friends."

"Are they relatives?"

"No."

"Very well. Don't mention it to anyone—anyone at all. You did right to report it to me. Now, forget it. It is my responsibility." I am pretty sure he took my report no further.

Anya married Volodya the following summer, after Volodya graduated as a forestry engineer, and they went to live in Kirov (formerly Vyatka), a town surrounded by forests in the northern part of Russia. We corresponded regularly and I often dropped in to see Rivekka Matveyevna.

In December, it began to look as if my long-awaited posting had come. I was photographed for my travel documents and filled out forms. In January, I was transferred to another center. Before I left, the Captain said he would like to talk with me. We went for a walk.

"Your documents are being prepared for departure," he said. "You will travel under your own name and will go home to your parents to await further instructions. Before you leave, you will undergo several weeks of intensive training at another center." He paused.

"Mary, listen to me very carefully," he continued. "If things work out as expected and you reach your home, forget everything you were taught here. Get out of this business. It is not for you."

I could not believe my ears. He repeated what he had said.

"B-but, Comrade Captain, how could I do that? It would be disloyal."

"Just remember what I said."

He did not caution me about not repeating that conversation to anyone. Evidently, he felt he knew me well enough to trust me.

There were only three of us at the center to which I was transferred, two very attractive young women and myself. The house was similar to the one at Khimki. The only staff was a housekeeper. There were radio and micro-photography labs. The women, Margo and Lore, were about six or seven years older than I was and already had gained practical experience as Soviet intelligence agents abroad. Margo was a native of Yugoslavia. Lore had been born in Poland and had lived in Austria and Palestine. They treated me with friendly condescension and did not include me in their private conversations. They were very serious and worked diligently in the labs. A pleasure we had that winter was skiing in the beautiful birch and pine woods. Margo and Lore were experts; I tagged along, far behind.

Soon after I arrived at the new center, two men turned up. The older man wore the uniform of a captain and had slightly Asian features. He spoke American English with a hardly detectable accent. The younger man, obviously his charge, was an American called Ben. They came a few mornings a week so that Ben could use the equipment, and left at the end of each day.

Ben was talkative. He told me that he had been recruited in Spain, and that he had been given both an apartment in Moscow and a good-looking blonde to keep him company. A month or so later he made me a proposition. He wasn't really interested in the girlfriend, he said. Besides, he'd be going home soon and she was not going with him. Why didn't we get married and go home together? He was sure his "boss" could arrange it.

I did not much like Ben and his proposition did not appeal to me. To this day, I do not know whether he had a better sense of the situation than I did and merely wanted to help me, or whether he was serious about wanting me for his wife. I turned him down (and said nothing to anyone about it). I did not need him to enable me to get back to the United States. Or so I thought.

It was another opportunity lost.

Thus, January and February went by.

Naomi and Bill had decided to return home. The year 1937 had been a bad one at the publishing house where Naomi was now a translator-editor. They left in February. I was officially instructed to ask them to get in touch with my parents and tell them to expect me soon.

After seven years in the Soviet Union, I was that close to going home. But it was not to be.

On March 8, 1938—I remember the date because it was International Women's Day—I was summoned to the Central Office on Arbat and informed that the whole plan was off. I was being "returned" to the Central Committee of the Komsomol. The new chief of the agency assured me that this decision had nothing to do with me personally, but that the arrests in the agency had put the entire network at risk. I was given the name of someone to see at the Central Committee who would help me make arrangements to return to civilian life. Meanwhile, I could stay where I was until I found a place to live.

My life, my future, my plans lay in ruins. I felt very much alone. In whom could I confide? Who could advise me? Who could help me through this crisis? What should I do next? Where should I go? Where would I live? For several days, I was too stunned to take any action. Margo and Lore were sympathetic, as well they might have been, for their turn was coming.

Among my first thoughts was how to forestall the message to my parents. I hated to think of their disappointment if they were told to expect me and then I did not come. There was no way I could get in touch with Naomi. I did not have her address and, anyway, she was probably still en route.

I need not have worried about that. Although she got in touch with my parents to give them my regards, Naomi did not convey the message. When I saw her next in 1961, she told me that their trip through Poland and Germany had been an eye-opener. Everybody was talking about the imminence of war and told them how lucky they were to be going to America. She decided not to raise my parents' hopes in so unstable a situation.

Finally, I pulled myself together and went to the Komsomol Central Committee. A very nice young instructor asked me what I wanted to do. Did I want to return to the university? My reinstatement could be arranged. Or would I rather go to work at the publishing house again, at least until the beginning of the next semester?

I could not face dormitory life and the financial hardships that returning to the university would have meant. Nor was I in the mood for intensive studying right then. I needed time to readjust and to think. The instructor made an appointment for me with the personnel director at the publishing house. The terms he offered seemed as good as I could expect at this point—a job in the English section and, most important, a place to live in the apartment building for publishing house employees that had been in the planning stages when I had left in 1934. I was hired as a proofreader–assistant editor and assigned to one-half of a room which I was to share with a Swedish girl named Aina Lindquist. I moved there in April 1938, just before my twenty-third birthday.

෴

# 11
## Purges and the Publishing House—
## Spring 1938 to Winter 1939

The apartment building was conveniently located on Kapelsky Lane number thirteen, halfway between Kolkhoz Square (formerly Sukharevka) on the B ring, and the Rzhev railroad station (formerly the Riga station). It was a five-story walk-up divided into sections with separate entrances, and the design was typical of residential buildings of the era. However, the building had a few extra features such as built-in wall closets and bathing facilities in the basement (in lieu of bathrooms in the apartments). It was divided into three sections with two apartments on each landing, all exactly the same—four separate rooms, two of them large, one medium, and one small. A small kitchen contained a sink with one cold-water faucet and a four-burner gas stove. There was also a separate washroom with a cold-water faucet (an extra feature) and a separate toilet. All the rooms opened onto a square-shaped foyer.

The bathing facilities in the basement were similar to those of the Russian bathhouses—they had hot and cold running water, tin basins (most bathers brought their own), wooden benches, and open showers. There was no steam room. The schedule specified two days a week for women, two days for men, two for washing clothes. The last day was probably for clean-up. The rationale for the basement bathhouse was that since the apartments were to be occupied by more than one family, common facilities in the basement would avoid conflicts.

"Living space" was parceled out economically and according to rank and the employee's (perceived) value. Most families of four had just one room, though the occasional family had two. Except for a few Russian families, most of the residents had come from foreign countries and had been living in privately rented rooms, in some instances paid for by the publishing house administration. In the main, the occupants were middle-rank employees, as the majority of those at the top level already had found living quarters through other channels.

Kapelsky Lane number thirteen was a veritable Tower of Babel. Every language, Western and Eastern, was heard. People speaking different languages and coming from varied cultures lived side by side, not only in the same building, but in the same crowded apartments, sharing their tiny kitchen and inadequate washing facilities. In some cases, this generated conflict; in others, lasting friendships. Because the building was always filled to capacity, I was considered lucky to have been given a place without having had a long wait. However, vacancies did occur: People went back to their native countries or were sent on assignments, changed jobs, or were arrested. I never knew or inquired about those who had lived in the room before I moved in.

I had been in the building even before, to visit Mussia who had lived there since its completion in 1936. Mussia had become involved with a German worker she had met in the print shop, and they had applied for a room together. They were expecting a baby and, because they were both valuable employees, were given a large room. Kurt was a skilled printer, many years Mussia's senior, an anti-fascist. He was neither as educated nor as bright as she was, so her friends considered them to be mismatched—nineteen-year-old Mussia carried away by her first romance. I visited them a few times, but had not kept in touch after I left the university. The marriage was short lived. It started breaking up when their son was only a few months old. They agreed to separate, but Kurt continued to live in the same room while he looked for other quarters, which he eventually found with a German girlfriend.

I dropped in to see Mussia the day I moved in. She had heard that I was coming back—Leon Talmy had announced it at a meeting—but knew nothing more. Mussia was surprised and pleased that we'd be living in the same building.

She had bad news. Kurt had been arrested at his girlfriend's place a few months earlier. He was still officially registered as living in Mussia's room, and their son bore his surname. She had reported the arrest to the personnel department (as if they didn't know!). So far, there had not been any repercussions (such as demotion or discharge), but she was very nervous and upset.[1]

Another devastating blow was the arrest of Joe Feinberg, the first in the English section. This was a shock to everybody, but even more so to Mussia, who had known Joe nearly all her life. The authorities arrived for him, atypically, at work, not in the middle of night at home. Joe was working on a rush job connected with a trial, and was dictating to a typist when they came for him. His brother Bram was working on the same job and went

---

1. Actually, she was treated with consideration. This may have been due in part to her youth and also because everyone knew that she and her husband had separated. Nevertheless, she carried the burden of that arrest for most of her life. Whenever she had to fill out forms for whatever reason—and that was often—she had to indicate that her husband had been arrested and convicted on a charge of espionage.

right on dictating. In fact, everyone in the office went on doing whatever they had been doing, stony-faced, not reacting. Recalling that day more than fifty years later, Mussia admitted to me that she still gets gooseflesh.

Joe's brother Bram was not fired. When his "personal case" (*personal'noye dyelo*—ominous words) was taken up at the Party committee, Bram refused to make the usual statement, which would have had him confessing to "lack of vigilance" and condemning his brother. He insisted that he was entitled to wait at least until his brother was charged. To everyone's surprise, the committee was not as harsh as expected, merely imposing a "strict reprimand"[2] on him. These events took place shortly before I returned to the publishing house. A few days after my return, an open Party-Komsomol meeting was held in the English section to discuss Joe's arrest, Bram's recalcitrance, and everybody else's "blunted vigilance." I noticed a marked change in Bram. He was no longer the arrogant star of the English section that he had been when I had last worked there. He was subdued, kept to himself, and responded gratefully to a friendly word or gesture, even from someone as low on the totem pole as myself.

Several of my coworkers lived in the building. Betty had a small room to herself. John Evans lived with his wife, a Russian woman connected with the film industry, and their infant daughter in a large room. David Fromberg, the new control editor and CPSU member who had come from England at the time of the revolution and who had fought in the Russian Civil War, occupied two rooms with his Russian wife and two young sons. Ahsia, now at the publishing house, lived with her parents in a medium-sized room. Toini, an American of Finnish descent who worked as a typist, had a large room with her Russian husband and small daughter. Mussia and I made up the English section contingent. I came to know most of these people quite well, and Mussia remained one of my closest friends. Betty became a good friend in later years. At that time, the difference in our ages was too significant, but she was very kind to me from the first. She was always ready to advise and help me in my work and often invited me over to share a meal.

Maria Rivkin, Mussia's friend from the German section, lived with her husband and two-year-old daughter in a large room on the ground floor. Among the other Germans who lived on Kapelsky were Willi Bredel, a well-known proletarian writer, and his wife Maya, as well as a printer named Freudenreich and his Russian wife. There were several other Germans, some Yugoslavians, a father and daughter from Poland, and various other East

---

2. A system of penalties applied throughout the Soviet Union in the Party, Komsomol, and trade unions. The lowest level of penalty was a warning, followed by a reprimand, then a strict reprimand with entry into one's work record or dossier, and finally expulsion, or, in the case of an administrative penalty, dismissal from the job. (Ed.)

Europeans. There was an Italian, Lombardi, with his Russian wife and two daughters; an Argentinean named Guerra, with his Russian wife and two children; a Cuban; a Korean family; several Chinese; and a man we thought was Malaysian. For several years, the latter, a slightly built, brown-skinned man of uncertain age who was always smiling, occupied the small room in Maria's apartment. He was apparently connected with the Comintern, but did not seem to rate much support from it. He managed on very little, though he would frequently "borrow" an onion, a carrot, or a potato from one or another of the neighbors to make himself a soup. Maria and her neighbor often gave him a bowl of soup or whatever else they could spare. It was difficult to communicate with him, as he spoke Russian with an atrocious accent.[3]

It was with a heavy heart that I went to work at the publishing house's new quarters on Mayakovsky Square. My old acquaintances welcomed me back. All except Helen (and possibly Talmy) assumed that I had just dropped out of the university and they expressed their regret. "If I were your age," my friend Liz said, "I'd be in school right now." I did not enlighten her.

Many of the old-timers were gone. Naomi, Sophie, and several of the typists had gone home to the United States. Lasker had not returned from his assignment. Scott was gone. Talmy was still in charge and Sareyeva still screamed, though not as much as before.

There were also several freelancers, known as "off-staff" employees. "Off staff" was a convenient way for the administration to fill a need without having to take responsibility for "lack of vigilance" if the off-staff person were arrested. The practice had become widespread as the number of arrests increased.

Among the off-staffers was seventeen-year-old Dorothy Furman, a copyholder with whom I often worked. I was very fond of her. Dorothy had come to Moscow from Baltimore with her family in 1931, when she had been eleven. Her father was a tailor and her mother a professional cook, and she also had an older sister and a younger brother. Theirs was an open house, filled with friends and acquaintances. A pot of soup was always simmering on the stove. Dorothy had dropped out of the ninth grade, bored, she said, by school. I assumed she would go back to school when she was ready. She was a bright, fresh presence and a good worker, very much in demand. She was not a member of the Komsomol—unusual for a person of her age—and no amount of persuasion could get her to join in any of our youth activities.

---

3. Leder became friendly with this man and used to hold long discussions with him on politics, philosophies, and other topics. Unfortunately, I cannot remember what I was told about those conversations, for the "Malaysian," Lev Kopelev told me many years later, was apparently Ho Chi Minh.

Where was Elsa Dobo? I had liked her and had looked forward to seeing her again. Had she gone home, too? Reluctantly, someone finally said, no, she had not gone home; she just wasn't working here any more. I inquired further and learned that her Hungarian husband had been arrested and she had been fired. Later, Rowena Meyer, another American employed in the English section, told me that Elsa was in dire straits with no job and two young sons to support. Rowena helped her by sending freelance typing and proofreading for her to do under Rowena's name, an illegal and courageous act in those circumstances. Rowena herself returned to the United States during the war.

Tamara, the beautiful young woman to whom Izzy had introduced me several years earlier, came to work as an off-staff typist in our office. She had lost her job at TASS after the arrest of several high-placed relatives. Upon her discharge, Tamara appealed to her uncle, the head of the State Bank, who himself would soon be arrested and later shot. He told her to take her husband's name and not make a fuss.[4]

Tamara was as charming as she was beautiful. She was also a superb worker, intelligent and capable, with an excellent command of both English and Russian. She was not at all interested in career advancement and projected an image of an empty-headed flirt and tease. More than anything, she was devoted to her husband Boris and was very serious about her wifely duties. Whether she projected this image deliberately or it came naturally, I do not know. However, her image probably prevented the powers-that-be from taking her seriously or approaching her for so-called assistance. It may have saved her life.

We became good friends and I often went home with her after work. The routine was always the same.

First, we'd go to the farmers' market on Trubnaya Square, which was walking distance from our office. I would watch as Tamara exerted her charms on the sellers to get the best buys. She knew what to look for, as she had been taught to market and to cook when growing up in Harbin and Shanghai. Then we'd go to her place on Karetnyi Row, which was also a short walk away.

She and Boris lived in a pre-war apartment house, one of the first rental apartment houses to have been built in Moscow. Before the Soviets had come to power, Boris's parents and three sons had occupied the entire apartment on the eighth floor of the elevator building—four very large rooms, and a large kitchen and hall. After the Bolshevik Revolution, they were compelled to give up two of the rooms and had to share the kitchen and bathroom with

---

4. In the 1980s, Tamara's uncle was posthumously rehabilitated.

strangers. When I knew Tamara, the eldest son had married and moved to his wife's apartment. When the second son married Tamara, the young couple was given the smaller of the two rooms. Then the youngest son married, and he and his wife, both musicians, shared the parents' room. The room was enormous, but with a grand piano and four adults, it was crowded; under the best of circumstances, this setup would have been difficult for young couples. It was made more difficult by the friction between the young wives and their mother-in-law, a strong, domineering woman who was proud of her three devoted sons and critical of their wives. A classic in-law case! Tamara, who had lived a great part of her life in China and gone to English schools, had definite ideas about privacy and independence. She insisted on separate households within the same apartment, not the usual way for families to live together, and this did not endear her to her mother-in-law.

Boris was usually at home when we got there, and he would be lying on the sofa and reading a newspaper. He worked as an engineer in a research institute and usually came straight home after work. He did not belong either to the Komsomol or the Party, and avoided "volunteer" duties whenever he could. Tamara would head for the kitchen and, in a very short time, have supper on the table. Her mother-in-law certainly could not fault her for neglect of her husband. Tamara took this aspect of her marriage for granted and did not seem to mind. In those early years of their marriage, Boris, a doting and proud husband, did not lift a finger around the house. What Tamara *did* mind was her mother-in-law's sharp eyes on her all the time.

I got to know the rest of the family superficially, at family gatherings and festive occasions to which I was invited. I had not met anyone like them before. Unlike my other friends and acquaintances, they were unmistakably anti-Soviet. Before the revolution, Boris's father, a quiet, unobtrusive man who now worked as a bookkeeper, had been a prosperous member of the merchants' guild. The mother had been a licensed midwife and, though a Jew, had permission to live in Moscow, outside the Jewish Pale of Settlement. The three sons had all been born in Moscow. I was shocked by some of the critical, not to say venomous, remarks I heard there. Tamara did not say much. She came from a different milieu. Her father had been a professional revolutionary who was killed during the Russian Civil War. Her uncles had held high government positions. However, by 1938 her uncles had been arrested, her mother and younger brother forced to leave Moscow and resettle in Sverdlovsk. No wonder she deliberately kept a low profile and followed her uncle's advice, changing her maiden name to her husband's.

They all knew that I was active in the Komsomol and a true believer, and I had heated arguments with them. To this day, I cannot understand how they risked talking so openly in my presence. They certainly knew about the system of informers! Years later, in New York, I asked this question of the eldest brother. The reply was that they were good judges of character. Incredibly, no one in Boris's family fell victim to the Terror of the thirties and forties. Perhaps it was not so incredible. The more politically active one was, the greater the danger of arrest.

A few days after I started my job at the publishing company, Kulkov, the head of the "secret department" (*sekretnyi otdel*—every enterprise had one in addition to the personnel department), sent for me. He stood up as I entered the room.

"Greetings," he said, shaking my hand. "We are very glad to have you here." Asking me to be seated, he continued: "These are perilous times. We need every person who can be trusted. We need people like you."

I murmured my thanks.

"We are beset by enemies," he went on. "Here in the publishing house, we are especially vulnerable. All these foreigners and others who have lived abroad have stories that cannot be verified. We are counting on you as a loyal member of the Komsomol to keep your eyes open and to report anything that looks the least bit suspicious."

He wished me well in my new job and said he'd like to see me from time to time. Then he delivered a parting shot:

"Be careful with whom you associate. Joe Feinberg may be the first, but he is not the last. Don't get too friendly with Liz Goldman. She won't be around much longer."

I was appalled. Liz! Kulkov could not know what he was talking about. Liz, a staunch Communist who had formerly held leadership positions in the American Communist Party and YCL! It was inconceivable that she could be mixed up in anything anti-Soviet.

No doubt, Liz would have eventually become the close friend she became later, but this warning actually precipitated our closeness. I was so worried about her that I began to dog her footsteps. When I did not have to stay late, I walked home with her. She was pregnant and walked from the office nearly every day, often accompanied by Fromberg, Evans, or both. Her home was only a ten-minute walk from where I lived. On weekends, I would drop in uninvited to make sure she was all right. Encountering me at Liz's so often, a close friend of Liz's remarked condescendingly that Liz had inherited my friendship from Naomi. Little did she know.

It had not been a good year for Liz and her family. Her husband Grisha had been dismissed from his high-level position for no reason except fearfulness on the part of the administration. He had lived and been educated abroad and therefore was a good candidate for arrest. This made his colleagues vulnerable to potential charges of "lack of vigilance," so they refused to take chances. Grisha was out of work for about eight months, but had recently been hired as a low-level engineer in a factory.

I did not tell anyone about my conversation with Kulkov. It had left me with an unpleasant feeling. He was a slimy character; his heartiness, conspiratorial air, and friendliness rang false, and his talk about arrests was alarming.

My job was humdrum. The novelty of getting acquainted with new ideas and an unfamiliar milieu was gone. Mostly, I did proofreading—and I was a rotten proofreader. I did not have the necessary patience or eye for detail. I did some assistant editing and found that to be more agreeable. My Russian had improved and I had no difficulty catching errors of translation and sometimes of interpretation. Komsomol work took up a good deal of my time: meetings, the wall newspaper, current events groups, and so forth. These activities were expected of me, but they were also what I wanted to do.

Vigilance remained the key word at work.

This was a very different place from the one I had left five years earlier. Gone was the strong feeling of camaraderie, the buoyancy, the sense of a worthwhile job well done. People worked as hard as they had, attended required meetings, and then went home. Not that there was an undercurrent of dissent or even doubt. It was just that people were frightened and unhappy, except for the "claques"—the fervent "announcers and denouncers" eager to demonstrate their support and prove their loyalty at every opportunity.

Fortunately, my roommate and I got along well together. Aina worked in the Scandinavian section as a typist and proofreader. Her father was connected with the Comintern. One evening about three weeks after I had moved in, I came home to find her in tears. She had been summoned to the secret department that day and told that her father had been arrested. The next few days were harrowing. She was called before the Komsomol committee, which recommended that she be expelled for "lack of vigilance." A special membership meeting was convened to confirm the recommendation. Aina did not defend or accuse her father, but kept saying over and over again that she did not and could not understand, that she believed and hoped it was a mistake. Aina was well liked. A few coworkers made feeble attempts to speak up in her defense, but these efforts petered out. As her roommate, I was called upon to make a statement. I said that I had only known her a short time, but I had no reason to doubt her loyalty and sincerity. Whether her father was guilty or not would be decided by the proper authorities, but in any case, children did not answer for their parents.

This was not the statement that the authorities wanted. Innocent people were not arrested, the Party representative said. The NKVD did not make mistakes. A vote was called for. One by one, the hands around me went up in favor of expulsion. No more than two or three souls besides me abstained. Aina was fired and ordered to vacate her "living space." She left and I never saw or heard from her again.

After Aina left, the housing distribution committee lost no time in moving me "temporarily" into a smaller room in another apartment. I lived there until the end of the summer in the bliss of comparative privacy, sharing the apartment with the family of a recently arrested Hungarian Communist—his wife, two small children, and the mother. The wife used to leave each morning; I did not know if she went to work or to stand in line at the NKVD building on Dzerzhinsky Square (the Lyubyanka) to seek news about her husband. She never spoke to me except to say hello. The mother-in-law took care of the children and kept house as best she could. I'd meet her in the kitchen sometimes. A frail, white-haired, sad-faced woman, she looked to be eighty, though she was probably only in her sixties. She confessed that they lived in fear of being evicted, of losing whatever small income they had. The situation was heartbreaking.

It was while I had the small room to myself that Captain Averikhin came to see me. He turned up one evening unannounced in full uniform, frightening my neighbors when they answered the doorbell. But I was delighted to see him. He had been kept informed about my situation after I left the organization and had found out where I lived. (Apparently, someone was keeping tabs on me!) The first time he came, he had waited outside until he saw the light go on in my room. He told me that the school had not reopened after the semester ended and that very few of the students had been given assignments. The others had gone back to their army units or jobs. There had been too many arrests among the top echelons of the military, and the intelligence network had been compromised. He came to see me a few times after that. I enjoyed his company, but before long it became clear that his intentions were romantic. (Ksena had hinted as much when we were at the school, but I had ridiculed the idea.) Apart from the fact that he was married and had a child, I could not see him as a lover. "Just friendship" was not going to work, so we stopped seeing each other.

In later years, I often thought of Averikhin with more affection than I felt at the time. I even still feel some regret. Of all the men I had known up to that time, he was undoubtedly the most interesting and the most mature, intellectually as well as emotionally. I came to have a greater appreciation of his intelligence, his integrity, and his courage, for it took courage to run the Commissariat of Defense school as soberly as he did at a time of great stress, as well as to give me such help and advice. It took courage to come and see me at a time when association with a "tainted" foreigner was no way to advance a career. I do not know what became of him. After the war, someone told me that he had been placed in command of a punishment unit for some breach of discipline and had been killed in action. Punishment units were made up of convicts, and they were sent on the most dangerous missions. Few survived the war. It would not surprise me if this were true.

Other sections had been hard hit by arrests. The top administration of the publishing house had been depleted. The director, deputy director, and others had been arrested. There was a new administration and a new director, named Paryshev. Some of the editors in the Russian section were gone, having been arrested or fired because family members had been arrested. Heads had fallen in the Comintern, and many in the publishing house had had close contacts with these victims. The German section was so hard hit that the new head of the section, Ozrin, was a Yugoslavian (who spoke German) and only a member of the Komsomol, not the Party. So far, however, with the exception of Joe Feinberg, the Americans and British had hardly been touched.

In 1938, a number of foreigners who were not Soviet citizens had their residence permits revoked. They were faced with a choice: Either apply for Soviet citizenship or leave the country. Among those who left were Harry Cantor, whose wife, a Soviet citizen, was unable to join him for years. Also leaving at that time was the man with whom Betty had been involved for about ten years. For Betty, this was a wrenching experience.

One day, I bumped into Izzy at the local post office. He now lived in the next building, a new apartment house that belonged to TASS, where he had been given a room in a communal apartment. He had been seeing Ahsia and knew I was back at the publishing house. I started seeing him again, not often and usually on my initiative. I'd call him when I was bored or wanted an escort. There was never any question of a return to our former intimacy, but he was available whenever I called.

Another surprise of a similar nature was in store for me. Ahsia often worked at home, and every now and then I'd be asked to deliver or fetch something for her or to leave a message. I had met her mother, but not her father, a printer by trade who was usually away at work when I came by. Then, one day, I dropped in when he was at home. I was astonished to recognize the slightly Asian-looking captain who had been Ben's "handler" (*vedushchii*).

We made no pretense of not recognizing each other. He had known that we would meet sooner or later. He had been demobilized a few months after I had been discharged and gone to work at his old trade. Both he and his wife were very cordial and I became friends with them even before I became an intimate friend of Ahsia. He was a sociable, fun-loving man, the life of any party. His wife was quiet and retiring. They were both kind and hospitable, welcoming me warmly whenever I stopped by.

My return to the scene led Ahsia to break off her relationship with Izzy. She told him she could not compete with me and refused to believe his assurances that there was nothing between us, especially since he continued to see me. At that time, I had only a nodding acquaintance with Ahsia and shrugged the matter off when Izzy told me about it. Long afterwards, when

Ahsia was a dear friend, we talked about this episode. I felt bad about my role in it. She told me, however, that she had been uncertain about the relationship and this factor had merely given her the impetus to end it. More importantly, she had already met someone else, a man named Igor, and the strong attraction between them was immediate.

Soon, she was in the middle of a new love affair and fighting a truly heroic struggle to get the publishing house administration to give her a room of her own. Quiet, soft-spoken Ahsia, who never put herself forward and hardly every spoke up, revealed an unexpectedly stubborn streak. Day after day, she could be seen waiting outside the office of one or another of the managers. Finally, she obtained an audience with the director and got his promise to give her the next available room of suitable size on Kapelsky. Then she had to go through the same procedure to get the promise fulfilled. After weeks—perhaps months, I don't remember—she was given a nine-meter room and Igor moved in with her.

Igor did not have a job. For an able-bodied man not to have a job was politically suspect, and for an able-bodied man to be supported by his wife was definitely frowned upon by society. Ahsia did not offer any explanations and no one ventured to question her. Igor would escort her to work every morning and call for her at the end of the day. He was very attentive. He did the shopping and cleaning. Ahsia's mother did the cooking and they had their meals at her parents' apartment. Ahsia was obviously very much in love and happy.

But her friends and parents were not so happy. Ahsia ignored the general disapproval and never discussed her personal affairs with anyone. Only many years later, when this part of her life was past history, did Ahsia tell me that Igor had been recalled from a special assignment for the agency where her father had worked and had been discharged in 1937 like so many others. He had been unable to find a job because of something in his dossier and could not do physical work because of an injury.

On the way to a movie one evening, Izzy said that he had invited a new colleague and his girlfriend to join us. The colleague, a specialist in Japanese, lived in his building and we were to call for him.

A tall, thin, very blond young man answered the doorbell. Izzy introduced him:

"Albert Case, an editor in my department."

The man smiled: "Call me Case. Everybody does."

"Why do you have an English name?" I asked.

"It's not English. It's Estonian. I am an Estonian from Leningrad."

He led the way down a long corridor to his room.

"Welcome to my hut (*khata*)," he said, holding the door open for me to precede him.

I stopped in my tracks. There, seated on the couch, her long hair down and looking rather disheveled, was Ksena! As Case proceeded to introduce us, I regained my composure and followed Ksena's lead. Neither one of us gave a sign that we were acquainted.

Ksena had made a plan. She had expected me, for she knew who Izzy's friend Mary was. She said she had a headache and did not want to go to the movie; why, instead, didn't we go without her? Case demurred. He'd stay with her. Then, as if we had rehearsed the scene, I chimed in: I didn't really want to see that movie. I'd stay and keep Ksena company. Would she like that? Yes, she would, definitely. The men were puzzled. Two young women, meeting for the first time, eager to spend the evening together, alone? But we insisted, and they were no match for us. They realized that there was something they did not understand, and they left by themselves.

It had been a little over a year since we had seen each other. We were both delighted at this turn of events. When Ksena had not returned to school in Khimki in the fall of 1937, I never expected to see her again. We talked non-stop for the few hours we had before the men returned.

I told her about my transfer to the other school, my sudden dismissal, my job. Our re-acquaintance occurred soon after Averikhin's first visit to my apartment, and I told her about it. She reacted angrily:

"What does he want? Get rid of him! Don't get involved with a married man! The next time he comes, you let me know. I'll tell him off!"

She was less open with me, out of pride rather than conspiracy. She merely hinted that she had broken with her lover, the general who had been in Spain. Out of tact, I did not tell her about my meeting with Lina. Without the general's backing, Ksena had been dropped from the school and had gone back to teaching English in a secondary school. She had met Case through her sister Marussia, who taught Chinese at the Institute of Oriental Studies where Case had been a graduate student. Marussia was soon to marry his best friend, a professor of Japanese.

Ksena finally told me about herself. She and her older sister Marussia came from the Far East, from a village not far from Vladivostok, and they had both studied in that city before coming to Moscow. The rest of the family—parents, two sisters and two brothers—still lived in the Far East. Many years later, Marussia told me that her oldest brother had been arrested in 1937 and never heard from again. That, too, may have had something to do with Ksena being dropped from the school.

Ksena moved in with Case, and after that evening we often made a foursome. Ksena and Case were very eager for Izzy and me to renew our former relationship and they tried hard, together and separately, to influence us. But nothing came of their efforts. Izzy was basking in the adoration of a pretty young secretary in his department, a far cry from what he had been accustomed to from me and probably from Ahsia. He once told me that American girls expected too much from a man. He eventually married the secretary.

I saw a great deal of Ksena that year. We enjoyed each other's company and always had much to talk about. She was often home alone as Case, like Izzy, worked long hours and odd shifts. At that time, Ksena was still trying to decide whether to marry him, as he was imploring her to do.[5] Meanwhile, her sister Marussia got married and I was invited to the celebration. She and her fiancé had been given a room, had set up housekeeping together, and had registered as husband and wife at the registrar's bureau (ZAGS).[6] Though there had not been a ceremony, civil or religious, tradition was observed—with the ribald jokes, the shouting of "bitter, bitter" to which the couple responded by kissing, the Russian dancing, the drinking, and the traditional foods.

At the end of the summer of 1938, the housing committee notified me that I would be moved back into a medium-sized room that I would share with a roommate. This meant the loss of the comparative privacy I was enjoying. I had expected this to happen sooner or later, but had hoped that they would forget about me for a longer time. It had been a vain hope. The room I moved into in apartment number twenty-six on the third floor would be my home for the next twenty years.

All my neighbors were Russian (as opposed to the foreigners in most apartments). One of the two large rooms was occupied by a mother and a daughter. The daughter, Natasha, a plump, brown-eyed, round-faced, pretty woman of about thirty, was fluent in English, French, and German, and worked in the publishing house. Her mother, Alevtina Vasilievna, was a contrast to her—she was gaunt, with white hair, high-cheekbones, piercing blue eyes, and a thin, aristocratic nose. They obviously came from the old Russian intelligentsia, but never talked about themselves. All I ever learned about them was that Natasha had been married for a very short time and that they had lived in the Crimea, but had left it after an earthquake.

---

5. Ksena wound up marrying Case, who had been appointed head of the TASS bureau in Estonia, and leaving for Tallinn with him soon after the country was declared a Soviet Socialist Republic. After that, my contact with them was by correspondence, except on the rare occasions when Ksena accompanied Case on business trips to Moscow. At first, Ksena took a job teaching English, but after their son was born, she became a full-time housewife. She had joined the Party and was active in community affairs. Ultimately, she became quite comfortable with her elite status and the privileges that went with it.

6. In 1917, the Bolsheviks decreed that marriage was a civil, rather than a religious union, and that marriages required no more than simple registration at the newly established registrar's bureaus (ZAGS). In keeping with the Communist goal to weaken the nuclear family and, somewhat contradictorily, with the need to provide women with child support, a law in 1926 provided cohabiting heterosexual couples with all the rights and obligations of husbands and wives (the so-called "de facto" marriage), whether or not they registered their union. This law remained in effect until 1944. (Ed.)

They were polite, but kept to themselves. They never borrowed anything from anyone and never loaned anything to anyone, never visited their neighbors, and never invited anyone into their room. In all the years I lived in that apartment, I never once "visited" with them, only spending a minute or two in their room if I had to deliver a message or ask a question. I'd have long talks with them in the kitchen, though, especially with Alevtina Vasilievna, about cooking, gossip, complaints about our neighbors, or cleanliness in the apartment. With Natasha, the talk was usually about office matters. Natasha liked to practice her English with me. She would go around humming "My Bonny Lies Over the Ocean." The two of them never expressed a political opinion and Natasha never criticized the administration of the publishing house. I once heard a rumor to the effect that Natasha had been married to an officer of the tsarist army and that she and her mother had gone to the Crimea to try to escape from Russia, but I never knew the truth of this for certain. The only visitors they had were a Russian woman who lived downstairs and, once in a great while, an old friend who would visit from Siberia.

The other two rooms—one large, and one the smallest room—were occupied by the Yegorovs—parents, son, and two daughters, who ranged in age from sixteen to twenty-four. They had no connection with the publishing house. The parents were semi-literate peasants who had left the village not long ago. We all shared the very small kitchen, toilet, washroom, foyer (which was used as storage space), and the telephone in the hall. There were three work tables in the kitchen. The Yegorovs had the largest table and wall space for cupboards, having moved in first. Natasha and her mother had a table against the wall between the sink and the stove. Our table was small and fit in against the window.

My roommate was a Spanish woman, a refugee who had come to the Soviet Union after the Loyalists' defeat in the Spanish Civil War. She had two teen-age children living in a home for Spanish children who had been sent to the Soviet Union earlier to escape the bombings of Spanish cities. We had no language in common and could communicate only on a primitive level. I don't think I ever even knew her name! She was a heavy-set, square-shaped woman with bushy black eyebrows and black hair streaked with grey. She told me that she had been a professor in Spain, but I don't know whether that meant a schoolteacher or university professor. I didn't know and I didn't care. All that I cared about was that she snored.

How she snored! Every night, all night, the room shook with her snores. No ruse of mine could stop it. I'd wake up and try to make noise so that she might turn over. My efforts were of no use. Sleepless night after sleepless night destroyed any feelings of compassion I might have had for her as a victim of the Spanish fascists. I did not care that her children were separated from her, and that she had no place to lay her head except in a room with a young girl with whom she could not even converse. In fact, I began to hate her with a passion. To make matters worse, she was always at home when I was at home. Every free day, her children came to visit and spent the whole day in our room. I never had a minute to myself.

Very likely, she was an interesting, educated woman from whom I could have learned a great deal, but all I wanted, fantasized about, was for her to vanish. I did not care how.

I don't know how I survived. I hated to go home. I accepted every invitation I got to stay with friends, but few had room for an extra person. I dreaded the nights.

This went on for about six months and then she left. I have a vague recollection that she took her children and went to Mexico. I sincerely hope that she and her children achieved a better life.

My next roommate was Elena Robotti, an Italian woman who worked in the publishing house. She had lived with her husband, Paoli, at the Lux, a Comintern hotel on Gorky Street[7] where many foreign Communists lived in comparative luxury. When her husband was arrested, she was evicted. Elena's sister, Maritsa, was the wife of the Italian Communist Party leader Togliatti, which is why she was not fired from her job or thrown out into the street, as had had happened to members of the families of other detainees.

Life became much more pleasant for me. Elena was a perfectly lovely person, quiet, understanding, helpful. She was away a great deal, too, which gave me some breathing space. She had a mentally retarded son in an institution outside Moscow whom she visited as often as she could. And like many other unfortunate women whose husbands had been arrested, she spent hours in line at the NKVD seeking information and to get parcels to her husband.

It was not easy for me to make ends meet. Elena asked me if I'd like to earn some extra money by tutoring her sister's son, who was doing poorly in English in school. She took me to see her sister at the Lux, and we agreed on terms. I started tutoring Togliatti's son Aldo, who was about twelve at the time. Now and then, Togliatti himself would look in, smile and say hello, but he never stopped to talk. The lessons did not go well. Aldo was not interested in English and I had no teaching experience. After several months, I gave up and recommended Dorothy's sister, who was a student at the Institute of Foreign Languages in Moscow. She took over and apparently succeeded in making the lessons interesting, because Aldo improved enough to pass the English exam.

---

7. The name of the street was changed from Tverskaya after Gorky's death in 1936. Now it is called Tverskaya again.

Living standards had begun to improve. Not only had rationing been abolished, but prices were also lower. There were lines in the stores, of course, but they were not as long as they used to be and the basics were usually obtainable. For the short time it existed, I often ate in a popular Jewish restaurant on Kolkhoz Square, not far from my house, where Dorothy's mother was the head cook. Anastas Mikoyan, member of the Politburo and then in charge of foreign trade, had returned from a trip to the United States, determined to introduce some of the things he had seen there. Soon, a soda fountain with American equipment opened right across the street from our office on Mayakovsky Square. Among its offerings were malted milk shakes and ice cream sodas. We ex-Americans patronized it enthusiastically until it closed down about a year later. (I was reminded of this restaurant in the 1980s when Moscow began negotiating for pizza parlors and fast-food restaurants.)

The summer of 1938 had gone by in comparative tranquility. There were no more arrests of anyone I knew personally; indeed, there were some releases. Families of detainees who had not yet been convicted hoped desperately for a miracle. However, the tranquility was deceptive, as I realized from my first encounter that summer with the system of informers.

Several weeks after Kulkov had "welcomed" me, he telephoned and made an appointment for me to see him the next day. There was a stranger in his office whom he introduced to me by a name and patronymic, Alexander Alexandrovich, shall we say. I don't remember his name, though I do remember him well: He was attractive, affable, and well-spoken. Our conversation began with the usual small talk.

"How are you?"

"Fine."

"Any problems?"

"Nothing special."

Kulkov gave his familiar spiel: We are surrounded by enemies. We must be vigilant. We need all the help we can get. There are so few who can be trusted. Then he turned to me and said:

"We'd like you to help us. This comrade has come especially to talk with you. I'll leave you two together." With that, he went out of the room and shut the door behind him.

I had no idea what was coming. For a moment my heart leaped. Perhaps they were going to send me to America after all!

The truth was nothing of the sort. Subtly, skillfully, Alexander Alexandrovich proposed that I "help the internal security organs" by keeping them informed about the reactions of my colleagues and coworkers to the issues of the day. Nothing special—I was just to report my impressions on a regular basis. I protested that I knew my duty as a Komsomol and did not have to be monitored. He increased the pressure: Surely, you are willing to help the Party and the government in its struggle against enemies of the people and to consolidate socialism. We need this information to help us shape policy. I agreed to another meeting in a few days. He told me to appear at a designated entrance to the Lyubyanka, and warned me against speaking to anyone about this or subsequent meetings.

When I arrived next time, he met me at the guard's booth and took me to the office of another man, someone who was apparently his superior. They were both wearing NKVD uniforms, though Alexander Alexandrovich had been in civilian dress at the meeting in Kulkov's office. The same generalities and the same arguments about my duty were repeated. With trepidation, I signed a paper agreeing to become a "voluntary" informant and promising not to divulge my connection with the security organs on pain of dire punishment. An appointment was made for the following week at an address I was told to memorize, not write down.

The address I had been given was of an ordinary apartment in an ordinary residential building in the center of the city. I went there the following week, and a middle-aged woman answered the doorbell, showing me into a room where a table was set for tea for two. She asked me to be seated and went out. A few minutes later, I heard the outside door slam. The doorbell had not rung and there had been no sound of a key turning in the lock, so someone must have left. Alexander Alexandrovich then came into the room. We talked in generalities, and nothing seemed to be expected of me at this point. Before I left, I was given an appointment for ten days later and told to bring with me a list of all the people I came into contact with—friends, acquaintances, colleagues.

The "relationship" developed slowly. I had nothing to report—and I assured him that everybody supported everything the Party and the government did. I told him continually that there was absolutely no sign of doubt or disaffection among my friends, coworkers, and acquaintances. We talked mostly about our work and had little time for anything else. Alexander Alexandrovich clearly did not seem very interested in my reports. He was obviously looking for something specific..

Finally, several meetings later, he revealed his focus of interest. I was instructed to cultivate John Evans and to report everything I managed to learn about him. On seeing my surprise, Alexander Alexandrovich remarked: "We have to know whom we can trust as well as whom we cannot trust. Just report everything. Let us professionals figure it out."

John Evans, who was not a Soviet citizen and had never been a member of the Communist Party, was probably the most talented editor on staff and one of the nicest to the junior staff members. Everyone liked him and enjoyed his wonderful sense of humor. He was witty in a droll, even dour way, and had a sharp mind. I used to meet him sometimes on the way to or from work, but never socially. Evans frequently walked home by himself, so I sought opportunities to join him "accidentally." Liz had given birth to a son in June 1938, so I did not often go home with her. I enjoyed the walks with Evans in spite of their object. At my meetings with Alexander Alexandrovich, I reported what the authorities already knew: where Evans was born, why he had come to the Soviet Union (he had been unable to find a job in England), what his wife's profession was, who his special friends in the English section were (Liz and Betty). His friendship with Liz was based on their common interests in their work and in writing and literature, while his friendship with Betty was based on their love and knowledge of music. Betty told me that Evans had an extraordinary command of music theory and she was certain he would compose music some day. My conversations with him were mostly about office gossip, but every once in a while, more frequently as time went on, he would say something outrageously critical about a local or national figure, a newspaper item or statement, or about some of the "information" we were being fed. I suspected that he knew why I was devoting so much time to him and was mocking me and my employers.

Nothing happened. I did not report on anything but the most innocuous conversations. Alexander Alexandrovich started getting annoyed.

"Why don't you ever visit the family socially?"

"Because I'm not invited."

"Get yourself invited."

"I can't. His wife is not friendly to me."

This was not conscious behavior on my part. I had no plan, but just followed my instincts. I did not doubt the system or even disapprove of the methods used "to protect the struggling young state" against the enemies surrounding it. But I believed that stupid people were doing stupid things, concerning themselves with unimportant matters. I thought they were suspicious of the wrong people and that they neglected the job of making the system work. I believed that the continuous calls for vigilance in the publishing house were misplaced. We were being urged to spy on one another and I, an ex-foreigner, found that system to be repugnant. The trade union officials were especially zealous, for they were supposed to be responsible for the "non-Party masses." I recall the head of the trade union (a tall, thin, unsmiling woman named Minquits) and her second-in-command (short, fat Levitan) and their ingratiating prying as they tried to discover something they could use in the vigilance campaign.

Above all, I believed that I knew better, that I could judge as well as anyone what was worth noticing. Therefore, I ignored the instructions to report everything and let the professionals sort it out. This attitude may have been arrogant, but it stood me in good stead.

My meetings with Alexander Alexandrovich became more acrimonious. As he became more frustrated with me, his veneer of politeness began to wear off. For my part, I resented the time I had to spend on this nonsense. I especially resented the requirement to submit a written report for each meeting. I tried to get released.

"How can you expect anyone to say anything anti-Soviet to me when everybody knows I'm a member of the Komsomol and that I'm an activist?" I asked him.

"You can ask leading questions, dissemble, act dissatisfied."

"I'm not an actress. I'm not good at that sort of thing."

Thus it went on for many months and I could see no end to it. None of my friends knew about my involvement. I had not told anyone, not even Ksena, who had been the first to try to alert me to the system of informers when we had been in the army school together.

The calls for vigilance never let up. We were constantly urged to watch for and report anything out of the ordinary, any criticism of the Party's policies, any expression of discontent. These admonitions applied to the work process as well. A mistake in translation could be construed as a deliberate distortion, hence, could be called sabotage. Criticism by an overzealous colleague could get the target of the criticism into trouble. The hunt for errors, which some enjoyed more than others in their eagerness to assert their superiority or win a point in personal rivalry, was now a matter of self-defense—the choice was to hunt or be hunted. In this highly politicized atmosphere, some of us closed ranks. It was more important to protect our fellow workers than to expose them. Controversial matters and errors were quietly pointed out to the culprit before anyone else noticed them. There was no consistency in our methods. A lot depended on personal relationships. And solidarity was stronger among the lower ranks than among the senior staff.

As I was no longer in a sheltered situation with special privileges, I was compelled to face reality and to do some thinking. I was troubled. Not that I doubted that publicized charges were true and convictions just. But the civics and history lessons I had learned in American schools had left their mark. I could see that the Soviet judicial system had no concept of due process; there was no presumption of innocence. A case was tried and decided in the preliminary procedures and interrogations before it got to court . . . and sometimes it never even got to court. Anyone could be framed.

These were painful thoughts for me, and the process of arriving at them was painful and solitary. I had to come all alone to revelations that seem obvious today and that may indeed have been obvious to many at the time, but there was no one with whom I dared to discuss my feelings. I know now, for example, that Ahsia already then had no illusions about what was happening. Neither did young Dorothy and her sister, but no one talked openly to anyone, except to trusted friends.

This is not to say that I was losing my faith. Not at all. Like many others, I attributed the "excesses" to the machinations of dishonest individuals who had somehow gained power. Such an attitude was sustained by the back-and-forth swing of the pendulum and the periodic "correctives" issued.

Kapelsky Lane number thirteen had, in just one year, gone through the same experiences as the building where my step-uncle and the Atlases lived. Residents trembled every time they heard a car drive into the yard after midnight. Whose turn was it next?

However, a lull set in at the end of 1938. Nobody knew why it happened or how long it would last. Kulkov's prophecy did not come true. Liz was not arrested, nor was anyone else in the English section. Since March 1938, there had been no public trials on a nationwide scale. Arrests continued, but at a lesser rate and with less publicity. Newspapers started carrying articles about unjustified arrests and chided some local Party organizations for hasty conclusions and "going to extremes." It was rumored that Yezhov himself had been reprimanded for uncalled-for harshness.

Then came a day of jubilation in the English section—Joe Feinberg was released and returned to work.

In December, Yezhov was replaced by Lavrenti Beria. This was regarded as a good sign.

The pendulum had swung back. But the seeming respite from the Terror in 1938–1939 coincided with increasing tensions in Europe. The events of those years made headlines in the Soviet press: the betrayal of Czechoslovakia, the Nazis' militarization of Danzig, their preparations for war, the sterile negotiations with British and French representatives in Moscow. The tenor of the press was strongly anti-Nazi.

One day in early 1939, I was standing in line in the basement cafeteria when someone tapped me on the shoulder. I looked up. It was Margo Pavlich, my Yugoslav housemate from the intensive training center. We arranged to meet later in the day. She told me that she and Lore had been let go a few weeks after my departure. They were given the same reason—that the network was penetrated and everybody was at risk. Both now had jobs at the radio committee—Lore in German, she in Serbo-Croatian. She had come to my office to use the publishing company's house library and had spotted me the moment she came into the cafeteria. Now she was living on the outskirts of Moscow with her nine-year-old daughter Inessa and infant son Felix. I'd known she had a daughter, but Felix was news to me. She also told me that her husband, who had been with the International Brigade in Spain, had joined her in Moscow and had expected a new assignment, but instead had been arrested. Felix was the result of their brief time together. She did not know her husband's whereabouts or what he was charged with and, as far as I know, never found out. She expressed no opinion to me regarding his guilt or innocence. I visited Margo and met the children—Inessa, an extraordinarily beautiful little girl with violet eyes and dark hair, and Felix, a roly-poly charmer. A Yugoslavian woman lived with them and took care of the children.

Maria, whom I had known only casually during my previous stint at the publishing house, became a close friend. She lived on the ground floor of the same section of the building in which I lived and I would often stop in on my way to work to see if she was ready to leave. Sometimes she was, but usually she was not and would come rushing in to punch the clock at the last minute or a few minutes late. No amount of nagging on my part or Mussia's could get her to leave a little extra time for her morning chores.

Maria's husband Yuri had formerly worked at the publishing house, but now he had a job on a factory newspaper and had to leave the house very early. They had a two-year-old daughter whom they left with their live-in domestic, a peasant girl, who slept on a folding cot in the kitchen, as did most domestics. In some apartments, two or three girls slept in the small kitchen or the foyer, one for each family. The domestic help was necessary, especially in families that had children, so that the women could go to work. The publishing house did not have a day care center and the district centers had long waiting lists. Attendants at these centers were usually untrained and the groups were too large. Children often got sick and the mothers had to miss work. Parents only sent their children to these places if they had no alternative. By contrast, there was no shortage of peasant girls eager to work as domestics in exchange for a place to live in Moscow or other big cities. Life was hard on the collective farms and there was a shortage of young men, who seldom returned to their villages after serving in the army. After completing their service, the men were entitled to internal passports that gave them the freedom to live and work in cities of their choice. The girls hoped eventually to find factory jobs that provided living space in a dormitory. They often met their future husbands at these factories.

Maria lived in one of the large rooms. The other was occupied by a Russian woman who was friendly with my neighbors, Natasha and her mother. From them, I knew that Maria's neighbor was married to a Bulgarian who was away "on assignment" for the Comintern. As far as I know, he never returned. She had some kind of office job and apparently received a small pension from the Comintern. Like Natasha and her mother, she was well educated, friendly, and yet kept her distance. The medium-sized room was like mine, occupied by two single people. At the time, the house electrician lived there. His roommate changed frequently and early in 1939, he was joined by a coworker of Maria's. The new roommate, Abram Leder, was a recent graduate of the German department of the Institute of Foreign Languages and had been hired as a junior control editor.

Leder did not receive a warm welcome in the German section. What was a non-native speaker doing in an editorial position? They gave him a hard time at first. But Maria liked him immediately and helped him both with the language and socially. She and her husband would invite him in for tea and German conversation. At first, I had no more than a passing acquaintance with him. As a matter of fact, if he was at Maria's when I dropped in, he'd quickly find an excuse to leave.

After the initial break-in period of a few months, his colleagues became friendlier toward him, for he was unassuming, hard-working, and well aware that he had much to learn. And, as an eligible young man—a scarce commodity in the publishing house—he was the object of attention for the many husbandless young women, a situation that seemed to embarrass him. Skinny, with a fair complexion and freckles, he reddened easily and looked much younger than his twenty-seven years. Maria kept me posted and we were amused to watch the women compete for his attention. One of the competitors was Maria's own sister, Dora, whose husband had been arrested in 1937, whom she had little hope of ever seeing again (she never did, as he disappeared into the Siberian labor camps).

"Why don't you join the fray?" Maria would say to me. "You don't have anyone now. You and Izzy are through."

I laughed.

"I'm not interested. Besides, he goes out of his way to avoid me. If we happen to get onto the same bus, he sticks his nose in a book and doesn't say a word to me."

"All the more reason. It would be fun," Maria retorted. "What have you got to lose?"

It was true that I did not have a boyfriend—a condition to which I was not accustomed—but I had no intention of competing. Despite my activist nature, I have always hated competition. I have never participated in contests, competed in sports, or played games.

But fate has its ways. There was a vacancy on the publishing house Komsomol committee (I had been a member since September 1938) and Leder was elected to it. We had to work together and usually found ourselves on the same side of the issues. We reacted similarly to petty bureaucratic annoyances and could count on each other's support. During the meeting at which his candidacy was proposed, he gave a routine account of his past activities and replied to questions. He had grown up in Rostov-on-the-Don. His father was a tailor, his mother a housewife; after the ninth grade, he had gone to work as a bricklayer and won awards for improving the efficiency of the work process. He had entered the Institute of Foreign Languages in Moscow, graduated in 1938, and taught German at a secondary school for one semester. (He later told me that that was a horrendous experience, with threatening parents, pregnant teen-age girls, and rowdy students who had not the least interest in learning German.) He had been Komsomol secretary in the German department and a member of the Institute's overall Komsomol committee. He proved a very suitable candidate, especially among the foreigners. He was supported by the Party committee and elected unanimously. Before long, he was appointed secretary of the committee.

Our relationship ultimately evolved. It came about unexpectedly and progressed rapidly throughout the summer of 1939. But at the same time that I was becoming involved romantically, I started having political problems.

In proofreading an article or speech by Stalin, I missed a huge number of typographical errors. I was accused of gross negligence and hauled over the coals at one meeting after another—a section meeting, a Komsomol committee meeting and, finally, a Komsomol membership meeting, where I was given an official reprimand with an entry in my dossier. At Kulkov's insistence, I was removed from the Komsomol committee.

Kulkov had become very cool towards me. Gone was the effusive welcome I had received when I had come to work there. He had probably received unsatisfactory reports from Alexander Alexandrovich and was generally annoyed that I had not become one of his retinue. I remember his words at the meeting because they upset me very much.

"In perilous times like these," he said, "we must trust only those who are crystal clear."

The implication was that I was not "crystal clear." My friend Helen was elected in my stead, to the relief of "our side," for Helen, in spite of her shyness, was not one to be manipulated.

Preparations were underway for the World's Fair, which was to open in New York in the summer of 1939. We English speakers were excited as we hoped that one or more of us would be chosen to act as guides. Candidates were screened, but no one who had lived abroad was considered. The only person who went from our section was a very pretty girl whose English was poor. Her brother was a prominent cameraman and it was rumored that he pulled strings to get her accepted. My parents and sister spoke with her at the fair. They found her only by asking the Soviet guides if anyone knew me. They had been crushed, as had I, that I had not been hired as a guide. It had seemed to them (and to me) that I was a natural candidate for the job.

One evening toward the end of the summer, I came home very late to find Elena waiting up for me. A bottle of wine and two wineglasses were on the table.

"Mary," she said, "I have wonderful news. My husband is coming home."

A week or so later, Paoli Robotti was released from detention, and he and his wife were sent to a resort in the south of Russia to recuperate. On their return a month later, they moved back into the Lux hotel. Though I visited them a few times, neither Elena nor her husband ever spoke to me or to anyone I knew about his experience in prison. Surely, he must have talked with his brother-in-law, who was instrumental in obtaining his release, but apparently he revealed details to no one else.[8]

Then, all of a sudden, without preparation, we were shocked by the announcement on August 19, 1939, that a trade agreement had been concluded with Nazi Germany. Before we had a chance to digest that piece of news, came another bombshell: the conclusion on August 23rd of a Soviet-German Friendship and Non-Aggression Pact. Newspapers splashed the pictures of Nazi and Soviet foreign ministers Ribbentrop and Molotov together.

Overnight, all criticism of Nazi Germany vanished from the press. *Professor Mamlock,* an anti-fascist film that had been showing at the cinema theaters, closed, as did all stage plays with anti-fascist themes. Now the press was filled with reports of the perfidiousness of the British and the French, who had planned for Germany to destroy the Soviet Union while they remained on the sidelines. The articles claimed that the British and French negotiators in Moscow had no decision-making powers and were procrastinating. Stalin had seen through them and turned the tables on them. (Later, after the Germans attacked the Soviet Union, the pact was defended as having bought time for the Soviet Union to prepare for war.)

Since my return to the United States I have had the opportunity to read Western sources. I now know that the issue was not as clear-cut as it might have seemed to my friends and me—neither in the first period when we accepted the official Soviet explanation, nor after our disillusionment when we rejected it in its entirety. Was it true that the British and French were deliberately playing a delaying game? Would the course of the war have been changed if the Western powers had been more forthcoming? If the Nazi atrocities had been taken more seriously in America? If America had not remained neutral for so long? If the Soviets had not concluded the pact with Germany?

No matter what the answer may be, it is an irrefutable fact that the Soviets did not use the two-year break to build up their defenses. On the contrary, Stalin continued to undermine the army by arresting its most talented leaders. He strengthened Germany by selling it the raw materials it needed to conduct its war.

---

8. Conquest writes that Robotti's teeth had been knocked out and his spine irreparably injured, but that he had kept silent about his prison experiences because he believed that it was the place of Soviet Communists, not of an Italian Communist, to speak out. See Conquest, *The Great Terror,* p. 432. I visited the Robottis in Rome in 1965. At that time, Paoli criticized de-Stalinization for hurting the Communist cause. "We kept silent," Paoli said. "They should have kept silent, too. The mistakes could have been corrected quietly, without publicity."

My German friends reacted to the pact most strongly, more with sadness than with anger. Maria and her sister Dora, however, expressed horror (in private, of course). The Soviet leaders do not know the Nazis, they said. They cannot conceive of the treachery of which the Nazis are capable. This is a disaster that will lead to worse disasters. They did not question the Soviets' motives, only their judgment.

One week after the conclusion of the pact, on September 1, 1939, Hitler's armies marched into Poland. Britain and France declared war. The Second World War had begun. When Soviet troops entered the Ukrainian and Byelorussian provinces of Poland, we did not doubt the official Party line that the action had been taken to protect the inhabitants of those regions. On September 28th, another agreement with Germany fixed the new borders and the factual partition of Poland. The campaign was an easy one. According to TASS, the local population welcomed the Red Army.

The Finnish campaign was quite another story. Preparation of public opinion began in October, when it was reported that Finland had refused to sign a mutual assistance pact with the Soviet Union or to agree to a readjustment of the frontier that would have improved the security of the Soviet Union by moving the border farther away from Leningrad. In return, the press reported that the Soviet Union was prepared to make territorial concessions to Finland that would more than compensate for the changes. The tone of the press toward Finland became increasingly hostile. Meetings were held in factories and other workplaces denouncing the Finnish "bourgeois rulers" and demanding that they be taught a lesson. On November 29th, Soviet troops crossed the Finnish border in what was supposed to be a brief campaign to end in a matter of weeks. The Soviets planned to set up a "Finnish People's Government" under Otto Kuusinen, an Old Bolshevik, when their armies marched into Helsinki.

They never got that far. The Finns put up a fierce resistance. Maria's husband, Yuri, took part in that campaign as a correspondent. He had business in Moscow several times, and he told us about the enormous losses the Soviet troops were suffering.[9]

The winter of the Finnish war remains in my memory one of the coldest I have ever experienced. The average temperature was minus twenty Fahrenheit and it often fell to nearly forty below. If you opened a window just a crack, the ink in the inkwell and the water in the glasses froze. Transportation

---

9. This part of the war lasted all winter and finally ended in March 1940 with a peace treaty under which the Soviet Union obtained the Karelian peninsula, the town of Vyborg, and lease of the Hango peninsula. Although the Soviets claimed that their goals had been achieved, the results were far short of expectations. The Finnish People's Government became the government of the newly formed Karelo-Finnish Soviet republic.

was in disarray, so most of the time I walked to work. Ordinarily a half hour's walk, it took longer because I was so bundled up. The sheepskin I had brought from America was still the only winter coat I had and it did not reach quite to my knees. I wore it along with felt boots, leggings, and a scarf wound round my neck and up to my eyeballs. I could hardly move. Many other people walked as well, and every once in a while, a passerby would call out to someone:

"Look out! Your nose is turning white."

It was no joke. The danger of frostbite was real. Stories about broken-off noses, fingers, and toes abounded. Some of the stories were probably true.

# 12
## Newlyweds—Winter 1939 to Summer 1941

That winter, I also got married.

No one had been moved in with me after Elena's departure. I knew that my privacy could not last, but I still kept my fingers crossed. It might take a while (I hoped) before a suitable candidate for the other half of my room turned up. After all, she would have to be an unattached female employee who had no place to live. Meanwhile, my relationship with Leder grew much closer. However, I was by no means prepared to make a serious commitment. The situation as it was suited me very well: I had my own room and a visiting boyfriend.

This lasted about three months. Then, Elvira Pulkka, a teen-aged American of Finnish descent who worked as a copy holder at the publishing house, asked the Komsomol committee for urgent help because she was having problems with her stepfather. Soon after, the Party secretary, a pleasant, middle-aged woman named Razvodovskaya, stopped Leder in the corridor.

"Listen, Leder," she said. "If you and Mackler are serious, you'd better hurry up and move in with her. Elvira Pulkka's application for housing has been approved and the housing committee is going to move her in with Mackler."

Leder did not wait for the end of the workday. He came into my office and asked to speak to me privately for a few minutes. I went out into the corridor with him and he repeated Razvodovskaya's conversation .

"You'd better make up your mind by tonight, Mary," he said. His mind had been made up for some time, though not without misgivings, because he foresaw us having clashes of personalities if we were together all the time. Besides, he felt he could not press me when I so obviously enjoyed living alone.

It did not take me long to make up my mind. I would rather be with him than with Elvira.

The next morning he spoke to Razvodovskaya, who told him to submit an application to the housing committee, saying that we were getting married. She would see our paperwork through the bureaucracy. On December 5, 1939—Soviet Constitution Day and a legal holiday—Leder, to whom I shall henceforth refer by his first name, Abram, moved his scant belongings from his room downstairs into mine on the third floor. That evening, Maria invited us in for a glass of wine with a few friends. Though we did not formalize our marriage at the registrar's bureau until over a year later, December 5th was the day from which we dated our marriage.

Not your usual starry-eyed approach to marriage, but our method was not that rare either, under the circumstances. Many a marriage was made or broken as a direct consequence of the availability of housing.

The neighbors were pleased when Abram moved in. They had apparently been expecting this turn of events even before we had. They preferred a stable couple to the constant changes of occupants.

Our first year together was rocky. The differences in our personalities were exacerbated by the cramped quarters in which we were compelled to live. Our small room served as a bedroom, dining room, living room, and study. We shared the common areas and the telephone in the hall with several people whom we had not chosen. We were lucky to have a washroom. In most apartment houses built in those years, people had to wash in the kitchen. Abram and I would keep our voices low inside the room, as every action outside the closed door was under scrutiny.

There was a schedule for maintenance of the common areas: sweeping the hall and kitchen every day and a general clean-up once a week. We had to alternate washing the floors, stove, washroom, toilet, and kitchen. Our turn came every eighth week for two weeks, the same for Natasha and her mother. The Yegorovs had five weeks every fifth week. Natasha and I also hired a woman to do the weekly cleaning. Even if I had wanted to, I could not have scrubbed the wooden floors until they were white, as that woman did with a bucket of soapy water and a stiff brush. The Yegorovs did the cleaning themselves and were often negligent, which led to recriminations.

Natasha never answered the phone. When a call was for her (which was often, as she frequently worked at home), she would wipe the telephone with a wad of cotton wool soaked in eau de cologne before talking. As in all apartments, there was a notice on the outside door giving the names of the occupants and the number of times to ring the bell for each family: one, general; two for the Yegorovs; three for Natasha; and four for us. With the five Yegorovs coming and going and none of them ever using a key, the bell never stopped ringing. I found this very annoying; a few months later, I persuaded the others with great difficulty and only by offering to bear the expense myself to have bells wired straight into each of our rooms. Ours was the only apartment in the building to have separate doorbells for each family—and this caused some muttering about "bourgeois individualism." When Abram moved in, I persuaded him to pad our door on the outside so as to reduce the noise level.

Now we were a family, with a change in attitude and lifestyle. All my friends and the neighbors, too, took an interest and were ready with all kinds of advice, especially culinary advice. Until then, I had tried only rudimentary cooking. I had my meals wherever I happened to be working or studying, and at the homes of friends. Tamara was the most helpful. She took me under her wing, showed me how to select meat and vegetables at the market, and told me exactly how to cook whatever I bought. She was a much more imaginative cook than my Russian neighbors. Abram used to laugh:

"Mary cooks by telephone. A couple of eggs, a frying pan, and the telephone, and she is all set."

He did not and would not cook. He did more than his share of the household chores, but they were of his own choosing. When he moved in, he immediately set about planning how to use our space efficiently. First, he'd draw several variations of a plan on paper—where to place the couch, the dish closet, the round table and the chairs, the lamps, the hangers for outer clothing (on the inside of the door), and where to build bookshelves. After selecting the variation he wanted, he'd start working on it—changing around the furniture, building shelves, and so forth. I did not mind. It was good to have someone around who was so handy. But everything took him much longer than he expected and he would often work late into the night, preventing me from getting to sleep at my usual hour. Our first quarrels were caused by his not stopping when I asked him to. He would promise to stop *seichas* (right away), but *seichas* could mean anything from a minute to an hour. This used to drive me crazy.

The daily routine that evolved in our first few weeks set a pattern for the rest of our life together.

Abram would get up much earlier than I in the morning and would be first in the washroom. Then he would wake me so I could take his place before anyone else got in. While I was washing, he would put the kettle on, make the bed, and set the table for breakfast, usually with tea, bread, and cheese or sausage, whichever was available. After breakfast, he would sweep the floor and we would leave for work.

One day, after several weeks of this routine, he said:

"Mary, don't you think you ought to sweep the floor?"

"Sweep the floor? Aren't you doing it?"

"I haven't swept for a week."

I hadn't noticed.

"I think it is your turn," he continued.

"Of course, if it's my turn, I'll sweep."

After a few days of my sweeping, Abram could stand it no longer. He took the broom from me and from then on, he swept the room, though I swept the hall and kitchen when it was our turn. He did not want to be seen doing "woman's work."

He had the same attitude toward my skills in making the bed. He was never satisfied with the way I made it. I tried my best, for I agreed with him that neatness was as important as cleanliness in such limited space. At first, he could not believe that I could not do better. He thought I was being contrary, and this too was a source of friction. After a while, however, he concluded that for some unfathomable reason, I was incapable of producing any kind of symmetry. When I finished cleaning, admittedly having done a thorough job, the room did not shine the way he wanted it to. So he took over its maintenance.

I complained that he was a pedant. He retorted that he had normal standards of neatness, but had been driven to extremes by my slipshod habits. However, his friends and former classmates confirmed that I was right and that he was, indeed, a perfectionist. They told me how he had browbeaten his two normally untidy roommates in the dorm and had them washing the floor several times a week, picking up their belongings, and hanging up their clothes. He turned their room into such a model of orderliness that its fame spread throughout Stromynka. That he had been less successful with me amused them. Actually, Abram's perfectionism did rub off on me and I changed a great deal over the years, but it took time. That first year we had a serious problem. Looking back, I can see how superficial and ridiculous our quarrels were, caused almost entirely by lack of space.

There were some things Abram would not do. He kept out of the kitchen as much as possible. I did the dishes. However, if we had had company and there were lots of dishes to do, he'd take them into the room and wash them there, bringing in basins of hot and cold water. He also would not take out the garbage. Taking out the garbage had been one of his chores at home from an early age and he hated it. I did not mind doing this chore, but after he had seen me carry the pail down three flights of stairs to the dumpster in the yard a few times, Abram devised a camouflage. He'd make neat packages of the trash, tying strings or even ribbons around them, and would take them out when leaving the house in the morning or the evening.

Neither did I have the wifely duty of caring for my husband's clothes. Two steamer trunks that we had bought from departing foreigners, which Abram had flattened out, curtained off and placed side by side against one wall, served as combined chests of drawers and clothes closets.

"The one on the left is mine," Abram announced. "Don't touch it. I'll take care of my clothes myself."

And he did. We had a washerwoman who collected and delivered our laundry, but he ironed his shirts himself, darned his socks, and sewed on his own buttons. Often he did the same for me, taking the needle out of my hand when I sat down to mend something. His closet was a model of neatness. He could find whatever he wanted whenever he wanted it. And he never seemed to have to do anything to achieve this order. I'd put everything in order in my closet, only to find a jumble within a few days. He ignored my closet and refrained from looking at it. (When my parents came to visit us nearly twenty years later, Abram was astonished to find them so neat. He had assumed that I came from an untidy home—an incorrect assumption!)

This division of labor was not typical of the average Soviet family. I know of no other couple, then or later, in which the wife did not do all the washing, mending, cooking, laying out of her husband's clothes for the day, and even the packing of his bags when he went on a business trip. Despite the state's insistence that women had been emancipated by Soviet power, there was still man's work and woman's work, and the dividing line was clear. Men fixed things. Men did the "heavy" work. But the only heavy work for a city dweller was helping to carry groceries. As for fixing things, some of the men I knew could not hit a nail on the head with a hammer. So a man's job was reading the newspapers and commenting on the articles to his wife while she did the housework.

The average married woman's day began early in the morning. She made breakfast, washed the dishes, and often prepared bag lunches for herself and her husband before they both left for their jobs. There might be a child to be taken to the day care center by her or her husband. During her lunch hour, she'd hurry out with her string bag to see what was available in the nearby shops. A string bag was called an *avoska*, from *avos*, meaning "just in case." On her way home from work, she might stop at a farmers' market or stand in line for groceries or manufactured goods. She would usually be the one to pick up the child at the day care center, her husband very likely having been detained at a meeting of one kind or another. It was harder for a man than for a woman to get out of attending a meeting. Children were seen as the mother's responsibility. When she finally got home, she would go straight into the kitchen to prepare supper. After supper and getting the child to bed, she might stay up late into the night washing clothes or cooking for the next day. Meals could not be prepared much ahead of time as there were no ice boxes and no refrigerators (the first electric refrigerators appeared in the 1950s). In the winter, we hung food, cooked or uncooked, in string bags outside the transom window, where it froze solid. A few years later, it became possible to buy hunks of ice at pharmacies, and we put these in basins. I wrote to my father, asking him how to make a simple ice box. He sent me a diagram, but other concerns intervened and Abram never got around to building one. The only appliances available were electric irons. Many women still used the coal irons or irons that were heated on the gas stove.

It was the woman who supervised the hired help if there was any, who dealt with household problems, who made decisions pertaining to the home or, at the very least, initiated discussions about them with her husband. In a word, she had the responsibility for running the household. Since nearly all these women had full-time jobs, they bore a double burden, physically and psychologically. My friend Maria used to moan:

"Where, oh where, are the oaks to lean on!?" There were very few.

The small minority of women who did not have jobs outside the home were usually the wives of the military or important officials. They were not the ordinary family.

In many families, the young couple lived with a set of one of their parents. Grandparents, especially grandmothers, had a useful function. They took care of the children, stood in lines to buy necessities, and, in general, kept house. This very valuable assistance was a mixed blessing because in-law friction could wreck a marriage.

Women's burden in the rural areas was even more demanding. In the villages I had occasion to visit, the women did most of the heavy work as well as the housework. The men drove the tractors and held management positions in the collective farms.

Abram was an only child in a Jewish family. One might have expected the usual pattern—that he was catered to and spoiled—but nothing was farther from the truth. On the contrary, he was, if anything, overburdened with chores. He was expected to fetch and carry and run errands for his parents. His father, a tailor, was officially employed by a government atelier, for which he received a nominal wage. The bulk of his income, however, came from his private clientele. Abram's habits of neatness and precision were developed during childhood. Everything in the home workshop had to be in perfect order so that if a financial inspector turned up unexpectedly, all signs of private work could be taken out of sight immediately. Small private enterprise was not illegal, but it had to be reported. The taxes levied on it were so high that few could survive. When his father did not have a chore for him, his mother did. Abram could hardly find the time to read a book just for the pleasure.

I met Abram's father soon after our marriage, and it was not an auspicious beginning.

Abram received a letter from his father saying that he would like to meet me and to see his son. He would be coming to Moscow in a few days.

Where would we put him? Ordinary citizens had no access to hotels and we had only our not-very-wide couch in our room for a guest. I arranged with Mussia to borrow a cot for Abram to sleep on and for myself to sleep at her place. To my dismay, Abram's father was mortally offended. He took it as an insult that I went away for the night. He saw no reason why he should not have slept on the cot; I should have stayed where I belonged. Considering that parents and married children often had to live in the same room, at best separated by a screen, his attitude was unremarkable. To me, however, it was preposterous. I would never have gone to bed with my husband had there been anyone else in the room, especially my husband's father.

This was one cultural difference, but there were others as well.

Another time, when I was home alone, three of Abram's cousins turned up, unexpected and uninvited. They were on their way to somewhere and planned on spending a few days in Moscow at our place. I told them that I was sorry, but they could see for themselves that we had no room for guests. In their eyes, of course, we had plenty of room—on the floor. A Russian saying, often quoted, goes: "Crowded but not offended." I asked them to wait until Abram came home, but they left. When Abram came home and heard my account, he was mortified. He asked, "How can I look my relatives in the eye after this?"

The word got around and we had no more uninvited guests. Later, when I got to know some of his cousins and friends, they would come to visit with us, invited, and no one took offense at the arrangements I made in those circumstances.

Though Abram felt very bad, he also saw my point. Some of his friends had come originally from Ukraine or Byelorussia and now lived in Moscow. They had a constant stream of visitors, with one, two or three sleeping on the floor for weeks—friends, relatives, and even friends or relatives of friends. Everyone wanted to come to Moscow—to see the sights and to buy food and clothing that was not available where they lived.

I was amazed and disapproving of the amount of effort Abram—and his contemporaries, too—would expend to track down a new gadget or an article of clothing or furniture. He would sometimes spend his entire day off going from store to store just to see what was available. If he saw something he thought I should have, he would phone me to come over to the store at once. He took great pleasure in the things my parents sent us in their annual parcels, as he enjoyed the workmanship and the design. As a matter of fact, all my Soviet friends of his generation had a similar interest in material things, especially in foreign-made articles. Good-quality merchandise was so hard to find that "what to buy and where" was a constant topic of conversation. Anyone who happened to locate a desirable article would immediately telephone friends and family to give them the information and the opportunity to buy it before it was sold out. Many of the people I knew would rather spend money on a hard-to-get article of clothing than on food. My first priority, however, was food.

We were very short of money, as neither one of us earned a good salary. On payday, we would put our money in a drawer and take it out as needed. Often, towards the end of the month, I'd find that there was no money left because Abram had bought a book that a sales clerk had saved for him, or a pair of shoes for me that I did not need, or another pair of gloves just because they were available. Once, for my birthday, he bought a beautiful Chinese lacquered jewel box decorated with mother-of-pearl figures. I had no jewelry at all and berated him for spending so much money (actually, much more than I knew, for he told me a very low price). I still have the box and am very attached to it.

I could not get him to budget our money.

Thus it went, give and take. On my part, my reactions were not planned. I responded to each situation on impulse. On Abram's part, as he admitted in later years, his refusal to give in to me on many small, unimportant matters was deliberate. He knew that I had a strong personality despite my helpless appearance, and he wanted to make sure from the beginning that he did not become a "dishrag that you could twist any which way!"

On the other hand, he was overwhelming in his solicitude. From the start, he decided that I was a homeless waif who needed someone to take care of her. Before we went out, he would look me over to see that my shoes were shined (he shined them), my collar straight, and my clothing suitable for the weather. He was very particular about his own clothes (unlike Izzy, whose trousers had been baggy and jackets ill-fitting) and interested and observant of what I wore. He was always on the lookout for something to buy for me and delighted to accompany me at shopping when I really needed something. When we were out together, he watched to ensure that I was not jostled or pushed in the street or in a crowded bus. I kept telling him that I was not made of glass, that I had managed by myself for eight years. He'd reply that I had only been lucky. He would quote the Russian proverb, "God takes care of drunks and little children." (Russians talk a lot in proverbs.) He enjoyed being protective. It was one of his many ways of showing affection.

In this, too, our personalities clashed. He was demonstrative; I was not. It took time for me to realize that I was no longer responsible for myself alone. This was brought home to me the day the secret police terminated my visits. In spite of the papers I had signed swearing me to secrecy, I told Abram about this matter, just as I told him about my stint in the Commissariat of Defense. He, too, had had dealings with the secret department at the Institute in his capacity as a Komsomol official and was knowledgeable about their methods. He worried about my involvement, but conceded that I had no choice in the matter.

My appointments were approximately every ten days, and they took place after working hours. My handlers were not happy with my performance and had been changed several times. Lately, I had been seeing a woman. I suppose they hoped she could elicit better results. I arrived one day in February 1940 to find that she was not alone. A man in the uniform of a colonel of the NKVD, whom she introduced as her chief (*nachal'nik*), took charge of the conversation. It started off with the usual amiable small talk: How was I? Was my personal life going well? Was I satisfied with my job? They could help me if I wished. They were pleased to hear that all was going well, but why wasn't I providing them with useful information?

"What useful information?" I wanted to know.

"Information about anti-Soviet activities."

"I don't have such information. Do you want me to make it up?"

"No, of course not. But we have other sources and we know that you are holding back."

A testy exchange developed. They said they had means to compel me to be more forthcoming. I retorted that this was not 1937, that I was not afraid of them, and that no one could compel me to go against my principles. I was more patriotic than they were, I said, for I knew that false information was misleading and could only harm our cause.

How naïve I still was! Perhaps that was fortunate, for I really believed what I was saying and was not afraid.

The colonel finally told me that they were terminating our connection and warned me of the dire consequences of revealing anything about it. I signed a paper and left.

The grilling had lasted several hours. It was about ten P.M. when I emerged. I was angry and upset, so instead of going straight home, I walked around the city for several hours. When I got to my corner at two A.M., Abram was pacing back and forth, frantic. Once he was convinced that I was all right, he burst into a rage. I had never seen him so furious. He had been worried sick. He had been certain that I had been arrested. Didn't I know the danger I'd been in? Didn't I know he would worry? He had known many instances of people not returning from just such a rendezvous. So far, I had been lucky. I should have come straight home; afterwards I could have walked to my heart's content. That I might have been arrested had not occurred to me. Neither had it occurred to me that Abram would worry.

Sometimes I felt smothered by Abram's attentions. Early in the marriage, however, I had a conversation I have never forgotten with a woman I knew only briefly. She left a deep imprint on my life. She was an American of Hungarian descent, about ten years older than I, a tall, attractive brunette whose flair for wearing clothes I envied. We were walking along Gorky Street and I was complaining about my husband's unceasing attempts to coddle me. Paula turned to me.

"Mary," she said, "if you want your marriage to work—or any relationship with a man—you've got to learn to make the best of what you have and not try to be what you are not. You look helpless, you look cuddly, you arouse protective instincts. Don't resist. Me—I am tall, striking, I look strong. No man wants to protect me. I have to emphasize my strength, my flamboyance. It doesn't matter that you are really very independent. Your husband knows that. Let him be protective and hope it doesn't wear off. It is not such a bad thing."

I took her advice seriously. Taking stock, I perceived that I had been resisting every step of the way. I tried, not always successfully, to stop. After all, my differences with Abram were not in matters of principle—we had the same values and much the same reactions to events and people, despite our different backgrounds. As I became more pliable, so did he. Gradually, after many ups and downs and considerable heartache that first year, along with a wonderful feeling of being cherished—I never doubted his love—our marriage evolved into a truly equal partnership. It was not until several years later that I appreciated how unusual this was.

Marriage is very much a matter of luck—of that I am convinced. Whether you start off wildly in love or have drifted into it, whether this is your first love affair or you have had several, whether you know what you want out of marriage or have not given it any thought—no matter how long you have known each other or how intimate you have been, it is practically impossible to tell in advance how the marriage will turn out. There are some things you can know beforehand—such as whether you are physically and intellectually compatible, whether you have similar interests and values. In my day and my circle, ideology counted a great deal. But the deeper qualities of character are not so readily apparent.

I got to know my husband slowly, through good times and through very bad times. I remember about a year and a half into our marriage being startled to hear an older couple who had known Abram only a few months, and who had just met me, refer to him as "noble" (blagorodnyi). With a sudden flash, I realized how right they were.

Abram had inner grace. He had an instinctive feeling for what was right, an awareness of other people, consideration not only for those he knew and liked, but for strangers too. He was incapable of being rude. Angry—yes, but not rude. His courtesy came from within. He did not have a trace of condescension towards women or of the brand of prudishness combined with lewdness that I had observed in many Russian men. He liked and respected women, never doubting that they were the equal of men intellectually and in strength of character. Abram was very conscious of the extra burden they bore and he sympathized with them.

He managed to combine such sensitivity with strength and courage. Abram had grown up in a rough neighborhood in Rostov in turbulent times and had had to cope with hoodlums and criminal elements. During the Civil War, he dodged the bullets of the marauding armies of the Reds and the Whites in the city streets. He learned to take care of himself at a very young age.

I had occasion to see him handle a threatening situation before we were married. We had been at Liz's and were walking home along a dark side street off the broad avenue that led to our home, when two or three toughs started to follow us. We were fifteen or twenty yards ahead of them and my instinct was to run. I pulled at Abram's sleeve to hurry him up. He held me back, merely increasing our pace a little. As we neared the corner, they caught up with us and demanded Abram's watch. Abram did not say a word, but kept on walking, holding me tightly by the arm. We turned the corner and they fell back. Abram said the worst thing we could have done was to show fear. If we had started to run, they would easily have caught up with us. This way, they did not know what to make of us, and so they lost the advantage.

I recounted the incident to Maria the next day. Maria, who felt almost as if she had a proprietary interest in our romance, was very curious as to whether he had conducted himself "as a man." We were both pleased to have had a glimpse of this side of his character.

Abram talked about his feelings. I did not, and this bothered him. Intellectually, we were opposites. I was quick, and often jumped to conclusions. He was slow, deliberate, and took more time than I did to consider, but once he made up his mind, it was hard to get him to change it. He was a much better judge of people than I was. He had artistic talent and was never without a pad and pencil. During his student years, he had augmented his stipend by designing and executing posters and decorations for festive occasions, and had earned more money than he did now. He was much more observant than I was and to go with him to a museum, the theater, or to the countryside was an enriching experience.

My understanding of him deepened when I learned of the troubles he had had at the Institute of Foreign Languages in Moscow. Throughout 1937, there had been numerous arrests among faculty and students. The German department was hit the hardest. Friends and relatives of the prisoners were expected to engage in breast-beating, and many were expelled from the Komsomol and sometimes from the Institute as well. As secretary of the German department Komsomol and a member of the overall Komsomol committee, Abram was held responsible for "lack of vigilance." When the district committee sent a representative to investigate, Abram was ordered to confess to lack of vigilance and to denounce his friends. He refused. At a meeting of the Komsomol membership of the German department, the district representative demanded his removal from his Komsomol positions. What happened next was unprecedented. In an open vote, the membership by a large majority rejected the district committee's recommendation. Abram served until the end of the semester, resigning only in order to give more time to his studies in his final year.

However, the district committee got its revenge when it came to job assignments. Whereas those of Abram's classmates who had weathered the storm were offered highly paid, prestigious positions in radio, the military, the NKVD, and in research institutions, he was assigned to a low-paid job teaching German in a secondary school in a factory district on the outskirts of Moscow. At the same time, he was pressed to move out of the dorm.

It was this chain of events that led to his job at the Foreign Languages Publishing House. Lev Kopelev, a classmate and close friend, recommended him to the woman who was married to Ozrin, the head of the German section. As a special favor to Lev, Ozrin hired Abram and arranged for him to be given a place to live on Kapelsky.

* * *

I had given up all hope of returning to America, even for a visit. It was clear that I was not going to be granted an exit visa, so there was no use applying. Moreover, now that my life was tied up with another's, I could not take steps of that kind on my own. Abram, too, was convinced that it was futile for me to apply at present; in fact, it might be dangerous.

My life was more settled than it had been since I left home. I no longer had to make all my decisions by myself. I felt personally secure. We had a circle of good friends. We were young, enjoying ourselves in this lull before the storm.

Abram's friends welcomed me. The friends he was closest to and whom I came to know best were four former classmates—Lev (Lyova) Kopelev, David Kugel, Max Gassel, and Yasha Liberman.

Lyova had a ebullient personality. His presence filled the room the moment he entered it. Everywhere he went, he attracted followers, both male and female. At the age of sixteen, he had performed some minor service for the Trotskyite opposition in Ukraine where he lived and, when he was a student at the Institute, someone informed against him. As a result, he was expelled from the Komsomol, despite Abram's recommendation that he be given only a reprimand. After appealing his case, Lyova was eventually reinstated. An outstanding student, he graduated with his class and was now in graduate school at the newly opened Institute of History and Philosophy (IFLI) where he was also a talented teacher. Lyova did not have a mean bone in his body. He never bad-mouthed anyone, not even the people who had tried and nearly succeeded in doing him in at the Institute. His trusting nature and gullibility had gotten him into trouble before and would do so later, but he himself did not change.

Lyova was an "old" married man. Abram and I were frequent visitors at his home before the war and I got to know the family quite well. He had married his boyhood sweetheart and now had two small daughters, Maya, three, and Lena, one-and-a-half. His wife Nadya was a student and then a graduate of the Mendeleyev Chemical Engineering Institute. His father was a highly regarded agronomist whose place of work had given him two connecting rooms in a communal apartment where they all lived. Lyova's mother, a tall, energetic, vivacious woman, whom Lyova resembled, dominated the household.

Abram had a very special fondness for Lyova, whom he placed in the category of people too brilliant to be judged by ordinary standards. (I, too, was fond of Lyova—it was impossible not to be—but I did not agree with Abram's assessment.) Therefore, he did not take offense when Lyova forgot or broke appointments ("He is so much in demand. What can you expect?"); nor did Abram judge him for his numerous sexual escapades ("What can he do if women throw themselves at him? Say 'no'?"), or for making promises and then not keeping them, ("He doesn't do it on purpose").

In a way, Lyova was not so different from David Kugel, though culturally, they had very little in common. Both were fervent believers in Marxism-Leninism long after some of their contemporaries had begun to question the tenets. It took a great deal to shake their faith—if indeed their faith was ever shaken.

David, from a small town in Byelorussia, had grown up in a religious home where Yiddish was the household language. He had strayed far from the fold. David was uncritically loyal to the Communist Party and the Soviet government. He was typical of the stratum of Jews of poor, working-class, or struggling artisanal origins for whom the revolution had opened the door to education and professional opportunities. Even when it became impossible to close one's eyes to the blatant anti-Semitism of the postwar years, David found excuses. But he was a devoted friend, always eager and available to give help when help was needed.

The only one of Abram's friends who joined the Party even before finishing at the Institute, David's record was clear. Upon graduation, he was assigned to a very good position in the NKVD. David's job came with a room in a communal apartment in central Moscow, and he sent for his parents immediately. His parents were sweet people, rather bewildered by their son's achievements. His mother tried her best to keep a kosher home and David, despite his views, did not argue or try to influence his parents. Their place was like a crowded railroad station, with visitors from the provinces coming and going all the time. I would hold that up to Abram as an example of what I did not want our place to become.

Max Gassel and I had a common bond. He had been in Birobidzhan when I had been there, though we had not met. Born and raised in Riga, Latvia, his family had gone to Birobidzhan in 1931 for reasons similar to my parents'—to help build a Jewish socialist homeland. He left Birobidzhan to enter the Institute of Foreign Languages in Moscow. Max knew Russian, Yiddish, German, and Latvian from childhood and spoke all four languages fluently. (My parents were impressed by his beautiful, literary Yiddish when they met him during their visit to Moscow in 1957.) He had a mother and a sister in Riga whom he had not seen since he left home.

We saw a lot of Max, for he dropped in often. Max had married recently, but he never came with his wife and I did not meet her at that time. She was a student in the French department and the couple lived with her family. Apparently, he did not feel free to invite his friends to his home. The wedding present Max gave us is the only one I can recall having received. It was a German sex manual entitled *Mann und Weib* [*Husband and Wife*] which he had found in a second-hand book shop.

Abram's other good friend did not fit in with the rest. Yasha Liberman was not a member of the Komsomol, nor was he active in extracurricular undertakings. Yasha came from a well-to-do professional family. As a child, he had been educated by governesses. Though an excellent student, he had had an unpleasant time at the Institute, and was constantly badgered and harassed. Abram seemed to have been his only friend. Yasha lived with his widowed mother and was the apple of her eye. As long as his mother was alive, Abram used to visit her regularly. Yasha used to come and see us often, always bringing flowers or candy. (He was one of the first of Abram's friends to be killed in the war.)

The first months of our marriage coincided with the escalation of the war in Europe, culminating in the fall of Paris in July 1940. From the press, we got only an approximate picture of the events. Germany, according to the Soviet press, merely wanted to end the war quickly and bring peace to Europe. Great Britain and France were "imperialist aggressors" who were to blame for the war in the first place. Whatever people may have felt about the Nazis and wherever their sympathies may have lain, the general population believed that Soviet foreign policy had kept the country out of the war. Now that the Western powers were fighting among themselves, the Soviet Union could feel secure after years of having been surrounded by enemies.

There were plenty of signs that such feelings of security were illusory: Soviet participation in the partition of Poland, the Finnish war, the annexation of Bessarabia, the annexation of the Baltic republics in 1940. These were not the actions of a neutral country hoping to keep out of the fight. There were domestic signs, too: the reorganization of the army after the Finnish war and, especially, the harsh new labor law enacted in June 1940. That law had such an impact on the public that it drove everything else out of their minds.

No attempt was made to prepare public opinion for the new law. Formally, it was proposed by the Central Council of Soviet Trade Unions, supposedly the representative of the working masses. The new law increased the workday for everyone to eight hours. (Until then, factory workers had enjoyed a seven-hour workday.) Moreover, the new law prohibited a change of jobs without the consent of the administration and imposed stiff penalties, including prison, for violations. The penalties for tardiness affected the largest number of people and were felt most keenly: If one were twenty minutes late, disciplinary action on the job with a twenty-five percent reduction in pay for up to six months; two minutes late—first offense, a reprimand; second offense, a strict reprimand with entry into your work record; the third offense was counted the same as a twenty-minute tardiness.

No excuses for lateness were accepted, despite the fact that public transportation was completely unreliable. Public conveyances were few and far between and usually so crowded that it was almost impossible to board. The early morning frenzy was palpable. Whoever could, walked to work. I walked. Abram walked. Mussia walked. But Maria was a last-minute person, and so was Ahsia. We worried about them every day. Punching the clock in their stead was out of the question, for there was always someone watching. Mussia would phone Maria early in the morning. Abram and I would knock on her door as we passed by. The situation was nerve-racking. Ahsia solved the problem by getting permission to work at home, as did several others (insufficient space at the office was the justification). Somehow, Maria would always manage to rush in at the very last minute.

That summer, Abram and I decided that I should return to the university and complete my education. I arranged to be reinstated in the fall of 1940, and in August, I joyously quit my job, which I had never liked and was not much good at. Abram took his vacation and we went to Rostov-on-the-Don so I could meet his family and friends.

Rostov, a growing urban center situated on the bank of the Don River, had several major projects as a result of the Five-Year Plans. The city had been the scene of fierce fighting during the Civil War. Abram had vivid recollections of the disruptions and dangers of those years. He also recalled with gratitude the American assistance given the famine-stricken, war-torn regions. He was surprised that I, an American, had never heard of these activities through the American Relief Administration led by Herbert Hoover. To Abram's generation, Hoover was a figure who deserved high regard.

The population of Rostov had a large proportion of Don Cossacks, black-haired, black-eyed, wiry men and women. A southern city (there is another Rostov in the north of Russia), it was livelier than Moscow and had more going on outdoors. Fresh fruit was plentiful and August was watermelon season (I was astonished at the quantities of fruit Abram and his friends could consume at one time). The housing situation in Rostov was not as critical as it was in Moscow. The influx of peasants from the surrounding countryside had caused crowding among the newcomers, but the old-timers had not been compelled to give up their private apartments.

Abram's parents lived on the ground floor in a large apartment, one room of which served as a workshop.

This was a very different milieu from any I had known. Abram's father was illiterate, even in Yiddish, which was very rare among Jewish men. He had learned his trade at a very early age and was a fine ladies' tailor with a citywide reputation. Despite poor health (he suffered from stomach ulcers), he worked very hard and was a good provider for his small family, much better than the husbands of his wife's five sisters who were engineers, book-keepers, and factory or office workers. Because Abram's mother was the eldest sister and the only one who had completed the gymnasium, the family felt that she had married beneath her station. However, they did not hesitate to accept the generous gifts of food, clothing, and money that she regularly gave them. She tried to keep her generosity secret from her husband, but of course he knew what was going on and resented it. This was a prickly situation of long standing. Not only did Abram's mother help her family, but she also had the reputation of a good angel in the neighborhood, ready to come to the assistance of anyone who needed her. I mistrusted her goodness, especially as I knew from Abram how demanding she had been of him when he was growing up. Abram had always sided with his mother, but was beginning to see his father's point of view as he once again carried pots and parcels of food to various relatives.

The main topic of conversation at the dinner table concerned money. Once, Abram's father told me how much his son had cost him from birth and indicated that he expected to be paid back. This immediately prejudiced me against him. Politically, too, we were far apart, and Abram and his father had been at odds for a long time. This had led to many quarrels when he had lived at home. Whereas Abram had joined the Komsomol, supported the government's policies, and believed in a socialist future, his father had a burning hatred of the Soviet authorities and the Soviet bureaucracy. I could not understand how this poor Jew from Liublin province, Poland, could fail to appreciate what the Soviet government had done for the Jews. I know now that I was unfair. Abram's mother's generosity must have been sincere or the entire neighborhood would not have been so fond of her. And what I took for avarice on the part of his father may have been an attempt by a hard-working man to get some of the appreciation he deserved. But youth can be intolerant. I was unhappy with my in-laws and they were unhappy with me.

Nevertheless, the two weeks in Rostov were enjoyable. I liked Abram's cousins, his friend Valya and Valya's girlfriend, Marianna, an Armenian girl who lived upstairs from Abram's parents. And, we were very well fed. Abram's mother was a good cook. I can still remember the taste of her specialty—paper-thin pancakes filled with meat, cheese, or pitted cherries. I never met anyone who made them like she did.

In September, I started school again, entering as a second-year student in the history department. My original class had graduated the previous June, but there were still students who remembered me, some of them graduate students. Every once in a while, someone would come up to me and congratulate me on my release from prison. Not everyone believed me when I said that I had not been arrested.

I was back in my element. I enjoyed studying. I enjoyed learning. My goals now were different from what they had been. I no longer had fantasies about being called upon to help bring about world revolution. Now my goal was to be recommended for graduate studies and, after that, to have a career as a research fellow at one of the Academy of Sciences institutes. Not only would I be able to spend the rest of my life doing what I liked best, but this career course would also give me a measure of independence, I thought, with a good salary and much more flexibility than was possible in most jobs.

Therefore, I was not overjoyed to find myself pregnant towards the end of that fall. If abortions had still been legal, I would undoubtedly have had one. I was perfectly willing to break the law, but I could not find a reliable doctor willing to take the risk. What could I do? There was not much choice. I would finish the school year and then we would see. The baby was due in June 1941.

Financially, our situation was difficult, and now we had a greater worry than before. My stipend was less than my salary had been. Abram was still in a junior position and did not expect to make much headway in the publishing house unless he took an administrative job—which he did not want to do. He was scouting around for another job, letting all his friends know that he was looking. In January, a friend called and told him that he had recommended him for a language job in the army. Soon afterwards, Abram was summoned for an interview. He filled out a long questionnaire, agonizing over whether my being foreign born might hurt his chances. In February 1941, he was offered a position on a German-language newspaper published by the political administration of the Red Army in (newly Soviet) Riga, Latvia. This was not a civilian position. It meant being commissioned as a political officer, the equivalent of junior lieutenant. The salary was much higher than what he was earning. There was also the attraction of living in what was still a foreign city. We both agreed that this was an opportunity not be to missed. Our main question was whether he should go by himself or whether I should drop my studies and go with him. We both felt that I ought to complete the semester. I assured him I would be fine without him. I would take my final exams as far ahead of schedule as possible, and join him in Riga in time for the baby to be born.

Before he left for Riga, we went to formalize our marriage at ZAGS. I was four months pregnant. It was Abram's sense of orderliness that prompted this action. The procedure was simple, with none of the "wedding palace" ceremonies that evolved in the later Soviet era. We signed the book and were given a marriage certificate dated February 8, 1941. I chose to keep my maiden name, Mackler.

A few days later, I saw my husband off at the Riga railroad station. He looked handsome in his uniform. As usual with me, I showed no tears, no fears. I had everything planned—exams at the end of May and early June, then Riga in the middle of June.

It never occurred to me that the war in Europe might interfere. As far as I knew, this would be a new beginning.

# 13
## The Outbreak of War—1941

Looking back, I wonder that I did not take the possibility of the Soviet Union's becoming involved in the war more seriously. The very fact that a German-language army newspaper was established in a border area should have alerted me. But the Soviet media played down Nazi policies and made no mention of the persecution, arrests, murders, and bombing of refugees. Reports of air battles over Britain were biased in Germany's favor. Germany seemed fully occupied consolidating its positions.

With my husband away, no money worries, an easy pregnancy, and no obligations, I concentrated on my studies, aiming to finish up my course work and take my exams as far ahead of schedule as permitted. Abram telephoned several times a week. He liked his job and his boss, editor-in-chief Colonel Jantzen. Those few months, February through May 1941, were a period of calm for me. I felt relaxed and detached from everyday anxieties, and planned to travel to Riga as soon as I finished my classes. When Abram started hinting that at such an advanced stage of my pregnancy, it was perhaps not such a good idea for me to leave Moscow and my friends, I paid little attention to him. As my departure date drew closer, however, Abram became more insistent, urging me to cancel my plans. But I dismissed his exhortations as his typical overprotectiveness and thought he was feeling a touch of panic at the prospect of fatherhood.

I had some bureaucratic details to deal with. Latvia was closed to ordinary travelers, as were all the newly acquired Baltic and Western Byelorussian territories. It was necessary to obtain a travel permit, and that meant filling out forms, always an anxiety-producing procedure for me because of my foreign background. To my relief, the papers went through without a hitch.

I arrived in Riga on Sunday, June 15, 1941. As the train drew into the station, I climbed onto my seat and stuck my head out of the window, which was open only from the top. Abram was standing on the platform, looking worried. When he caught sight of me, however, his face broke into a surprised smile. He had not expected to find me so spry.

He was billeted in an apartment that belonged to a young Jewish couple with one child, a boy of about eight. They welcomed me warmly and invited us in for a delicious meal. It was immediately obvious that they were very fond of Abram.

The apartment was in a solid old building with high ceilings and thick walls on a quiet, tree-lined street. Our room was large and airy, completely private, much nicer than our room in Moscow. Surely, I was better off here. Why had he tried to dissuade me from coming? He could see that I was in good condition.

Yes, he was pleased to find me so well and he was happy to see me, but concern for my condition was not the reason why he had tried to keep me from coming. What he had to say was a complete surprise to me. In Riga, everyone listened to foreign broadcasts. For the past few weeks, he said, the British Broadcasting Company (BBC) had been broadcasting warnings claiming that the Germans were about to attack Russia. War between Germany and Russia was imminent! The rumors had been rife there for weeks, though in Moscow we had had no inkling of them. Very few people had access to uncensored information from abroad; and those who did were not talking.

Abram had not been able to tell me this over the phone because the official response to the warnings was that they were the work of provocateurs attempting to undermine the Soviet Union's friendly relations with Germany. Abram, as well as his colleagues on the newspaper and the local population, did not subscribe to that view. They took the warnings seriously. Abram wished that I had trusted his judgment. However, here I was. All we could do was hope for the best. Perhaps it was indeed a false alarm.

My first few days in Riga went by pleasantly. I took long walks, exploring the city. Riga still retained the ambience of its recent past—it had small shops and privately owned, well-kept apartment buildings on tree-lined streets, Gothic churches, and stone buildings hundreds of years old. One of the things that struck me about Riga was how quiet it was at night. All street doors were locked at ten o'clock. There were no intercoms. A late-arriving visitor would have to be met at the entrance to the building. Complaints about noise were taken seriously. After noisy Moscow, this was a relief to me. Browsing was fun. Because of the travel restrictions, there had not been a great influx of people from other parts of the Soviet Union and there were still many things to buy that were not available in Moscow. There were few Russians in Riga, except for the military, their families, some visiting writers, and performers.

At five A.M. on June 22, 1941, the phone rang. It was for Abram and it was a summons to his headquarters. Abram left immediately, calling me an hour later. He said that the Germans had attacked at three o'clock that morning! They had bombed Minsk and other border towns! I was to go to the railroad station at once and take the first train back to Moscow, leaving my luggage behind.

"What about you? When will I see you?" I asked.

"I don't know. Don't wait for me. In a few hours, everybody will know and it will be much harder to get out of the city."

"If this is war, who knows when we will see each other again? I'll wait until you come home," I replied.

I was adamant and I persisted. I would not leave without seeing him first.

How I wished I had not been pregnant! Had I not been pregnant, I could have stayed with my husband, gone with him wherever he went. With my knowledge of English and my serviceable German, I could have been useful. Here I was—trapped!

At twelve noon, Molotov addressed the nation in a radio broadcast. He announced that the Germans had "perfidiously" attacked the Soviet Union without a declaration of war and that the two nations were now at war. Shortly afterwards, Abram came home and we hurried off to the railroad station.

The station was so mobbed, we could not get near the ticket office. The boarding gates were locked and the area cordoned off, probably in anticipation of people trying to board without tickets. The crush was dangerous and we decided to go back to the apartment. It was not far and we walked. Planes flew overhead. As we stood under a bridge, Abram pointed out the swastikas on their wings. I was absolutely unafraid. Many years later, Abram told me that he had marveled at my calmness and wondered whether I fully understood what was happening. Perhaps I was in shock. Perhaps pregnancy had something to do with it, nature's biological defense. When the planes were out of sight, we hurried on our way, taking shelter in doorways whenever planes appeared. My head was empty. Not a single thought about what the future might hold for us entered my mind. I left everything to my husband.

The Germans did not bomb Riga then or later. They knew they had many supporters in the city, both trained "moles" and ordinary Latvians who hated the Russians. We termed them the "fifth column," an expression from the Spanish Civil War, meaning the enemy within: Franco had four columns in the field; his supporters behind the loyalist lines were called the "fifth" column.

At the apartment, we found the family distraught. Our return only deepened their distress and undermined their faith in the Red Army as protector. They had no illusions as to what awaited them if the Germans took Riga. Neither did they trust their fellow countrymen. The fascists had been strong in Latvia before the Soviet occupation and Latvia had a history of anti-Semitism. What would happen to them? What would happen to us?

Abram went back to his office. Later in the day, I had visitors, his friend Max Gassel's mother and sister, whose acquaintance I had made earlier in the week. Max had told his mother and sister to get out of Riga by any means possible, to go to Abram for help.

The two women took in our situation at a glance. I can see them now, the sad smile on the old woman's face, the desperation in the eyes of the younger woman. They stayed a short while, said good-bye, and left. We never heard from them again or learned what became of them. The Red Army retreated from Riga so precipitously that many whose lives were especially at risk, including some Soviet army families, were stranded among a hostile population. The situation was even more desperate because many regular army officers had been summoned to take part in maneuvers and were nowhere near the border areas where they had been stationed. They could not get back home, so their families were left to fend for themselves. The Soviet military was completely, criminally, unprepared. Over the years, the true story of the war and Stalin's role and responsibility for the enormous losses of lives and territory has come out in bits and pieces from Western sources. To some degree, we found out about it in the Soviet Union during Khrushchev's regime. More was learned in the 1980s.

But that day, Jantzen gave Abram a letter addressed to the Riga station master and told him to go home and not come back until he had put me on a train going to Moscow. The office staff was packing to leave almost immediately so Abram would have to find out where they went and catch up with them. I have much to be grateful for to Colonel Jantzen. He could have ordered my husband to remain on duty and leave me to deal with the situation as best I could. That is what happened in many instances.

At daybreak the next morning, we set out for the station. It was pandemonium, worse than the day before. Outside the station master's office, people were pushing, shouting, waving official papers, calling for special treatment. Abram's requests to make way for me were ignored. Nobody paid attention to the rules that permitted pregnant women, women with young children, and invalids to go to the head of the line, any line. We stood at the edge of the crowd, not knowing what to do next.

Then we had a stroke of luck. A young woman came out of an office in another part of the station, surveyed the crowd, and beckoned to me. We responded as unobtrusively as possible. She invited us into her office, asked us to be seated, examined our identification papers, and told us to wait for her. She was the station master's assistant and, having noticed me earlier when she reported for work, she realized how badly I needed help. She returned in ten or fifteen minutes with a ticket for me, reserved seat, lower berth, "soft" class. She told us to come back later that afternoon, one hour before boarding time, and she would see me through the gate.

We spent the few hours left to us at the apartment, then took leave of the family, and walked to the station. Abram carried my two small suitcases. He himself left the apartment for good that night. We never heard from the family and I am afraid that they perished. They had my Moscow address and would surely have written to me had they survived.

The young woman was as good as her word. She escorted us through the gate and spoke to the conductor, who allowed us onto the train so I could settle in before the rush. She gave me a letter to mail to her family. With her straight blond hair, blue eyes, and fair skin, I had taken her for a Latvian but, no, she was Russian from a small town near Moscow. She wished she were going with us, she said, but all railroad personnel had been placed under military orders and could not leave their posts. I've often wondered what became of her, another person to whom I probably owe my life.

Abram stayed with me until the train pulled out. When the other three occupants of my compartment arrived, we went out onto the platform and talked in whispers. By now, I was no longer in shock and we spoke of what lay ahead. Abram was worried about his parents and asked me to keep in close touch with them. We did not pretend to be optimistic. Although he acknowledged that we might be out of touch for long periods, Abram said that I was never to lose faith in him or in the final outcome. His last words to me were a warning that the war would be a long one, that the Germans might succeed in capturing Soviet territory.

I remember his words well. They were contrary to everything we had been taught. Over and over again, we had been told that the Red Army was strong, prepared to rebuff any attack. Right was on our side and right would always win. An ubiquitous slogan for years had been: "We don't want a foot of anyone else's territory, but we won't yield an inch of our own."

The departure bell rang. We embraced. I felt the tears on his cheeks. Or were they my own? My last image of Abram was of him standing on the platform and waving until he disappeared from sight.

The train crawled along and came to a stop on the outskirts of the city. It remained there for twenty-four hours.

It took four days to get to Moscow (normally, it was an overnight journey). The train stopped frequently, sometimes for several hours. German dive bombers attacked railroad stations, junctions, and trains. Miraculously, our train got through unharmed. We picked up passengers from the bombed trains behind us and ahead of us, mostly women with children who told us of low-flying planes strafing people as they ran from the trains for cover. Before long, we were eight women and several children in a compartment meant for four. The air was so thick, I could hardly breathe. My food did not last long, shared among so many, but I did not feel hungry, only horribly uncomfortable.

As if the enormity of the events was not enough, two of the ticketed passengers from Riga were rah-rah trade-union officials in the Party. These two middle-aged women constantly mouthed clichés and slogans, and were contemptuous of personal feelings. Consequently, they would not leave me alone with my thoughts and my grief—for now, at last, I was grieving, grieving for my husband, for myself, for my future child. They kept telling me that I should be proud that my husband was defending the Soviet homeland, and they denounced my slightest expressions of anxiety, sadness, or doubt as weakness of spirit, unbecoming to a member of the Komsomol.

There was no one at the station to meet me. Abram had cabled my friends, but the train was so off schedule that no one knew when it would arrive or what had become of me. I phoned my apartment. Marussia Meshcherina, who had been staying in our room, answered and hurried to the station, which was only a few blocks away. We walked slowly, Marussia carrying my suitcases. The farmers' market across the street from the station was empty, as were the shops we passed. There was very little traffic on the usually busy avenue. The few worried-looking pedestrians all seemed in a hurry.

Marussia brought me up to date about events at the university. The remaining spring session exams had been deferred. All able-bodied students had been drafted and formed into work teams to build anti-tank barriers on the approaches to Moscow. There had been a run on the stores right after Molotov's speech. As a result, they were empty of food, soap, and other essentials. (Soap, sugar, and salt were always the first to go in hoarding panics.) The city was tense, agog with rumors of German parachutists, spies, saboteurs. She warned me to be careful, as anyone speaking Russian with an accent might arouse suspicion. Marussia had volunteered for the service and already had orders to report for duty. She expected to join a partisan outfit in her native Byelorussia. She left the same day and I never heard from her again.

I left word with Maria's neighbor that I was at home and, later that evening, Maria came upstairs to see me. Her husband had been drafted. She was terribly worried about her five-year-old daughter whom she had sent earlier in the month to the Comintern's summer camp for children near Gorky in the upper Volga region. A large group of children of publishing house staff had been sent there, among them Mussia's five-year-old son, Liz's three-year-old son, and her sister's three-year-old daughter. Fortunately for Maria, her mother-in-law, a trained art historian on the staff of the Pushkin Museum, had taken her vacation and accompanied the child. Eventually, Maria heard from her. She had rented a room in a nearby village and planned to stay there for the duration. She took a menial job at the camp and remained there until the children were allowed to come home nearly three years later. It was a long time before parents were able to visit their children. A school was established and life was as normal as it could be for the children under the circumstances. Maria, Mussia, and Liz managed to visit the camp a few times.

Maria, too, cautioned me about the rumors. She told me that all Germans (that is, persons who had "German" as their nationality in their identity papers) had been ordered to report to the local police and were shipped out of the city, often without being allowed to go home for their belongings. The Germans in Moscow were either Volga Germans[1] or anti-Nazi refugees from Germany. The publishing house administration managed to extricate some of its employees who had been caught in the net, among them the printer Hans Freudenreich (who later held a high position in the East German government) and Hilda Angarova, who, though Jewish, had given her nationality as German in her internal passport.

There had been arrests, too. The Argentinean Guerra and the Italian Lombardi who lived in our building had been arrested the day after war was declared. Guerra left a Russian wife and two young children; Lombardi left a Russian Jewish wife and two young daughters.

Maria was not working at the publishing house any more. The outbreak of the war had given rise to an immediate need for persons with language skills. As a result, the publishing house was asked to send some of its staff to various institutions. Maria and a senior staff member in the German section were loaned to the Chief Political Administration of the Soviet Army. Soon afterwards, Mussia was co-opted as a translator at the radio committee.

Mussia came to see me the next morning. She told me that Liz's husband Grisha had joined the Home Guard (*opolcheniye*), thus named after a similar civilian defense in the war of 1612 against the Poles who had occupied Moscow. The majority of the present volunteers were ill-adapted, untrained intellectuals who were decimated in fierce battles in the early months of war.

At Mussia's urging, I decided to spend the night at her place. In the middle of the night, I began to have labor pains. The maternity hospital was about two blocks away. Mussia walked me to the hospital and hurried home to get ready to go to work.

I had a prolonged and difficult labor. Much of the time, I was all alone in the delivery room. The nurses' aides, middle-aged peasant women, were not sympathetic. They thought I was making too much fuss and dubbed me *prichitalka*, which means "one who laments," because I talked to myself constantly, most of the time in a language they did not understand. On June 30, 1941, after thirty-six hours of labor, I gave birth to a daughter.

Afterwards, I became critically ill. I had an extremely high fever and was delirious. My arms and thighs were black and blue from injections. I was given oxygen to breathe and cups of a revolting liquid that the nurse said was

---

1. Volga Germans were descendants of Germans invited to settle in Russia by Catherine II in the eighteenth century. They were to serve as models of efficiency and industry for surrounding Russian peasants.

blood. The head doctor told the Laskers, when they came to inquire, that there was little hope that I would survive. This information surprised me very much when Reba Lasker told me about it later. It had not entered my head that I might die. I followed the doctor's orders without a murmur and was held up as a model patient to women suffering from inflammation of the nipples. These women were in great pain, though they were in no danger and complained loudly. I was not in pain—I was just very, very tired. The official paper from the hospital said that I suffered from complications due to a previous condition, but I do not know whether that assessment was accurate.

All this time, I nursed the baby. She was brought to me at three-hour intervals when I was at least semi-conscious. I loved having her near me and was reluctant to let her go when they came to take her away.

From mid-July on, there were almost nightly air-raid alerts. Only a few enemy planes got through, as the anti-aircraft defense did a fine job of driving off the German bombers. However, since there was always a chance that a plane might penetrate our defenses, many people did not wait for the alerts, but spent the nights in shelters, most of them underground in subway stations. In the hospital, all patients and their infants were moved into the basement shelter after supper. I hated being cramped there with hysterical women and crying babies. After a few uncomfortable nights, I persuaded the nurses to leave me alone in the ward. All alone on the top floor, silent after the day's commotion, I felt at peace. I paid no attention to the sirens.

Visitors were not allowed. Now and then a friend would come by, talk with the doctor, and send me a note. Most of my friends were bound by a state-of-emergency work schedule and had very little time. Only Ahsia and Igor came to the hospital nearly every day to bring me my mail.

Igor was now house superintendent of our building. The former superintendent had been drafted and Igor had taken his job, his first real position since he had moved in with Ahsia. The position of house superintendent was a sensitive one, especially in a building full of foreigners, and especially now, in wartime. The house superintendent was in daily contact with the local militia and was responsible for reporting visitors and illegal residents. He was connected with the local housing authorities and was often questioned by the secret police. In addition, he was now in contact with the military authorities. A charming, well-spoken man, much better educated than the run-of-the-mill house superintendents, Igor easily ingratiated himself with these agencies and, before the summer was over, had acquired access to the tenants' dossiers. He looked up his own dossier with the military and removed damaging material from it. He also did us a favor without being asked. He discovered that neither Abram nor I was registered in the room we occupied. I was still supposed to be living in the room I had moved into when I had first come to Kapelsky; Abram was registered in the dormitory room downstairs. Such a bureaucratic snag could have caused us a great deal of trouble. Igor corrected the record.

During those early weeks of the war, Abram wrote to me nearly every day. His letters were on scraps of paper, on the back of forms, even on wrapping paper; sometimes in envelopes, other times folded into triangles. Postage was not required of servicemen. His letters followed the Soviet retreat in the northwestern sector of the front: June 29th, Pskov; July 7th, Novgorod; July 29th, Krestsi; August 9th, Valdai. After that, place names were no longer mentioned. His letters were also filled with anxiety. "I don't know what to think. I haven't heard from you. I don't know whether you arrived safely or what has happened to you. I don't know where you are. Do you have enough money?" He wrote to our friends, to our neighbors, to my step-uncle. I wrote, but my letters did not reach him. The army was retreating so fast that the mail could not keep up with him. His first letter indicating that he had heard from me was dated August 9th. He had received my card dated July 2nd, telling him that he was the father of a daughter and asking him to suggest a name. In that letter, he wrote that he and his buddies had drunk to our health and had suggested the name Victoria as expressing our faith in our final victory in the war. When I came home from the hospital, I entered that name in the birth certificate, but I never thought of her as Victoria and never called her by that name. Victory was so long in coming, and so many tragic things happened before it did.

Abram's letters were wonderful for my morale. As long as they kept coming, I knew that he was alive. In his first letter, he wrote that he had returned to the newspaper office to find Jantzen and the entire staff gone. There was a note for him stating the general direction they had taken. A driver and another stranded officer from a different department were waiting for him and they set out at once. The other officer, who had spent part of his childhood in the United States, spoke English and German. His name was a well-known one. He was the son of Martens, an Old Bolshevik, famed for his part in one of the Russian Civil War episodes. The driver was the nineteen-year-old youth I believe to have been the Black child that Loren Miller and I tried to talk with long ago, at in the children's home in Bolshevo.

I had been in the hospital for nearly a month when the head doctor's turn for night duty came around. Horrified when she discovered that I was not being moved to the shelter with the other patients, she gave orders that I was to be moved with everybody else. This was unbearable and I begged her to discharge me. She was reluctant—I was still very weak—but she agreed when I promised to leave the city. Though there was no organized evacuation as yet, the city authorities were urging women with young children to leave Moscow. I told the doctor I would go to my husband's parents in

Rostov and, on that condition, she discharged me. I had been in the hospital for twenty-eight days.

Home was an empty room, no loving husband, no solicitous relatives. I was alone in a new and unfamiliar situation, for I knew next to nothing about caring for an infant. Most of my friends had either left the city or were working round the clock and had no control over their time. My step-uncle and his family had left Moscow immediately after the war broke out to join their elder daughter who had been assigned to a librarian position in Novosibirsk upon graduating from college. I sat down and wept.

Help came from an unexpected quarter. Among the residents of Kapel-sky was a widower named Krause and his teen-age daughter, Polish Jews from Germany. Krause had been a colleague of my husband's. Father and daughter came to see me. They told me that they had spoken with their domestic, Frossia, and that she was willing to work for me as long as I needed her. They themselves were planning to leave Moscow within the next few days. They had offered to take Frossia with them, but she had declined their offer.

I don't know what I would have done without Frossia. She came that very day and took over the grocery shopping (which was an activity more akin to foraging), the cooking, and cleaning. She also found time to sit outside with the baby.

Money was no problem for the time being. Immediately after he was commissioned, Abram had arranged for me to receive a family allotment (*attestat*), a document entitling me to receive a portion of his salary at any military commissariat (*voenkomat*) in the country. The allotment was made out for 500 rubles a month, a considerable sum, and the maximum he was allowed at the time.

Frossia stayed with me only a short time, but her help came at a crucial point in my life and I remember her with gratitude. She was an illiterate peasant woman, short and round, with a weatherbeaten face. She was probably only in her thirties, but looked older, and was kindhearted and scrupulously honest. When the Krauses left, she moved into their room. Like other domestics, she had slept in the kitchen—and unlike many who stayed behind in Moscow when a German breakthrough seemed imminent, she did not pilfer or steal. When the Krauses returned from evacuation three years later, they found all their belongings intact and the rent paid up (they sent her money regularly). Many evacuees returned to find their homes looted or, worse, occupied, even though they had sent rent money all along.

A nurse from the natal clinic came to check on me and instructed me in the care of my child. She told me never to pick the baby up when she cried, once I had determined that she was dry and that nothing was hurting her. Otherwise, she said, I'd become a slave to her. (Aunt Liza gave me the same advice when I had come to see her during my pregnancy.) I tried to follow instructions, but the baby cried incessantly, especially at night. I'd sit by her and cry, too. Finally, I'd give in and pick her up. She would stop crying, but would not sleep, and neither would I. Only when Frossia took her outside was I able to snatch some rest.

The air raids continued. The bath premises in the basement had been fixed up as a shelter, and for the first few nights, I went down. Maria, when she was at home, or Dora, her sister who was staying with her, would come upstairs to help me when the sirens sounded. But I found it too much of an effort to run up and down the stairs. What would be would be. I was too tired to worry. After I stopped going down to the shelter, Maria or Dora, or both, would come to stay with me until the all-clear signal.

My entire being was now centered on my daughter. Not only the practical, time-consuming aspects of caring for her, exacerbated by the difficulty of obtaining the basic necessities or anything that might have lightened my burden, but all my thoughts and all my emotions were concentrated on her. The intensity of my feelings overwhelmed me. I had not expected to feel as strongly as I did. I had never been one to gush over babies and I used to be amused and a bit bored by my friends' talk about their children. Of course, I had said, I would love my baby, but I would maintain a sense of proportion. I would be a sensible mother.

It did not happen that way. I became obsessed. I hated to let her out of my sight. I felt her pain, for she must have been in pain. Why else did she cry so much? I felt inadequate and, at times, desperate. And I had no one to turn to for the mature advice and loving help I needed so badly.

I decided to go ahead with my plan to go to Rostov. As far as I can recall, I was not aware of the precarious military situation in the south of Russia. I left for Rostov in the second week of August, receiving a letter forwarded from Abram advising me *not* to go only after I had already arrived. The letter was dated August 9th. He wrote, "I have seen so many refugees lately that I really don't know whether it is better to head for some place else or to stay where you are." But, in any case, he recommended that I stay away from Rostov because of the Don Cossacks' well-known anti-Soviet and anti-Semitic sentiments. As he put it, "I don't much like the population there."

Rostov was a very different city from the one I visited two summers before. Gone were the lively crowds in the streets and the parks. People hurried about their business, eager to get home before dark and the blackouts. Dusk came earlier than in Moscow. The absence of men in the streets was noticeable.

All of Abram's male cousins and friends were in the army, gone to the front either as draftees or volunteers. The women and children came to see me and the baby, and they offered their help. I would not accept help, however, either from them or from my in-laws. My obsession—I can only call it that—became even stronger. I would not let my mother-in-law help care for the baby, nor would I follow her advice. We did not argue. No one crossed me. They must have felt terrible, but were positively meek, much more understanding, apparently, than I was. Marianna Allakhverdova from upstairs, whom I liked very much, could not understand my attitude. Aunt Zina, as Abram's mother was known, was beloved throughout the neighborhood for her kindness.

This is an episode of which I am not proud and over which I continue to feel regret and shame. I still do not fully understand my behavior. I can only think that my hostility to Abram's family's political views was sharpened in this time of the country's life-and-death struggle, for Abram's parents did not believe the accounts of German atrocities. His father recalled the German occupation in the last war and asserted that Germans were civilized people. He believed that the press reports about Nazi atrocities against the civilian population were the usual lies of Soviet propaganda. His denial of the situation was aided by the press's silence about the Nazis' efforts to single out the Jews.

My days were filled with dread of the coming nights. The Germans were not bombing Rostov regularly, but incendiary bombs were dropped occasionally and reconnoitering planes flew over us frequently. There were air-raid alerts nearly every night. The improvised shelter was down the street in the cellar of a house, and could not provide adequate protection if a bomb actually hit it. The wardens would not allow anyone to remain at home, so when the siren sounded, we had to stumble along a bumpy, pitted sidewalk in the pitch dark and back again the same way. I was worse off than I had been in Moscow.

Worse off in more ways except one—I did not have to concern myself with food or housekeeping. Abram's father had always been a good provider and was managing well enough. He had stocked up on staples and obtained whatever else was needed through barter or tailoring.

As the days went by, I grew more uneasy. News was skimpy, much of it rumor. My uneasiness deepened when a swarm of relatives from Odessa descended upon us, all women and children. These were my father-in-law's nieces and wives of nephews. They had made their way by whatever means of transport they could obtain with the stream of refugees fleeing from the embroiled city. They were hungry, tired, hysterical, and worried about their men, who had all been drafted to defend Odessa. This must have been at the end of August, because by August 30th, Odessa was encircled and they could not have escaped. They told horror stories of the bombing, the anti-Semitic outbursts among the population, and the German atrocities in the captured areas on the approaches to the city. They had no intention of remaining in Rostov, for they were convinced that the German onslaught could not be stopped. They stayed with us only a few days, just long enough to replenish their supplies the best they could and for the children to calm down. They urged us all to come with them, and when my in-laws refused, categorically tried to persuade me to join them. My in-laws did not try to influence me one way or another. I knew I had to do something, but I decided against going with them. I did not know them and did not want to become a part of a stream of women and children who had enough problems without me and my baby.

One afternoon, I was walking up a cobblestone hill along Rostov's main street when I fell in step with a young Cossack woman who was headed the same way. We got into a conversation about mundane things—how hard it was to get food for the family, the frequent air alerts, and so forth.

"It will be over soon," she remarked. "The Germans will be here before long. They'll take care of the Communists and the Jews."

Either she did not realize that I was Jewish or, more likely, did not care.

From the day I arrived in Rostov, I sensed the antagonism of the population and knew that if the Germans captured the city, we'd be in great trouble. This episode intensified my fears—an ordinary woman, gloating over the approach of the Germans and not afraid to show how she felt. She must have been pretty sure that her time was at hand.

"I am going back to Moscow," I announced after recounting the incident. "There will be a pogrom in Rostov if the Germans get here. You had better come with me or go somewhere else," I said to my in-laws.

Abram's father was not worried. "The Germans will keep order," he said.

From my husband's letter dated September 7, 1941, in reply to my letter from Rostov dated August 16th, I see that I must have described my impressions of the atmosphere in Rostov and the friction with his parents (information he could have done without). He wrote that he could not understand how differences could loom so large in the midst of the present dangers and hardships. "It seems unreal," he wrote. "In any case, get out of Rostov." (By the time that letter reached me, I was back in Moscow.)

In the same letter, he wrote that Lev Kopelev, his friend from the institute, was there. "He is battling the Germans with poems, which he composes on the spur of the moment and at times that are most inappropriate for poetry." I was pleased to learn that Lyova was there, as I knew how fond Abram was of him.

It was by no means certain that we would be able to return to Moscow. A state of emergency had been declared and no one was being allowed to enter the city without legitimate business. Fortunately, Moscow University had not yet been evacuated. The fall semester had just begun. I presented my student ID at the train station and asked for three tickets (my in-laws might change their minds and come with me). The ticket agent would sell me only one. I did not dare insist or say that I needed help, as I was afraid that if the agent found out that I had an infant with me, I would not be permitted to buy a ticket at all.

When my baby and I left for Rostov, the Germans had been close to Moscow. Now, upon our return to the Soviet capital in September, they were closer still and were advancing. Towns were being surrendered one after another. From the official reports, you'd think that the surrenders were a matter of strategy—like Kutuzov's strategy, in the war of 1812 against Napoleon, of leading the enemy deeper into the interior of the country in order to rout him there.

October 1941. The enemy was within one hundred miles of Moscow. Official Moscow was preparing to evacuate. Most women with young children had long since left. But I made up my mind to stay put until I received a letter from Anya Atlas. Her husband had a deferment because of his position in a vital industry. Anya wrote that she lived with her husband and six-month-old daughter in the middle of a forest, that the air was pure, the war far away, and food obtainable in the surrounding villages. She urged me to come and stay with them for the duration of the war.

My spirits lifted. This was an ideal solution. I went to the railroad station and bought a ticket out of Moscow for the first available date—October 15th.

October 15, 1941. No one who lived in or near Moscow will ever forget that day. Panic gripped the city. All over Moscow, in government offices, research institutes and factories, staff members were burning papers to keep them from falling into German hands. The great evacuation of Moscow had begun, both organized and unorganized.

The organized evacuees departed by train. The unorganized took what they could carry, and walked or hitched rides whenever and by whatever means they could. For days, a stream of Muscovites moved eastward along the Highway of Enthusiasts, one of Moscow's main roads.

But, unaware of the situation, that morning I set out for the station, accompanied by Frossia. At the station, I found that the trains were not going where they were supposed to go: They were all heading east! Tickets were useless. The trains had been commandeered by various organizations for their employees and their families. It was a madhouse. We turned around and went home.

The next morning, I had a phone call from Razvodovskaya, who was still the Party secretary at the publishing house.

"Mary," she said, "someone told me you were still here. I was certain you had left long ago. What are you planning to do?"

I explained my situation and said that I would wait and see what happened.

"Wait and see!" she exploded. "Do you know what will happen to you and the baby if worse comes to worst? Leder went into the army from our organization and we are responsible for you. Listen carefully. The evacuation of the publishing house has begun. Be at the Kazan station at seven A.M. tomorrow morning." She told me the platform number. "I won't be there, but say that I sent you."

Razvodovskaya would not be there because she chose to stay with her husband and his institution. She was later censured by the publishing house Party committee "for putting personal interests above the interests of the collective." There was bureaucratic rigidity, even at a time like this.

My two suitcases were still packed. Once more, Frossia accompanied me to the station.

It was October 17th. The evacuation of Moscow had been in progress at full steam for about three days.

The unheated suburban train reserved for the Comintern and publishing house was already full to capacity. Men and women shouted and pushed, trying to get themselves and their luggage aboard. They had been instructed to take no more than two pieces of luggage per family, but some had brought more—seven, ten, fifteen pieces. They did not care that there was not room enough for other people. I stood on the platform not knowing what to do, when I heard my name called. I turned around to see Paul Alpari, a colleague and close friend of Maria. Abram and I knew him quite well. He and his wife had already settled in on the train. Paul came out to help me and made room for me in their coach.

When the train pulled out, there were still people and many pieces of abandoned luggage on the platform. The evacuation of the Comintern and publishing house continued for several days. Some of the people who left later picked up luggage to deliver to the rightful owners; others, I was told, took the remaining suitcases and bundles for themselves.

*Mary and her mother.*

*Mary at her eighth grade graduation
in New Haven, Connecticut.*

*Mary with her friend Miriam Brooks
in Santa Monica, California, 1930.*

*Mary with her Moscow University classmates on a geological outing in 1935.
Mary is in the front middle; Mira Katz is wearing a white hat
with a band in the back row.*

*Mary with her Moscow University classmates in Gelendzhik on the Black Sea in 1936. Mary is lying down in the front middle.*

*Mary in Gelendzhik.*

*Mary, 1938.*

*Mary Mackler and Abram Leder in February 1941*
*when they registered their marriage.*

*Abram and his parents in the early 1930s.*

*Abram, 1942.*

*Publishing House English Section, 1949,*
*including Helen Altshuler and the Laskers.*

*Galya Babushkina.*

*Sasha, the machinegunner, in 1949.*

*Mary and Abram, 1952.*

*Abram, 1954.*

*Mary and Abram, 1955.*

*Mary and her friend Maria Rivkin, 1955.*

*Liza Mikhlin.*

*The Mikhlins with their daughters, Sara and Liuba; their granddaughter, Sonia; and Mary in 1958.*

*Mary and her friend Miriam Brooks in 1961 during Mary's visit to the United States.*

*Mary, 1985.*

# 14

## Evacuation from Moscow and Return— Fall 1941 to Spring 1942

Thus began our journey into the unknown, for no one seemed to know where we were going. The train changed direction as orders came at station stops. There was a rumor that we were going to Kuibyshev (formerly and now again Samara), a city on the middle Volga where TASS, the Radio Committee, some military academies, and several government institutions had resettled earlier. Other rumors had it that we were going to Ufa, the capital of the Bashkir Autonomous Republic, about 750 miles from Moscow, where the Comintern had been set up. Other places were mentioned as well. Our destination might have been any one of the main centers of evacuation, several of them located in Central Asia. (Moscow University had started a partial evacuation to Ashkhabad. My friend Helen ended up in Tashkent. Ahsia and her family eventually went to Samarkand.)

No one could tell how long we'd be on the road. The train was not suited for a long journey. It did not have sleep shelves, toilets, or washrooms. The nights are cold in October and they became colder as we traveled farther east and north. The train moved slowly with frequent stops, no one knowing for how long. Whenever it stopped, there was a mad rush for the toilets, for boiling water from the *titan,* and to barter or buy food. If the stop was in the middle of nowhere, well, you managed the best you could.

The majority of passengers in this particular train were connected with the Comintern. They had been given coaches of their own that outsiders were not allowed to enter. They had been given rations at the start of the trip and the administration personnel had taken along a limited supply of provisions for staff members to be distributed en route. All others had only what they had managed to bring with them. Even in this time of uncertainty and travail, rank counted. The Comintern people felt superior to the publishing house employees. The publishing house personnel who were higher on the staff ladder looked down upon those on the lower rungs. Cliques formed. There was eating in secret, whispered rumors. Some shared what they had. Most did not. These people, mind you, were all supposed to be idealists, many of them foreign Communists and anti-fascists who had fought and sacrificed for the "cause." But in most instances, it was everybody for himself.

Among the passengers in my coach were my neighbors Natasha and her mother. True to their nature, they had been very prudent. They had brought pots and pans, utensils, and even their chamber pot. Their behavior was consistent with how I had known them to be in the apartment. They kept to themselves, shared nothing, and asked for nothing. My other neighbors, the Yegorovs, had remained behind. As they pointed out, they were neither Jews nor Communists, just simple folk in ordinary jobs, not connected with foreigners or with politics. They believed they had nothing to fear from the Germans.

Without Paul Alpari, I would have had a much harder time. He went searching for food and water, and watched my baby when I had to do other things. His wife was seldom around. She spent most of her time in the VIP coach with a man with whom she had been having an affair. They supposedly were working together. Paul did not seem to mind. He had been having an affair himself.

Paul and I talked a lot as we traveled across Russia. Once he really surprised me—in fact, shocked me.

"Mary," he said, "you have an allotment. As the wife of a frontline officer, you can travel more freely than most. You are not tied down. When we get to wherever we are going, you must continue on your way. Go south. Head for the border areas with Turkey or Persia. In all the confusion, it might be possible to get across. Contact the Americans, your parents. Go home!"

This was surely in the realm of fantasy. Besides:

"What about Abram?"

"Abram is at the front. Anything can happen. If you can get out, get out."

So Paul did not believe in our coming victory over the Germans! I asked him the question point blank.

"That, and other things. The war will go on for a long time. No one can foresee the future."

Talk of this kind would have been remarkable coming from anyone. No one else I knew expressed defeatist sentiments. Coming from Paul, it was even more remarkable: Paul Alpari was a member of the Communist Party and the son of a legendary Communist killed in the Hungarian Revolution of 1919 after whom the post–World War II government would name a Budapest street. We never again referred to that conversation.

After three or four days, we arrived in Ulyanovsk, a small town on the middle Volga. Ulyanovsk (formerly and now again Simbirsk), was Lenin's birthplace and was named after him (Vladimir Ilyich Ulyanov). Everybody piled out. Ulyanovsk was a transfer point and there were crowds of people milling about. Some had arrived on earlier trains; others were from our train. There were scenes of reunion among friends, acquaintances, and relatives, with people questioning one another as to who had seen whom where as they sought news of separated families.

Tamara had been in my train in a different coach. She had come aboard at the very last minute. Some time later, she told me what had happened. Several days before the panic of October 15th, Ozrin had sent for her and told her in strict confidence that she had been selected to be part of a work team that would be evacuated immediately. The team would consist of a translator, editor, assistant editor, and typist, and its purpose would be to assure continuity of the production of urgent material. She was not told where the team was going, but they were to leave the next day. Tamara refused. She said she was going instead with her husband, whose factory was preparing to evacuate any day now. When Ozrin insisted, Tamara pointed out that she was not a staff member and could do as she pleased. With that, she went home. Ozrin kept telephoning and she kept refusing. Then, on October 15th, Boris was summoned by his factory director and told that there had been a change in plans. He was ordered to leave within a few hours to deliver a packet of documents to a destination that would be revealed to him en route. He was not permitted to take anyone along, not even his wife.

Boris had no choice. His factory manufactured armaments and was under military orders. He left, uncertain as to when and how Tamara would get out of the city, and Tamara had no idea where he would end up.

Tamara telephoned Ozrin. He told her to meet his wife Eda at the station the next morning and gave her the platform number. When she got to the station, she found Eda there with a typist from the French section. No one was being allowed to board the supposedly overcrowded train. The three of them, all very attractive young women, had given up hope of leaving that day when they heard male voices calling, "Girls, girls, come here." A couple of young men were calling to them from another coach. "Come with us. We'll make room," they said.

They turned out to be on a security police escort coach. Tamara admitted that she had to fend off their sexual advances, but that, otherwise, it was a good trip with plenty to eat and drink. We knew that we were on the same train because she came through the cars, looking for the publishing house contingent and for any other acquaintances.

In Ulyanovsk, Tamara found, quite by chance, a man who had met her husband at some station stop and who had a message for her about Boris's destination. Boris had given messages to anyone he thought might possibly encounter his wife.

The Comintern people left us in Ulyanovsk to continue due east to Ufa. The rest of us were told to go to the pier, where we would board a steamboat going down the Volga. The pier was a short distance away, but the landing stage was at the bottom of a long, wooden staircase. The steps were covered with slippery mud. People fell and bundles scattered. I was petrified. Paul took his own luggage down, then came up for mine, and then came up again for me. With him and Tamara holding me tightly on each side, my baby in my arms, I got down the stairs and aboard the steamboat.

Our first major port of call was Kuibyshev, where many passengers disembarked. A crowd of evacuees who had reached Kuibyshev earlier now met the boat to look for friends or family. Several publishing house employees who had left before the official evacuation joined us too, among them Krause and his daughter. The boat continued downstream to Saratov, where we disembarked and took a ferry across to the town of Engels, where earlier groups from the publishing house had settled in.

Engels, on the Volga River directly opposite Saratov, was the capital of the Volga German autonomous republic. Though the roots of its residents could be traced back to the eighteenth century, to the time of Catherine the Great, all ethnic Germans had been expelled in a one-day operation with no advance notice. This was done in response to a rumor that German parachutists had landed in the region soon after the outbreak of the war and had been welcomed by the populace. No one of German descent was exempt, not even high-ranking Party and government officials. Local Russians described the shock, the clamor, and the disruption. The Germans' farms and houses, of much higher than average standards, had now been taken over by Russian peasants.

We were housed in a five-story building that had formerly been a school. There was electricity, but no indoor plumbing, no elevator, and very little heat. The primitive toilets were in a freezing cold outhouse at some distance from the building and could be reached by a narrow path over icy planks from which the snow had been imperfectly cleared. The desks had been removed from the schoolrooms and narrow iron beds put in. People were "billeted" according to rank. The higher the rank, the fewer people in the room. The top people had separate rooms that they only had to share with their families.

Food, too, was distributed according to rank, the quantity per person determined arbitrarily on a day-by-day basis, depending on availability of supplies. A regular item of the "menu" was watery farina with a bit of machine oil or linseed oil—six portions for top administration and Party officials, five for senior staff, four for middle staff, and so on down the line to one portion for the few people like myself who were not on staff. Fortunately, I was not entirely dependent on them. I had my allotment and could buy a little milk and cheese for exorbitant prices at the so-called collective farm market.

The rooms set aside for the rank-and-file contained from six to ten beds. Each room was supplied with an electric hot plate. Beds were assigned on a first come, first served basis, people seeking as much as possible to be with friends and colleagues. Most had never lived in dormitories before and did not adapt readily. There was a great deal of squabbling—for a better place in the room, for the use of the hot plate, about lights, cleanliness and noise, over the differentiation of rations.

A work schedule was set up. Officially, the publishing house was operating again. Manuscripts in progress and other materials were shipped from Moscow. The schedule gave some structure to the days, and people were glad to have something to do, even though they understood that this was make-work, more for morale and discipline, since no one knew where and whether their "output" would ever be printed. The immediate orders for materials used for propaganda and defense purposes were being filled by a skeleton staff in Moscow, with Ozrin in charge. The publishing house director, Paryshev, had gone to the front as a volunteer, despite his right to a deferment on account of his age and his position.

From the English section, there were Liz, Tamara, Joe Feinberg with his wife Yetta, among others. Many of the staff had brought spouses, but except for two infants—mine and another young woman's—and an eleven-year-old daughter of someone in the French section, there were no children. All young children had been sent to summer camps in early June, as was the custom in Moscow.

Liz had not heard from her husband for a long time. She had received several letters after he had joined the Home Guard, but had not heard from him again. Long afterwards, she was notified that he was missing in action.

"Missing in action" is hard information to live with. I came to know many women whose husbands, sons, fathers or brothers had been declared "missing in action." For years, they nurtured the hope that their loved ones may have survived, may have escaped to another country and would turn up some day. There were some such instances of this, but very few. By far, the greatest number of MIAs had been killed in battle or in enemy prison camps.

Ahsia, her parents, and Igor arrived in Engels two weeks later. Igor had left his job as house superintendent without notifying anyone. (If he had, he most likely would have been ordered to stay.) They told us that the only people left in Moscow, apart from the military, were those who were prepared to welcome the Germans or who were prevented from leaving by sickness or disability. Ahsia and her family stayed only a few days, continuing on to Central Asia at Igor's insistence. He wanted to get farther away from the front, which was getting closer by the day.

The extremity of our situation gave rise to extreme behaviors. Outbursts of pent-up resentments, backbiting, gossip, envy, sycophancy, jockeying for position, and wheedling for favors made for a generally unpleasant atmosphere. Some people withdrew into themselves and fell into what I now recognize as depression, but at that time I regarded them as indifferent and passive due to self-absorption. Others proved to be very energetic and enterprising, foraging for food, bartering clothing, and bargaining. Complete strangers sometimes turned out to be considerate and kind, ready to help those in greatest need. Lucy Paryshev, for example, the wife of the publishing house director, was among the evacuees. I had never met her before, but she came to me in the train, introduced herself, and offered to help with the baby, something she continued to do while we remained in Engels. Joe Feinberg was another exception. As the senior staff member from the English section and a member of the overall Party committee, he was one of the privileged. He and his wife had a room to themselves and maximum rations. They were outraged by the caste system, especially in the distribution of food. When he was unable to change the system or to obtain special rations for me as a nursing mother, he and Yetta insisted on sharing some of their food with me.

In the struggle to survive, cliques were formed of friends, colleagues, or merely of individuals who could be useful to one another. They shared among themselves, but kept all others at arm's length. And some, especially those at the top, were downright mean and cruel. The "ruling" group in Engels included Grigorian, a political editor in the Russian section who was now in charge of production; two Communists originally from Poland, both of whom later held high positions in the postwar Polish government; a senior editor from the German section; and a Hungarian Communist named Koenig (called "Big Koenig" to distinguish him from another Hungarian with the same name) who was in charge of provisions and equipment and thus was the most powerful of all because his decisions affected our daily lives.

Most vicious, at least where I was concerned, was Big Koenig. Because he was the provider of food and was in charge of living space, he had the power to do favors for those who toadied to him. He could also make life difficult for those who did not cultivate him or who were low on the totem pole. Since I was not on staff and had no official work assignment, he ordered me to do heavy work in the kitchen. He expected me to carry pails of water. When I refused, having all I could handle to take care of myself and the baby, he screamed and shouted at me, threatening to deprive me of my meager ration and to throw me out of the building. He did not dare go that far, but did his best to make my life miserable in small ways. After a while, Joe Feinberg intervened and Big Koenig left me alone (he returned to Hungary after the war and held an important position in the Communist government).

And then there were the Chinese, the only group that did not quarrel among themselves. They were unfailingly cheerful and helpful. I ended up living with them in their crowded room. No one else would have me. The baby cried too much. After two or three nights of being shunted from one room to another, I accepted an invitation to stay with them. We had no common language. I don't remember a single name or person among them, but they smiled reassuringly, and made it clear that I was not to worry about disturbing them. They even invited me to partake of the strange-smelling concoctions they cooked on their hot plate. I shall always remember them with gratitude and recall thinking sadly that they were the only true Communists among us, idealists who practiced what they preached. They showed true concern for ordinary people, decency and equality, and the primacy of the common good over individual self-interest.

My first encounter with bedbugs had been in Birobidzhan. My first encounter with lice was in Engels. I was horrified one morning to discover insects on myself and the baby. I did not know what they were and asked Liz to take a look.

"Lice," she said. "Body lice, and they are dangerous. They cause typhus. You must get rid of them."

I demanded and obtained kerosene from the kitchen. With Liz's help and repeated "treatments," I got rid of the lice. It turned out that the infestation was extensive, but most people had been too ashamed to admit they had lice and were too inexperienced to do anything about them. After my outcry, the extent of the problem became apparent and the administration took action to eliminate the infestation with kerosene, boiling water, and pyrethrum.

The reports from the battlefront were unbelievably bad throughout October and November 1941. The Germans came within five to twenty miles of the Moscow city limits. A fierce battle was raging in the Rostov area. The Germans captured Rostov on November 19th; then the Red Army recaptured the city ten days later. I received a letter from my mother-in-law, to whom I had written upon my arrival in Engels, saying that they were all right (this was not entirely true, but we did not learn the whole truth until after the war). The first letter from Abram to catch up with me in Engels was dated November 19th, forwarded from Moscow by my neighbors. He did not find out where I was until he finally received a letter from me in December. He replied at once. He had not heard from anyone in Rostov and was worried about his parents.

The general mood was somber. Families were separated and everybody had somebody to worry about—a young child who had been sent to camp in June and was not equipped for the winter, a spouse at the front or evacuated with another organization, a family member left behind in Moscow. For some, the feelings of despair were expressed in a "live-today-for-tomorrow-we-die" attitude that led to sexual competition and torrid affairs. Since it was impossible to conceal anything in our beehive, gossip was rampant. The most talked-about affairs were those of the top brass who got together with attractive young women while their wives were safely tucked away in Ufa, Kuibyshev, or farther still.

A break in the bad news came in December. Soviet forces launched a month-long offensive and drove the enemy back to one or two hundred miles from Moscow. This turn of events lifted the morale tremendously. By mid-January, some of the partially evacuated organizations such as the radio committee, TASS, and government agencies began to recall staff members. The Comintern and the publishing house, too, recalled some of their staff. Because everybody wanted to return to Moscow, competition for the good will of anyone who could influence the selection became intense.

Meanwhile, after weeks of dealing with the local bureaucracy, the administration arranged for the two babies, mine and the other mother's, to live in the town's child care center on a permanent basis. I was not given a choice. However, at the time I believed that this solution would be better for the children. The other mother was a Russian typist on staff who had to keep to a work schedule, but I was able to spend most of my time at the center. I breastfed my baby, took her outside for fresh air, and sometimes brought her to the building where I lived so that my friends could see her. But leaving her each evening was a wrenching experience. Each morning when her face lit up on my reappearance, my heart turned over. She was a beautiful child with huge grey eyes in an oval face, dark hair that formed a widow's peak like my husband's, and a dimpled chin, also like my husband's. She did not resemble me at all. She was not developing at a normal rate, but I was only vaguely aware of that. At six months, when she should have been crawling, she only managed to hold up her head and follow me around with her eyes. She did not look undernourished and had good color, but I myself was thin and haggard and my nursing could not have provided her with much nutrition and no supplementary food was available. Her resistance must have been very low.

Disaster struck. First, it was pneumonia at the end of January. She was taken to a hospital and I stayed with her day and night until she finally pulled through. Then, on February 12th, she started breathing with difficulty. I recognized the signs of croup from my anatomy course and I remembered our teacher's statement that all physicians, whatever their field, were obliged to take emergency action to save the life of a child with croup. But no one at the center could help me. No hospital beds were available. Every minute counted. With my child in my arms, I went on foot from one hospital to another, pleading with the doctors to do something. I was turned away everywhere. No room—the hospitals were overcrowded with war wounded. At one hospital, the head doctor said right out that infants and old people were expendable when young men were dying in battle.

Finally, at the end of the day, a hospital admitted us and the doctor made the necessary incision. But it was too late. Four days later, on February 16th, my daughter stopped breathing. She was seven months and fifteen days old. The death certificate gives diphtherial croup as the cause of death. But she was as much a casualty of the war as anyone who fell in battle, a victim of the callousness and indifference that arose when the horror was so appalling and the fatalities so great that the mind refused to absorb them.

Liz, who was officially at work, asked her boss Grigorian for time off so that she could go to the hospital to bring me back. Grigorian refused, an act of pure malice as Liz was not engaged in urgent work. He had the same attitude about my baby's funeral. He refused to give anyone time off to accompany me to the cemetery, which was two or three miles away. Krause's daughter, who was not an employee, went with me. Someone, I don't remember who, hired a horse and wagon. It was a cold, grey day. The ground was covered with snow. There was no ceremony. The driver placed the tiny coffin onto the wagon and we, two mourners, trudged along in silence. At the cemetery, the driver and the graveyard attendant lowered the coffin into a shallow, unmarked grave. The driver waited for us the few minutes we remained by the grave and then gave us a ride back. It was February 18, 1942. Victory was nowhere in sight. I never went back. I could not have found the grave if I had.

Several days later, I came down with a high fever. Tamara had a good friend who was a doctor in a nearby hospital for contagious diseases (mostly typhus and typhoid). She asked him to examine me. He diagnosed my illness as paratyphoid and had me admitted to his hospital. However, he did not put me in a ward with other patients, but in a cubbyhole all by myself. I did not believe that I had paratyphoid and am convinced that neither did he, though he never admitted, even in later years, that his decision had been a ruse to get me into the hospital where I could rest, calm down, and get some passable food.

The hospital was a twenty-minute walk from where we all lived and most evenings Liz, Tamara, or Krause would come to see me. (That was a special arrangement with the doctor, as visitors were not allowed in the regular wards.) One day, when I had been in the hospital for about three weeks, Liz informed me that she had received an official summons from the publishing house and would be leaving for Moscow in a few days. Her news sent me into a dither. I had already decided that I had to find a way to get out of Engels. I hated the place and the associations it held for me. I made up my mind that I would go when Liz went.

First, I had to get out of the hospital. The diagnosis with which I had been admitted required a longer stay, so the hospital would not or could not discharge me. I needed clothes. All I had was a hospital gown and robe and slippers. As was the custom in Soviet hospitals, my own clothes had been sent away with whomever accompanied me when I had been admitted. I told Liz my plan and asked her to bring me my clothes a day or two before she was scheduled to leave Engels. She did so, and I sneaked out of the hospital in the middle of the night.

Very early the following morning, Liz and I took the ferry across the river to Saratov and the railroad station.

There was no way I could return to Moscow legally. The state of emergency had not been lifted and no one was allowed to come within sixty miles of the city without a permit. Persons apprehended trying to enter illegally were dispatched to haul logs in lumber camps or to dig trenches or build fortifications. By and large, the illegal entrants were women because the men were either in the army or were employed in the defense industry. It was not possible for me to obtain a permit since my status was that of a student of Moscow University and the university had been evacuated to Ashkhabad. Liz had her ticket, a reserved seat in a compartment in a second-class coach.

As usual, the station was crowded, mostly with women and children. Many of them had been trying to buy tickets and board trains for days. There was also a smattering of disabled men and men in uniform. My identification as the wife of a frontline officer entitled me to purchase my ticket at the special ticket office reserved for military personnel. I asked for and obtained a ticket to the small town of Mikhnevo, just sixty miles southeast of Moscow, where most trains made a scheduled stop. My ticket was unreserved and for no particular train. To have tried to fight my way into an unreserved coach was out of the question. I could not have done it. We decided that I should stay with Liz.

We boarded the train together, planning that I would hide when the conductor came to collect the tickets. The important thing was not to be forced off the train before it started moving. We stored our luggage on the top shelf of the compartment and went into the corridor to wait for the departure bell. Departure time came, but no bell rang. The passengers settled down, and the conductor deposited the packages of bedding on the four reserved shelves. Still no bell. We stood in the corridor in our coats, looking out of the window, not knowing whether I should settle in as if I belonged there or remain standing as if I were planning to get off. The conductor, a middle-aged woman, walked by several times, eyeing us suspiciously, Liz in a shabby old coat and scuffed shoes, I in a handsome new coat my father-in-law had made out of fabric my parents had sent me. Finally, the conductor approached Liz and demanded her ticket. With aplomb and an air of injured innocence, Liz produced her ticket and an imposing looking document indicating that she was a Very Important Person. Abashed, the conductor apologized and suggested that we get settled, as the train would not leave until the snowdrifts from yesterday's heavy storm were cleared from the tracks. She did not ask for my ticket. Apparently, my prosperous appearance put her off. It was March 1942.

We entered the compartment. There was only one other passenger in it. When the train finally pulled out the next day, we showed the conductor my ticket and told her that I would get out in Mikhnevo. She said I could stay at least until ticket-holders for the two vacant seats showed up somewhere along the way. We probably gave her money. The two seats were claimed by military men, but no one objected to my staying and sharing Liz's shelf.

The trip to Moscow took three days. As we came closer to the forbidden zone, soldiers came aboard from time to time to check passengers' identification. Each time, I managed to evade them, sometimes in the toilet, sometimes by going into another coach. One afternoon, the soldiers came when I was napping. There was no time to warn me. Liz covered me with blankets and prayed I would not wake up suddenly. The other passengers in the compartment did not give me away and neither did the conductor.

In a few hours, we would reach Mikhnevo. What should I do? Should I get out and try to make my way to Moscow by other means? Or should I stay on the train and take my chances?

The problem was solved for us. The train whizzed past Mikhnevo without stopping. We arrived at the Paveletsky railroad station in Moscow. I left my two suitcases with Liz and went off on my own. We arranged for Liz to go straight home. I would get in touch with her as soon as I was able.

I knew Paveletsky station well. It was near Mira's home and it was also the station I used to go through when I visited Izzy. The street entrance to the waiting room and the ticket offices opened onto a large square in front of the station. The back entrance to the waiting room opened onto the boarding platforms. The train area was separated from the square by high iron gates, usually left open so that trucks and baggage carts could get through. The picture that met my eyes was discouraging. The iron gates were locked, except for a narrow passage for pedestrians, a sort of sub-gate in the lower left-hand corner flanked by mounted policemen. Arriving passengers were being allowed through the gate single file as officials checked their papers. Adjacent to the gate were several wooden steps that led to the back entrance to the waiting room. The door to the waiting room was guarded by a soldier with a rifle.

As I stood there wondering what to do, I suddenly saw that the soldier guarding the back entrance had vanished. I'll never know where he went, but I did not hesitate. In an instant, I was through the door, into the waiting room, and out the front entrance into the street. I turned right into the square, positioning myself near the gate as I waited for Liz. When I caught sight of her, a drab, worried figure, dragging my suitcases and hers, I began to jump up and down to attract her attention. She looked up and a slow smile of amazement spread across her face. I met her as she came through the gate and, together, we managed to carry our bags to the A streetcar, which took us near her apartment.

The first winter of the war is legendary for its severity and the effect that it had on the battles around Moscow and farther north. By March 1942 winter was on its way out, but the signs of it were still everywhere. Stove-pipes stuck out of windows all over the city. The central heating in most residential building had not functioned all winter and Muscovites got by with makeshift iron stoves called *burzhuiki*, which were heated with newspapers, peat, wood, furniture, and whatever else was at hand. A curfew was in force. Volunteer block and building wardens saw to it that not a sliver of light shone through windows at night. After dark, the streets were deserted except for the patrols and an occasional hurrying figure. Anyone out after curfew had to have a special night-time pass.

The day after my arrival, I went to my apartment. The Yegorovs acted pleased to see me and asked for news about Natasha and her mother, who were still in Engels. They commiserated with me, speaking of the hard winter and the food shortages. They had a *burzhuika* in their larger room. I told them I was on a special job and would be staying somewhere else for a while. I did not trust them enough to tell them that I had come back illegally.

It would not have been wise for me to move back to my room. I had to be re-registered, and for that, my presence in Moscow would have to be legalized. On the other hand, by showing up, I ensured that my neighbors would spread the word that I was back and that my room would be safe-guarded for the time being. I decided to stay at Liz's until I found a job.

Of my close friends, only Mussia and Maria were in town. Mussia had recently been recalled from Kuibyshev by the radio committee. Maria had not left Moscow at all: She was a civilian employee of the armed forces and was subject to military orders. Division VII of the Chief Political Administration of the Soviet Army, where she worked, was responsible for propaganda in the languages of the enemy. She and a German Communist refugee named Frieda Rubiner, the only two civilians in the division, were closely involved in the composition and production of leaflets, brochures, appeals and other materials in German to be dropped behind the German lines or broadcast over loudspeakers stationed on the forward line or in the "no man's land" between the opposing sides. Initially, Maria's role was to have been a clerical-secretarial assistant, but her talent was quickly recognized and she participated in all stages of production on a par with everyone else. Consequently, she worked long hours and did not come home for days at a time.[1]

Tamara had returned to Moscow about the same time as I had, and her husband arrived soon after. Tamara was now on the publishing house staff and Boris was back at the factory. Boris's work often took him away from Moscow on assignments at the front—often dangerous assignments—but

---

1. Later, the division also prepared materials for use in prisoner-of-war camps. Division VII was responsible for the staffing and supervision of subordinate departments of various sizes at all army levels.

not even Tamara knew about the dangers until long after the war. Their apartment was in tolerable shape. However, the elevator was not working and did not start working until near the end of the war, so that they and their visitors had to trudge up eight steep flights of stairs. This did not deter anyone and their place was always filled with friends and acquaintances.

I had to break out of a vicious circle: to establish legal residence I had to have a job, but to be hired, I had to be legally registered. (Incidentally, this situation was part of the system. It held true before the war, during, and after.) No job meant no rations. And my March rations had ended. We took it for granted that I would stay with Liz until my affairs were settled. Unlike my other friends, she worked at home and could regulate her hours. Liz's rations were sufficient for both of us.

I needed to find a job with an organization that had enough clout to get me registered in Moscow. Mussia steered me to the radio committee where I passed a test for an announcer, a desirable position with short hours, high pay, and extra rations. I filled out an application and was told that I would be contacted when the paperwork was processed. Not long after that, I met Izzy in the street. I had not seen him since my marriage (Abram refused to meet him) or his, about a year later, to his pretty secretary. His wife and son had been evacuated but he, like most of the TASS staff, had not left Moscow. I told him of my predicament and he said he would make inquiries at TASS. He thought that his former boss Chernov needed translators into English. A day or two later, he telephoned me at Liz's and said that Chernov would like to see me as soon as possible. Chernov, whom I had met several times when I was seeing Izzy, received me cordially and had me fill out an application. Now I had two irons in the fire. There was nothing more I could do but wait.

As a matter of fact, I had been thinking along other avenues as well—of joining my husband at the front. When I made up my mind to leave Engels, that had been my first thought and I wrote to Abram, asking him to arrange it. When I arrived in Moscow, I tried to persuade Maria to pull some strings for me, but she did not feel that it would be ethical to do so. Besides, she did not approve of the idea.

Neither did Abram. In a letter dated April 5, 1942, forwarded from Engels, he not only vetoed my suggestion about joining him at the front, but cautioned me (too late) against returning to Moscow. He described the work he was doing as "hard and often very unpleasant," and told me, " I'd worry terribly about you every minute." Without his cooperation, there was no point in my going ahead. My motives were not primarily patriotic. If they had been, I could have gone to the local military authorities and volunteered. Then, if accepted, I could have been sent anywhere, least likely of all to join my husband. But my overwhelming feeling was that I wanted to be with him, to share whatever he was going through, and, above all, not to lose our young years together.

I made a few more attempts to persuade him to agree to my joining him, but as things developed for him, that was the last worry he needed.

Meanwhile, I waited.

Food was strictly rationed and obtainable only in the shops to which the ration cards were attached. The rationing system was complex and highly stratified, much more so than it had been in the early thirties when I had first arrived in Moscow. Apart from the especially privileged—top Party and government officials, factory directors, and so forth—who had their own sources, the population was divided into categories, based (theoretically) on their relative value to society. Job title was very important. The top level for general rations was reserved for factory workers and manual laborers. Below that, came rations for secretarial and clerical employees and others who were not entitled to one of the higher categories. There were special rations for children, redeemable for milk and dairy products (when these were available). Skimpiest of all were the rations for dependents—housewives and the elderly, of whom there were few in Moscow, but many outside in the provincial towns and among the evacuees. Supplementary rations were introduced later. The highest rungs on the employment ladder had the status of *liter A*.[2] Below that was *liter B*. Eventually most of us received *liter B*.

Rations categories were not all equal either. Much depended on the shops where the coupons were redeemable and on the perceived importance of the given organizations. The stores to which the more important organizations were attached received better supplies, often including extras to be distributed among employees at the administration's discretion. Designation of rations categories for employees was often arbitrary, depending on the whim of the boss or, even more, on the good will of the head of the rations distribution office, who was more often than not a Party hack with no special skills or education, now suddenly risen to a position of power. Opportunities for corruption were limitless.

Liz had moved up the ladder since I had first met her in 1933. She was now a senior editor-translator and as such was entitled to *liter B* rations. This provided her with more than enough staples—bread, sugar, potatoes, flour, cereals, and cooking oil. Neither of us was a big eater and though our diet was not varied, we were never hungry. Some of the surplus bread could be exchanged at the market for milk and cheese. The farmers' markets were not what they used to be, but peasants came from afar to barter or sell whatever they could spare.

---

2. *Liter* was originally a railroad term for a travel warranty. Now it meant a warranty entitling the holder to special privileges.

For a week or two, things were fine. Liz worked at home, and I ran around following up on job leads and contacts and helping with the marketing. All went well until Liz's brother-in-law George arrived, recalled from Kuibyshev by the radio committee where he was a leading translator.

George Hannigan[3] was a tall, good-looking, ginger-haired Irishman. He was a member of the British Communist Party, and was a gifted linguist who had spent ten years in the British army in India. He knew Hindi and Urdu as well as Russian, and was a highly valued translator at the radio committee, where he exhibited an extraordinary capacity for work and, consequently, earned above average wages. He was arrogant, ambitious, rude to those whom he regarded as inferiors, and eager to be admitted to the corridors of power. But he was wonderful to Liz's sister Rose, who had been a single mother at the radio committee. They had married not long before the outbreak of the war, after which he formally adopted her daughter and proved himself a kind and loving husband. Rose worshiped him.

Liz invited George to stay at her place and pool their resources. By Moscow's standards, she had plenty of room—two adjoining rooms in a communal apartment—and the location was much more convenient for him than his own room, which was on the outskirts of the city. He, too, had *liter B* rations and there was plenty for the three of us.

But plenty was not enough. From the beginning, it was obvious that he resented my presence, and resented having to share with me, who had nothing material to contribute (money was not the problem). He became very nasty, baiting me, making snide remarks, and pushing me to leave. He made my life there so miserable that I finally took my bags and departed. I did not speak to him again for five years.

Throughout this episode, Liz did not intervene. She went about her business, seemingly oblivious to the bad feeling between the two of us. Actually, Liz's behavior was in keeping with her personality. Liz was a reticent person, not given to expressing her feelings. I used to envy her ability to shut out the world and do her work amidst all kinds of tumult. When I visited her before the war, I often witnessed scenes of acrimonious bickering between her husband and her mother, during which Liz did not react outwardly.

This may have been her way of dealing with a fate that she must have felt was an aberration. She had never considered emigrating to the Soviet Union before she met her future husband, and her life in the USSR had been full of disappointments. Her fate had included her rejection by the Soviet Communist Party; her husband's loss of his job and the long period of unemployment that followed and, though they never spoke of it to me, the

---

3. George Hannigan is a pseudonym.

fear of arrest; her husband's status as missing in action; and, of course, her separation from the rest of her family, including her son who had been born in 1938.

Since it would have been imprudent to return to my own apartment before my job situation was resolved, I gratefully accepted Mussia's invitation to stay with her. Food was very important to Mussia. She had always been a compulsive eater and was a very neurotic person. Yet never once during the month that I shared her rations and her room did she indicate in the slightest manner that my presence was a hardship for her. She was under a great deal of pressure on her job, working three shifts and coming home at odd hours. She had to use some of her food coupons for meals in the canteen, but she scrupulously divided everything else she was able to buy and did not touch it until she got home. We wasted nothing. We concocted strange combinations to stretch our supplies, such as potato peels fried in linseed oil or pancakes made of flour and water (this brought to my mind the Okies in John Steinbeck's *The Grapes of Wrath*). Once, Mussia succumbed to temptation. On her way to the night shift, she stopped in the store and found that chocolate was available for sugar coupons, a rare treat. She used up the entire month's sugar ration, intending to bring the chocolate home. Then, she started nibbling. Little by little, by the end of the shift, she had eaten it all. I was shocked by her appearance when she arrived in time for breakfast the next morning.

"Mussia, what's wrong?"

I thought something terrible must have happened. My first thought was that someone we knew had been killed in battle.

"I ate all the chocolate," she said in a voice from the grave.

"What chocolate? What are you talking about?"

From her confession, you might have thought she had committed murder. Nothing I said could make her feel better. For years, she'd recall the incident and how guilty she felt.

I really did not mind, for I never felt hungry those first months after my return to Moscow. It was not that I had enough to eat, for I was very careful about sharing my friends' food when I had no food coupons of my own. Even when I got a ration card—an employee card with no extras, hardly enough to subdue hunger pangs—I did not suffer from hunger. I thrived. I had been thin and haggard when I left Engels. Now I grew plump, with good color and firm skin. Soon, I could not get into my clothes and had to improvise skirts and blouses. I looked so well-fed that sometimes people in the street gave me dirty looks, no doubt thinking I was the wife of some big shot or myself in charge of supplies (a category of people traditionally disliked by the general public). And I had become very placid, which was not my nature at all.

The war conditions affected people physically in strange ways. Many women stopped menstruating. Stomach ulcers and liver ailments, instead of getting worse, often got better. Eczemas that people had had for years disappeared. After the war was over, most pre-war conditions returned.

Finally, a doctor I consulted about the inexplicable weight gain sent me to an endocrinologist who diagnosed an inactive thyroid and prescribed medication. Gradually, I returned to normal. My appetite increased and I became as concerned about food and rations as everybody else.

Food was, indeed, a constant topic of conversation. When we got together to share pot luck at Liz's with her colleagues, or at Mussia's or somewhere else, we fantasized about eating, especially about the foods of our childhood and younger years, which many of us had spent in distant countries. We did this in fun, not in self-pity. After all, we were not starving. Our stomachs were seldom full, but we had enough nourishment to keep our bodies and souls together.

On those rare occasions when Maria came home, she always brought a special treat. The canteen where she worked was well-stocked. Seeing Maria was in itself a special treat. She was witty and entertaining, no matter what fears we might all have had. Her verbal sketches of the people with whom she worked were so vivid that when I met some of these individuals later, I had no trouble recognizing them. The officers with whom she worked most directly were not career officers, but had been drafted because of their special knowledge. Her immediate superior had been a professor of Oriental languages and was fluent in several European languages as well. Among her colleagues was Yuri Zhdanov, son of the Leningrad Party head, Andrei Zhdanov.[4] Maria liked and respected him, and said he was hard-working and unassuming and did not take advantage of his privileged position. Maria derived great satisfaction from her job. She felt she was doing something useful and doing it well.

TASS was the first to complete the formalities and offer me a job. Personnel gave me a letter for the local militia and I was re-registered in my room without further ado. I started my new job at the end of April 1942. Now that my papers were in order, I could make arrangements to resume my studies at the university starting in September. Moscow University was still officially evacuated and operating in Ashkhabad, but a partial reopening was planned for the fall.

Once I settled in my room, I noticed what I had not noticed the times I had dropped in briefly—some things were missing. Among the missing articles of clothing was a silk maternity dress I had borrowed from an

---

4. Andrei Zhdanov was architect of the post-war repressive policies on art and literature. Yuri Zhdanov married Stalin's daughter Svetlana after the war. (The marriage ended in divorce.)

American woman who had had a baby the year before. She had planned to alter it, but said she would wait until I no longer needed it. The loss of that dress bothered me most of all and probably gave me the nerve to do what I did next. On a day when I was alone in the apartment, having worked night shift, I took the Yegorovs' key from its hiding place and unlocked the door of the smaller room, which was the younger daughter's, who was then about eighteen or nineteen years old (the elder daughter had married and moved out of the apartment). Taking a quick look around, I spotted a bottle of *Krasnyi mak* (Red Poppy) perfume on the night table. Ksena had given me such a bottle for my birthday and since I hardly ever used perfume, it was still full when I left. *Krasnyi mak* was a popular brand and ordinarily it would have been impossible to prove that this bottle was mine. But when I lifted the bottle out of its pretty cardboard box, I saw the message that identified the real owner. It read: "Happy birthday, Mary, from Ksena."

I did not bother to look further. I put the bottle back, locked the door, and replaced the key. When Dussia came home from work, I knocked on her door and entered before she had a chance to come into the hall and talk with me. When I told her that some of my belongings had been stolen and asked her what she knew about them, she angrily denied all knowledge. Indicating the bottle of perfume, I said:

"You took that from my room."

"Are you crazy? Anyone can buy a bottle of perfume!"

"I can prove it is mine," and taking the bottle out of the box I showed her the inscription.

She was speechless.

"Dussia," I said, "return everything you took and I won't make a big fuss. Otherwise I will report the theft. It is wartime and there are laws against looting."

She burst into tears.

"I don't have everything. I sold some things. We thought the Germans would take Moscow and you'd never come back."

"But you did not return the things when the Germans were driven off, nor tell me about them when I came back. Return what you have."

Among the articles Dussia gave me was the dress, ripped apart at the seams, ready to be altered. I returned the dress when the woman got back from evacuation and apologized for the condition it was in. She was pleased to have it even as it was. Every scrap of clothing counted and it would make a pretty dress for her.

One day, soon after I returned to my apartment, I met Margo in our courtyard. She had been visiting a friend who lived in the building. She was still employed at the radio committee, working shifts as I did, and lived in the same place out of town. She herself had not left Moscow, but she had sent her two children away with a woman who had been taking care of them along with the sixteen-year-old son of Josip Tito, the Yugoslavian Communist Party leader and partisan. Tito's son had lost an arm in an accident. The four of them were living in a Siberian village not far from Novosibirsk. Margo asked me if she could stay at my place on the days when our different shifts made it convenient. The radio station had promised her a room in the city, but it might take some time until the paperwork came through. We worked out a schedule that suited us both, not getting into each other's way, pooling some of our resources, and sometimes meeting over a meal between shifts. The arrangement continued for about six months. Among the few belongings Margo left behind when she moved out of my room was a small wooden-handled copper Turkish coffee pot that I still have, one of a number of cherished possessions that remind me constantly of long-gone persons who shared my life at one time or another.

On April 25, 1942—I remember the exact date because it was my twenty-seventh birthday—I returned from night shift early in the morning to find Margo preparing to leave for her job. She seemed rather excited, wished me a happy birthday, and asked if I was planning to go out.

"Not for a couple of hours," I said. "I'll get some sleep first. Then I have errands to do. Would you like me to do something for you?"

"No," she said, "but don't go out until you hear from me. I may have something interesting to tell you."

With that mysterious statement, she left.

I had been awake for some time and was eager to get out of the house. Still, Margo did not call. It was not until late afternoon that the phone rang, and it was not Margo but the operator who asked for me and told me to hold on for a long-distance call. In a few seconds, a man's voice came on the line.

"Happy birthday!" I could not believe my ears. It was Abram!

He was calling from Kalinin (formerly and now again Tver), a town about eighty miles away. He had been sent there to be reassigned and had called early in the morning and spoken with Margo. He asked her not to tell me he had called, but to make sure I stayed home, as he could not tell when he would get another chance to telephone. That it was my birthday was coincidental. He had not remembered until she told him.

It seemed like years since I had waved goodbye to him from the train in Riga just ten months before. So much had happened. What can you say in an unexpected telephone conversation which might be cut off at any moment? From a recent letter forwarded from Engels, I knew that he had received my letter informing him of our child's death and of my plans to leave Engels. Obviously, he had received my letter from Moscow. Now I told him that I had a job and he told me that he was being reassigned closer to the battle front. Above all, what mattered was not what he said, but hearing his voice again, knowing that at least for the moment he was safe. I felt both sad and elated as I hung up. When would we see each other again?

In his next letter, Abram wrote that it had taken him three days on foot and hitching rides to reach his new unit, but that he had discovered old friends there and was making new ones. He seemed to be in better spirits (I knew from earlier letters that he had detested the outfit he was in and was not getting along with his superior officer). He was sorry he would not be able to telephone me again; he was too far away. He had sent me 600 rubles with an acquaintance and hoped I had received it, and he was dispatching a letter with the *Krasnaya zvezda* (*Red Star*—the army newspaper) correspondent to be mailed in Moscow. He was worried about his parents and kept urging them in his letter to leave Rostov, but his mother had written that they could not make up their minds. "I'm so afraid we may all lose each other," he wrote.

# 15

## TASS and Moscow University— 1942 to 1946

TASS had not been evacuated, but it lost many staff members who had to leave for various reasons. Consequently, many of the departments were shorthanded, which was probably why speedy action was taken on my application. I was hired to translate from Russian into English at RIDZ (an acronym for *Redaktsiya informatsii dlya zagranitsy,* which means "Editorial Office of Information for Foreign Countries"), the department where Izzy had started his journalistic career. The Russian editors selected news items and articles from the Soviet press to be translated into English, French, German, and other languages. We dictated directly to the typists and the translations were then transmitted by teletype. RIDZ had several fabulous typists who had an excellent knowledge of English, French, and German. One of the "perks" of my job was my access to the foreign press. Ordinarily, such access required clearance, but Chernov managed to obtain it for us on the grounds that we needed to keep in touch with the contemporary languages in which we worked. After ten years, a window to the outside world had suddenly opened up for me, and I read American and British news magazines avidly every spare moment I had.

Three translators into English were on staff, and none of us was very good. It was my first translation job. The other two translators were not native speakers of English. Nina Shapiro had learned English at a short-term language course in Moscow; Alexander Gurevich had lived in England for a few years. However, the texts were simple and the vocabulary limited to official reports from the battlefield, articles by war correspondents describing the heroism of the troops, and political commentary. All the well-known writers and some who would become well-known were at the front, reporting on the exploits of Soviet soldiers. The most difficult to translate were the regular features by writers Ilya Ehrenburg and David Zaslavsky.

We did our best, helping each other in whatever way we could. Everyone cooperated in the effort to prevent our translation errors from going on the air. The friendly atmosphere was a contrast to that of my earlier experiences at the publishing house. It may have been so because there was a war going on, but I also attribute it to the fact that I was not working with foreign Communists who were trying to prove themselves.

TASS was located in a five-story building on Gorky Street between the Nikitskiye Gates and Pushkin Square in the heart of old Moscow. However, the entire department of RIDZ had been moved to offices below street level in the Byelorussian metro (subway) station. The purpose of this move was to ensure uninterrupted transmissions, despite the air-raid alerts. The department remained underground long after the danger to Moscow had passed, chiefly because it proved difficult to dislodge the "temporary" occupants from TASS's offices in the main building. Space was always a problem.

The Byelorussian station was one of the deepest in Moscow at the time. It was dank and dark in its lower depths; not a ray of daylight penetrated, and the air was thick and musty. I remember buying a rose one day on my way to work. I thought it would surely die before the day was out. Instead, it opened up and filled the room with fragrance. After that, I brought roses to work whenever I could get them. They thrived in the jungle-like atmosphere.

About twenty of us worked on the RIDZ staff—editors, translators, typists, and teletype operators. We worked three shifts, with the night shift often ending as late as three A.M., long after the escalator and public transportation stopped running. We could either climb the hundreds of steps and walk home, or wait until five o'clock when the escalators were turned back on and public transportation started operating again. Chernov, who always stayed until all the work was done, had a key with which to turn on the escalator, but he refused to use it except in dire emergencies. He was too dedicated to "waste" electrical energy for us. I argued with him that our energy was important, too, but it did no good. So I would climb the escalator and walk home.

Summer nights are short in Moscow. At three in the morning, it is already dawn. I had a night pass entitling me to be out after curfew. As I walked home in the half-light through deserted streets, past armed patrols, many of whom got to know me and who waved me on without checking my papers, I could shut out thoughts of the war. It seemed so peaceful. When I would arrive home, I'd tumble into my bed and sleep until noon.

My route home was the way Abram and I used to walk to and from work: The Byelorussian metro station is only a few blocks north of Mayakovsky Square. Now I walked alone—there was no one to hold onto, no one to make sure I was all right, no one. . . . I would then recall my impatience with my husband's protectiveness, his tendency to treat me as if I were fragile, his "untimely" manifestations of affection. I vowed to myself that if we survived this war and were ever together again, I would be more giving of myself. I would not hold back my feelings and I would show my appreciation of his love and tenderness. I missed him terribly. The sight of couples in the street filled me with sadness and envy. Who were they? Why were they so fortunate as to be together?

Daytime Moscow was still a busy, bustling city. Unlike other towns around the country, its streets were full of men, the majority in uniform: men from the Commissariat of Defense located in the side streets around the Arbat; men from other military establishments; soldiers on their way to or from the front (which was nearby for a long time); officers on various errands; directors and engineers from defense plants on business trips to their headquarters; civilians employed in vital areas such as government agencies, the radio committee, Sovinformburo, TASS, the central newspapers, and some publishing houses. Many of the women were in uniform, too. Some had high rank, but most were secretarial and clerical employees of military establishments. It was a city of youth, energy, vitality. This combination of individuals formed a vibrant mix, complemented by the Muscovites who had not left the city in the fall exodus because of circumstances beyond their control or because they were not afraid of the Germans.

The singles' sector was much larger than in ordinary times. Wives and children had been evacuated or, in the case of men from outside Moscow, were at home in the provinces. Husbands and sweethearts were at the front or stationed elsewhere. Men and women were thrown together, working hard, long hours, often through the night. As in the town of Engels, wartime romances developed. War separates some, but it binds others—by common purpose, by job pressures, by the same responses to the same news from the front or from home, and, for many, the same feelings of being cheated out of the best years of their lives. It was not uncommon for men, concerned about their families and sending them parcels of food and clothing when they could, and women, depriving themselves to send goodies to husbands at the front, to be involved in liaisons on the spot, some of which were very serious. No young woman in Moscow needed to have been without a man, some man, in those days.

Among the frontline forces, too, life went on, as I knew from my husband's letters and from the gossip that reached my ears. The women at the front were mostly in auxiliary positions—radio operators, dispatchers, medical personnel, typists, secretaries, and, in outfits like my husband's, translators and interpreters. Though not in actual combat—except for the occasional female snipers and machine gunners—they were often in danger. Some were volunteers, but the majority had been drafted. There had been a partial mobilization of girls age eighteen and over who had completed their secondary schooling. The pressures on them were enormous. With few women and so many men, competition for their favors was fierce. Some of the liaisons were lasting, some broke up long-established marriages, but most army romances ended in heartbreak and disillusionment, especially when the women involved were very young and inexperienced. Many of the young girls found it easier to choose a "protector" than to fend off importunate suitors. The "protectors" were invariably officers, more often than not with wives and families in the rear. The army had a name for the female half of these liaisons—"PPZh" (pronounced "peh, peh, zheh"), which stood for "field campaign wife" in Russian. There was no term for the male half of the affair.

There must have been many officers as well as enlisted men who were envious of those who had field campaign wives. In the Soviet army, there were no periodic home leaves or discharges after a term of duty. Only the wounded or sick were entitled to furlough. All others were granted leave on an individual basis, and whether the individual got leave depended on his relationship with his superior and his ability to wangle the favor. The great majority of enlisted men and officers did not get to see their families for the entire four years of the war.

One day late in the summer of that first year at TASS, I, who seldom received personal calls during working hours, was summoned to the phone. "A man," whispered our secretary. "He wouldn't give his name." An unfamiliar voice introduced himself as a colleague of my husband and asked if I could meet him on the subway platform at the Mayakovsky metro station at four o'clock that afternoon. He had a parcel and regards for me.

I went there and waited. Suddenly, someone grabbed me from behind. It was Abram! He had disguised his voice on the phone in order to surprise me. He had unexpectedly been sent to Moscow on an errand and had the rest of the day and night free, but had to leave early the next morning. We went back to my office, where I got released from the rest of my shift. I telephoned Margo not to come to the apartment that night.

There was hardly enough time to tell each other everything—all that had happened in the year gone by. Abram described the hectic drive through the countryside in the company of Martens and their young driver as they tried to catch up with their unit. I noticed a small, round hole in his forage cap: It was a bullet hole. He laughed and told me how it had happened. "Don't worry," he said. "The longer you've been at the front, the better your chances of survival. You acquire a sixth sense for anticipating danger and skill to cope with it." We talked about the future and about our feelings. He said over and over again, we must never cease to trust each other no matter what lay ahead.

That summer day was the only time we saw each other during the war.

Soon after our meeting, I was approached again by the secret police, this time not through personnel, but directly by telephone. A man called me at home to arrange an appointment. I tried to get out of the involvement, pointing out that I was no good at these activities and that they had been dissatisfied with me in the past. I said that I was very busy. I was going back to school in the fall and I hadn't time to socialize, but I did not refuse point blank. I don't think it occurred to me that I could do so. This operative was much smoother than his predecessors, invariably polite, even charming. There were no specific targets—I should just keep my eyes and ears open and report to him at scheduled intervals on the general atmosphere in the office and, later, at school. I never had anything of interest to report, but he remained polite and friendly. In a letter, Abram warned me to be careful: "I am skeptical about it [the connection]. Often, the attitude towards those who inform is no better than towards the targets."

I knew that. I had no illusions that I was helping out or that their approach to me meant that I was trusted more than others. In fact, a curious incident confirmed my suspicions about the extent of the informer system. In the office one day, a phone call came for one of the French translators. I recognized the voice at the other end of the wire—it was my operative's. I smiled to myself as I summoned my colleague, but said nothing to anyone about my discovery. No wonder it was said that one out of three Soviet citizens was an informant!

One of the most unpleasant aspects of our existence was the need to scrounge for better ration cards. We were dependent on the people in charge of their distribution. At TASS, each department was allotted a specific number of ration cards in each category; these cards were distributed among staff according to job title, and also at the discretion of the department head. The more aggressive the department head was, the better supplied the staff was likely to be. Chernov was highly respected in the organization and could have obtained whatever he requested, but it was hard to persuade him to make more than minimal demands. He believed that everyone had to make the same sacrifices that he himself was willing to make. Our first hurdle was to prevail upon him to demand the best possible deal for the department. To that end, we combined our efforts, cajoling, arguing, and trying whatever worked. After that, we each took care of ourselves. This, of course, affected relationships among the staff. There was envy, suspicion, and resentment as each worker sought a bigger share of the pie. The psychological aspect was important: One's rations category was a status symbol, the expression of a person's worth and a mark of appreciation.

Real nastiness showed when we went to pick up our monthly coupons at the rations distribution office. Management had their coupons delivered to them by messenger, but the rest of us had to wait in a long line. The tension was palpable, for one was never sure that one would get the category expected. There could always be a snag. The tight-lipped, pale-eyed woman in charge had been suddenly catapulted into a lucrative position of low-level, but vital authority. This ordinary, half-educated former Party clerk could and often did question the list, ostensibly in the performance of her duty, but actually just to display her power. For example, a typist may have been listed as an editor by the department head so that she could qualify for a better rations category. In fact, the typist may have been performing more valuable duties than an editor, and her "promotion" in title was a way to get around the rules in this status-conscious society. The head of the rations office knew very well what was going on and could overlook it, but she could also make trouble. Moreover, she often had extra coupons to hand out—for specific items of food or other necessities—and she distributed them at her discretion. She reveled in her power and enjoyed the way people curried favor with her, brought her gifts, and danced to her tune.

This scenario was not limited to TASS.

After several months in a lower category, I was given *liter* B-level rations, and that was how my situation remained for the time I worked at TASS.

After September, however, when I resumed my studies at the university, I worked only the evening and night shifts. I had an exhausting schedule, but it enabled me to make good use of my time. I was not required to attend any but the most important meetings either at TASS or at the university and I took no part in the so-called voluntary extracurricular and free-time assignments. The majority of young men with whom I had started studying in the fall of 1935 had graduated in 1940; most were now in the army. The women had jobs, several at TASS. Of the class that I had joined in 1940, many had missed all or part of the fall 1941 and winter 1942 semesters, as had I. My present class was made up of these people and of students who had caught up with us from junior classes or who had lagged behind from senior classes. We were rescheduled to graduate in January 1945, not in the usual June ceremony that was firmly fixed in the Soviet educational system. Though we formed just a small class and knew each other well, we rarely socialized. Everybody was too busy struggling to obtain their mundane necessities.

Because of the pressures on me, I departed from my usual practice of studying alone. I joined two classmates, both very good students, and found that studying in a threesome was productive, especially before exams. We got along well. Our friendships continued after we graduated.

I did not regard school as a burden. On the contrary, it was something that I was doing for myself that could never be taken away from me. I still strove to do well enough to be recommended for graduate studies (*aspirantura*), to earn a graduate degree (*Kandidat nauk*), and to obtain a position in academic research, where I would be well-paid and sheltered from the everyday aggravations of most jobs.

The history department's program remained heavily ideological. Not only was Marxism a significant part of each year's curriculum (a curriculum that included the history of the Party, political economy, and dialectical and historical materialism), but all other subjects were presented through a Marxist prism as well. In the history of philosophy course, we were given an overview of pre-Marxian philosophers, but once Marx appeared on the scene, no one else counted except in terms of a relationship to him (this was true of the approach to Hegel, for example). The same went for political economy. Adam Smith and David Ricardo were acknowledged, but with the publication of Marx's *Capital,* the final word had been said.

Much of the material was available in English and I managed to obtain a smattering of other views from books referred to in the text or in footnotes. I found these sources in the university or Lenin library. I really gave no thought to the one-sided aspect of our instruction, however, until one incident caught me up sharp. During a class break, I congratulated a classmate on her brilliant presentation at a seminar in political economy. Suddenly she burst out, "How do I know that what I said is true, or even correct?! We are not given any other point of view, no other literature to read. It may all be lies, for all I know!" and she walked away.

I was stunned. I had not realized that she or anyone else had doubts. I was suddenly aware of the intellectual isolation that prevailed in our environment. Naïvely, I thought I had an advantage, having lived in another kind of society and thus having a basis for comparison. This was the first time I thought seriously about the intellectual deprivation which I had come to feel so keenly as the years went by. Until then, I had chafed at the unavailability of the foreign press to me and of the lack of access to foreign books, but mainly I resented this lack because I was eager for news, for information.

The girl who had made the comment avoided me for the rest of the year. She may have worried that I had reported our interchange.

As winter approached, the nights grew longer, and it would be pitch dark when I left the office at TASS. My eyes grew so accustomed to the dark that I could make out shadows and outlines. Besides, I knew every inch of the way and for the most part, could manage to avoid pitfalls. This winter, like the one before and the ones that followed during the war, was extremely cold. Snow was on the ground by the middle of November. This made it easier to see, but harder to walk. On moonlit nights, with the sparkling white snow covering the gaping holes and dilapidated buildings, Moscow looked like a picture postcard.

\* \* \*

We understood the events surrounding World War II strictly through what we were told by the Soviet media. What had taken place in Europe prior to the attack on the Soviet Union seemed unreal and was not to be compared with Russia's struggle. The German conquest of Europe had been swift and presented in the Soviet press in a neutral, not to say favorable, light. We had only a vague idea of what the bombing of Britain had wrought. It was not until I returned to the United States in 1965 that I saw the other side and began to read about the war and to watch the BBC programs on the struggles of the times. I do not recall that the bombing of Pearl Harbor and America's entry into the war made an impression on me or my friends. Certainly these events are not mentioned in any memoirs by Soviet authors that I have read. In December 1941, the battle for Moscow had been raging, driving everything else from our minds because we were living through it.

During the first two years of the war, when the Germans were advancing and the Soviet armies were sustaining enormous losses and the outlook was bleak, Abram wrote often and regularly. His letters helped me through the hardest times. They followed me from Riga to Moscow, from Moscow to Rostov-on-the-Don, to Moscow again, to Engels, and back. A constant theme of his letters in the early years of the war was his fear of losing track of me.

He also worried about his parents, especially after July 1942, when Rostov fell back into enemy hands. Despite Abram's urging, his parents had not left the city. "I have no news from my parents," he wrote. "What has happened to them, poor things?"

Abram was prepared for the worst—and the worst happened. His parents and every member of his family who was not in the army were slaughtered—uncles, aunts, cousins, old people, and children.

The massacre in Rostov followed a pattern similar to the massacre at Kiev's Babi Yar. The German command ordered all Jews to gather at a designated place and to bring their valuables with them. They were then taken to a ravine outside the city, were forced to undress, and were machine-gunned down.

Abram learned this only after Soviet troops marched into Rostov in 1943 and a cousin in the military wrote him with the news. Further details were provided later in a letter from Marianna Allakhverdova, their upstairs neighbor to whom Abram wrote, imploring her to tell him everything she knew. According to Marianna, at some point after the Germans had been driven out of Rostov the first time, Abram's father was arrested by the Soviet authorities for "speculation" (the Russian word for profiteering). He had been bartering needles and thread for food in the open market. When the Germans recaptured the city in 1942, he was in prison, and that may be the reason why Abram's mother did not leave. When the Germans issued the order for all Jews to report, Marianna begged "Aunt Zina" to come and live with her, to pretend to be her aunt. She could have done so, as she did not look particularly Jewish. But she refused, not wanting to jeopardize Marianna. On the designated day, she left home in the early morning. She was never seen or heard from again. And Abram's father apparently died in prison.

Some time after the end of the war, in 1948 I believe, a relative of Abram's by marriage came to see us. A non-Jewish colonel in the army, he had been married to a cousin of Abram's who had perished in the war along with their young son. He had just returned from Rostov and I remember him seated at the table, his head in his hands, repeating over and over again, "Why did they go? Why did they obey the order? Why didn't they leave the city when the others left?"

Why did they obey the order? What else could they have done? A neighbor would surely have informed on them had they disobeyed. And where could they have gone? As for not having left the city when they had the chance, they might not have realized the danger of their situation. They had been kept ignorant of the Nazis' treatment of Jews in the areas they conquered. Compounding the problem was the skepticism that Abram's father and, presumably, many others had about the reliability of anything they read in the Soviet press.

After the war, Abram always intended to go to Rostov and see for himself, but he never did.

Another thread that ran through Abram's letters was his unhappiness with his job.

By the fall of 1942, sections of the Soviet army's political administration (Division VII) had been set up in all the political departments of the main army groups. These sections, in turn, staffed small sections at all levels, down to one-man sections on the forward lines of the battlefront. The job of these divisions was to disseminate material prepared by the central office (where Maria worked) and, depending on the circumstances and the availability of qualified personnel, to write, translate, and disseminate material produced on the spot. When required to do so, they also interrogated prisoners of war.

From the very first, Abram had doubts about the usefulness of trying to demoralize the Germans. As time went on, he grew stronger in his belief that the meager results of the demoralization campaign were not worth the expenditure of effort and personnel, not only while the Germans still expected to win the war, but later, too, when they were in full retreat. Officers of Division VII were often sent on assignments that placed them in dangerous situations close to or at the front lines, despite the fact that they were not combat officers. Though some of his fellow officers were sincere, patriotic, and highly qualified, there were others whose only qualifications were their rank and connections and who were ignorant of the history, culture, and psychology of the enemy. Abram tried unsuccessfully to get released from Division VII and transferred to intelligence. Instead, he was moved down the line to more dangerous units until he ended up on the forward edge, forming an independent outfit consisting of himself, a tommygunner, a horse and cart, a driver, and a loudspeaker. He wrote bitterly, "I have had a career like no one

else in the army—all the way down instead of up." He had started out a lieutenant and ended the war a captain, having risen only one notch.

Actually, he felt much better on his own, away from the politics and
intrigue that dominated the higher ranks.

Lev Kopelev, too, was having his troubles with the petty intrigues and
incompetence of others, but it took him longer to find out the kind of people
he was dealing with. Echoes of Kopelev's difficulties reached Abram. Lyova's
tendency to take people at their own evaluation and to be open about his
own feelings (so sure was he that his sincerity and patriotism were justification for any criticism he might have) would be used against him later. But, at
this juncture, he was much too valuable to be put down or harassed. He
spoke German far better than most of his colleagues, having learned it as a
child, and was already a university professor and distinguished scholar with
a doctorate in German language and literature. He had a magnetic personality that gained him loyal followers, but it also earned him jealous enemies.
He had absolutely no guile and was incorruptible, a combination of qualities that, unsuspected by him, aroused resentment in some of the people he
trusted, who concealed their true feelings for the time being. Abram had
remarked to me long before, in talking about the events of 1937–38 at the
Institute of Foreign Languages: "Lyova trusts everybody. He will always get
into trouble."[1]

As for Abram, he'd be away on frontline assignments for weeks at a
time, unable to pick up his mail, which seemed to distress him more than
anything else. Whenever he got the chance, he'd send me a letter with someone who was going to Moscow, often a newspaper correspondent. In these
letters, he gave more details about his whereabouts and the military situation. If the messenger was someone he knew well and could trust, he would
send money or a parcel. Typically, the parcels contained rock sugar, candy,
and fatback. One parcel contained a length of fabric that had been issued to
officers for uniforms. He often also sent books that were unobtainable in
Moscow but available in the small towns he passed through. He had always
collected books, a source of one of our ongoing conflicts, for he bought
books when we had neither money nor space for them. Once in a while,
he'd ask for something that revealed the lack of basic necessities in his unit.
In one letter, he asked for tooth powder. Another time, he asked for carbon
paper and typewriter ribbons. The need was acute, he wrote, and if I managed to get a large quantity, he might be permitted to come to Moscow to
pick it up. But it was impossible for me to buy or procure typewriter ribbons

---

1. Kopelev described his growing conflicts with peers and commanding officers and his arrest and
interrogation vividly and honestly in *Khranit' Vechno* (Ann Arbor: Ardis, 1975), the English-
language version of which is titled *To Be Preserved Forever* (Philadelphia: Lippincott, 1977).

or any kind of paper in Moscow, and I was unable to get them where I worked nor was anyone able to get them for me. Thus was lost a chance for us to see each other once more.

"Don't send vodka," he wrote. "We have plenty of that here."

At the front, as in the rear, rank got you goodies. Abram described how someone on his staff had been given a sack of apples and pears to deliver to a high-ranking commander. The sack wound up with Abram and his group, who "divided the fruit into equal portions and paid for it happily, anticipating the pleasure in store for us." When the aide for the commander who had ordered the fruit showed up, Abram and the others panicked. "We set to devouring the wonderful fruit," he wrote, "the likes of which I had not seen for at least three years, thus making it impossible for Voentorg (the commissary) to take it away from us. The story spread and even those who had not benefited from the mix-up enjoyed it."

By the 1942–1943 academic year, all the leading professors and most of the students had returned from Ashkhabad. Understandably, there was a preponderance of females at the university. The only males were those whose military status had been deferred, usually because of a physical disability, and those who had been wounded and demobilized. The atmosphere was subdued. The excitement of young people getting acquainted, falling in love, competing intellectually and otherwise, was missing. Students came to class and hurried off to do chores at home.

Though I seemed to settle down for the duration of the war with work and school, I had not entirely given up the idea of getting sent to the front. Abram objected strenuously. On January 5, 1943, he wrote, reminding me that "There is no guarantee that we will be together, and if we are not together, what is the point?"

In early 1943, the Germans were defeated at Stalingrad. The entire army of Fieldmarshal von Paulus was taken prisoner or destroyed. A lull set in that ended in July with a German offensive in the Oryol-Kursk region; this was followed by a Soviet counteroffensive. Fighting was fierce. The liberation of Oryol and Byelogorod in August was marked in Moscow by a twenty-gun artillery salute, the first of many that from then on marked the liberation of every major city. Those salvos became the sounds of hope and victory. The next salute was for Kiev in November.

The tide had finally turned, even though there were still fierce battles ahead. The Germans had fought back at every inch of their retreat. They dared not do otherwise, for they knew what they had wrought and were terrified of falling into the hands of Russian soldiers. There were setbacks, but we could nevertheless look ahead with confidence to a victorious end to the war.

Abram's letters came much less frequently now. Weeks would go by without a word from him. I'd beg Maria to make inquiries through her contacts, but he was away from his home base much of the time and Maria was not always able to find out where and how he was. It was an anxiety-filled summer for me. Adding to my fears for his safety was my worry that his feelings for me might have changed.

It was Margo who sparked these doubts. She came to me one day and said she had something to tell me. She had agonized for days as to whether she should speak up and had come to the conclusion that I ought not to be kept in the dark. A colleague of my husband, a young woman lieutenant named Lyuba, had boasted to Margo that every man in the unit was in love with her, not excluding Abram. She did not claim that she and Abram were having an affair, but stated only that he found her "very exciting and wished he were free to pursue her." I knew Lyuba superficially. Before the war, she had worked for the censorship bureau (*Glavlit*) in several languages and had been connected to the publishing house as well as with the radio committee; that was how Margo knew her. As a matter of fact, she had brought me a letter from Abram on one of her periodic trips to Moscow. It was the "wished he were free" that troubled me. I would not have taken a casual affair seriously, considering the circumstances.

I wrote to Abram, imploring him to tell me more about his friendship with Lyuba. However, he ignored my questions, which I repeated in several letters. Finally, I stopped writing to him. After about two months, I got a letter from him asking why I had not written for so long. He had not been able to write, he said, as he had been moving around a great deal and was hardly ever at home base. Besides, he had been grieving. He had received a letter from his cousin telling him about the deaths of his parents and all the family who had remained in Rostov. As to my questions and hints, he did not know what kind of nonsense I had gotten into my head, but he could not deal with my worries and advised me to stop being foolish. His next letter was uncharacteristically angry and bitter. If I could not put myself in his place and understand that he was mourning for his parents, and if I continued to ask him nonsensical questions not worth the paper they were written on, there was nothing he could do except to add this experience to the series of misfortunes that had overtaken him and to which he was becoming accustomed. In the same letter, he wrote movingly of the death of a comrade. They had been on an assignment together. Abram had gone ahead while the other man had stayed behind and been killed "on the very spot I had just left."

That was a short letter. Two days later, I received a long and detailed letter answering all my questions. He hoped that his response would mark the end of the matter. He said that more than ever, he hated his job. His repeated requests for a transfer to intelligence had been refused. His boss, with whom he had been on bad terms all along, reported to superior officers that Abram had been so affected by his parents' death at the hands of the

Germans and was so filled with hatred that he could not perform properly. His boss recommended that Abram be moved all the way down to a frontline unit "so that he could vent his anger more directly." Abram was outraged at this underhanded move. He had been doing his job and felt that his grief was nobody's business but his own. A visiting officer from headquarters discovered what had been done to him and moved him up again almost immediately. "This is a hard time for me," he wrote. "The hardest ever in my life."

A few days later I received a short, but warm, letter. Apparently, Abram had heard from me and felt a little better, at least on the score of our "misunderstanding." That was the end of the incident. I saw Lyuba after the war and she immediately apologized for the trouble she had "unwittingly" caused me, and blamed Margo for misinterpreting her words.

As I reread Abram's letters now, I wonder how I could have been so wrapped up in my own feelings that I failed to give him the support and sympathy he so badly needed. War, separation, and tragedies so numerous that they could not be absorbed put everything out of focus, so that what was important seemed unimportant. Trivialities took on exaggerated dimensions. It took years for events and feelings to fall into their proper places; some never did.

Moscow was returning to a semblance of normality. By the end of 1943, many of the evacuated institutions had returned to the city and many of the evacuees had come home. Most staff members at the publishing house staff were back at work. Maria's sister Dora returned to find her room occupied, so she was staying at Maria's. Seriously ill when she came back, Dora died a year later while Maria was on frontline assignment and Liza, their older sister, was in the army. I was with Dora in the hospital when she died.

Helen and her mother, who had been living in Tashkent where Helen earned a living as a bookkeeper, returned to find their apartment occupied. They had nowhere to go and moved in with me temporarily. It was their bad luck (and mine) that the occupant of their apartment was a high-ranking official in one of the ministries. It proved impossible to have him dislodged. Though, by Moscow standards, to find three adults living in one room of a communal apartment was not unusual, the quarters were very cramped for our particular group. At first, the situation was not too bad. For one, I was in better health and was eating more regularly. Helen's mother performed miracles with our combined rations. Helen and I did the grocery shopping. I remember how Helen came home one day with three dozen eggs in a cone fashioned out of a newspaper—she had carried the package over her head in a crowded bus all the way from Arbat! I shall never forget the look of triumph on her face as she entered the apartment with not one egg cracked. Still, even though both Helen and her mother were low-key and easy to be with, the closeness began to wear us down. As the months went by, our nerves became frazzled and I could not wait for the two of them to leave. Our friendship survived nonetheless. They had stayed with me for nearly nine months while they waited for the courts to evict the official from their apartment. Though all the legal decisions were in Helen's favor, that made no difference. In the end, their move was made possible because Helen's uncle, a member of the Writers' Union, had strings to pull. They were given two rooms in a three-room apartment, much less desirable quarters than they formerly had possessed.

Late in 1943, we learned that Ahsia's husband Igor had been drafted soon after they had reached Samarkand. Ahsia had then gone to work at a clerical job, and her father had found a job as well. They managed until Ahsia came down with typhus. She was still in the hospital when her father and then her mother came down with the same illness. Ahsia recovered, but her father died. And because her mother was still in the hospital, she was the sole mourner at the funeral. Now, she wrote, she and her mother were very weak, and she was unable to do much work. They were having a hard time making ends meet.

Tamara, Liz, and I got together and mailed her a considerable sum of money. Then Tamara started scouting around for an organization that would bring her back to Moscow. A number of organizations needed translators, and finally VOKS (USSR Society for Cultural Relations with Foreign Countries) agreed to hire her. She and her mother arrived in Moscow in mid-1944. Their rooms, of course, were occupied, so they stayed with Ahsia's uncle for several months until the courts compelled the publishing house to give them a room. Ahsia was very touched by our help, and the events of this period marked the beginning of our close friendship.

While she was living at her uncle's, Igor came to Moscow for a few days home leave. He and Ahsia stayed at Tamara's. Igor was now an officer: The black marks in his dossier, whatever they may have been, were now eliminated and forgotten, and he was on his way up. He had come to Moscow to collect his belongings and to break off the relationship with Ahsia. Ahsia did not tell Tamara what went on between her and Igor, but her unhappiness was obvious. Tamara, who had never liked Igor, could hardly conceal her outrage. Ahsia never spoke to her or to me about Igor, not even many years later.

One day, not long after Ahsia had moved back to Kapelsky, she phoned me and said:

"Come on down. There's somebody here who would like to meet you."

"Mary," she said, ushering me into the room. "This is Alyosha. Alyosha, this is Mary."

Smiling broadly at my surprise was Alex, our charming instructor from the Commissariat of Defense school whom I had last seen in 1937. He told me that the school had been closed down early in 1938 and that he had been hired to teach conversational English at a military academy. When the war broke out, he had volunteered for active service. But he had been seriously wounded early on and was discharged from the army. He now worked for the North Sea Route Company.

Alyosha Ulanovsky and his wife Nadezhda (Nadya), whom I met later, were old friends of Ahsia's family. They had two young daughters when I met them, the elder born in the United States around 1932, the younger in Moscow in 1936. The girls had been evacuated together with their grandmother.

Alyosha dropped in at Ahsia's whenever he was in town. His wife had a job as secretary to a foreign correspondent and had a room at the Hotel Metropol, where she spent most of her time. It was always interesting to talk with them. Alyosha was very independent-minded and outspoken. He was a loyal Soviet patriot at that time, but had never been a Communist and never became one. He had been an active revolutionary and a leading member of an anarchist group. He had even spent some time in Siberian exile under the tsar and had become acquainted with a fellow exile, Josif Stalin. Alyosha was something of a celebrity in old revolutionary circles, famous for his exploits during the Civil War battles in the Crimea. I got to know his story in bits and pieces, the final piece when I returned to America.

The Soviet offensive continued on all fronts, with fierce battles interspersed with setbacks and lulls. Abram was much closer to the fighting than he had been but, paradoxically, his letters were more cheerful. As he put it, "The war is going full blast and it is so exciting that there is no time to think of oneself." For the first time, he described an actual battle, an attack that began on December 24, 1943:

> Early that morning, when it was still dark, our artillery opened fire so fierce that it became light as day. Behind us was a solid wall of artillery fire. Overhead, an ocean of fire raged. This lasted a whole hour. Shells burst without let-up on the German side, nothing living remained there. Then we attacked. By evening we were already very far ahead.

Abram wrote that this pattern repeated itself over the ensuing days, with the Soviet army so close in pursuit of the retreating Germans that the Soviet troops often sat down to meals that the enemy had left uneaten!

Yet the war was nowhere near over. In the same letter, Abram described how the Germans had come from behind and trapped half his squadron. They succeeded in breaking out, but his commanding officer and several others wound up in a village held by the Germans. When the village was retaken by the Soviet army, Abram saw the mutilated bodies of his officer and the other men; they had been tortured to death.

He wrote that the Soviet offensive gave him access to goodies that had been stored behind the enemy lines:

> For a whole month now, we have not eaten army food. Chicken, goose, lamb, veal are on the table every day. We are actually tired of honey, sour cream, butter, and milk. We drink gallons of tea because every outfit has plenty of sugar and honey. We captured eight sugar refineries, hundreds of trucks and railroad cars with cargoes and fuel. We are sometimes faced with absurd choices to make—between a sack of chocolate and a sack of hard candy, between vodka or champagne, Narva herring and Ukrainian fatback.

In a short note dated January 24th, Abram said that he was working all by himself now; instructions from headquarters hardly ever reached him.

In January 1944, the blockade of Leningrad was ended.

A letter dated February 5, 1944 detailed how in January the Germany army had several Soviet divisions surrounded for three days near the town of Lipovetsk.[2] The Red Army soldiers fought their way out:

> We came up very quietly to the village where we were to break through. When we got there, we had to fight a fierce battle. The Germans clung like crazy to every ruin and fired from every kind of weapon. No sooner did one group break through, then the circle would close again. All the houses were in flames and were convenient cover for the Germans to fire from. On one street, they nailed us down so that we could not move for three hours. We were in the direct line of fire. We started up our artillery and launched a frontal attack. That way, we managed to break out of the first circle. The road was strewn with bodies, dead horses, equipment. It was hell! We moved five kilometers away from the village, under fire all the time, and then had to fight our way out of another circle. At last, we were close to the place where the final breakthrough was to occur. We were all terribly agitated. Here it was, nearly daybreak, and we had not yet broken through. The area we had to cross was flat, with not a shrub, and nowhere to take cover. But we knew that if we did not break through now, we would perish. Our division was a Stalingrad Guards division and well known. Anyone taken prisoner would be treated with especially vengeful brutality. At dawn, we were not far from the railway station held by our troops. But

---

2. Anyone who remained in encirclement for more than three days was considered suspect. If he eventually escaped and returned to the Soviet army, he was usually arrested and imprisoned.

it was light and German tanks saw us and started a wild chase after people and wagons. Many were crushed. We were forced to scatter. I was lucky, I managed to leap onto a wagon and jump out at the station, but many others were cut off by the tanks and killed. It took me a whole day to find my unit—the part that had remained in the rear. When I found them, they were sitting around and crying, certain that we had all been killed. We embraced like brothers. Afterwards, we learned that many of our people had not made it. All four colonels and many staff officers were killed. Three out of the five political officers who were inside the circle did not return. Our entire political staff suffered huge losses.

That was one of the most vivid letters I had received from him. It conveyed the horror of the experience, the elation of survival, and the sadness of loss.

On March 18, he wrote about the "rotten spring" he was having and the way the newly unfrozen, muddy roads were "drowning" the army's equipment. "The mud never dries, yet the men push ahead and practically strangle the Germans alive. No one wants to take prisoners. Our troops are killing Germans without mercy everywhere and in every situation. . . . I cannot say that I feel sorry for them. My official job is neither here nor there in these circumstances. All that lofty stuff is all right farther back in the rear. Out here, the only thing you know is to kill as many Germans as you can." He closed by saying that he had just been summoned to headquarters: "That means forty kilometers on foot through thick mud."

In April, Odessa was liberated.

For nearly two months, I got no mail from him at all. Then on May 3rd, he wrote that the "war has become wild. . . . Everything is on the move. Often we don't know at one end of a village what is happening at the other end. Sometimes we discover that we have spent the night in the same village as the enemy."

He also wrote me about his first encounters with Jewish survivors: "They don't resemble human beings. They lived in the forests and in dugouts, ate whatever they could find. The horror of what can be done to people; yet it is impossible to destroy them completely."

In May, Sevastopol was liberated. Then we learned of the liberation of Karelia in June; of Minsk and Vilna in July; of Bucharest, Romania in August; of Sofia, Bulgaria and Tallinn, Estonia in September; of Riga, where the war had begun for Abram and me, in October; of Belgrade, Yugoslavia later that month. A month-long battle for Budapest, Hungary, where a large group of Germans were encircled, ended in a Red Army victory just before the end of 1944. In Moscow, we looked forward to the frequent artillery salutes celebrating the liberation of each city.

Starting that summer, Abram was on his own for the rest of the war. He had a horse, a wagon, a driver, a megaphone, and a tommygunner. I met his tommygunner, Sasha, after the war. When the Germans took Kiev in September 1941, Sasha was a blond, blue-eyed twelve-year-old Jew living in an orphanage. The Germans, following their usual pattern, ordered all Jews to appear at a designated place, after which they were transported to Babi Yar, a ravine on the outskirts of the city. At Babi Yar, the Jews were given shovels and ordered to dig a pit, and then to undress and stand on the edge of the grave they had dug for themselves. Instead of following those orders, Sasha had grabbed a wheelbarrow and pretended to be one of the helpers, carting away the belongings of the doomed. For two years, he survived on the streets, picking up the German language and learning to handle weapons. When Kiev was liberated, he persuaded some of the first officers who entered the city to let him join their unit. Abram had heard about this young tommygunner who spoke German. When he set up his outfit, Abram asked that the boy be transferred to it. By the end of the war, Sasha was a seasoned, decorated soldier of sixteen.

Abram's job was to get as close to the German lines as he could and broadcast whatever material he chose. He wrote on July 10th: "I heckle the Germans any way I can and they go wild with fury. They'll soon find out that we are not wasting our time here." No one badgered him. It was dangerous work, but he felt at ease with the independence it gave him.

As for me, 1944 was the year I was rejected for membership in the Communist Party.

Both Abram and I had been active in the Komsomol and were dedicated to the stated goals of the Communist Party. The war experience had intensified our political feelings, as it had for many others. Like them, we believed that things would be different after the war, the Soviet people having proved their loyalty and made tremendous sacrifices. (Of my friends, Maria, who was two years older than I, had recently been admitted to the Party, recommended by the political officers with whom she worked. Helen, also two years older, had simply let her Komsomol membership lapse. Galya, of course, had joined years before.) The age limit for Komsomol membership was twenty-eight. I had always planned to join the Party and would have applied sooner, except that the situation had not been favorable for persons like myself who had been born abroad and had ties outside of Russia. Abram had applied for membership before the war and had been admitted as a candidate, obtaining provisional membership as the first stage of admission. We had been very nervous when he went before the district committee, fearing that having an American-born wife would mean trouble for him. When he was asked about my occupation and he replied that I was a student at Moscow University, they nodded approval and asked no more questions about me. This may have been on oversight or just pure luck. He applied for and received full membership at the front.

The Party secretary at TASS was a man named Kuzyuren, an Old Bolshevik and a former member of the Kremlin's Latvian guard. I discussed the matter with him and he encouraged me to apply. So did Chernov, who too was an Old Bolshevik, highly respected by TASS. Ordinarily, three recommendations from Party members were required, but as a Komsomol member, I needed only two, plus a recommendation from the Komsomol district committee. Chernov and Galya's mother gave me these. Then I came before a TASS Komsomol membership meeting, after which it was recommended that the district committee approve my application. That, too was routine. Next was usually the most critical stage of the procedure, the TASS Party membership meeting. Izzy, Chernov, Kuzyuren, and others spoke on my behalf, and the membership voted unanimously to recommend my acceptance to the district committee, the body whose approval was the final step in the admissions process.

Prior to the Party district committee meeting, applicants were interviewed by an instructor. From the questions the interviewer put to me, I sensed that all was not well. After the interview, I went straight to Kuzyuren and asked him to sound out the district committee because I believed that I was going to be denied admission. Kuzyuren ridiculed my fear, assuring me that the district committee would not go against so authoritative a body as the TASS membership. He did not set my fears at rest, but I was unable to persuade him to take action. I also told Chernov about my misgivings. No one took me seriously.

Then came the day of the full district committee meeting. Two other applicants from TASS were on the agenda, a former classmate of my husband's and a TASS war correspondent. The questions were the usual ones— family background, education, Komsomol activities, and the history of the Soviet Communist Party. It all went smoothly. One by one, we were asked to wait outside. The two others were admitted. But I was turned down, ostensibly because I had not been active enough in the Komsomol. Patently, this was an excuse. No one in my circumstances—working and studying full time—was expected to do more than a minimum of outside work, and I had a long record of activism. I took the situation to mean that I was not trusted.

I was devastated. I had not contemplated life outside the Party. Abram, who was also upset over this development, reminded me in a letter, "If we are destined to survive and be together again, time will heal everything. All we can do now is to be patient."

Little did I dream that in the not-too-far future, I would thank my lucky stars that I had not been admitted to membership in the CPSU. You did not resign from the Party if your views changed. You were in it for life or until expelled, which could make life very difficult indeed.

But at that point, it was not my way to accept a setback without a fight. With the encouragement of Kuzyuren and Galya's mother—not Chernov, for he knew better—I wrote a letter to the Central Committee of the CPSU asking for a hearing. I was given an appointment some time in April 1944. A pleasant-looking, grey-haired man greeted me warmly, complimented me on the good letter I had written, and said that perhaps the district committee had not thought through their decision. He suggested that I undertake some special Komsomol assignment for the record and then reapply. (Though he assured me that I would not be turned down a second time, I did not reapply.)

Then he said something that astonished me:

"You know my name. [Kagan, I think it was]. I am Jewish and you can see that I have a responsible position."

It had not occurred to me that my being Jewish had anything to do with the rejection (and I don't think it did; I still believe it had to do with my American background). But the implication was clear: Jewish heritage had become an issue.

Despite repeated instances that smacked of anti-Semitism—for example, the replacement of the (Jewish) Commissar of Foreign Affairs Maxim Litvinov with the (non-Jewish) Molotov; TASS's recall of its Jewish correspondents from abroad in 1942; its failure to appoint any more Jewish correspondents; and the increasing number of Jews who had job offers withdrawn suddenly—it was not until that year that I became convinced beyond a doubt that the Soviet government was fostering discrimination against the Jews.

Creeping anti-Semitism from below had been evident from the early days of the war. It was manifested in anti-Semitic remarks in public, and in the expressed belief of the populace—contrary to reality—that Jews were sitting out the war in cushy positions. Jewish evacuees returning from other parts of the country, especially Central Asia and the Tatar republic (which received the major waves of refugees), described the hostility they faced. I also heard accounts of anti-Semitism in the army and among the partisans.

The rise of anti-Semitism among the population coincided with the newly formed alliance between the Soviet government and the Russian Orthodox Church. Immediately after the war broke out, the Soviet government initiated an entirely new policy toward the Russian Orthodox Church, restoring it to a position of power and influence after years of harassment. Obviously, the government did not believe that Communism was a sufficient battle cry to rally the country's support. The leader of the church, the Patriarch, called upon the nation to save Holy Russia. There was much fanfare connected with church activity. Parishioners were urged to contribute money, valuables, gold, and silver to the war effort. The response was enormous. With funds thus collected, the church donated aircraft, tanks, and materiel to the armed forces.

Just as the Soviet authorities deliberately downplayed the Nazi policies toward the Jews, reporting massacres and death camp horrors as directed against "Soviet citizens," they did nothing to curb expressions of anti-Semitism from below. One reason for this, given by apologists for the Establishment, was that to call attention to Jews as the special objects of Nazi persecution might arouse even more popular resentment against them and encourage the idea that the war had in some way been caused by the Jews and was being fought for them.

Still faithful, we rationalized: The penetration of enemy propaganda, the influence of church dogma, the unwillingness of the Soviet government to "rock the boat" were to blame. We noted the economic basis for the rise of anti-Semitism in the regions of evacuation where the influx of refugees brought pressure on the limited supplies of food and clothing. We believed that when the war was over and the Soviet government once again stressed internationalism and fraternity, anti-Semitism would diminish and disappear.

But when it became indisputable that discrimination was emanating from above as well as from below, no excuse was acceptable. For me, the straw that broke the camel's back was an incident at the university that was impossible to misinterpret or to excuse.

Classes ended in May, with exams scheduled through June. Students spent the time between exams studying at the library or at home; few showed up at the departments. One day in June, I stopped by the faculty office and found an unusually large number of students gathered in the hall, talking excitedly.

"What's going on?" I asked.

One of my classmates replied, "The list of students recommended for graduate study has come back from the university administration with all the Jewish names crossed out."

"How do you know?" I asked, for this concerned the graduating class just ahead of us.

"Someone saw the list and the rejected students have been told."

Some of the students in the corridor were Jewish, some were not. All were upset. I remember thinking that anywhere else, certainly in the United States (I thought), there would have been protests, possibly a strike.

As usual, it was hard to get the facts straight. It was rumored that the professors whose recommendations had been rejected had demanded an explanation and had been told that the orders came from above, from outside the university.

This was proof positive of anti-Semitism at the government level, the first incontrovertible evidence I had of the official anti-Semitism that was to become rampant in the postwar period.

I did two things.

First, I went to Chernov, knowing that he was a dedicated longtime Communist, and demanded an explanation. Chernov did not pretend to doubt my story. He did not say that I must be mistaken or that there must be a misunderstanding. What he said was that the Nazis claimed that Russia was run by Jews, and that we did not want to add grist to their propaganda mill. That was why TASS was not sending Jewish correspondents abroad for the time being. I did not find this explanation convincing and told him so. I doubt that he did either, but what else could he say?

I also telephoned my contact in the secret police, whom I still saw infrequently but on a regular basis. I told him I had something special to report and he made an immediate appointment with me.

I told him that there must be saboteurs somewhere in the university administration or even higher up because of the outrageous incident that had occurred in the history department—shameless discrimination that went against all our principles of internationalism, brotherhood, merit, and so on and so forth. I was putting on an act. I was not so naïve by then as to expect him to do anything about the situation. He responded that surely I was exaggerating, that Jews were often hypersensitive and jumped to incorrect conclusions. He instructed me to write up the incident and mention by name which students had said what. I replied that I had not paid attention to who had said what. Besides, I did not know the names of most of them, as they were not in my classes. I would write up the report as I saw it—which I did, giving my opinion and no one else's (no doubt causing another black mark in my dossier).

Most of the Soviet Jews I knew were Jewish only in name, only because they had been designated a nationality and were entered as such in their internal passports. The majority of Jews of my generation were assimilated. Their language and culture were Russian. They neither knew nor were interested in Jewish religion, history, or culture. For most, awareness of their Jewishness was aroused, perhaps for the first time, by the combination of fascism in Germany and its local manifestations during the war and the official discrimination that began in the Soviet Union in the 1940s.[3]

The official discrimination against Soviet citizens with Jewish names and the refusal to combat it at the lower levels produced the first crack in my faith in the Communist cause and in the Soviet Union's interpretation and implementation of Communist theory. In my mind, there was no possible excuse for ethnic or religious discrimination. Expediency was not a justification. The basic tenets of the brotherhood of man and justice for all

3. The American journalist Ella Winter visited the Soviet Union during the war. Despite having heard first-hand accounts of arrests and anti-Semitism, she refused to take them seriously.

were being violated. I was very upset and angry and, among friends, I did not conceal my feelings.

There was another significant event that year, one that also shook my faith in Soviet Communism and to which my friends and I reacted strongly. I'm referring to the promulgation of a new marriage law preceded by a phony nationwide discussion similar to the one before abortions were banned in 1936. In addition to making divorce extremely difficult to obtain, the law reintroduced the concept of illegitimate (out-of-wedlock) birth. According to an entry in the *Great Soviet Encyclopedia* (1953 edition): "Until 1944, registered and unregistered but factual marriage were equal. With a view to strengthening the Soviet family, the USSR Supreme Soviet issued a decree on July 8, 1944, to the effect that only marriages registered with the proper civil authorities would be entitled to the rights and obligations provided by Soviet laws on marriage, the family, and guardianship."

This concept went against the grain of the new, revolutionary morality that had prevailed after the Bolshevik Revolution. Under the new law, the father was no longer responsible for the support of an out-of-wedlock child. His name was not entered on the birth certificate even if he acknowledged his paternity. The unmarried mother was given a (subsistence-level) monthly allowance by the state. While its stated goal was to strengthen the family, the law also purported to protect unmarried mothers, for now they would be the responsibility of the state and would not have to worry about whether the father would help support the child. It was not difficult to perceive what the real motive was: to relieve men of financial responsibility so that they would produce more babies to replenish the population when the war was over. It was also intended to reassure the wives of men in the armed forces that they would not be displaced by frontline liaisons. Actually, the new law caused anxiety and confusion among couples who had not formalized their marriages; these couples could not react because they were separated by the war.

The TASS general meeting that was called to discuss the proposed law was unusually well attended. Every seat was taken, with people standing in the back of the hall. There had been much private discussion prior to the meeting, especially among the younger people, and there was an air of expectation in the audience, despite the foregone conclusion that the law would be enacted. And, indeed, along with speakers who supported the law, there were some who offered mild criticism, presented more as suggestions for improving details than as opposition. Then a young editor, active in the Komsomol, asked for the floor and flung a challenge to the audience. In a well-reasoned speech, she argued that the proposed law was reactionary and that it went against all socialist principles. She concluded with the assertion that many capitalist countries—Switzerland, for example—had more progressive family legislation than the Soviet Union. No one in the audience responded. Afterwards, a special Komsomol meeting was held to discuss her "outburst." She was reprimanded, but no further action was taken.

One of the consequences of the 1944 law was a rush to the registrar's office by long-established couples. In my building, for example, a dignified white-haired couple who had met in Siberian exile before the revolution and who had grown children and grandchildren formalized their marriage. I happened to meet them on their way back from ZAGS and the wife said, smiling, "He has just made an honest woman of me."

Common-law marriage (which the decree called "de facto but unregistered marriages") was no longer recognized. Gradually, new moralistic attitudes took over. Unmarried mothers were looked down upon (though their children were not stigmatized). As always, the housing shortage was a factor. Cohabiting couples no longer had equal rights. To be registered in your spouse's "living space," you had to produce a marriage certificate. As time went by, the simple act of registration of a civil marriage evolved into a ceremony that combined traditional church wedding customs with a contemporary veneer.

Also distressing was an unmistakable trend towards rising nationalism and the reintroduction of pre-Soviet nomenclature. Personal ranks were instituted for the highest army command in 1940, after the Finnish war. In October 1942, the institution of political instructors in the armed forces was abolished. Before that, the political instructor, representative of the Party, had as much authority as the unit commander. Now that authority was no longer divided. In January and February 1943, personal ranks were conferred on all commissioned and non-commissioned officers. Political instructors were recertified and given personal ranks. The new army uniforms with their insignia and epaulets resembled the uniforms of the tsarist army. Rules on subordination to rank and saluting were made more stringent. The stated aim of the changes was to strengthen discipline. Actually, in my view (as with the rehabilitation of the Russian Orthodox church when the war started), the aim was to instill a strong nationalist spirit on the assumption that the people were more likely to fight and make sacrifices for the "motherland" than for socialism and internationalism.

In the summer of 1944, tragedy struck from a completely unexpected quarter. It started with good news.

Margo called me.

"My children are coming home." Her voice was joyous. "I don't know how long it will take, but I hope it will be soon. I've sent them four train tickets." The tickets were for Inessa, now twelve years old; Felix, five; the Yugoslavian woman who was caring for them; and Tito's son.

A week or two later, they arrived in Moscow—without Felix. The woman from Yugoslavia was in hysterics; the story she told incredible. When they arrived in Novosibirsk where they had to change for the Moscow train, she left Inessa to look after Felix and their luggage while she and Tito's son went to the ticket office to validate their tickets. Novosibirsk, always a busy railroad junction, was mobbed. Every inch of bench space was occupied. Men, women, and children were sprawled on the floor with their boxes, sacks, and cases. Some had been there for days. When the woman and Tito's son returned to their spot several hours later, Felix was gone. Inessa told an incoherent story of how Felix had wandered off and she had caught a glimpse of him being led away by a woman.

Two days later, Margo left for Novosibirsk by express train. She could find no trace of Felix, no one who saw anything, and no help from the local authorities. She returned empty-handed.

Felix was never heard of again.

This was worse than death—not knowing what had happened. In those days of food shortages, there were rumors of cannibalism in distant regions. We never uttered the word, but I am sure it was on Margo's mind as it was on mine.

Not long afterwards, horror was added to tragedy. Inessa and I were seated on a bench, waiting for her mother, and I asked her to tell me once again exactly what had happened in Novosibirsk. She repeated the story, adding nothing. Then she turned to me, her violet eyes ablaze, her cheeks flushed, and said:

"It's better for me now. I'm the only one my mother loves."

I never told Margo about that conversation.

To complete the story of Margo Pavlich: Toward the end of the war, she was parachuted into Yugoslavia to join Tito's partisans. Tito never quite trusted her, regarding her as a Soviet stooge (which she may have been), and she returned to Moscow after the war. In 1946, she committed suicide by shooting herself through the head with a pistol, muffling the sound with a pillow.

The beginning of 1945 was an unhappy time for me. The end of the war was in sight, but I was receiving no letters from my husband. I was frantic. Added to the worry about Abram's safety were the stresses of the final semester at the university.

Our class was scheduled to graduate in February 1945. I had to finish writing my thesis and prepare for state exams, one on the principles of Marxism-Leninism and one in my major, modern European history. My thesis was on the development of the Constitution of the United States, 1787–1789. My advisor was Professor Alexei Yefimov, a Corresponding Member of the USSR Academy of Sciences and a leading scholar in American and French history. Yefimov was a gentleman of the old school, rather aloof, but highly respected in the department and a member of the faculty

Party committee. On several occasions, I went to his home, either to pick up or deliver material or to consult him. He and his wife always received me graciously.

Professor Yefimov approved my thesis and said that he would recommend me for graduate studies. But two months before graduation, there came a thunderbolt. First, we heard rumors that Professor Yefimov was being brought up before the Party committee on a "personal case," indicating that some sort of transgression had been committed. Then we learned that someone had discovered that Yefimov had been an officer in the tsarist army and had fought with White Guard troops in the Civil War. He was expelled from the Party and removed from his academic positions. Eventually, he weathered the storm. After the war, with all the emphasis on Russian patriotism and a new interpretation of Russian history, a tsarist officer's background was considered to be a minor offense. He appealed and was reinstated in the Party with a reprimand for concealing his past; he was then restored to his academic positions. However, when I needed him he was unable to help me, and my plans to enter graduate school went up in smoke. I was lucky my thesis was accepted and that I was not held guilty by association. I passed my state exams and finally graduated from Moscow University after ten years, years that had been interrupted by the Commissariat of Defense interlude, childbirth, war, and evacuation.

Like all final-year students, I had to come up before the placement commission for a job assignment. TASS put in a request for my services. The commission denied it and, instead, appointed me senior instructor in history at the Pedagogical Institute in Vologda, a town about 250 miles north of Moscow. This was undoubtedly a vengeful act, possibly connected with my association with Yefimov, because ordinarily a request from so prestigious an organization would have been honored. In fact, several graduates were placed in TASS, among them one of the trio with whom I had studied. I had no intention of going off into the wilds where it would be so much harder to keep in touch with my husband. Nor did I want to abandon my room and take the chance of someone being moved into it. I took my assignment paper to Chernov, who said TASS would take care of the situation.

Several weeks later, I came home from the night shift one morning to find a summons in my mailbox, ordering me to appear in court on charges of having broken the law by not reporting for my assignment in Vologda. I hurried right back to the office with the summons, very much disturbed that TASS had not done anything about the matter. Chernov took the summons from me and told me to calm down. TASS sent its lawyer to court in my stead, and that was the end of the episode.

In March and April 1945, our troops were fighting in Germany. Though the end of the war seemed within sight, I still had no letters from Abram.

On May 8th, Germany surrendered. On May 9th, the country celebrated Victory Day.

That was a never-to-be-forgotten day. People poured into the streets and headed for Red Square and the Kremlin walls. The square was jammed. The air crackled with excitement. Strangers embraced. Everybody talked with everybody else. Some people were smiling, laughing joyously, shouting. Others had tears streaming down their cheeks.

At the victory banquet in the Kremlin, Stalin addressed the nation and rather perfunctorily thanked the Soviet people as a whole for their sacrifices and war effort. Then he singled out the *Russians* "who had sacrificed the most and fought the hardest." In his speech, Stalin said that the Russians were the most outstanding of the nations of the Soviet Union and that they had demonstrated their keen intellect and strength of character. The emphasis on the Russians made me and some of my friends uneasy, but we did not attach the significance to Stalin's words that we would when we looked back a few years later. As things turned out, this speech was a harbinger of the chauvinistic interpretation of Russian history and culture and the discriminatory policies that would mark the postwar years up to Stalin's death.

It was true that the Russians had borne the brunt of the fighting. The two other Slavic republics, Ukraine and Byelorussia, had been occupied early in the war. Entire ethnic groups in the Caucasus and the Crimea had been accused of collaborating with the enemy and later were deported from their homelands. Greeks who had lived along the Black Sea coast of Georgia for generations were forcibly relocated when the Germans were advancing in their direction. Central Asians were rumored to be reluctant soldiers with a high incidence of self-inflicted wounds that they used for avoiding the battle front. And, of course, the (only newly Soviet) Baltic republics had been occupied in the very first days of the war.

Yet it seemed wrong to have glossed over the other nationalities who comprised about half of the total population of the Soviet Union. The omission was contrary to the rhetoric of internationalism that had been drummed into our heads all these years. There were strong partisan movements in Byelorussia and in Ukraine. Jews had served in disproportionately large numbers to their share in the population. They constituted only 1.8 percent of the population and 2.8 percent of the fighting force, yet were fourth in the number decorated for bravery.[4] Nevertheless, the myth persisted that Jews had avoided service and that those who were in the army had cushy quartermaster jobs and avoided the fighting. It would have been easy to set

---

4. Data from Solomon Schwartz, *Jews in the Soviet Union,* Russian edition (New York: American Jewish Labor Committee, 1966).

the record straight. The power of the controlled press was such that a word in any one of the central newspapers, *Pravda* or *Izvestiia,* would have been sufficient to curb at least overt manifestations of anti-Semitism. The fact that no such word came was not an oversight. This would become clear in the not-so-distant future.

From Red Square, I went to Liz's. It had been the custom of Liz's friends to gather at her place on July 4th, her birthday. That July 4th was also American Independence Day added to the festive spirit, but also brought on nostalgia, especially during the war. Gradually, Liz's apartment became a gathering place for important occasions during the war, both happy and sad. On this day, the apartment was more crowded than usual. People came and went until late in the evening. Everyone talked about where he or she had been when the surrender was announced.

Our joy was mixed with sadness and anxiety. Grisha, Liz's husband, had still not been heard from. I, too, had not heard from Abram for much longer than usual and Maria had not been able to get any news of his whereabouts. But that day, we put our cares aside and rejoiced.

Another three weeks went by before I heard from Abram. Finally, I received a short note dated May 19th, written on a picture postcard from somewhere in Hungary. In it, he congratulated me and all our friends on victory. A subsequent letter must have gone astray because in the next letter I received, more than two months later, he wrote as if I already knew that he had been ill. That letter, dated July 23rd, was brought to me by Maria's older sister, Liza. I learned that Abram had contracted typhus during the liberation of a death camp in Austria and had been lying unconscious in a hospital in Vienna when the war ended. Liza was a Lieutenant in a Department VII section and had met him by chance in Hungary.

The general tenor of the letter was unhappy. He was anxious about his future, about where he would be sent, and about when he could expect to come home. The opening lines were uncharacteristically brusque: "Enough of being angry and worried. The war is over and now we can probably hope to be together again." He also assessed his overall situation: "I'm a little better after my illness. In general, I've come out of the war comparatively whole and unharmed, except for a sprained finger, loss of hearing in my left ear, and a weakened heart after typhus. But that is all right. It is possible to live and work with that."

After being discharged from the hospital, he was not returned to his division, but sent to the reserve of a different army. The outlook for coming home was bleak. It would take months, he wrote, to complete the demobilization of all those who were entitled to it. He begged me to "push all buttons" to get him out of there or at least to get him transferred to a situation where his knowledge of German would be useful. He also sent a gold watch.

Meanwhile, with Professor Yefimov out of the picture, I looked around for some other way to gain admission to graduate studies. I consulted Professor Guber, whose seminar in Latin American history I had taken and for which I had written a paper on the Incas and the conquest of Peru. The USSR Academy of Sciences consisted of a number of specialized institutes, all of which had post-graduate programs. He offered to recommend me for *aspirantura* at its Pacific Ocean Institute. My application was approved with the usual condition that I pass the exam in the history of philosophy.

Under the Soviet system of higher education, the student seeking a graduate degree had three years in which to take courses and pass exams in the history of philosophy, two foreign languages, and in a field of specialization, after which he or she had a year in which to write and defend a thesis. Unlike the other Soviet institutions of higher education, the Academy required its graduate students to take and pass the history of philosophy exam *before* starting classes. The exam was given in August for all the Academy Institutes. I took time off from TASS to study. I also decided to take the two foreign language exams (English and German) to get them out of the way. I passed and was enrolled with the usual first-year stipend of, if I recall, 750 rubles, nearly as much as I was earning at TASS. I quit my job and looked ahead to an easy, pleasant three years, doing what I liked best—learning—and then writing my thesis, earning a degree, and gaining a research position.

Maria was back at the publishing house. All she had to show for her service during the war was a medal and Party membership. Mussia stayed at the Radio Committee. The children had all come home. Families were reunited, losses chalked up. Finally, in October, Abram came home for one month's leave to await further orders.

He did not look well—he had a rash that he had picked up in a Romanian fleabag hotel where he was quartered while being processed for leave. He was worried about his future, but was also deliriously happy to be at home, to see old friends again, to pour out everything that had happened to him in the last four years, and to hear how I had fared.

However, the joy of home and reunion was marred by more bad news.

Lyova Kopelev was in jail. He had been arrested a few weeks before the end of the war, charged with anti-Soviet agitation and slandering the Soviet army. The case against him had been building for some time, though he was not aware of this. Envious colleagues, many of whom he had considered his friends, produced "evidence" based on distortions and deliberate misinterpretations of opinions he had expressed in public or in private conversations. Abram went to see his family. The case was being appealed, they told him. Friends in very important positions had come to his assistance, and hoped the situation would be "straightened out" soon.

Max came to see us. He did not know what had become of his mother and sister. After weeks of waiting in 1941 for permission to go to Riga to see them, he arrived there on the day war was declared. When he returned to Moscow, he went to Nalchik to see his wife and newborn son. That was the last he saw or heard from them. Nalchik was captured early in the war. After Max was demobilized, he went back to Nalchik, but was unable to learn anything definite. Nor had he been able to find out what had happened to his mother and sister left behind in Riga. He assumed that they had been killed.

It was also at this time that the death of Abram's parents was confirmed in the letter from Marianna Allakhverdova. We learned, as well, that his friends Yasha Liberman and Valya had been killed in action.

Yet another calamity befell our group: Liz had a massive stroke. She was only thirty-eight years old. Slowly, very slowly, Liz recovered enough to function independently, but she was never able to work again. Her son Donald was eight years old in 1946. He had been away between the ages of three and six. He never knew his mother as we knew her—a remarkably intelligent, talented woman and devoted friend.

October went by very quickly. Before the end of the month, Abram received orders to report to the headquarters of the Soviet Military Administration (SVA) in Berlin. His assignment turned out to be with the censorship department that dealt with German publications. We had no idea how long our separation would last.

What happened next was incredible, a truly unexpected stroke of luck. Around the middle of December, Abram wrote that arrangements were being made for SVA officers to send for their families. An officer had been delegated from his outfit to go to Moscow to escort the wives and children. The date had not been set, but I was to be ready at a moment's notice.

No forms to fill out. No red tape. No questions asked. Just a blanket order, and me under that blanket.

I obtained a leave of absence from the Academy, drew up a plan of study in Berlin with Professor Guber's approval, and arranged to report back in six months to present a progress report and thereby hold onto my place in the graduate program.

In January 1946, I left for Berlin.

☙◉☙

# *16*
## Berlin—1946

Not until I boarded the train at the Byelorussian railroad station did I believe that I was actually going. A man had telephoned me about ten days before, introducing himself as the officer who was to escort our group. He told me where and when to meet them, but I half expected to be told at the last minute that there had been a mistake and that I was not included. Germany was "abroad." I could not believe that I would be permitted to go to a foreign country. However, all went smoothly. There was not even a border check at Brest.

Abram had arrived in Berlin in October 1945, by which time some order had been restored after the chaos that followed Germany's surrender. Municipal services were functioning, and the population was receiving food rations. Politically, it was a time of transition. Among the immediate tasks of the four powers in the zones of occupation was to deal with former Nazis and Nazi propaganda and to set up local governments.[1] In the period immediately following the occupation, the stress was on democracy. Several legal parties existed. The largest were the Social-Democratic Party of Germany (SPD) and the Communist Party of Germany (KPD). These parties had their own newspapers and other periodicals. The Soviet censorship group consisted of German-speaking officers, all of whom had served in Division VII during the war.

Abram was at the station to meet me and take me to his room in the heart of the city. The rest of the group from Moscow, only a few of whom we met, continued on to Karlshorst where SVA headquarters were located and where all but a few Soviet citizens were required to live. Karlshorst, a section in southeastern Berlin, had been cleared of all Germans except service personnel and was for all intents and purposes a Soviet town within the city.

Abram was now censor of the German Liberal-Democratic Party's daily newspaper. This entailed working late into the night at offices in the

---

1. A detailed account of how the government of the Soviet zone was set up and its subordination to the Soviet Military Administration is given by Wolfgang Leonhard in *Child of the Revolution* (Chicago: Henry Regneri Co., 1958).

center of Berlin. Therefore, he and the other censors who wished to do so were permitted to live closer to their places of work. Abram had decided to wait until I arrived before looking for an apartment and had, meanwhile, rented a room in the apartment of two middle-aged sisters in Mitte, a block or two from Unter den Linden, where the Russian sector ended and the American began.

Aside from the few days I spent in newly Soviet Riga, this was my first trip outside the Soviet Union since I arrived in 1931, and my first ever to Western Europe. Even war-torn Berlin, with its small shops, varied architecture, and billboards looked good to me. I did not pay much attention to the political situation; I was enjoying myself too much.

All of Berlin bore the scars of battle, but Mitte was the worst. The area had block after block of gutted buildings, roofs off, walls blown away, and piles of rubble. It seemed as if no human being could live there. Yet it *was* alive. Every habitable edifice was inhabited. And shops were open amidst the ruins. It was in one of these buildings, only slightly damaged, that the local young German Communist in charge of finding housing for Soviet officers had found Abram his room. The two sisters owned the building as well as a flower shop on the ground floor.

It was a large apartment, furnished with heavy mahogany furniture, fine china, crystal, and Japanese porcelain. Abram, who loved and appreciated beautiful things, bought several crystal bowls, a Venetian glass vase, and a Japanese tea set when we left the apartment. (I have them still.) Our landladies had the saccharine friendliness I was to encounter among so many of the Germans. Yet, undoubtedly, they were genuinely pleased to have us. We brought extra income and food and, perhaps, protection from prowling soldiers.

Abram told me that he too had worried about whether I would be allowed to join him, but no one had asked any questions about me. It seems that there was increasing concern in high government and military circles about fraternization between Soviet troops and local German women. Toward the end of 1945, an order had been issued for all married officers to send for their wives and children. Officers were delegated from the units to fetch the families.

It took some time for us to find a suitable apartment. We stayed with the German women through April. I remember this because I celebrated my first postwar birthday there: I was now thirty-one. I had mentioned the date to the ladies in earlier conversations and on the morning of the twenty-fifth, before I got up, they reminded Abram who, as usual, had forgotten it. One of the women went downstairs with him to open the shop. He pointed to the flowers he wanted—orchids. When he heard the price, he had to go upstairs for more money. He had never seen orchids before. Neither had I, except for the lady's slippers that had grown wild in the woods near New Haven where I lived as a child.

The housing shortage in Berlin was acute, especially in the center of town. We were finally shown an apartment that seemed right for us on the third floor of a solid brick building about a mile away from where we were living. It was a large one-bedroom with a living room, dining room, and kitchen, fully furnished with the usual heavy furniture and machine-made carpets. It had been occupied by a Soviet officer who had been transferred.

Tieckstrasse was a neighborly sort of street—women sitting on stoops in front of apartment buildings like ours, children playing, small shops along the block. The women would nod to me in a friendly manner. Once, to my horror, I saw a woman dangling a baby out of an upper floor window across the street. I was afraid to gesture to her for fear of startling her into loosening her hold on the child. Apparently, no one else on the block thought anything of this.

We did not stay in Tieckstrasse long. One day, an emergency brought the editor of the Liberal-Democratic newspaper to the house. He was a very proper-looking gentleman with a goatee, and he carried a walking stick. After he and Abram had attended to the business at hand, he hemmed and hawed and apologized for the comment he was about to make. He said he could not conceal his surprise at where we lived. Tieckstrasse, he said, was in the heart of the red-light district. Many of those pleasant *Hausfrauen* seated outside or in open windows were prostitutes, and most of the apartments in the buildings were *Absteigskwartiere,* that is, he explained, rooms for rent by the hour. It was damaging to the prestige of an officer to live there, he said, and he was astonished that the young gentleman from the municipality had not warned us.

The "young gentleman from the municipality" had not seen anything wrong. Tieckstrasse was a working-class neighborhood and we had a very nice apartment, he had told us. Indeed, it was the nicest apartment either of us had ever lived in (since I left the United States, of course). Nevertheless, we asked him to help us find another.

This time, it did not take very long, as Abram went looking by himself. Walking to and from his office along Friedrichstrasse, he noticed a group of houses set back from the street with parts of a fence around the site and an iron gate. The buildings caught his eye because they were different from the others on the street. He found out that they had been built by French Huguenot refugees in the seventeenth century. The four-story buildings had been severely damaged. Some were in complete ruins, but others, less damaged, had been repaired and were inhabited. Trees and grass sprouted among the ruins. He made inquiries and discovered that there were still a few unoccupied apartments that could be restored. He found an apartment that required only minor repairs. It was sparsely furnished and there were books on the book-shelves, including *Gone with the Wind* in German. (I read it then for the first time. I read it again in English, years later.) It looked as if the occupants had left in a hurry.

It was a lovely apartment, with five large rooms and a balcony. Though we knew that our stay in Germany was temporary—how temporary we did not then guess—Abram set about remodeling. He had the old-fashioned bathroom tiled and a new bathtub installed, new kitchen cupboards built according to his specifications, the gas refrigerator connected, and the balcony enlarged and glassed in at the expense of the adjoining room. He bought rugs, an entire dinner set for twelve, and every gadget he could find. I guess he finally had found an outlet for his strong architectural and home-building inclinations. He directed the German workmen every step of the way, demanding perfection and getting it. Since his own workday started late in the afternoon, he was able to devote his mornings to the repair work.

I had never felt so fortunate. I was free from financial worries, living in a spacious private apartment for the first time in my married life, and had the daily assistance of a woman who did the shopping, cooking, and cleaning. The reunion with my husband after years of danger, hardship, and tragedy was like the honeymoon we had never had. It was actually even better than a honeymoon, for the years apart had given me a fresh perspective on my marriage, a new appreciation of my husband, a new tolerance, and a new determination to recognize and cherish my happiness. And we were happy.

The most enjoyable thing about the apartment, for me, was its spaciousness. The hammering and sawing did not bother me as it had when Abram had worked in our small room in Moscow. I would often go off by myself to the farthest corner of the farthest room to read or listen to the radio, but if Abram were at home, I did not remain alone for long. He would come looking for me.

"What are you doing here all by yourself? Can't you read in the front room?"

He could not understand why I wanted to get away from him. He did not want to get away from me, he said. I never succeeded in making him understand my craving for space and my need to be alone from time to time.

I could have taken a job. Sovinformburo offered me one, but I declined. I did not want to be tied down to a routine. Besides, I intended to do some research for my dissertation. I went to the library a few times, but found little that was useful.

The atmosphere of postwar Berlin excited and stimulated me. I enjoyed exploring the city on foot with Abram when he was free or alone when he wasn't. Though there were no barriers to movement between the occupation zones, we seldom encountered Soviet officers in uniform in the Western sectors.

We went to French, German, and American movies. The Russians were flocking to *Die Frau Meine Traume* [*The Woman of My Dreams*], a musical extravaganza starring the beautiful redhead, Marika Rokk, with elaborate sets and pretty chorus girls in sexy costumes. Some of the men had seen it five or six times. They were fascinated by the glitter, the tuneful songs, and the high kicks. It was certainly a change from the kind of entertainment to which they were accustomed.

The Berlin circus in the Soviet sector was another popular attraction for the military personnel. They especially loved the scantily clad "Fraulein Nummer" who introduced each number. She was always greeted with shouts and applause.

A high point of our movie-going was *The Gold Rush*. I had seen it as a child and had a vivid memory of some of the scenes, but Abram had never been able to see it. I was so excited at the prospect of seeing it again and talked so much about it that I was afraid Abram would be disappointed. But he wasn't. He had been a Charlie Chaplin fan ever since seeing the only two Chaplin films shown in the Soviet Union before the war—*City Lights* and *Modern Times*.

Theater flourished in Berlin. In the American sector, there was the Hebbel Theater; in the Soviet sector the opera the Deutsches Theater of Drama, and the Brecht Theater. I went everywhere, usually with my husband, sometimes without him when he was at work, sometimes escorted by someone who was free. Among the productions I saw were Thornton Wilder's *The Skin of Our Teeth,* Friedrich von Schiller's *Maria Stuart*, and Jerome K. Jerome's *Three Men in a Boat* with a then very young Hildegarde Kneff. I saw Ellen Weigel in *Mother Courage* at the Brecht Theater, known at the time as the Theater on Schifferbaumstrasse.

At home, I listened to the American Forces Radio network. I remember Dinah Shore singing "Let it Snow," and I was shocked to hear the German war song "Lili Marlene" broadcast over American radio.

Fred Astaire, Rita Hayworth, Bob Hope, Dinah Shore—these had been unfamiliar names to me. I never tired of listening to them on the radio or of watching them in films. I saw Olga Chekhova and Zara Leander in German movies, and I saw French stars whose names I do not remember but whose films I enjoyed very much.

This torrent of impressions—some new, some remembered—coming all at once after so many arid years kept me in a constant state of exhilaration. I lived entirely in the present, hardly thinking of the past or the future.

The senior member of the censorship group was Colonel Haskin, a long-time member of the Party who had held a series of high positions in civilian life until his brother was purged in 1937. Colonel Haskin got off with a reprimand, but lost his position. His last job before the war had been director of the popular Leningrad Theater of Miniatures, which starred Arkady Raikin, a stand-up comedian and satirist. In Haskin, we recognized a kindred spirit, although he was careful about what he said, and so were we. He was intelligent, witty, and fun to be with. We became very fond of him and his wife Nyura, a lovely-looking woman with classical features and prematurely grey hair. They had a young son and lived in Karlshorst. Haskin astonished me by detecting my American accent the first time we met, before he knew anything about me. (Most Russians took me for a native of one of the Baltic countries.)

Only a few of the censorship group lived in the city, and we were the only married couple among them. But after we moved to Friedrichstrasse, others followed, finding and repairing suitable apartments, so that we soon had a small community of our own. One of the officers, Lieutenant Neiman, lived with a girlfriend, which was strictly forbidden. He could not have gotten away with this had he lived in Karlshorst, but here, no one bothered him for the time being. The girl kept house for him and moved about freely. She was from Ukraine, and had been among the young women drafted for labor in Germany by the Nazis. Apparently, Neiman had come across her in a displaced persons camp. She sometimes dropped in to see me, but she did not talk about herself.

We were closest to a lieutenant named Drescher, a short, stocky man of about forty, originally from Bessarabia (now independent Moldova), who held a law degree from a European university and was fluent in German, English, Russian, French, Romanian and, probably, Hebrew. He told us little about himself. It was strange how one could be good friends with someone without knowing much about the person. No one questioned anybody's reticence. Who could tell the reasons behind it?

Drescher used to drop by whenever he had some free time. He was far better educated and more knowledgeable than I, and yet we seemed to have more in common with each other than with the others, possibly because of his Western education. He was always a welcome conversationalist and often accompanied me alone or with Abram to the theater and cinema.

Unlike the other Soviet officers we knew, we had personal friends among the Germans. Maria's sister Liza arrived in Berlin not long after Abram (though we did not think of her as German, because she was Jewish). A Soviet army lieutenant, she had been posted to a job on the German Communist Party newspaper *Neues Deutschland*. She was married to a man named Erich, who became a good and trusted friend with whom we could talk openly.

Erich and Liza had come to Moscow in 1933 or 1934. Their daughter was born in Moscow in 1936. A year or so later, Erich was sent abroad on a Party assignment (I did not know them then. I met Liza after Erich was gone). For a while, Liza heard from or about him, but by 1938, they had lost all contact. One day, soon after she came to work at *Neues Deutsch-land,* Erich walked into the office. He had just returned from England where he had spent the war years.

They were stunned. Neither had ever expected to see the other again. Liza was certain that Erich had been killed by the Nazis. Erich had tried and failed to establish contact with her. He was certain that some calamity had befallen her in the Soviet Union during the war.

As it turned out, Erich had been in Czechoslovakia when the Germans invaded in 1938. He had escaped at the very last minute and made his way to England. There, believing Liza to be dead, he met and married a German Jewish refugee with whom he had a daughter in 1944. He had returned to Germany with his new family at the first opportunity. The Party newspaper office was the natural place for him to come to.

The next few weeks were happy and sad as they talked about their years apart and agonized about the future. In the end, Erich divorced his second wife and remarried Liza. Erich provided for the family he left and, after things settled down, a distant but friendly relationship developed between the two families. It was all very civilized. Liza was demobilized and arranged for permanent residence in Germany. Soon their older daughter, who was then about ten years of age, joined them in Berlin.

Erich and Abram took an immediate liking to each other. The four of us spent many enjoyable evenings together. There was much to talk about: Erich's experiences in the West, Liza's and ours in the Soviet Union since Erich had left Moscow, the current situation, and our hopes for the future. There were the troubling subjects of the behavior of the Soviet troops in Germany before and after Germany's surrender, and about the relations between the Soviet occupation authorities and the East German government. Some members of the East German government and other German Communists were distressed by what they felt was the excessive dismantling of factories by the Soviets. They felt that this destruction hampered the economic recovery and development of socialist East Germany. In all instances, the Germans knuckled under to the Soviet administration. There was friction between the Germans who had spent the Nazi years in the Soviet Union and those who had been in German concentration camps or in the West. The returnees from the Soviet Union pulled rank, whereas returnees from the West and local Communists often found it difficult to deal with them and to accept their decisions.

The Russians were very much the conquerors. Frieda Rubiner, the German Communist who had worked alongside Maria in Division VII, now held a high position in East Berlin. We saw her now and then, and listened to her concerns about the psychological effect of power on the Russians and the leading German Communists. Privilege, she said, alienated them from the masses and impaired their judgment.

In Moscow, we had met Liza's friend, Trudi Kramer. Toward the end of the war, Trudi was parachuted into Germany on an assignment. Back in Moscow, Liza had given us the name and address of someone who might be able to tell us how to find Trudi. Thus we met Regina, an out-of-work actress who had been a friend of Trudi long before the war. Regina described in vivid detail how Trudi had appeared on her doorstep in 1945 after having vanished without a trace ten years before. Trudi stayed only a few days, but before she left, she gave Regina a piece of valuable advice: She taught her two Russian words and told her to use them if she had any trouble with Russian soldiers when they captured Berlin. The words were the same ones I had heard when I had whistled indoors or failed to use a fork to spear pieces of bread when I had first arrived in Moscow: *nye kul'turno*. Regina said they worked like magic.

We saw a lot of Regina. She was an interesting person and we enjoyed her company. She had a bulldog from which she was inseparable and a husband who lived in West Germany. He was a journalist whom Regina visited from time to time. She said their living situation was an ideal arrangement. Through Regina, we met other Germans, mostly from the theater world. They described the fighting in Berlin, the first days after Germany's surrender, and the earliest days of the Soviet occupation. Everyone had a horror story to tell. Worst of all, they said, were the indiscriminate rapes by Soviet soldiers of young and old.

We did our best—not to justify, but to explain. We spoke of Nazi Germany's unprovoked attack on the Soviet Union and the Germans' atrocities in the captured territories (not Germans, they objected, but the SS). We pointed out that there was hardly a family in all of Russia that had not lost someone in the war. What impressed them most was the fact that, with few exceptions, enlisted men had been fighting for four years without home leave.

"Without a woman for four years?!" Regina and her friends were appalled. "Why didn't they ask? They didn't have to use force. There were lots of women who would have accommodated them."

They knew what they were talking about. Abram had told me amusing stories about his sixteen-year-old tommygunner's sexual escapades as they advanced into enemy territory. Sasha would sometimes disappear for a whole night, in spite of my husband's scolding.

"Aw, Comrade Captain," he'd say. "They're so willing and it doesn't hurt anybody."

We did not associate with the Karlshorst crowd at all, and we did not attend meetings or holiday celebrations. We always had the excuse of Abram's working hours. The majority of wives of Soviet officers occupied themselves acquiring possessions, looking for bargains in exchange for food and cigarettes. Imitation seal coats made of dyed rabbit were the rage. Abram urged me to have one custom made. I refused. Rabbit was not sturdy enough to withstand the wear and tear of Moscow's buses and street cars, so why wear it? Once, I tried on a chinchilla coat that looked marvelous—it changed my image completely. But I saw no practical use for it and passed up the opportunity to own a genuine Argentinean chinchilla coat.

Abram had a few suits made, but he mostly was interested in books and gadgets. Among his books in Moscow, he had a collection of "Lilliput" editions of dictionaries and German classics that had been printed in Leipzig, which he had bought, over the years, in shops that sold old books. He made inquiries and discovered that the publisher still lived in Leipzig, though the firm was no longer in business. He telephoned him and arranged an appointment to look at the stock that the publisher had in his home. We went to Leipzig one weekend, and Abram bought all the Lilliput editions he could find, including several Shakespearean plays in English. The owner was delighted by the windfall and "charmed to meet such a refined Russian officer."

Leipzig was the hometown of Maria and Liza's family, and I had heard so much about it from them. We walked around the city and visited its most famous sight, the monument to the Peoples of the World commemorating Napoleon's defeat in 1813. It was my one and only trip outside Berlin and I enjoyed it very much.

Leipzig was well known as a publishing center. We bought other books there, among them beautiful editions of Russian classics issued long before the war by Petropolis Berlin. With plenty of time to read, I found my perceptions to be quite different from what they had been when I first read them many years ago, mostly in English translation. Nikolai Gogol, especially *Dead Souls,* was a revelation to me. How little I had understood when I had read Gogol ten years before! How much more I understood now after having lived in Russia for fifteen years! *Dead Souls* was like a flash of light, providing insights into the Russian character. For the first time, I thought of the Soviet Union as a continuation of tsarist Russia, with the roots of bureaucracy, inefficiency, and deviousness stretching deep and far back. Socialist rhetoric was merely a veneer. For me, the thought was original. I was unacquainted with Western scholarly writings on the subject.

Sometimes, when Abram and everyone else were busy, I'd take our excellent map of Berlin and go riding the subway and trolley cars. I'd walk through the city streets, getting into conversations with strangers. One way of starting a conversation was to ask for directions (something Abram hated to do). Often, I myself was approached for directions. My accent would arouse curiosity. If I revealed that I was American, the immediate response would be cordial and respectful. If I said I was Russian, there would be withdrawal, wariness, and false politeness. The most interesting conversation occurred when I said I was an American married to a Soviet officer. I talked with housewives, workers, students, and professionals, and I could discern no feelings of guilt or regret on the part of ordinary Germans. (By "ordinary," I mean Germans who were not Communists, socialists or returned anti-fascists.) They did not even bother to say to me, a passing stranger, that they had been against Hitler. Germans who provided services to the Soviet military—tradespeople, drivers, maintenance personnel—were obsequious. Rank was terribly important to them and everyone was addressed by a title. It was "Herr Doktor" and "Frau Doktor" (the wife not a doctor in her own right). Military men were consistently addressed one rank above their insignia, even after they had corrected the person. Drescher was "Herr Doktor-Kapitain" to make sure nothing was left out.

Once in a while, Germans would forget themselves when dealing with Soviets who spoke their language. Abram paid frequent visits to a dentist in one of the Western sectors. The dentist was a slight, dark-haired, wiry man, not at all an "Aryan" type. The going was slow, as it was difficult to obtain high-quality dental materials, so they had ample time in which to get acquainted. One day, we arrived to find that nothing had been done since Abram's last appointment. My husband was annoyed. The dentist explained: The source which supplied the necessary gold had not delivered.

*"Leider haben wir den Krieg verloren"* ["Unfortunately, we lost the war"], he said, completely forgetting who we were, though Abram was in uniform.

*"Leider haben Sie den Krieg angefangen"* [Unfortunately, you started the war"], I retorted angrily.

He paled and apologized profusely—he hadn't meant it the way it sounded; he was only referring to the shortages. He must have thought we would inform the authorities and that his days were numbered. I never went there again. Abram continued until the job was finished—it was a very good job, much better than the dental work he had had at home. The dentist was very careful about his words after that, but in my opinion, his conversation had indicated accurately how the majority of Germans felt.

The Germans looked down upon the Russians. Even the Germans we knew—the young man from the municipality, our landladies from the flower shop, a hospital administrator we knew, a doctor at a medical clinic (the Charité) whom we had occasion to consult, and Regina herself, spoke disparagingly of the Russians, declaring that they were "primitive," present company excepted, of course.

It angered me to hear Germans speak of Russians in that manner. It was not a question of truth or falsehood, but of attitude—who were *they*, who had caused so much destruction and tragedy, to pass judgment?

Indeed, a large number of enlisted men from remote areas of Russia and from Central Asia had never been out of their villages before the war and were not accustomed to city ways, much less to European city ways. And it could not be denied that there were still too many infringements of the disciplinary rules. I myself was accosted by a Soviet soldier. In the middle of the day at a busy subway station, he put his hand on my shoulder and said, *"Kom, Frau."* I shook him off and told him in Russian to get lost. He persisted. Though he spoke terrible Russian with a heavy Central Asian accent, he detected my slight accent and took me for a German. He became quite nasty. I managed to get rid of him, but it was an unpleasant experience.

Another time, Nyura Haskin and I were on our way to meet our husbands at the theater when a group of Russian soldiers called out to us in broken German. We turned around and took to our heels through back alleys that I knew to be in the neighborhood. We did not want to risk an encounter, even though we could easily have proven our identity. They may have been out to pick up women, or they may have wanted to check our papers (which could have been even more dangerous). Wives of Soviet officers were not often seen unaccompanied outside of Karlshorst, and there was no love lost between SVA and the internal security troops that performed police functions.

Generally, though, I felt perfectly safe roaming about the city on my own. When I was alone, I blended in with the people going about their everyday tasks. It was when I was in the company of Soviet officers in uniform that I had to be cautious. As a rule, I did not let on that I understood English when we encountered the British or American military. Once, when I was with my husband, some American officers made snide remarks about the Russians' "comic opera uniforms." Abram asked me what they were saying and I made something up. I was afraid he'd get angry and confront them. Most of the time, however, the encounters were friendly. The French were noticeably warmer toward the Soviet military than were the other Allies.

The one time I was drawn into a conversation with Americans was at a Sunday picnic in Wannsee, in the American sector. Several American officers who were passing by asked if they could join us and were invited to do so. The conversation was partly in German and partly in English. Several of our people spoke English well enough to keep a conversation going. For a while, I kept quiet, but when one of the Americans addressed me directly, I instinctively responded in unaccented English, thereby arousing curiosity. I evaded their questions and their cameras. It was hard to explain my aversion to having my picture taken, even to myself. I think it went back to my time at the Commissariat of Defense. But the others all posed together for snapshots. Someone, somewhere in this country, may still have those pictures— Berlin, Wannsee, 1946.

Prostitution was rampant in Berlin. Though Friedrichstrasse was not Tieckstrasse, it was still a regular thoroughfare for prostitutes after dark.

Abram used to walk home from his office late at night and at first they used to accost him. After a while, though, they got to know him and used to greet him with *"Guten Abend, Herr Kapitain."* One morning we went into a neighborhood grocery store and a young woman greeted us. Abram responded: *"Guten Tag, Fraulein."*

"Who is she?" I asked. "Why didn't you introduce me?"

"She is a prostitute from Friedrichstrasse. I see her out there almost every night," was his reply.

How ordinary they seemed when they were not on the job.

Drunkenness was common, too. It was not unusual to see a tipsy German winding his way home after work in the late afternoon or early evening, quietly, politely, not bothering anyone, not at all threatening. You never saw anyone lying on the ground dead drunk or picking a fight, as you so often did in Russia. They were so *orderly.*

As I look back, I am amazed at how I barely reacted to the wider political scene that year. The war crimes trials were in progress in Nuremberg and other German cities. I am a news addict and was reading newspapers and periodicals in three languages, yet I do not recall my reactions or those of my acquaintances. Nor do I recall giving serious thought to what was going on in the Soviet Union. In August 1946, Andrei Zhdanov made his infamous speech on what were deemed mistakes and shortcomings in Soviet literature, art, and music, thus ushering in years of savage cultural repression which culminated in the "cosmopolitan" period. Surely, a sophisticated analysis of Zhdanov's attacks on such luminaries of the Soviet cultural world as Anna Akhmatova, Mikhail Zoshchenko, Dmitri Shostakovich, Sergei Prokofiev, and others should have signaled danger ahead. How is it that we paid so little attention? Perhaps my memory is failing me, not letting me recall my true reactions. I had always corresponded with my parents regularly; while in Berlin, I wrote even more often, mailing my letters from the Western sectors. Unfortunately, my family did not keep my letters. (Neither did the FBI. I sent for my file and that of my parents, hoping to find copies of my letters, but all I found were copies of all the letters I wrote to my Soviet friends between 1965, when I returned to the United States, and 1972.) In these letters I was able to give them a much more detailed and truthful picture of my life in Russia and of the way that I felt about some of the government policies over which I had no control. My parents could not respond candidly, of course; the correspondence remained one-sided because I could not receive mail in the Western sectors.

In October 1946, SVA finally got around to documenting all its employees and their families. Questionnaires were sent to everyone. This was the first time I was required to provide information about myself for the SVA records. I knew at once that as soon as they discovered my background, I would be sent back to Moscow.

We should have realized that our nonconformist behavior (especially mine) and our association with Germans—though most of them were Communists we had known in Moscow—would attract the attention of the Soviet authorities. Indeed, it did, although we did not then realize the full extent of the attention.

One night at two o'clock in the morning when Abram was away on night duty (which happened about once a month), the doorbell rang. At first I thought I was dreaming, but it rang again—insistently. I went to the door and asked who was there.

"Soviet military police. Open up!"

I replied that I was alone in the apartment (which they already knew) and would not open the door to strangers at that hour of the night. They began to shout and threaten me. I told them to wait, that I would telephone my husband.

Abram answered the phone on the first ring. He said that under no circumstances was I to open the door, no matter who the callers said they were. I returned to the door and said that my husband would come home as soon as he could get a replacement at work. Until then, I would not open the door. The police started pounding, evidently trying to break the door down, but it was a sturdy old German door that would not yield without a battering ram. Finally, they went away.

Meanwhile, Abram called Colonel Haskin in Karlshorst, who immediately telephoned military police headquarters, but got no information. The next morning, Abram went to the military police headquarters to demand an explanation. He was threatened and insulted in what he said were unmistakable anti-Semitic overtones. He came home terribly upset and would not talk much about it. I don't know whether he ever told me the whole story. If they had been acting on information that he was living with a foreign woman, then, logically, they should have come when he was at home, to catch him "red-handed." That they had come when they knew he was not at home seemed to indicate that they were after *me* and wanted to pick me up with the least possible fuss.

In a way, it was lucky for Abram that he had not been at home. He might have felt obliged to open the door, and heaven knows what might have transpired. Short of threatening them with his pistol, he would not have been able to prevent the police from taking me away. Once in their hands, I doubt that any power on earth would have been able to save me. Innocence or guilt was not an issue. For a few days, we were very nervous, but the incident was not repeated. Haskin went to the top officials of SVA and got them to put an end to the harassment.

We saw 1946 out and 1947 in at the home of one of my husband's colleagues. We were joined by others from the Karlshorst contingent, and everybody had a merry time.

But our merriment did not last long into the new year. A few days later, Lieutenant Neiman's girlfriend was taken away by the Soviet military police. Neiman tried to help her, but was told to consider himself lucky that he was not arrested. We never found out what became of her. Soon after, Abram received his demobilization orders and was given one month to wind up his affairs and return to Moscow. He was told that a replacement would arrive before the end of the month. No explanation was offered, but we did not doubt that I was the reason. However, I did not think Abram would be sent back, too. He was a professional officer, having been commissioned before the war, and professional soldiers were not being demobilized.

Our apartment was very desirable and several of my husband's colleagues asked us to let them move in before we left. Maria's husband Yuri had been posted to Berlin and had been to see us a few weeks earlier. Their marriage had been in trouble before the war and it was clear that they would not get together again. Maria had asked him one last favor before they were divorced: to send for her so that she could return to Germany. Dora had died; Liza and Aida (the eldest sister) lived in Germany; and Irina, her daughter, was only ten and the change would be easier for her at this time than when she was older. But Yuri had a liaison with a woman at the front and would have had to end it if he were to send for his lawful spouse, so he stalled, not refusing, and yet not doing anything. He wanted very much to move into our apartment and Abram was willing, but I was angry with him—I felt he owed it to Maria to do what she had asked—and opposed it so vehemently that Abram was compelled to turn him down. (Subsequently, Maria and Yuri were divorced and Yuri married the other woman. Maria and Irina did not return to Germany until 1955.)

Did it occur to us not to return to Moscow? It did to me, and I raised the question very tentatively with Abram. I had fantasized about returning to America, but I had never shared my fantasies with anyone, not even with my husband. For an officer to desert is an overwhelming step to take. Abram was not ready to take it, so I dropped the subject.

Once and once only, the officer who now shared our apartment spoke to me alone about not returning to the Soviet Union. He said he had recently visited his family in Ukraine and that anti-Semitism was pervasive. If he were in my husband's situation—with an American wife and no living relatives in the Soviet Union—he would not hesitate to desert. We were insane to go back, he said.

I repeated the conversation to Abram. We were very worried. What if the man was a provocateur? If we did not report him, we'd be in trouble. If he were not a provocateur, he had taken a huge chance in saying the things he had said. We decided to ignore the conversation, to behave as if it had not occurred. If he reported us, we would say that Abram did not know anything about it, that I had not taken it seriously and had not told him about it (as if that would have saved us!).

We left for Moscow in February 1947. The officer was not a provocateur. A year or two later, we saw him in Moscow and talked about old times. He told us that many of Abram's colleagues had been demobilized and that the Jews were being sent home. No mention was made of the conversation in Berlin.

# 17
## Postwar Moscow—1947

After a hectic month preparing for our departure—obtaining papers, deciding what to take and what to leave behind (I wanted to leave most things behind, whereas Abram wanted to take everything, including a huge rug that would be much too large for our Moscow room), packing, saying goodbye to our friends—we had two days on the train with nothing to do. We were in a compartment for four and consequently could not talk freely, but we could think and look back over the past year. What lay ahead? We were both very quiet.

I recalled a line from a poem I had learned in grammar school, in my other life: "Opportunity knocks but once." Had Germany been our opportunity? Had I missed it?

Until Abram received his demobilization order, I had not given serious thought to defecting (for defection it would have been; there was no legal way for us to leave the Soviet Union). When I did start to think about it, I felt ambivalent. Emotionally, I wanted to go home. I wanted to see my family. I was sick and tired of the hard life I had been living in Moscow. I dreaded returning to our cramped room in a communal apartment and to the neighbors with whom we had to share it. But, ideologically, I was not certain. Like many others, I believed that the Soviet people had proved their loyalty by fighting so valiantly and suffering such hardship. I presumed that things would be different, more liberal, and more democratic. I was convinced that good people would work hard to prevent the recurrence of the "excesses" of the past. This belief was shared even by many who had been affected by those "excesses" and who had not believed the official reports given during the "enemy-of-the-people" trials of the 1930s. During the worst period of the mass arrests and public trials—from 1936 to 1937—I was isolated at the Commissariat of Defense. The doubts that I had, especially after I returned to the publishing house in 1938, concerned the "excesses," not the system. Not yet.

Unsure of myself, I felt that I had no right to pressure my husband, for if I myself was not quite ready to reject the system, he was even less so. He had been an army officer for the past five years; desertion was much more of an enormity in his mind than defection was in mine. He had fought hard and endured much in the war for a cause and country in which he believed. Abram was still a dedicated Communist who hoped that the ideal of social justice and a good life for all could be achieved. Moreover, he wanted to go to Rostov-on-the-Don to find out for himself the fate of his parents and the rest of the family. I did not feel that I could ask him to make the mistake I had made—to leave his native land and face mistrust and uncertainty in a strange country—for I had long known that emigration had been a mistake, irrespective of ideology.

It takes time for an idea to sink in, especially an idea that would have changed our lives so completely. Abram's demobilization was unexpected. As a rule, SVA officers served at least two years. We had not been thinking about the future at all, and when the crucial moment for a decision came, we did not have enough time to prepare ourselves mentally. If we had felt then as we did less than a year after our return to Moscow, we would have known what to do.

But Abram was thinking of other things, of friends who had been killed and those who had survived, of the kind of job to look for and where to look for it. He had been given six months severance pay, a very large sum for us, and would be entitled to ration cards for that period, so there was no urgency. Still, he was worried. Our homecoming was not jubilant.

Life was hard at this time in the Soviet Union, especially in the war-ravaged towns and villages to which demobilized soldiers were returning throughout 1945 and 1946. There were many visible signs of the war—war invalids hobbling around on crutches, often drunk and belligerent, a short-age of men of marriageable age. There were rumors about institutions for the legless and the armless in remote parts of the country where they were kept out of the sight of the public. The psychological trauma caused by the battle experience, about which so much has been written in the United States, was not dwelt upon. Either there was much less trauma or the phenomenon was ignored. I believe that the physical effort of providing for daily needs—shelter, food, clothing—left little room for less obvious concerns. The only psychological problem (if that is what it was) that was raised chiefly in the fiction of the period, was that of the soldier coming home to find that his wife had been unfaithful to him.

As we neared Moscow, my thoughts turned to more immediate matters: In what condition would we find our room? The publishing house administration had put someone in it, without our consent of course, but as owners of the building, they had the legal right to do so. The sub-tenant was a young Frenchman of Russian descent who had been seduced by a postwar Soviet government campaign that urged the children of Russian emigrés to return to the "land of their forefathers." We had notified the publishing house administration that we were returning and had asked our friends in the building to follow through. Fortunately, there were no complications about the young man vacating the room. Nikolai, the returnee, had been given a minor position in the French section and was obviously finding life very different from what he had expected. He moved in with a French woman who also lived in the building. The woman had come to Moscow in the 1930s with her husband, but he had been arrested in 1937 or 1938 and not heard of since. Before the year was out, Nikolai disappeared into Siberia, which was the fate of the majority of the Russian returnees.

Our feelings of sympathy for Nikolai were tempered by our dismay at the condition in which he had left our room. Obviously, he had never had to look after himself. The floor was black with dirt, the furniture covered with greasy dust, the books in disarray, and worst of all, there were swarms of bedbugs. The neighbors had been sorely tried by the young man's sloppiness and were pleased to have us back.

It did not take us long to become aware of ominous currents in the atmosphere. The first blow came when I reported to the Academy of Sciences to arrange the resumption of my graduate studies and discovered that I had been dropped without anyone having bothered to inform me. I had written from Berlin, requesting an extension of my leave, but had not received a reply. I had considered returning to Moscow when my six months were up, but we had decided against this, never doubting that I could straighten the matter out later. What I did not know was that the political situation had changed radically in the year I had been away. The harassment of the intelligentsia that began with Zhdanov's 1946 speech vilifying Soviet cultural luminaries had frightened many people, leaving the field open to place-seekers and petty bureaucrats. Anti-Semitism and xenophobia were on the rise. Professor Guber, my advisor, had not even been consulted when I was dropped from the rolls. At any rate, he was in no condition to concern himself with my problem. He had recently lost his nineteen-year-old son in a drowning accident and I did not ask him for help.

I went to see Professor Yefimov, who was now back in official good graces. As a Corresponding Member of the USSR Academy of Sciences, he was entitled to have a certain number of special students. He had not yet filled his quota and invited me to become one. He was certain he could get me approved and was distressed when he had to inform me shortly afterwards that he had been unable to do so. He urged me to write my thesis anyway; he would be my unofficial adviser and, meanwhile, the situation might change and I would be reinstated. However, I was not willing to work hard without definite prospects for acceptance and no remuneration. Besides, I was beginning to realize that I would never get anywhere in so ideological a field as history. I thanked him and declined.

We were happy to see our friends again. There had been some changes. Maria no longer lived downstairs from us. She had moved into a room the same size on the second floor in another section. It was an improvement over the ground floor for her, but she had acquired some very unpleasant neighbors—a Russian family who had been moved from Mayakovsky Square. They were quarrelsome, frequently drunk, and they bullied others to whom they felt superior by virtue of being neither Jewish nor foreign. Maria suffered in silence along with her other neighbors.

Maria's former room was occupied by Liz's sister Rose, her husband George, and their two small daughters. The offer of this room, which was a great improvement over the room they had from the radio committee on the outskirts of Moscow, had induced George to leave the radio committee to work for the publishing house. He was now a senior translator-editor in the English section.

A day or two after our return, Rose came upstairs to see us.

"Mary," she said. "I don't know what happened between you and George. I don't want to know why you are not on speaking terms. I've come to ask you to let bygones be bygones."

I had not spoken to George since he had driven me out of Liz's room during the war, five years ago. Abram, who always had a tendency to forgive, seconded her, though he knew quite well why I had broken off relations. Consequently, a polite peace was established.

Mussia was having a rough time. Her mother had had a stroke in 1944 and was paralyzed from the neck down. The building in which she lived with her husband was not heated, so Mussia had taken them in to stay with her temporarily. They were still there, all in one room: Mussia, her eleven-year-old son, her mother and stepfather, and the domestic, a young peasant girl who slept behind a screen. They finally returned to their home the following summer, taking the domestic with them.

Ahsia and her mother lived in a room the size of ours on the ground floor. Evans had gone back to England. His wife and daughter remained in their room on Kapelsky. The publishing house could not evict them because they had given up "living space" when they moved in.

The great news among my friends was that Betty had gotten married. To me, however, this was not news. She had written to me in Berlin about a man she had met in a neighborhood cafeteria who was paying her a great deal of attention. For a while, she wondered whether he might have an ulterior motive. We knew what she meant—that he might be an agent of the secret police. She asked me to keep her secret and kept me informed about the progress of the romance. She probably would not have told me had I not been so far away. Now they had decided to formalize their union because they wished to exchange their two separate tiny rooms for two rooms together. To obtain permission for the exchange, they had to be legally married.

Betty's ability to attract men was always a mystery to me and my friends. She was not good-looking in face or figure, she lacked a scintillating personality, and was not even particularly erudite. Nevertheless, as long as we knew her she was never without a man. Betty never spoke to anyone about her sex life, but I remember the excited buzzing among us at one time when we observed her in the morning with Bram Feinberg at the bus stop. Another time, we saw Chernov leaving her apartment. Both of these men could have had their pick of attractive women. Puzzled or not, we wished her well.

Betty invited us over to meet her new husband. He was a big, burly man who spoke with the rounded "o's" of Russians from the northeast and the Volga region. He was a *revizor*, an auditor, at one of the ministries. By virtue of his job, he knew a great deal about conditions in various parts of the country and understood how the national economy operated. He spoke freely and critically. He was not a Party member and had no interest in ideology—he was, indeed, an ordinary Russian, a type with which most of us had had no contact at all. We found him intelligent and enjoyed talking with him. I don't think Betty, who had never really mastered the Russian language, understood half of what he said, but it did not matter. In him, she found a mainstay and protector who helped her through some very bad years ahead. She called him "Eugene" and addressed him in the formal second-person plural. He called her "Betunchik." The incongruous marriage lasted over thirty years, until Eugene's death in the mid-1970's.[1]

At Liz's, the picture was depressing. Liz's face lit up when we came to see her. She tried hard to talk, but became frustrated because she could not express her thoughts. She was on disability and slowly learning to do things for herself after having suffered her stroke the year before. The publishing house administration arranged a personal pension for her, which, though not large, was about five times the usual disability pension and gave her valuable privileges such as free transportation, lower rent, better rations, and better medical care. The story of Liz's struggle to survive and become independent is one of heroism and stamina. She eventually learned to do everything necessary for everyday living, especially after her mother died, but she never learned to count money or figure and used to thrust a handful of bills at the cashier or peasant in the market and tell them to take what

---

1. I saw Betty when I visited Moscow in 1986. She was in her eighties and a little confused, but she told me that Eugene's son by his first marriage, whom I remember being a difficult teenager, and the son's wife took good care of her, visited her regularly, and saw that she had everything she needed.

was required for her purchase. She kept house, cooked, and read a great deal, though only in English.

There was good and bad news about Lyova Kopelev. Throughout an investigation that lasted longer than a year and during which time he was imprisoned, his influential friends from the army and literary circles wrote letters to people in high places, attesting to his loyalty, honesty, and the absurdity of the charge of anti-Soviet agitation and slander against him. Their efforts bore fruit. He was tried in December 1946, acquitted, and released the following January. But in February, shortly after our return to Moscow, he was informed that the verdict had been challenged and that there would be a new trial. Clearly, he had powerful and determined enemies. At the second trial in April, he was convicted and sentenced to ten years of "deprivation of freedom."

Lyova's second trial took place in a different atmosphere from that of his first trial. It reflected the unmistakable trend toward intensified ideological control and rising chauvinism to which many of us had not paid enough attention in the euphoria of the war's victorious end. Despite the ominous air, people continued to hope for and expect more liberal policies, more concern for the "little man."

In 1945 and 1946, Lyova's friends did not hesitate to give him and his family their support. But by the spring of 1947, there was no longer any doubt about which way the domestic political winds were blowing. Many of Lyova's better-known supporters were summoned to the Party Central Committee and ordered to cease and desist. Most were intimidated. Those who stuck by him were expelled from the Party and/or lost their jobs.

Abram, who did not hold a position of any importance and was not involved in the case, was one of the few friends who visited the family regularly through all the years of Lyova's incarceration.

Very early one Sunday morning in April, our doorbell rang. I opened the door to find Rose standing there, disheveled and distraught. She made no move to come in.

"George has been arrested," she whispered.

"Come in," I said.

"Are you sure?"

"Of course, I'm sure," I said, pulling her into our room.

They had been awakened at two o'clock in the morning by a loud banging on the door. Two men entered, accompanied by the house superintendent. They carried a search warrant and an arrest warrant for George. The men searched the room for several hours, pulling books off the shelves, inspecting papers, letters, notebooks—anything they could lay their hands on—while the family looked on in silence. George seemed bewildered as they led him away.

We tried to comfort her as one did in such circumstances, saying it was surely a misunderstanding, that George would be back in a few days. She stayed only long enough to tell her story and would not have breakfast with us. The children—Alla, nine, and Lucy, five—had fallen asleep and she was afraid they would wake up and be frightened if she were not there.

This was an even greater blow than Lyova's arrest had been because it seemed so preposterous. Lyova, by contrast, had always been getting into trouble. Abram knew the people whom he had antagonized and was not surprised at the lengths to which they had gone to "get" him.

But George, who was no friend of mine and whom Abram hardly knew, was another story. A longtime British Communist, a pillar of political orthodoxy, a highly respected member of the publishing house staff and before that of the radio committee staff, who never uttered a syllable of criticism of anyone in power—what charges could be brought against him? I never doubted for a minute that he was innocent of whatever the charges may have been.

For his wife, it was the start of eight years of struggle to survive, a struggle for shelter, food, and clothing for herself and her children, a struggle to maintain her sanity. The publishing house immediately ordered the superintendent to move all her belonging into a tiny, damp room in the cellar and started proceedings to evict her and the children from even that room. She spent days in line at the secret police headquarters on Lyubyanka, seeking information about her husband, and in the waiting room of the local housing office, begging for a place to live before she and her children were put out into the street. Sometimes her mother looked after the children. More often, they were left alone. She needed a job, but no one would hire her. After a month or two, she was told that her husband was in Butyrki prison and that she could bring a package for him to the prison gate once a month. She scrimped and foraged for that parcel, never missing a month. She learned the "ropes" from the people in line, most of whom were other women seeking information about husbands, fathers, brothers, and sons. George ended up with a twenty-five-year sentence, of which he served eight years in Magadan, a notorious prison camp in the Far North on the edge of the Sea of Okhotsk.

All those years, Rose did what people in trouble did in the Soviet Union: She wrote letters. She wrote to the Central Committee of the CPSU, to the Minister of Internal Affairs, to British Communists residing in Moscow, and to Stalin—above all, to Stalin. She did not seek justice by way of the law courts—there was no point in that. We helped her write the letters, as she did not know Russian well enough to write them correctly herself. Besides, two, three heads are better than one.

Many friends turned away from her. She would tell us about meeting so-and-so in the street and so-and-so would avert his or her eyes or cross the street. Every time that happened, it caused her pain. Other friends rallied round. Tamara managed to obtain freelance typing jobs for her, which she did in Tamara's name. We all helped with money and food. If my memory does not fail me, Abram and I, Ahsia, Tamara and her husband, and Mussia each contributed ten rubles a month. It was not much, but it helped. Rose, who had always been so sickly—she had some form of encephalitis—was so thin and haggard, that it was a miracle she kept going. Yet she never whined, never wallowed in self-pity; she did what she had to do and appreciated what was done for her. There was something very appealing about her, and now and then she got a bureaucrat to listen to her. She was finally given a room in a wooden barrack without conveniences on the outskirts of Moscow. Tamara and her husband, who helped her move, were appalled when they saw the place. Rose also managed through letters and personal appeals to compel the publishing house after many months to pay her the money they owed George for work he had completed before his arrest.

George's arrest impoverished Liz's family as well. He had always been very generous to them. Now they had to live on Liz's pension exclusively.

Tragedy and stamina—those are the words that best describe that family, the two Goldman sisters, who had been born and raised in Boston. Tragedy to have ended up sick, humiliated, and rejected by the cause to which they had been devoted, thousands of miles from their native land.

Meanwhile, Abram was looking for a job. There were no employment agencies in the Soviet Union, nor was there advertising, except at the lowest levels of manual and clerical labor. Factories posted lists of their needs outside the factory gates. But unless one was a member of the *nomenklatura,* the privileged caste whose jobs were handed to them from above, jobs were generally found by word of mouth. The natural places for Abram to explore were the radio committee, TASS, prisoner-of-war administrations, and foreign language periodicals. There were vacancies everywhere and he had a few irons in the fire, but it looked as if it would take some time before he would get results.

When I had left the publishing house before the war to go back to Moscow University, I never expected to work there again. I had my future all planned: After graduation and an advanced degree, I'd do research and writing in an academic setting where I'd be left much to myself. Those plans had gone up in smoke. I had to find a job and, after some inquiries, I realized that my choices were limited. Personnel departments were being very careful about whom they hired and I was in the high-risk category. They were careful, not because they feared that a spy or nonbeliever might infiltrate their organization, but because if someone they hired were later arrested, they would be held responsible for "lack of vigilance." Everybody was responsible for everybody else. Anyone who recommended anyone for anything—Party or Komsomol membership, a job, a room—was held responsible for the person's actions in the future. Research positions were closed to me: They required clearance. Chernov would have given me back my old translation job, as they badly needed translators into English, but that would have meant working three shifts and I did not want to work at night. Professor Varga, whose seminar in economics I had taken in the university and who had been a member of the state examining commission when I graduated, invited me to apply for a position at the Institute of World Economics, of which he was the director. Varga showed more courage than most when he was in a position of power, hiring "tainted" people when he wanted to and speaking his mind. However, my experience with Professor Yefimov's efforts had made me cautious and I thanked him and refused his offer.[2]

Reluctantly, I decided to apply for a job at the publishing house. Even that was not a sure thing. People were very jittery there. Talmy was no longer head of the English section, and was now a senior editor-translator. The new head, Katya Kosinskaya, happened to be a former classmate of my husband's at the Institute of Foreign Languages and she remembered that when she got into trouble as one of Lyova Kopelev's entourage, Abram had been able to prevent her expulsion from the Komsomol and the Institute. The director of the publishing house, Boris Suchkov, had also been a class-mate of theirs. Kosinskaya hired me, implying that she had done so over the objections of the personnel department. That was as far as her gratitude went. She was an arrogant, high-handed boss and together with her assis-tant, an uneducated Communist from Brooklyn, made life miserable for all but the "stars" of the section. I went to work there as a junior translator and assistant editor in April 1947.

The weeks stretched into months, yet still no job materialized for Abram. He'd be invited for an interview on the recommendation of a friend or ac-quaintance, be asked to fill out an application . . . and that would be the end of it. The application forms were many pages long and asked for detailed information not only about the applicant's qualifications and personal his-tory, but also about the applicant's spouse and often about the applicant's and the spouse's parents and grandparents. Obligatory questions were "Do you have relatives abroad?" and "Do you correspond with anyone living abroad?" There was no doubt that I was the obstacle—American-born, hav-ing close relatives in the United States with whom I corresponded regularly. There was probably a thick dossier on me in the secret police files. Here was a paradoxical situation: I, the source of the trouble, had a job, while my husband was not able to find one because of me. Abram gave up applying to

2. My decision turned out to be correct. In 1948, Varga was criticized for the "incorrect analysis of postwar Western capitalism" and dismissed from his post. The institute he headed was closed down.

"sensitive" organizations and started looking for any kind of position. Here, too, he encountered a stumbling block: Why was a person with a college degree and specialized experience applying for a position that did not require his skills? This situation aroused suspicions of the personnel bureaucrats and he was turned down time and again as being overqualified.

Abram took his joblessness very hard. He was hurt and embarrassed and bitter. He did not want the neighbors or casual acquaintances to know that he was not working, so he would leave the apartment in the morning and stay away until evening when people came home from work. He would spend the day in the park or walking the streets in good weather, at the movies or in stores in bad weather. He became irritable and touchy and we began to quarrel about money. That I was the only earner diminished him in his own eyes and he imagined all sorts of slights. I pointed out that he had supported me for two years and sent me money all through the war years, but he shrugged that off. A husband supporting a wife was different from a wife supporting a husband.

It was a miserable time. We wrote letters to important personages. The context of the letters was that he was a dedicated Communist who had served his country for the entire four years of the war and had been decorated for bravery. He also had good work experience, but now was being refused an opportunity to earn a living. The letters did no good. In fact, in one instance, we had proof that a letter had made things worse. In one of the organizations where Abram was interviewed, they wanted him, but were afraid to take a chance. A letter that Abram wrote elicited an inquiry to the organization couched in terms that made them shy away. (We were told this by the friend who had steered him there.)

The year 1947 was unhappy for us. Our hopes for a better future ebbed slowly. Manifestations of anti-Semitism were increasingly frequent, though anti-Semitism was not yet openly and officially condoned. The newspapers were filled with the usual paeans to Stalin, reports of achievements by workers and collective farmers, fulminations against the imperialists, especially and continuously against the United States. Ilya Ehrenburg was a strong voice in the anti-American campaign. In an article entitled "Voice of a Writer," he wrote that Americans were takers, not givers. He characterized the Marshall Plan as a diabolical attempt to enslave the peoples of Europe.

One anti-American cartoon showed the Statue of Liberty with the face of General Marshall. The statue's figure was holding aloft a money bag with dollar signs in one hand and a pair of scissors with "Marshall Plan" inscribed in the other hand. A circle of men were groveling at the base with only their posteriors showing, across which was written "Europe." As I know now but did not know then, the Czechs, Poles, and Yugoslavs were eager to join the Marshall Plan. Needless to say, the Soviet government did not allow this.

The first use of the word "cosmopolitanism" in a maledictory sense appeared in an article by the literary critic Vladimir Yermilov entitled "For a Militant Theory in Literature." Published in the Soviet Union's leading weekly journal, *Literaturnaya gazeta* [*Literary Gazette*], the article commemorated the anniversary of Zhdanov's notorious speech and called for a fight against "rootless cosmopolitanism" and *"nizkopoklonstvo"* (literally "servility," but meaning in this case "the worship of foreign things"). Yermilov wrote that the glorification of alien bourgeois cultures and the rootless cosmopolitanism that went with it were among the most harmful survivals of capitalism.

It would not be long before "rootless cosmopolitan" became a euphemism for Jew.

To counter *nizkopoklonstvo,* Soviet scholars claimed that every scientific discovery and every technological advance had been made by the Russians first. Russians invented the electric lamp, the telephone, discovered penicillin fifty years before Fleming did, and so on. "Priority" was the key word. Whether people believed this information or not, it made them very careful about what they wrote and said. And, of course, most people did in fact believe what they read and what they were told. They had no other information.

Whoever could—that is, those who had not already been damaged beyond repair—jumped onto the bandwagon: writers, journalists, philologists, historians, theater and literary critics. Many who did so eventually became victims themselves, but meanwhile they joined the chorus. Objects of attacks beat their breasts and admitted their mistakes. Some of those who recanted managed to survive and continue in their professions. Many did not. All became very cautious in their work, careful not to praise or give credit to anything that had been achieved outside the Soviet Union and Russia.

As usual, letters poured in supporting the official viewpoint and calling for patriotism, for "genuine" music, literature, and art. Most of the letters were undoubtedly genuine. Who could have made up such silly letters as the response to the words of a ditty sung by Ruslanova, one of the country's most popular singers? A major of the guards at the Frunze Military Academy was roused to indignation by the line, "With my lace skirt and my lace blouse, I'll surely catch a lieutenant and become his wife." "Are our military men so backward," wrote the major, "as to be interested in lace blouses and foolish girls?"

Of special interest to me and my friends was the creation in the autumn of 1947 of the Cominform (Communist Information Bureau) to replace the Communist International. By this time, I had severed my formal connection with the Communist movement—I had resigned from the Komsomol.

In 1947, I turned thirty-two years old. I handed in a statement to the publishing house Komsomol committee, pointing out that my application for membership in the Party had been rejected and that I was not planning to reapply in the foreseeable future. I was, therefore, resigning from the Komsomol. I was subsequently summoned before the Komsomol district committee. *No one* resigned from the Komsomol. It could be interpreted as an act of defiance, they said (which it was). They suggested that I apply for Party membership, perhaps later. After all, that was what the Central Committee instructor had suggested. I asked the committee members whether they thought I had a chance of being accepted, considering the present relations with America and my background. They shrugged and told me to hand in my membership card. I did not have it with me (deliberately) and said I would bring it to them. I never did. I kept it as a memento of my youthful dreams.

There was much fanfare in 1947 in connection with the celebration of the eight hundred years since the founding of Moscow. Medals and decorations were handed out right and left. Many of my friends and acquaintances received medals with a picture of the Kremlin on one side and the number "800" on the other. They got to go to the Kremlin, which had not been open to the public in those years, where the medals were given out in mass sessions. Some of my coworkers who were not recommended for an award felt bad (apparently, there were quotas for institutions), but by now I was so completely alienated from the regime that the pangs of not being appreciated did not touch me. After sixteen years in the Soviet Union, I was an outsider, would always be an outsider, and I did not care.

Tension was mounting and the number of arrests increasing. The press was not shouting about the arrests as it had been before the war when the main thrust had been against prominent people in the upper echelons of the Party and the luckless lower ranks connected with them. These arrests were hitting closer to home. The next casualty in our circle was Dave Fromberg, who was arrested in November 1947. Fromberg was a staunch Communist who had never wavered in his loyalty. He was also a very decent person, ready to help colleagues, not wont to see a saboteur behind every mistake or an enemy in anyone who disagreed with him. We were completely unprepared for his arrest, especially as he was practically blind and known to have a brain tumor. Fromberg refused to sign a fake confession, despite torture. We knew this from a letter he managed to get out to his wife. Apparently, he dropped the letter out of the train window en route to a prison camp and some good soul put a postage stamp on it and mailed it. In that letter, he named three persons whom he blamed for his arrest. One was the boyhood friend with whom he had come from England in 1919. Another was George. Both men were under arrest. The third was the Frombergs' Korean neighbor, Anya Kim, who had not been arrested, only interrogated. Dave was convicted and sentenced to ten years imprisonment on the basis of their testimony. Ten years was regarded as a very light sentence, the type of punishment given when the secret police had *not* succeeded in developing a case. Fromberg died in camp less than a year later. He left a wife and two young sons.

Years later, when we knew more about the methods used to extract "confessions," we were more tolerant and had more compassion for those who signed anything to appease their tormenters. At the time, though, we were horrified. We ostracized Anya Kim (I had been rather friendly with her, for we had been drawn together by common misfortune, both having lost a child). Neither Fromberg's wife nor any one of us to whom she showed the letter told Rose or Liz about George's alleged role, and I don't believe that they or their children ever found out.

One person from whom we learned a little of what went on in the dungeons of Lyubyanka was an Italian Communist who worked at the publishing house. Tina Parodi was arrested, but released after about six months. She came to see Abram and me and told us about the torture. Not everyone, she said, was tortured to the same degree, and women were better treated than men. But I never understood why she had come to see us. We were not close friends, not even close colleagues. Perhaps she was trying to warn us, perhaps to elicit information, perhaps both. Her quick release was strange, too. Was it paranoia to suspect everyone? That was the way we lived.

A common technique in developing a case was to go through the prisoner's address book and tie in all the names to a concocted plot. At some point in the endless interrogations, the prisoner would break down and implicate others. A joke, current at the time, went like this: After weeks of torture, especially the "no-sleep" torture, the prisoner tells his operative that he is ready to confess. He is given pen and paper and describes in detail how he and his fellow conspirators planned to assassinate the Civil War hero Marshal Semyon Budonny. Pleased, the operative reads it through and says:

"Very good. But why Budonny?"

"He's not important. The sentence will be lighter," was the reply.

It was probably fortunate for me that I had not been on speaking terms with George for a long time. There was no way I could be implicated in his case, for someone, somewhere, was trying hard to find incriminating evidence against me.

One day in the autumn of 1947, Ahsia said to me out of the blue:

"Mary, tell Abram to take any kind of job he can get, even manual labor, as quickly as possible."

It was a strange outburst, for she knew that it was not Abram's fault that he could not find a job. She was very tense and obviously upset—unlike her usual controlled self. I questioned her and she told me that she had been contacted by two secret police operatives in the usual manner, but for the first time for her. She assured them that she could be of no use to them, that she led a very quiet life, that she worked at home most of the time and socialized very little. They were insistent, using the customary arguments: There are enemies all around; didn't she want to help the authorities; it was her duty, and so on. In the end, she signed a paper in which she agreed to become an informant and not to reveal the connection to anyone under pain of dire punishment. I was familiar with the procedure. They made another appointment and instructed her to bring a list of all her friends and acquaintances. Only one of the operatives was present at the next appointment. After the third or fourth meeting, it became clear that we were his main interest. Subsequently, it turned out that it was I who was the target, but Ahsia did not know this when she spoke to me. She thought it was Abram's joblessness that had attracted their attention to us.

Ahsia's appointments with the operative took place at ten-day intervals. The day after her meeting, she would come to our room and the three of us would go over every detail, trying to analyze the questions and her replies. We spoke in low voices so that the neighbors would not overhear us (in those years we did not have to worry about electronic eavesdropping devices). We would work out a strategy for her next appointment, a strategy that we hoped would protect her so that she could say a lot without telling them anything. After several meetings, the operative dropped the pretense of being interested in anyone but me. He seemed determined to find something in my words or actions that could be construed as anti-Soviet. He asked Ahsia leading questions over and over again. He particularly tried to get her to say that I had expressed a desire to return to the United States.[3] Ahsia had the impression that there was something in their dossier on me that concerned the Berlin period, but that whatever it was, it was not quite enough to build the case they wished to build.

The meetings with the operative were a tremendous strain on Ahsia. Each rendezvous was a duel of wits, guile, threats, and an enormous burden of responsibility. She suffered from the fear of falling into a trap and inadvertently saying something damaging. When I had been in her position a few years earlier, I had been naïve enough to believe that innocence always triumphed and I had been confident in my ability to handle the situation. We had no illusions now. We knew that we were rabbits for whom traps had been set. We were fighting for our lives.

Ahsia began to stay up until two or three in the morning, chain smoking and listening for the sound of a car stopping in front of the house and, when

3. An expressed desire to return to the United States would be the main charge against Fannie Leib, an American-born mathematician who was sentenced to ten years' imprisonment in the early 1950s on the basis of a friend's testimony. The friend, also from America, was arrested later.

one did, wondering who it was for this time. Staying up late into the night became a lifelong habit of hers.

This went on for over two years. It changed our way of life. Our every thought and every action was affected. It shocked me into silence. By nature open and quick to express an opinion, I withdrew into a shell. I stopped seeing anyone but a few close friends, and the only reason I continued to see them was so as not to excite suspicion and thereby give Ahsia away. Abram kept in touch with Max, David, some other friends, and with Lyova's family, but I no longer accompanied him on his visits. Once in a while, someone would drop in unexpectedly, but we did not encourage visitors. This was to protect them from guilt by association. Our friends did not know what was going on. Maria disapproved of my new closeness with Ahsia, for Ahsia had not been part of our "inner circle." She admonished us, saying that this was not a time to make new friends, to trust people whom you did not know very well. In fact, I still believe that I owe my life to Ahsia. She was the first to make me aware of the danger I was in. If I had not known about the investigation, it would have taken some time for me to become scared enough to be discreet and cautious in my associations.

Abram became a nervous wreck. He was convinced that if I were arrested and imprisoned, I would not survive. It was not the physical conditions of incarceration that he feared most for me. It was the brutality of the hardened criminals with whom I would most likely be imprisoned, for persons convicted under Article Fifty-Eight—anti-Soviet propaganda and actions—were jailed with habitual criminals. He knew the type from encounters in Rostov and had no hope that I would be able to hold my own against them.

I had devised an escapist mechanism. I had observed, or thought I had observed, that most arrests took place on Saturday nights. I theorized that the secret police operatives had Sundays off and that making the arrests on Saturday allowed for an extra day before the news got around at the person's place of work and alerted co-workers. What difference this made I don't know, but I guess I wasn't looking for logic. At any rate, I decided that I would worry only on Saturday nights, and I would stay up until two A.M. On other nights, I pushed my anxieties aside and slept. Abram was not able to do this. Neither was Ahsia. They worried every night.

Another shocking casualty that year was the arrest of Talmy's son Vova in Berlin. Vova, who was bilingual—having been born in the United States and raised in an English-speaking family—was in the army in 1945 and was sent to Berlin to serve as an interpreter at the Allied Joint Administration Headquarters. We had come across him from time to time in Berlin. He was a handsome, charming young man in his early twenties who enjoyed his job and, in the free and easy manner of the Joint Administration staff, socialized with his counterparts. His parents were very proud of him.

Talmy, who usually worked at home, came into the office one day, pale as death. He had come to report his son's arrest to the Party committee. I do not know what transpired at the closed Party meeting held later, but for the time being, no action was taken against him or against his wife, who was also a Party member who taught English at the Moscow Institute of Foreign Languages.

\* \* \*

Shortly before the end of the year, we had a letter and then a visit from Sasha, my husband's former tommygunner. He had been demobilized in 1945. All alone, without family or friends, he had gone to work at a construction site near Moscow and been given a place to live in workers' barracks. His entry into civilian life was not a happy one. He reproached Abram for his idealism, for not having prepared him for the corruption, dishonesty, and bureaucracy he was encountering. He told us that the workers were not paid on time and were mistreated when they complained. He came to see us a few times. Then, when he turned eighteen, he was drafted and stationed in Germany. He seldom wrote and we lost touch.[4]

For many weeks, rumors of a monetary reform circulated in Moscow. It was a guessing game as to whether it was better to keep one's savings in the bank or as cash under the bed. When the reform came in December 1947, cash was exchanged at the rate of ten old rubles to one new one, whereas a limited amount of money in the bank was redeemed at three to one. Many people who had large amounts of cash for which they could not account lost it rather than take the chance of trying to exchange it. The devaluation of the ruble did not hurt us, as we had no savings. Abram's severance pay was long gone and my salary lasted from approximately one payday to the next.

New Year's Day remained an important holiday in the Soviet Union. It took the place of Christmas, from which it borrowed some of its customs. For a week or two before the end of the year, the smell of fir trees fresh from the forest pervaded the air on street corners where trees were piled up for sale. Most families decorated a tree that they set up on New Year's Eve. (The tree would not be taken down until the following week, so that for those who wished, it served as a Christmas tree. Russian Orthodox Christmas is on January 7th.) Gifts were exchanged among family and friends. For a week or two preceding the new year, parties were held for children at schools, kindergartens, offices, and factories. Grandfather Frost, dressed exactly like Santa Claus,

---

4. The last time I saw him was in 1960, soon after my husband's death. He had stayed in the army, been sent to officers' training school, and became a career officer. He was married and raising a family. After talking about Abram, the war, and shedding a few tears, he left. I did not hear from him again.

presided and distributed goodies to the children. New Year's Eve parties for grown-ups began late. Supper would be served at midnight and the eating, drinking, and merrymaking would go on into the wee hours of the morning. There was no public transportation in Moscow after one A.M., and it was well nigh impossible to find a taxi on New Year's Eve, so either you stayed until five or you walked home. Many was the time I walked home at two or three in the morning through snowy streets in the company of one or more friends. And even in the most difficult years, our spirits were high, lifted by hope for a better year ahead.

Not so on the eve of 1948, not for us. The way things were going, 1948 augured no good.

# 18
## Postwar Anti-Semitism—1948 to 1950

Food rationing was abolished as of January 1, 1948. There was some hope that perhaps life would become a little easier, but events soon suggested otherwise.

Open anti-Semitic rhetoric was not apparent as yet. The Jewish Anti-Fascist Committee was operating, and its newspaper *Einikeit* [Unity] was being published, as was the Yiddish language *Der Emes*. The Yiddish Theater and its distinguished company, the most famous of whom was Solomon Mikhoels, was also still going strong, showing plays like *Freilakhs, Three Raisins,* and *The Uprising in the Warsaw Ghetto.* Early in January 1948, a meeting commemorating the thirtieth anniversary of the death of the Yiddish writer Mendele Mosher Sforim was held at the Polytechnic Museum and was attended by luminaries of the theater and literary world, among them Mikhoels.

All the more startling, then, was the news of Mikhoels's death later that month. On January 15th, all the central newspapers carried an obituary that began: "A great actor has died. Solomon Mikhailovich Mikhoels is no longer with us." And it went on to recount Mikhoels's accomplishments and his significance for the theater. On the roster of illustrious signatories were several well-known Jewish writers including Ilya Ehrenburg and heads of various theaters. Mikhoels was given a state funeral.

Curiously, none of the reports said anything about how he died. But as some of the details were spread by word of mouth, a rumor emerged that he had been murdered, killed in an automobile accident staged by the secret police while he was on official business in Minsk.[1] "Why?" we asked ourselves. "Why this great actor who had performed for Stalin himself and had been praised by him?" We sensed that there was something going on behind the scenes, but we did not yet know that, just a few years after Hitler's slaughter of most European Jews, the bell had begun to toll for the ones who still remained in the Soviet Union.

---

1. The murder rumor has been credibly substantiated. On Mikhoels, see Nataliia Vovsi-Mikhoels, *Moi otets Solomon Mikhoels: Vospominaniia o zhizni i gibeli* [*My Father, Solomon Mikhoels: Memoirs about Life and Death*] (Tel-Aviv: Iakov Press, 1984).

The next blow that struck close to us was the arrest in February of Nadya Ulanovsky. Alyosha came to Ahsia's with this news and said that he had better stay away in the future, but Ahsia insisted that he do nothing of the sort. The Ulanovskys' other daughters, Maya and Irina, were fifteen and twelve at the time.

Finally, Abram found a job in February after having practically lost all hope. This change of affairs helped financially and was a boost to our morale. By pure chance, cold, from the street, Abram was hired as an editor and producer of publicity materials at the Ministry of Labor Reserves, the ministry that recruited labor power for large-scale enterprises all over the country. The page-long application form asked no questions about the applicant's spouse except for the name and place of work. The salary was low and the job had nothing to do with his education or experience, but Abram was glad to have it. He had been out of work for a whole year.

Abram's job entailed a considerable amount of travel. To make sure I was all right, he would telephone me each morning from wherever he happened to be. And each morning, our close circle of friends would exchange calls, for the casualties were becoming numerous and fear walked among us. We felt as if we were living on borrowed time.

I did not go to the official functions usually attended by family members. In fact, it was years before I met any of his colleagues. No one knew about the skeleton in his closet—an American wife.

Each day brought fresh newspaper reports of American "crimes." The Western powers were accused of locking up and preventing Soviet citizens in displaced persons camps from returning home. A publishing house in Moscow was chastised for publishing a translation of an American book on U.S. political parties and was accused of manufacturing propaganda for enemy ideology. "Specialists" in American literature, many of whom I knew or met later, expatiated on the "plight of honest writers in America," naming as examples Howard Fast, Don West, Ira Wolfert, and other well-known leftist authors. A much-touted film that year, *The Russian Question,* portrayed "the fascistization of America," as one reviewer wrote. And so on and on in every single newspaper and periodical in the entire USSR. As always, *Pravda* and *Izvestiia* set the tone and the other papers and journals followed. Editors all over the country not only reprinted leading articles from those newspapers, but sought to prove their zeal by providing colorful horror stories of their own.

At the same time, the press emphasized the difference between the "masses" and their rulers in Western nations. Soviet readers might have concluded that "ordinary people" in the capitalist countries did not support and were not responsible for their governments. The fact that all these anti-American articles quoted American sources to substantiate their claims did not strike average Soviet citizens as strange. Nor did it start them thinking about such issues as freedom of the press and freedom of speech. The great majority believed what they read and did not know that the American press presented a variety of viewpoints and interpretations of events.[2]

We former Americans residing in the Soviet Union had every reason to take the official anti-American rhetoric personally. The cumulative effect was to make everyone with American connections suspect. Most ex-Americans stopped writing to family and friends abroad. My instincts, however, told me that this was not a wise move. Besides, I did not want to worry my parents. Instead, I wrote to them even more frequently than before and repeated from time to time that if they stopped receiving letters from me, they should make inquiries, since I would not stop writing to them of my own free will. As I discovered when I saw them again, they did not understand my hints: They proudly pointed out to their left-wing friends, who had lost touch with their own families in the Soviet Union, that *their* daughter wrote to them regularly. Therefore, they concluded, nothing was wrong—their friends' relatives were simply negligent.

It was becoming increasingly difficult for Jews to find professional jobs and for Jewish youths to gain admission to the best institutes and universities. There were persistent rumors that certain institutes and universities had quotas for the admission of Jews—revealing shades of tsarism when there had been an official five percent quota for admittance of Jews to institutions of higher learning. (Some people said that out-and-out limits were better than the unofficial and arbitrary quotas—at least one knew where one stood.)

I described earlier how I had argued with the militia chief when I had been issued my internal Soviet passport in 1934. I had finally persuaded him to put me down as American rather than Jewish. Now, with the experience of the war, of official and unofficial anti-Semitism in the Soviet Union. and the Nazi atrocities against the Jews, my attitude underwent a change. Whatever Marx, Lenin, or Stalin may have written about the nationality question and the Jews—namely that the Jews were not a nation because they did not have a common language, territory. or culture and that the solution to the Jewish question was assimilation with the predominant population of the countries in which they lived—I now realized that assimilation was a hoax. Jews were Jews wherever they lived and whether or not they were religious, if only because in times of historical crisis they were so often made scapegoats. Just a few short years ago, it had happened in Germany and it was now happening in the Soviet Union.

---

2. My impression was confirmed when I met Russians from all walks of life during my husband's long stays in hospitals some years later.

In this connection, I remember an exchange that took place at one of the annual reunions of the class with which I had started out in the biology department of Moscow University. I occasionally attended these gatherings, though I had been in the class only one year. This reunion took place during the war. In the course of a conversation, one of the girls remarked that Jews were too touchy and that they stuck together. Why didn't they assimilate and forget that they were Jewish? And she reiterated the received wisdom of the Marxist-Leninist theory of nationhood. My friend Mira Katz, the other American-born student, then flared up.

"When your ancestors were monkeys, hanging from trees by their tails," she said angrily, "the Jews had an alphabet and a literature. Why should they assimilate?"

The girls were taken aback. They had never thought about Jews in those terms. As I listened in admiration, Mira proceeded to present a short course on the history of the Jews. She was well versed in the subject, for she came from a family of Jewish intellectuals who, though dogmatic Communists, were "Yiddishists" as well; they wrote and published in Yiddish.

To be Jewish in Soviet Russia was bad enough. But to be American was worse. I decided that I had to shed the American part of the double burden, at least in my internal passport. Besides, I no longer felt American and never expected to see America again.

I wrote to my parents, asking them to send me a copy of my birth certificate. It arrived in due course, though with no indication that I was Jewish. I prepared a statement requesting that the nationality in my passport be changed from "American" to "Jewish" and went to the central militia office. An officer received me, read my statement through, and asked me if I had proof of my Jewish origins. I showed him my birth certificate and he, too, was surprised that there was no mention of nationality—just the dates and country of my parents' birth (Russia, 1886 and 1890).

"I believe you," he said, "but I need documentation. Why don't you ask your parents to send you a notarized statement indicating that you are Jewish?"

That was going too far. I could imagine my family's perplexity on receiving such a request, so I dropped the matter and remained "American" in my Soviet documents.

The establishment of the state of Israel in May 1948 did not arouse enthusiasm in Abram or me. We had no particular feelings for Palestine as the Biblical homeland of the Jews. We foresaw insurmountable problems in the Middle East, and were afraid that the creation of a Jewish state would make Jews unwelcome in other countries and that it would intensify the already existing anti-Semitism all over the world. The Soviet Union's initial support of the establishment of Israel went against all that Communists had preached about the Jewish question (not that we believed it any longer) and that made us wary as well. We wondered what the true motive was.

Some of the literature in the West has pictured the response of Soviet Jews to the establishment of the state of Israel as one of great enthusiasm and has linked that response to the rise of Soviet official and unofficial anti-Semitism in the following years. That was not my experience at all, or of anyone I knew. The response was moderate. Soviet Jews who were enthusiastic would probably have concealed their enthusiasm. It is true—at least so I have been told since leaving the Soviet Union—that when the Israeli Embassy was opened in Moscow, some Soviet Jews wrote letters welcoming Golda Meir, attended Embassy receptions, and even inquired about the possibility of emigrating to Israel. If there was such a response, it was not publicized and, therefore, was not widely known. The assertion that the Jews were not trusted because they were perceived as disloyal is putting the cart before the horse. It was *because* the Jews were distrusted and discriminated against, despite years of loyal service to the regime, that so many finally became disillusioned and discontented.

Anti-Semitism is endemic to Russia—it existed before and after the revolution. Some of us thought that it had been eliminated by the Soviet government's policies—good policies that gave Jews equal rights to jobs and education. We found, to our distress, that it had been there all along, merely latent, ready to raise its head at the first opportunity.

Over the previous several years, the Soviets had consolidated their power in the countries of Eastern Europe. At first, coalition governments of local Communists and other parties were set up when the Soviet armies marched in. Then, non-Communist members of the coalition governments were gradually forced out, leaving the Communists in complete control. I cannot say that I paid much attention when this happened in Poland, Hungary, and East Germany. But Czechoslovakia was another matter. The main events of the takeover occurred in 1948, by which time I was seeing things very differently than I had in 1945 and 1946. I was now following newspaper reports very closely. In September 1947, the Czechoslovak Communists and Socialists had signed a Joint Action Agreement. On February 19, 1948, the Central Committee of the Czech Communist Party issued a statement accusing the non-Communist members of the government of subversion. The next day, all the non-Communist members except President Eduard Beneš and Foreign Minister Jan Masaryk resigned. Over the next few days, the Communist head of the coalition government addressed crowds of Communist-organized demonstrators. On February 2nd, it was announced that an "anti-government plot" had been uncovered in Prague. Arrests followed. On February 28th, a new government was formed, made up exclusively of Communists, except for Beneš and Masaryk. Ten days later, the body of Jan

Masaryk was found on the pavement in the courtyard of his home. The official announcement said that he had committed suicide by jumping out of the window. But rumors persisted that he had been pushed. We never doubted for a moment that he had been murdered.

All these turbulent events around us, having, it would seem, little to do with our personal lives, affected us in one way or another. Each day brought something new to worry about and we opened the daily newspapers with trepidation.

The break with Tito that summer dismayed everyone, not just us. Tito was an enormously popular figure in the Soviet Union. The heroic exploits of the Yugoslavian partisans and his personal heroism had been widely reported in the Soviet press during the war. He had a charismatic personality and, because he had been in exile in Moscow before the war, was well known in Moscow's foreign Communist circles. Now, a Cominform resolution accusing him of Trotskyism and other heinous crimes demanded that the Yugoslavian Communist Party discuss and admit its mistakes and, if necessary, remove its leadership. The Yugoslavian Communist Party rejected the Cominform resolution. The Yugoslavian side was not given in the Soviet press, but we recognized that it was Tito's independent spirit and refusal to accept Soviet demands that had brought about the current situation. Our sympathy for Tito was strong.

It was not long before soon-to-be-confirmed rumors reached us that Tito was treating those who disagreed with him just as harshly as his Soviet and East European counterparts treated *their* opposition. Not only did he order the arrest of confirmed Stalinists, but he used the occasion to settle old scores with some of his former fellow exiles. Among his victims were two of our past colleagues from the publishing house, Ozrin, who had been in charge of both the German and the English sections, and Stumpf, with whom Abram had worked closely in the German section. Both men had gone to Yugoslavia even before the end of the war, with their families following later. It was from their returning families, especially Ozrin's wife Eda, that we learned of the arrests, torture, and executions.[3] Our sympathy for Tito evaporated.

The pretense that all was well with Soviet Jewry came to an abrupt end with the publication in *Pravda*, on September 21, 1948, of a lengthy article by Ilya Ehrenburg entitled "In Regard to One Letter."[4] The article purported to answer a letter received from a German-Jewish medical student who had

---

3. In 1990, Yugoslavian newspapers started carrying articles revealing Tito's torture, including pictures of Ozrin and Eda.
4. Ilya Ehrenburg, "Po povodu odnogo pis'ma," *Pravda* (September 21, 1948).

returned to Munich after the war and was upset to find that anti-Semitism still existed there. He asked, "What is the Soviet Union's attitude towards Israel?" and "Is Israel the solution to the Jewish question?" The article laid out official Soviet policy on Israel and on Jews.

Ehrenburg began by reminding the letter writer that the Soviet government had been the first to recognize Israel. He also asserted that the Soviet people had sympathized with the Jewish people when they were fighting the Arab Legions, admiring their courage in their struggle against the British hierarchy. According to Ehrenburg, the Russian people had never been anti-Semitic. Anti-Semitism in pre-revolutionary Russia had been artificially instigated by the tsarist regime to divert the people's wrath from itself. Lenin, he wrote, had always castigated anti-Semites.

This was fine as far as it went, for even if it was mostly untrue, positive statements in the central press could influence the public in the right direction. However, his opening was merely a sweetener.

Ehrenburg then warned that the invasion of Anglo-American capital was just as dangerous to Israel as were the Arab Legions. In other words, now that the British and the Americans were gaining the upper hand in Israel, Soviet support of Israel would be tempered with caution. The only way the Jewish question could be solved, he wrote, was in a social context, that is, by the victory of socialism.

However, the article continued, the establishment of Israel had nothing to do with Soviet Jews. The Soviet government supported the establishment of Israel as a haven for the victims of Nazi persecution. But that problem did not exist for Soviet Jewry. Israel was just another country. Soviet Jews had best keep their distance from Israel. Moreover, for Soviet Jews to have ties with Jews in other countries was unpatriotic, subversive, and dangerous.

Less than two months later, in November 1948, the Jewish Anti-Fascist Committee was disbanded, its periodical *Einikeit* closed down, as was *Der Emes*. The Jewish Anti-Fascist Committee, which had raised millions of dollars for the Soviet war effort, was declared a nest of spies in the service of Western imperialists. The arrests of Jews began. Prominent Soviet Jews, including the late Mikhoels, were branded as spies. By the end of 1948, scores of Jewish writers, poets, actors, artists, and musicians had been arrested.

This was very frightening, even to the still dedicated Jewish Communists. Job applications asked whether the applicant had relatives in foreign countries. A great many Jews had relatives abroad, especially in the United States. These links left Jews vulnerable to charges of treason. In addition, Jews were easily identifiable by their names, patronymics, by their internal passports which stated nationality, and, to a certain extent, by their looks (it always amazed me how Russians managed to spot as Jews individuals who did not look at all Jewish to me).

It was becoming increasingly difficult for Jews to find jobs "on the ideo-logical front"—in journalism, the radio, academia. This created another in-escapable paradox: Jews were discontented, and if they were discontented, they could not be trusted. If they were discontented, they might sympathize with the Western imperialists and spy on their behalf. Since all hardships were attributed to external hostile encirclement, Jews were to blame for the hardships. They were also to blame for the war in which they had not fought, but in which they had let the heroic Russians do the fighting for them. Such was the tenor of the times.

Drunks ranted in public against the *zhidy*.[5] Anti-Semitic remarks be-came commonplace in the long lines to buy food. Jewish children were taunted in the schoolyard. No attempt was made to curb such outbursts, which was signal enough. Whereas before the war, anyone who ventured to utter a racial or ethnic slur in public could be hauled before a court of law and punished, it would be a foolish person indeed who tried to take a tormenter to court now.

Thus 1948 came to an end. We had little reason to hope for a better year ahead.

The undercurrent of anti-Semitism, which had been growing stronger and which was neither publicly condoned nor countered, was still being denied by some and ignored by others. However, it suddenly burst through the floodgates with the force of a natural disaster. Attacks against "rootless cosmopolitans" came fast and furious, surfacing in the press in all the Soviet republics. The Union of Soviet Writers held a plenary session for the pur-pose of "exposing and destroying" anti-patriotic groups. *Literaturnaya gazeta* led the pack. It now appeared three times a week and we cringed every time we opened it. There was certain to be a vicious attack against a Jewish writer, artist, musician, academic, or scientist. Some of the victims admitted their mistakes publicly, but their protestations were not accepted; the victims were deemed insincere. Others remained silent. They were ha-rassed and told that they would not be allowed to avoid stating their posi-tions. "Rootless cosmopolitanism," "kowtowing to the West," and "worship of foreign things" constituted the vocabulary of the witch hunt.

The attacks were not just verbal. They were reinforced by continued arrests.

The *Moscow Daily News* was hit early in 1949. The police swept in the editor, along with practically the entire staff of the newspaper, some of whom we knew personally or knew people who knew them. The American journalist Anna Louise Strong, a close associate of the editor at the time, was denounced

---

5. *Zhidy* is a Russian derogatory term for Jews.

as a spy and was expelled from the Soviet Union. That was a sensational piece of news. Her friends and associates did not get off so lightly. One of them was Harry Eisman, who was sent into Siberian exile.

Alyosha Ulanovsky's turn came in March 1949. He had been expecting it ever since his wife's arrest one year earlier. In that year, he had failed in his attempts to find out where she was, what the charge was against her, or anything at all. He had written a letter to Stalin, reminding him that they had been in Siberian exile together under the tsar and vouching for his wife. However, he did not receive a reply and was not surprised when he later found that his letter was part of the incriminating evidence in his file.

Maya was all alone now. Her younger sister had been sent to live with their grandmother in Ukraine. For the next two years, Maya was a frequent visitor at Ahsia's, where she always received a good meal, money, and, when needed, clothing. Maya told Ahsia (and Ahsia told me) about a group of friends, all students, who met weekly in someone's home to study Leninism, which, they said, had been distorted after Lenin's death. Ahsia implored her to keep away from groups, whatever their purpose; it was asking for trouble. But Maya, nineteen years old, ignored Ahsia's advice. She was arrested along with the other members of the group in January 1951. Two of her friends—an eighteen-year-old and a nineteen-year-old boy—were shot. The others received long prison sentences. Maya herself was sentenced to twenty-five years hard labor.[6]

One after another, people we knew were struck down. Later that year, Leon Talmy was arrested. Since being released from his managerial position, Talmy did most of his work at home on Kapelsky, and I often worked with him as his assistant editor. On the evening of his arrest, I had left his apartment after midnight. Less than an hour after my departure, the secret police came for him.

Talmy was generally a quiet man, not given to spouting his opinions, passive rather than active, and much too intelligent to get involved in anything dubious, especially after his son's arrest. But he knew the Yiddish writers who had been arrested, and guilt by association was a widely used technique for dragging victims into the police's net. Talmy's wife had always been very loud in her support of the Party line. At the Foreign Languages Institute where she taught English, and beyond its walls, she was known for her "vigilance." Now, she was the only member of her family still at large. Before long, she too was expelled from the Party and sent to Siberia.

The Wattenbergs and the Talmys were old friends from New York. When Chaika Wattenberg did not report for work one Monday morning, my heart

---

6. Maya was released in 1956. She now lives in Israel. The Ulanovskys' story is told in Nadezhda and Maiia Ulanovskie, *Istoriia odnoi sem'i* (New York: Chalidze Publications, 1982).

sank. Sure enough, she had been arrested. Her husband had been arrested, too. Though Chaika was quite a bit older than I, a sort of friendship had developed between us. She often talked to me about her life in New York, the people she knew, the parties they had, the theater and the concerts. I was impressed when she told me that she had never locked the door of her apartment in Manhattan and that friends were welcome to drop in whenever they wished and could help themselves to whatever they wanted in the icebox. Since the war and my marriage, I had not spent much time with her outside the office, but I felt her arrest deeply as a personal loss.[7]

Toward the end of 1949, Paul Robeson gave a concert in Moscow. Robeson was very popular in the Soviet Union, so it was difficult to obtain tickets without connections. The concert was broadcast live over the radio and we heard it. Robeson used to sing songs of many nations in their original languages. We could not believe our ears: The very last number he sang was a Yiddish song. Was this a statement? Did Robeson know about the anti-Semitism and the arrests, or was the song merely part of his repertoire? The concert was re-broadcast many times, but we never heard the Yiddish song again. It had been cut.

The secret police finally gave up on Ahsia. Once again, she had to sign a paper saying that she would never under any circumstances divulge the connection. Although we assumed that someone else was performing her function, we still felt that we had been given a breather. We did not have to cudgel our brains every week to meet the immediate danger, and it was a relief for Ahsia.

The breather did not last long.

A few months later, Maria came to us with the same story. She had been recruited to spy on me. Maria! My closest friend! The secret police must have been hard pressed indeed to have had to resort to my close friends. Maria was very frightened, her situation made more difficult by the fact that she was a Party member and obligated to "help out." The whole procedure started all over again: discussion, analysis, working out strategies. For their own protection, we did not tell Maria about Ahsia or Ahsia about Maria. The less they knew, the easier it would be for them to dissemble if need be. (It was not until long after Stalin's death that we told them about each other.)

All told, for five years we were hunted. We knew who the hunters were and where the traps were laid, but we could do little about them. I was lucky to have good and true friends like Ahsia and Maria. Perhaps there were also others who did not confide in me, who also displayed such courage and decency.

---

7. Neither Leon Talmy nor the Wattenbergs survived. Talmy's son now lives in the United States.

During this period, we got rid of whatever possessions we thought might compromise me if I were arrested—works by Trotsky and other opposition figures that Abram had acquired in his bibliophilistic zeal, early editions of Lenin's works that differed in some respects from current editions, and the diary that I had kept for the first four or five years after my arrival in the Soviet Union—an irreparable loss.

It is not easy to destroy a book when one lives in a communal apartment. Each page has to be torn into little bits and flushed down the toilet when none of the neighbors is at home. How else could it be done? There was no place to burn it and it was far too risky to throw it away in the trash.

Though it was illegal to keep firearms, Abram had a German revolver that he had brought back from the war. Many of the men had picked up such trophies and kept them after relinquishing their general issue weapons, but all weapons were supposed to have been turned in upon demobilization. Abram got rid of his revolver by taking it apart and dropping the parts in rubbish bins widely scattered throughout the city. Years later, I read a description of just such a scene in a Soviet novel.

I had a recurring dream. I seldom remember my dreams, but this one was unusually vivid and occurred several nights in a row, imprinting itself on my mind. It would recur with different details, but always the same underlying theme: I'd be running away from pursuers. Sometimes it would be a whole pack of pursuers, sometimes just one or two. Sometimes they were faceless, and other times I knew them. Among the pursuers I recognized most often were Minquits, the tall, gaunt, thin-lipped woman who was head of the publishing house trade union, and her fat, round-faced assistant. The former ran very fast. The latter waddled. They were always among the first to speak up at meetings exposing "enemies" or relatives of "enemies," and to call for harsh measures and demand "vigilance" of the rest of us. They had been at the publishing house long before I had first worked there, and they had formerly been quite friendly toward me. Their cool attitude now led me to deduce that they had been informed that I was under surveillance.

The dream was not a nightmare. I always got away. I'd wake up with a feeling of elation, having outwitted the hunters.

I used to talk in my sleep, usually in English. Abram would wake me and demand to know what I was saying. He'd repeat my words, but most of the time I could not figure them out. Once, he said, I kept saying "brown and black, they are both the same," and when I told him they were only colors, he wanted to know whether I was referring to fascist symbols. I thought that very funny, but he was not amused. He said that if I talked in my sleep elsewhere, I might get into trouble. It was another thing to worry about!

In one dream that I had quite often, I was back in America, usually revisiting the places of my childhood, always Albany or New Haven, but never Los Angeles. That dream persisted until I returned to this country in 1965.

Early in 1950, Boris Suchkov, the former director of the publishing house, was arrested. Suchkov had been a very popular director—young, intelligent, well educated, approachable, efficient. Then Kosinskaya herself, who owed her job to Suchkov, vanished from the office without a word to anyone. Apparently, she had decided not to wait to be fired.

The English section did not get a new manager to replace Kosinskaya for several months. In the meantime, the assistant manager was in charge. Scared out of his wits, he groveled to his superiors and treated the rest of us as potential "enemies of the people."

My health had been affected by the stresses and anxieties of the past few years, and my doctor advised me to spend my vacation in Yessentuki, a mountain resort in the North Caucasus. Accommodations became available in June 1951. Yessentuki is one of a group of spas famous for their hot and cold springs of varied chemical composition. It was a place that was recommended for the treatment of a variety of illnesses. The diet, waters, structured regimen, and, above all, the surrounding natural beauty did me a great deal of good and I returned to Moscow after a month, refreshed and feeling much better.

But unpleasant news awaited me. I had been fired. The bad news was imparted to me by the publishing house director, Pravdin. He expressed his regret and wished me luck. I had the distinct impression that it was not he who was responsible for my dismissal, that the order had come from somewhere else.

The arrests continued to reach deep into our circle. In 1937–1939, the Terror had been aimed primarily against high-ranking Party, government, and army officials, as well as the unlucky people connected with them. Huge numbers of known and unknown victims disappeared into the camps, but they were rarely people we knew personally. Most of the ex-foreigners arrested in the publishing house and the Comintern had been East Europeans. Now the terror was directed chiefly against intellectuals and cultural figures, many of them Jewish, and Soviet citizens who were ex-foreigners, including those from Western Europe and America. These groups had hardly been touched in the earlier Terror.

Abram traveled extensively for his job and got an uncommon view of living conditions around the country. It was a depressing picture. There was hardly a family that did not have a jailed relative. Petty thievery was regarded as a crime against socialist property; and a collective farmer or factory worker could be sentenced to ten years "deprivation of freedom" for taking a handful of nails because he could not buy nails anywhere. Abram remarked that the whole country was a prison camp—only some were fenced in, while others were not.

# 19

## Respite—1950

Abram was away on business in Kemerovo, an industrial town in Siberia. He was not expected back for several weeks. Ahsia had not yet had her vacation. Moscow was having a cold, rainy summer, and Ahsia was eager to get away. We agreed to go south together, to the Black Sea coast of the Soviet Republic of Georgia.

This was not the usual way one reacted to loss of a job. It caused some comment.

We decided to go to Sukhumi, where Tamara and Boris had a friend who could possibly put us up or help us to find a place to stay. No hotels or hostels were open to the public, so we were going "wild"—that is, without sanatorium or rest home reservations. Later, the practice of going wild became widespread, but in July 1950, few venturesome souls attempted to travel in this way.

Train tickets had to be reserved long in advance, but plane tickets were easy to get, so we flew. This was my first airplane flight and I looked forward to it with some excitement and a little apprehension. The eight-hour flight to Adler, the only airport to serve that entire section of the Black Sea coast, was smooth, and I enjoyed every minute of it. We planned to spend a day or two in nearby Sochi and then go further south to Sukhumi. We had no trouble renting a room for the night. There were local people with offers at the airport.

It took me a while to shed the anxieties of Moscow. My first day in Sochi, I shied away every time I saw a militiaman. I was afraid of being asked for identification and hauled off for questioning because of the word "American" in my internal passport.

I couldn't believe the warm weather and brilliant sunshine. Back in Moscow, I had been unable to imagine that it was warm anywhere, so I had packed a suitcase of woolens in spite of Ahsia's attempts to dissuade me. It was thirteen years since I had been in the south of Russia, and I had forgotten the lush subtropical vegetation, the oleanders, the palm trees, the eucalyptus, the roses, the relaxed atmosphere. It was a delightful change.

In Sochi, we hired a taxi and set out for Sukhumi over winding mountain roads amidst breathtaking scenery, a drive of about three hours. In some places, the mountains came right down to the sea; in others, they receded and the road ran parallel to the rocky shore. Valya Skulte, Boris and Tamara's friend, lived in Kelasuri, a village on the outskirts of Sukhumi. To our surprise, the driver knew the house and deposited us practically at the door. Valya, as we soon learned, was something of a character in the area—everybody knew her.

Valya's house was built on a high bluff overlooking the sea. It was a two-story frame house with windows and balconies facing the water, unlike most of the houses in the villages through which we had driven, which were turned away from the sea. Every inch of the small garden was planted with fruit trees and grape vines. There were oranges, peaches, figs, and a fruit I had never heard of—feijoa. A crooked wooden staircase led down to the beach. Valya's house and a squat log cabin about two hundred yards farther along the shore were the only two houses on the beach as far as the eye could see.

Valya's two guest rooms were occupied, but she had spoken with her neighbors in the log cabin and they had a room we could rent. We could also look for a room in the village, she said, but she thought we'd be more comfortable with her neighbors, who were Ukrainian, than with Georgians. We left our suitcases at Valya's and walked along the beach to the cottage.

It was a typical peasant cottage, more spacious than some, with one large central room and two rooms off it. Its wooden floor was scrubbed white and was spotlessly clean. The house was turned away from the sea, all its windows facing the dusty trail that led up to the village road. In the back of the house was a chicken coop with a few chickens, a doghouse, a cowshed, a privy, and a well with a pump. The cow, they said, was led out to pasture with the village herd every morning and brought back at dusk. That meant there would be fresh eggs and milk. It looked good, except that they asked for twice as much as we had expected to pay for lodging. Besides, we had our hearts set on a room with a view. We said we would think it over and set out for the village.

In the village, we immediately attracted attention. Groups of men sat in front of the houses, smoking, talking, and playing dominoes. There was not a woman in sight. The women, we discovered later, were at work in the collective farm fields. The men were supposedly at work, too. They had "leadership" positions in the collective farm: They were mechanics, tractor drivers, bookkeepers, and the like. Apparently, they worked when they felt like it. The men's real job was selling the fruit and vegetables from their private plots in the open market locally and as far away as Moscow.

They shouted questions at us. Where did we come from? Where were we staying? When they heard that we were looking for a place to stay, they made suggestions, none of which turned out to be acceptable. We stopped to watch men working on an unfinished building that had caught our attention because it had a second floor and windows facing the sea. The men called to us, asked us if we had found a place (everyone in the village knew we were looking), and said they had all but finished the second floor—all but the staircase. They urged us to climb the ladder propped up against the wall to see for ourselves, which we did. We entered a large, bright room, completely bare, but with a view. And what a view! With the sea in front and the mountains behind, it was stupendous. The men assured us they would have the staircase finished and installed the next day and would put in two mattresses, a table, and chairs right away. For the one night, we could use the ladder. There was a well in the yard and a privy farther off. They did not seem to care what we paid them or even whether we paid at all. We said we'd let them know within the hour.

As we sat on a bench discussing the situation, a woman came over to talk to us. Clearly not from Georgia, she was rather tall, wore a long skirt and blouse and had a cotton kerchief on her head. Her Russian was that of an educated person. She told us that she used to live in Ashkhabad and had come here after the recent earthquake (as many Russians and Ukrainians had done).[1] We told her of our dilemma and she said she'd be happy to have us stay with her, but that her place was a steep climb up the hills. With visions of a more *kul'turnoe* place than those that we had seen, we climbed the hill with her.

The higher we climbed, the more spectacular the view. Finally, we passed the last peasant house.

"Not much farther," she encouraged us. At last, she stopped. "Here," she said.

We looked around. We saw nothing that resembled a dwelling. She pointed to a clump of bushes. We came close and saw a shack, more like a hole in the ground than a dwelling, and a couple of mattresses on the earthen floor. There was no water. She carried buckets of water from the nearest well in the village. We asked about the outhouse.

"Oh, go anywhere," she said. "Hardly anyone ever comes this way."

We thanked her, said the climb was too steep, and left.

We never came across her again, never found out who she was. We wondered whether we were so insensitive as not to have noticed something strange about her at once. Or perhaps she was not strange, just different. Even Valya had no idea who she was.

---

1. Ashkhabad (now Ashgabat, capitol of Turkmenistan), close to Iran's border, was the capital of the Turkmen Soviet Socialist Republic. A devastating earthquake in 1948 nearly destroyed the city. (Ed.)

Dusk was approaching and we had to make up our minds. We went back to the unfinished house and arranged to return for the night. Valya thought we were making a mistake, but we stuck by our decision.

The men helped us take up our things—our night clothes and sheets and pillow cases that Valya had loaned us. True to their word, they had put down two mattresses, a table, and two chairs. The room was brightly lit by a naked bulb in the middle of the ceiling (all the places we saw had electricity). There was a bowl of fruit on the table. We were charmed. We were very tired, turned off the light, and went to sleep.

We did not sleep long. I woke up. Something was biting me. Ahsia was moving about on her mattress too. I turned on the light. The mattresses were swarming with bedbugs. We had no means to fight them. Unable to sleep any more that night, we decided to go outside and sit on a bench in the fresh air. We opened the door, only to discover there was no ladder! They had taken away the ladder! Short of jumping out of the second story, there was no way to get out. Why in the world had they taken away the ladder? Did they think we might make off with it in the middle of the night? We looked at each other and burst out laughing. What a pair of idiots we were! Virtual babes in the woods! When the men arrived with the ladder in the morning, we took our things, left, and rented the first room we had seen.

The place turned out to be ideal. We had only to walk out the back gate and down a few steps and we were on the beach, which we had all to ourselves. Absolute peace! It was possible to shut out the world, to forget all our worries. Ahsia expected to be fired from her job momentarily and I had no idea what I would do when I got back to Moscow, but we did not talk about the present. We read no newspapers, talked no politics, and put everything unpleasant out of our minds. The beach was rocky, as it is nearly everywhere along the Georgian coast. We'd flatten out a bed of stones, throw a blanket on top, and lie down. Then we'd recall the wide, sandy beaches of our youth, of Ahsia's childhood in Boston and New York, of mine in New Haven and Santa Monica. Those beaches were worth recalling! We read, reminisced, and sometimes sang the songs we remembered from the twenties and early thirties. I cannot carry a tune and Ahsia had to guess what I was trying to sing, but we enjoyed ourselves immensely.

On our first day at the beach, we had a bit of a scare. Two soldiers in border guard uniforms and carrying rifles came by. No one had told us that the beach was patrolled! Our hearts were in our mouths as they approached. It was too late to get up and leave. They stopped, greeted us, asked where we were from and where we were staying, saluted, and continued on their way. The patrols came by in the early morning and late afternoon, young, fresh-faced boys—Russians, never Georgians.

Food was no problem. We had fresh milk, eggs, potatoes, fruit, and once in a while, chicken. We had brought canned goods and coffee, and we left the coffee grounds to the cow, who loved them. I did the cooking, Ahsia washed up and swept the room. In relationships with other friends, I always did the unskilled chores while someone else did the cooking, but Ahsia was even more inept in the kitchen than I.

There was a restaurant in the village and one day we decided to try it. We had misgivings the moment we entered. There were no women inside, only men talking, laughing, and smoking. We ordered *kharcho,* a thick, spicy stew made with mutton and local vegetables, and wine. As the steaming bowls were set before us, the laughing, talking, and eating stopped. Everybody was watching us. We each swallowed a spoonful and our mouths felt as though they were on fire. We did all we could do to keep from spitting the food out. We sputtered as the tears ran down our cheeks. The men burst into laughter and pointed to the glasses of wine, gesturing to us to drink. We asked for water, paid our bill, and left.

We had eaten Georgian food before, but it had never been as spicy as this. We suspected that it had been specially prepared for us this way. Later in our stay, we risked eating in restaurants in Sukhumi. The service was always friendly and the food good. Our meal must have been a Georgian peasant's idea of a joke on strangers, especially when the strangers were women.

Night fell much earlier than it did in Moscow. It was so dark before the moon rose that we seldom ventured even as far as Valya's. We sat outside on the beach or talked with our hosts. They were Ukrainian peasants who had come to this area many years before to escape the famine in Ukraine. They had lost a son in the war and, more recently, a daughter in the Ashkhabad earthquake. They did not belong to the local collective farm—apparently, no outsiders did—but they lived off the produce from their vegetable garden and their livestock, selling and buying on market days in Sukhumi. They had a roof over their heads and enough to eat, and expected nothing more from life. The rent that vacationers paid was a bonus. Their paying guests were usually the overflow from Valya's.

We realized why their cottage and most of the village houses were turned away from the sea—to deaden the sound of the waves crashing onto the beach. The villagers seldom came down to the beach and, as far as we could tell, never went into the water. I don't think they could swim. That was the case all along the seacoast: The people lying on the beaches were vacationers from other parts of the country. Valya was a strong swimmer and so was Ahsia. Valya would swim off and be away for two hours or more. Ahsia deferred to my anxiety and did not swim out of sight, though sometimes I could hardly discern her head bobbing in the distance.

Valya! I had never encountered anyone like her. A free spirit in this rigid, regimented society, seemingly unaware and certainly unconcerned about its restrictions, living by her own rules and her own standards. When I first met her in 1950, she had already turned forty, a statuesque, blue-eyed, blond beauty with a perfect figure and golden tanned skin. I did not get to know her well that summer as she was busy with her guests and her garden, but I spent more time with her in later years. She came from a conventional family of Moscow white-collar workers, summer neighbors of the Milman family whom she met when she was twelve years old. After completing secondary school, she studied English at an accelerated six-months course and went to Stalingrad to act as interpreter and translator for the American engineers who were helping to build a tractor plant in Stalingrad. That was around 1928, at the beginning of the First Five-Year Plan. She had a generally poor opinion of the Americans she worked with—found them ill-mannered, doing things like blowing their noses with their fingers and urinating behind trees. (I wondered about that. I had never known educated Americans to behave in that way. Were the men she worked with really engineers?)

For about two years after she left Stalingrad, she was a close friend of the son of the noted Russian writer Maxim Gorky. Together they crisscrossed the Crimea and Ukraine on foot or hitching rides, sleeping in peasant huts, and doing odd jobs now and then. In the early 1930s, she was deeply moved by the scenes of disruption and starvation in Ukraine, so she begged the famous author to report this to the authorities, for he had access to the highest among them. Gorky became very angry, accusing her of lying, and told her to stop spreading enemy propaganda. That, I gathered from her account, turned her off the political system and its leaders for good.

She came to Kelasuri in the mid-1930s because doctors had recommended the climate for her husband, who had tuberculosis. At that time, Kelasuri was a tiny village and the coast was deserted. Valya had no difficulty obtaining permission to build a house on the beach. The doctor's written recommendation helped; besides, no one was interested in the land. Valya and her husband built the house, doing most of the work themselves, and begging, borrowing, purchasing materials and tools from the villagers who, at first, regarded them with cautious curiosity but then got accustomed to them. The distance between the water's edge and the bluff on which they built was much greater then and the bluff was not so high. As her husband got sicker, Valya did most of the work and cared for him as well. He died two years later. Valya stayed on alone.

Valya worked on the house, put in the garden and planted the trees, and earned a living of sorts by giving private English lessons to young children in Sukhumi. Her pupils were the children of the elite—Party and government officials, scientists employed at Sukhumi's famed botanical gardens and zoological laboratory where monkeys were bred—and this probably gave her the protection she needed to live outside the normal channels of society. Until very recently, she had had no official status—she was neither peasant, employee, or academic, nor a member of a trade union or of any other organization. She had never joined the Komsomol or the Party. When we met her, she had started a part-time job as a translator at the Georgian Research Institute for Subtropical Vegetation, located in the village beyond Kelasuri. She had done so in order to qualify for the minimum old age pension, a pittance, but better than nothing if there came a time when she could not work. To our delight, she brought us *batata* from the Institute—sweet potatoes, much smaller and not as sweet as the ones we remembered, but the first we had had since we left the United States.

In Moscow and in most others parts of the Soviet Union, Valya could not have lived as she did, but Georgia, as we soon perceived, was another country and it, too, lived by its own rules. For the most part, its collective farms were a facade. They produced the minimum of the taxes-in-kind required by the government, but often not even that, for bribery was common and there were ways to get around the tax collector. The line between collective and private property was blurred. Several men would be delegated to fly the villagers' produce to the markets up north, especially to Moscow, Leningrad and other cities in central Russia where it would be sold for very high prices in the so-called collective farm markets. The black market, or as it became known as, the "second economy," thrived quite openly in Georgia. If you wanted services or merchandise, you paid extra. Bus conductors never gave you change unless you asked for it and then they let you know that you were a cheapskate. Transactions of every kind had to be sweetened. There was a great deal of this kind of corruption in Moscow and everywhere else, but nowhere was it as pervasive and blatant as in Georgia. A system such as this had its advantages—if you knew whom to bribe, you could cut through a lot of red tape.

Sometimes we'd take the bus into Sukhumi to go to the market and to visit the botanical gardens and the monkey-breeding lab—Valya got us passes— or to walk around the town. There were always a great many people at the bus station and we invariably became the center of attention. The locals did not hesitate to ask us questions. Where were we from? Where were we staying? How old were we? Were we married? Did we have children? If not, why not? What language were we speaking? And, above all, what was our nationality?

Nationality! That inordinate interest in ethnic background that I had encountered when I first arrived in Moscow and still encountered now and then was more intense than ever, here in the Transcaucasus, where dozens of ethnic groups lived side by side and were intermingled.

We always replied "Jewish," but they never believed us.

"You are not Jewish," they would say. "You are hiding your national-ity." Pointing to Ahsia, they'd say "Armenian," and to me, they would say "Greek." The Greeks had been deported from the area during the war, and the Georgians and Armenians were frequently at loggerheads. Apparently, it was better to be Jewish than Armenian or Greek. As for Russians, all the local nationalities were hostile to them and the hostility was reciprocated in full measure by the local Russians.

All too soon, it was time to return to Moscow and to reality. We took the train, having bought tickets in advance. Abram met us at the railroad station and was happy to see us looking so well. He told me that someone had telephoned me from TASS and that I was to call the Editorial Office of Information for Foreign Countries (RIDZ) as soon as possible. I called and made an appointment to see the new head of the department. (Chernov had left because of ill health. He died a few years later.)

Chernov's replacement welcomed me warmly, saying that Pravdin from the Foreign Languages Publishing House had called him and recommended me. I was offered my old job back off staff. I accepted gladly. He introduced me to a round-faced, worried-looking little man who was in charge of the translators.[2] We arranged that I would report in a few days. My off-staff status was mere formality. I'd be working three shifts like everybody else and I'd be paid by the hour. Although I hated the night shift, I was in no position to make conditions.

Of my former coworkers, all the typists were still there. The French and German sections were intact, but the only English translator I recognized was Nina Shapiro. Alexander Gurevich had been arrested. The third trans-lator was Leo Lempert, a Russian-born former American citizen whom I had met casually over the years, but did not know well. Like myself, he was not officially on the staff. We worked different shifts and met only at depart-mental meetings or when changing shifts. Whatever conversation we had concerned our work. The staff editors who checked our translations for inaccuracies, political errors, distortions and, God forbid, sabotage were all new to me. Of the four editors I worked with, three were Russians who had lived in America and gone to school there when their fathers were posted in the USSR trade mission or embassy. I had no problem with them. The fourth editor, a pleasant-looking, grey-haired woman, was a former American Com-munist named Aerova. She smiled when I was introduced to her. She said what a pleasure it was to meet me and that she was sure we'd make an excellent team.

---

2. He was the father of the well-known refusenik, Alexander Slepak.

Aerova was a complete stranger to me. Over the nearly twenty years I had lived in Moscow, I had met or at least heard of most of the Americans, British, and Canadians who lived in Moscow and worked for Soviet organizations. Before the war, they had kept more or less to their separate clusters: the publishing house, the *Moscow Daily News,* the foreign language institutes where they taught, the Comintern. After the war, with their numbers diminished and the redistribution of forces, most of us got to know one another, though superficially. Yet I had never heard of Aerova, nor had I known anyone who knew her. Obviously, Aerova was not her real name. She told me nothing about herself, but hinted that she had been very important in the Communist Party of the United States and that she was temporarily between missions.

It did not take me long to discover that beneath that affable exterior was a vicious, rigid, bullying defender of the faith. From the beginning, she tried to establish herself as my superior, entitled to criticize, reprimand, and give orders. Her Russian was atrocious, yet she argued points of translation, citing her political "intuition." She lectured me on current events, joining in the anti-American rantings of the press and in the attacks on "enemies of the people." She sensed an adversary in me, but could not put her finger on anything, except that I never expressed an opinion, which infuriated her. After taking her bullying for quite a long time, I finally lost my temper and had an all-out, shouting fight with her (entirely about job-related matters) with an amazing result. She turned into a lamb and stopped pestering me. I learned a lesson—bullies will back off if you stand up to them.[3]

I went to work for TASS in August 1950 and stayed until the summer of 1953, when I felt secure enough to quit. I never again had or sought a staff job in the Soviet Union, and I never rejoined the trade union or any other organization. During my tenure at TASS, I took no part in the so-called volunteer "social work" and I refused to attend the political classes in which all employees were expected to participate. I pointed out to the RIDZ Party secretary, when he tried to pressure me, that not only was I not on staff and had no obligation toward him, but that I had a degree from Moscow University and was qualified to teach those classes myself. I had no intention of wasting my time just for the record. I also refused to train "young talent" from the foreign language institutes who were eventually supposed to replace us "bourgeois specialists," as the Party secretary explained, referring to Lenin's statement in the early days of the revolution on the need to make

3. Aerova died in China. She went to Beijing soon after Stalin's death and worked on the *Jenminjibao* [*Beijing Daily*]. Lempert saw an obituary and a picture of her with Chairman Mao. It gave her real name which, if my memory does not fail me, was Manya Reiss. Reiss, who lived from 1900 until 1962, was a founding member of the CPUSA.

use of the skills of bourgeois specialists until the Soviets could train their own. I was furious at the implications and wrote a memo to the TASS Party committee, demanding an explanation. I was assured that I had misunderstood, that it was a slip of the tongue, and that my work was needed and appreciated. After a while, I was left alone and I settled into a groove.

The job was boring and stressful, as we always had to meet deadlines, but the money was good and the job had an important perk: limited access to foreign newspapers and magazines. The basis for this privilege was that it was necessary for translators to keep up with the languages into which they translated. Above all, I was lucky to have the job. A job, more than anything, else defined a person's status in Soviet society. For me, it was especially important in those dangerous years. I would have been much more vulnerable had I not had a regular job. I still think of Pravdin with gratitude. Pravdin had been the head of the TASS bureau in New York and had good connections in TASS, but he did not have to do what he did for me. It was heartening that there were decent people around who held out a helping hand when they could do so. And, as I already knew from the war years, I could never tell who they were until it came to the crunch.

# 20
## During Stalin's Final Years—1950 to 1953

The years from 1950 to Stalin's death in March 1953 were times of mounting tension and danger, particularly for Jews and ex-foreigners. Anti-Semitism had become a way of life. The press in Moscow and outside, especially in Ukraine, regularly printed articles accusing persons with Jewish names of fraud, swindle, bribery, and nepotism. Jews were no longer accepted in the diplomatic service; neither were they sent abroad as foreign correspondents. They were squeezed out of the Party and government apparatus and fired from the secret police. Jews who had jobs held on to them for dear life, trying to be as unobtrusive as possible, for if they lost their jobs, it would be extremely difficult to find another. They were afraid to criticize, to take any initiative, and consequently, they accepted all kinds of humiliation. Their children were having a hard time getting admitted to prestigious universities and institutes. Children of my friends who graduated from secondary school in those years applied to schools in which they had no interest at all. For example, Mussia's son went to a horse-breeding institute in Udmurtia.[1] He never worked at the profession for which he was trained. After graduation, he returned to Moscow and got a factory job. When the situation permitted, he completed a correspondence course in German from a foreign languages institute and found a position in that field. Before her arrest, Alyosha's daughter Maya Ulanovsky had been a student at an institute run by the food ministry, despite the fact that she had no interest in the food industry.

Most anti-Jewish measures were not made public, but were handed down as instructions to personnel departments. Nevertheless, the measures were common knowledge and they permeated every aspect of people's lives. The "masses" were quick to respond. The number of anti-Semitic incidents "from below" increased, and there was no recourse. For example, the Jewish cemetery in Malakhovka, a small town outside Moscow, was desecrated and no one did anything about it.

---

1. Udmurtia, located in southeastern European Russia, had been an Autonomous Soviet Socialist Republic since 1934. It is still part of Russia. (Ed.)

It was not only the ignorant and uneducated who rallied to the banner of anti-Semitism. Persons in middle-echelon positions often benefited from the easing of competition, and many rationalized: Yes, this is a Russian republic. Why do so many Jews have good jobs? Yes, Jews engage in nepotism. Yes, everybody knows that they look out for their own. Yes, Jews are touchy, they imagine slights, and so on. Many mixed marriages, never before thought of as such, were affected and fell apart. Their children were now being urged by their own parents to choose the non-Jewish parent's nationality for their internal passports so that life would be easier for them.

One result of the cosmopolitan period was that it made many Soviet Jews rethink their feelings about being Jewish. The majority of the Jewish intellectuals I knew had believed that assimilation was the solution to the "Jewish question" and anti-Semitism. Many Soviet Jews, especially in the mid-1920s through the 1930s, had actively sought assimilation. It was a rude awakening when they discovered that they could not get away from being Jewish, no matter how assimilated they thought they were. Bitterly, they resisted. They tried to close their eyes to the fact that they were not allowed to assimilate. They protested that they had been raised on Russian culture, the Russian language, and that they knew nothing about Jewish history and culture (which was true). But the battle had been lost. Like the Jews in Nazi Germany, the Jews in the Soviet Union were compelled to realize that they could not get away from being Jewish, whether they liked it or not.

The anti-American tone became increasingly aggressive. Soviet journalists in the United States painted a picture of unmitigated horror for ordinary Americans: unemployment, harassment, crime, racism, warmongering. The Soviet reader was told that America was preparing to wage bacteriological war and was deliberately infecting Europe with the Colorado beetle. (The Colorado beetle story kept coming up in the Soviet press for months.)

As usual, *Literaturnaya gazeta* was in the forefront, with pretensions to authority as a cultural mouthpiece. No one was safe from its barbs. Established Soviet writers like Valentin Katayev and Veniamin Kaverin, for example, were told that they had not depicted Communists as sufficiently heroic in their latest novels. Some foreign writers who used to be praised by the critics were now out of favor. Upton Sinclair, for example, was called a warmonger for his Lanny Budd books. Articles critical of America by American writers were prominently displayed. Howard Fast, in a long article published in *Literaturnaya gazeta*, complained that very few bookstores in the United States carried his books and that he had not been permitted to give a talk at Columbia University. He compared universities in the United States to those of Hitler's Germany. Stefan Heym, author of *The Crusaders*, a 1948 novel in which the chief protagonist was an American army officer in the same kind of outfit as my husband during the war, wrote an article about the deplorable plight of writers in America (as contrasted to those in the Soviet Union).

We laughed at these articles. Soviet writers who dared to offer much milder criticism would have had their books removed from shops and libraries. In the USSR, there would have been no outlet for these sorts of complaints. Any Soviet authors who criticized their society in the way that Fast did would be lucky not to end up in a Siberian labor camp.

Fast's *Thirty Pieces of Silver*, a play about guilt by association during the McCarthy years in the United States, was translated into Russian and produced on the Soviet stage in the 1950s. We went to see it. We identified with it because it applied directly to our lives, from the individual held responsible for recommending someone for a job to the unfortunate person who happened to have known someone charged with a political crime. However, the events he wrote about were an all-encompassing fact of life in the Soviet Union, whereas in the United States the events referred to an episode that lasted a few years and affected only a limited number of people.

Needless to say, we had neither seen the foreign plays and films nor read the books that aroused the ire of Soviet critics. Foreign travel was a rare and highly-prized privilege. Those who enjoyed it, whether journalists on assignment, or scholars and cultural figures, were very careful to write that which was required of them. Their articles were read avidly by average citizens who had no hope of ever being allowed to travel abroad and see for themselves what life was like in other countries. I resented those articles.

Access to information was also a highly prized privilege, whether to foreign periodicals or to the "secret" ("white") TASS review of the foreign press, or to sources that knew what was going on in the upper echelons of Party and government power. The Lenin Library had copies of every book published in the Soviet Union and of major works published abroad, as well as of all books published in Russia before the revolution, but only a small part of its resources was open to the general public. An institutional request was required for access to its "closed" funds, and permission was limited to a particular field of science or scholarship. There was a foreign languages library in Moscow with a good selection of classics up to the early twentieth century and a closed section of more recent fiction and current periodicals, but access to these was restricted. Foreign films were rare and always attracted long lines at the box office, whether they were the wonderful Italian neo-Realist films such as *The Bicycle Thief* or sentimental films from India. Many more foreign films were shown to selected audiences at the writers', cinematographers', and composers' clubs, and at special showings for government and Party officials. A friend of mine who used to do simultaneous translation at such showings was sometimes able to take me along, and that was a treat. Thanks to her, I saw some good films, among them *Twelve*

*Angry Men, The Best Years of Our Lives, San Francisco,* and *Casablanca.*
But the great majority of the Soviet people were able to read, see, and hear
only what the powers-that-be deemed suitable.

The inaccessibility of information, the absence of freedom of choice
with regard to what one could read or see, and the forced ingestion of pre-
masticated pap had always troubled me. The explanation that the Russian
people were not sophisticated enough to interpret diverse points of view did
not satisfy me even in the early days when I first asked such questions, but I
accepted this. Who was I, a new arrival, to contradict them?

As the years went by, my anger grew. In the university, I saw how one-
sided information and interpretation affected young minds. The information dulled the critical faculties of those who accepted all they were taught
and made cynics of those who did not. Even when I was a true believer, I
was convinced that the restrictive policies were both unnecessary and harmful. I strongly resented the intellectual deprivation much more than the material hardships I had endured and was still enduring. I stopped reading the
Soviet newspapers and periodicals altogether. Abram read them very carefully and commented on them, often finding significant indications of policy
directions. Now and then, I'd read an article he recommended. We used to
joke that an important conjugal duty of husbands was to read the newspapers so that the wives would not have to do so. Other couples we knew had
the same division of labor.

The arrests continued. Mostly we learned of them by word of mouth.
Each day, we braced ourselves for more bad news. I no longer saw the
Mikhlins. My step-uncle asked me not to come any more and ordered his
daughters not to visit me. I was hurt, but Abram was not offended. He said
that you could not blame anyone for being frightened. Anya Atlas's mother
lived in the same building, but since I had no reason to go there, I no longer
saw her either. Anya and her family had moved from Kirov to Ordzhonikidze
(formerly and now again Vladikavkaz) in the North Caucasus. Her brother
Dodya was in exile. He had served his ten-year sentence, but could not return
home. Released convicts were issued identity cards that listed cities in which
they were not permitted to reside, a practice inherited from tsarist times.
Moscow, Leningrad, Kiev, and most big cities were on the list. I had drifted
away from Galya Babushkin and her mother, not because I was afraid of
endangering them or their endangering me, but because my views differed so
much from theirs and I could not talk freely with them.

One morning, I came to work and found that my scheduled editor, Hans
Vladimirsky, had not turned up. No one said anything, but I knew at once that
he must have been arrested. I remember the precise date—November 4, 1950.

Among the former Americans in Moscow arrested between during this
period were George Green and his sister Lee. George had worked with foreign

correspondents during the war. The Greens—the parents and the two children—had come to the Soviet Union from Los Angeles a few years after we had. The parents went back to Los Angeles, but the children remained in Moscow. I had known them casually in California, but had not kept up with them in Moscow. Others arrested were Fannie Leib, who had come to Moscow with her mother, brother, and stepfather in the mid 1930s; Jack Guralsky, a translator; Pauline Rose and her husband, Sam Friedman. These were all people I knew slightly, some only by name.

We felt that we were living on borrowed time. Our only respite was our vacations, when we could get away from it all—or thought we could.

Abram and I planned a very special vacation in 1951. After more than ten years of marriage, it would be our first vacation together. We would fly south in September, the very best time for a vacation in the south of Russia. First, we would spend a few days visiting his relatives in Odessa. These were the relatives on his father's side whose wives and children I had last seen in Rostov fleeing the German advance in 1941. Abram had not seen any of them since long before the war. After that, we would board a ship that sailed between Odessa and Batumi on the southernmost tip of Georgia, spend a day or two there, and then backtrack by train to Sukhumi and spend the rest of the month at Valya's. We made all our reservations, including arrangements with Valya.

Odessa, with its wide, tree-lined streets, its European architecture and its seaport, was a pleasant contrast to Moscow. We climbed the staircase made famous in Sergei Eisenstein's film *The Battleship Potëmkin,* and then went on a tour of the opera house, said to be a replica of the Viennese opera house (there were no performances at the time). Old-timers talked about how different present-day Odessa was from the former lively city with foreign shops in the harbor and sailors from all over the world in the streets. There were no foreign ships docked there nowadays and no sailors. It was a quiet city, uncrowded and unhurried. Except for the beach! One day we went to a sandy beach not far from the city. I laughed out loud when we got there—it reminded me so much of my one visit to Coney Island as a child—with fat women screaming at their children, and bodies lying like sardines on a beach so crowded you could hardly find a place to put your feet as you stepped over the bathers.

We were wined and dined by numerous cousins and we caught up on the family news. All the men had fought in the war and most had survived. Their families had been evacuated from Odessa in good time. They lamented the lack of foresight of Abram's parents, whom they had tried so hard to persuade to leave Rostov. The women recalled how Abram's aunts and cousins—his mother's side of the family—had gathered to hear them describe what was going on in Odessa, yet no one had been willing to leave. From us, they learned that every last one, including several young children, had perished in the Rostov massacre of the Jews. They spoke of the anti-Semitism they had encountered in evacuation and upon their return to Odessa. Their apartments had been looted and were occupied by local people. They had a hard time getting their living quarters back, and solved their problems in the tried and tested way—by spreading money around, a much faster and more effective way than going through the courts.

The boat trip was a delight. The *Pobeda* [*Victory*] had been a Germany luxury liner and had been acquired by the Soviet Union as part of the reparations agreement. We had a comfortable, first-class cabin with its own bathroom and excellent meals which we augmented with fruit bought in the markets of the towns where we docked. We spent a whole day in Batumi's renowned botanical gardens, where we talked to a gardener about this and that. (One of our pleasures of travel was talking with strangers.) In the course of the conversation, the gardener pointed to the mountains in the distance and said:

"That's the Turkish border. There are mountain passes there that have been used for centuries."

I started to ask questions—were the passes still used? How far away were the mountains?—but Abram became nervous and pulled me away.

As we strolled into town the next day, Abram suddenly stopped short.

"Look," he exclaimed. "That's Misha Eidelbaum from Rostov. I'm positive it is he."

Abram had an extraordinary memory for faces. Time and again in Moscow, I had seen him stop someone in the street whom he had not seen for ten, twenty years. He never made a mistake.

He called out the name and the man turned around. For a moment, he looked puzzled, then broke into a smile and ran towards us.

"Abram! Of all people! What are you doing here?"

The men embraced. They had not seen one another since their grammar school days.

We went into a teahouse to talk. The story Misha told us was fascinating. He was about Abram's age (forty), had black hair, black eyes, and a luxurious black mustache. He had been startled when Abram called out his name because he had not used that name for years. He had fled Rostov in the early days of the war, both from the Germans and, he unashamedly admitted, from the draft. He ended up in Baku where he obtained documents in another name and passed himself off as Azerbaidzhani. Much better than being Jewish, he remarked. He had succeeded in avoiding the draft by getting a deferred job. He was doing well and had come to Batumi on business. He gave us his new name and address and urged us to visit him. Abram enjoyed the meeting and was amused at his old schoolmate's enterprise, but he destroyed the name and address as soon as we parted.

"With a man like that," I remarked, "we could have got across the border to Turkey."

"That, or Siberia," was Abram's comment. He was not an adventurer.

At Valya's, we spent the days on the beach or exploring the area, and the evenings sitting around the stove in the kitchen, talking. The weather was perfect. It was harvest time and fruit of all sorts was abundant, some of it straight from the trees in Valya's backyard. We were enjoying ourselves enormously. Valya told us a great deal about local customs, about the friction among ethnic groups and the hostility toward Russians. The top official in local government was usually a native of the region, but the real power was in the hands of the second-in-command, a Russian.

On the tenth day of our stay, we were awakened in the middle of the night to banging on the door. Valya opened it to find two militiamen whom she knew personally. They demanded the passports of her guests—and we were the only guests. They pretended to examine our papers carefully and then handed us an already-prepared paper ordering us to leave the area by morning.

It could have been worse. For a moment, I thought my time had come. Valya was outraged. Nothing like this had ever happened before and she wanted to put up a fight. We dissuaded her. It was best for us to leave as quickly as possible. Understandably, we were upset. We felt humiliated, unable to defend ourselves. We did not even have the meager rights of ordinary Soviet citizens.[2]

We caught the first bus from Kelasuri to Sukhumi and, from there, took a bus to Lake Ritsa, a high mountain lake several hours drive away. The drive took us through spectacular mountain scenery and, by the time we reached our destination, we felt better. The sight of the lake pushed our cares out of our mind. Lake Ritsa is situated about 10,000 feet above sea level in the midst of a mixed forest of conifers and subtropical vegetation with snowcapped mountain peaks in the distance. There were several empty buses parked near the hotel, but we did not see many people. They had scattered round the lake and into the woods or were in the hotel restaurant. We had no trouble booking a room for a few days. The receptionist told us that the bus tours always departed in early afternoon, so as to get back to their coastal resorts before dark. Darkness fell early here because of the mountains. Few people stayed overnight.

We were given a large room with a view of the lake. It had a private bathroom with hot and cold running water, an unheard-of luxury for citizens

---

2. Valya wrote us that the reason for our expulsion was that Stalin and his cortege had passed through Kelasuri on their way to one of the several government vacation houses in Georgia. The local authorities had orders to clear out all "suspicious" persons. The following year, we spent our vacation at Valya's without incident.

of no importance. We were told that the hotel had originally been built as a hunting lodge for high Soviet officials. By the time we settled in, most of the buses had left. Absolute peace descended. We spent four days there. In the mornings, we were far away on the other side of the lake or deep in the woods before the buses arrived. We stayed away until they had left. We'd return to the hotel tired and hungry, ready to spend the rest of the day over a leisurely dinner of freshly caught lake trout. We would watch the lake change colors, and then go early to bed. It was a perfect setting for our frazzled nerves.

We returned by way of Adler, where we boarded a plane for Moscow.

As we neared Moscow, all my anxieties returned. I had a sinking feeling every time I returned home from vacation. Home? I had no home. Home is a place where you belong, where you feel safe and secure among people you love and who love you. Home is a place where you can shut out the world if you want to do so. I lost my home when I left my family and lost my native land. I had not found another, not in the narrow sense of family and domicile, not in the larger sense of love of country. After twenty years in the Soviet Union, I felt more than ever a stranger in the land. I truly was a rootless cosmopolitan!

I still feel that way—homeless. I have adjusted and adapted and made new friends. Yet I do not feel that I belong anywhere. I gaze in wonder at my cousins who have lived all their lives in the cities where they were born and raised and see how they identify with all that goes on around them. I do not feel part of anyone's life, and that, I believe, is the meaning of homelessness. That is what being uprooted does to a person.

I do not recall my reactions to what may have been the most important event of 1951, the Soviet Union's acquisition of the atom bomb. The news was made public in an interview with Stalin that was published in October. In reply to a journalist's undoubtedly prearranged question as to whether it was true that the Soviet Union had developed an atom bomb, Stalin replied, "Yes, the Soviet Union successfully tested an atom bomb on October 4th." Neither do I remember my reaction earlier, when the Americans dropped the bombs on Hiroshima and Nagasaki. The horrors of the war had been so great that this seemed like just another horror.

Of the political trials in the Communist-controlled countries of Eastern Europe, the culmination and the one that had the greatest impact on us was that of Rudolf Slansky, former general secretary of the Czechoslovakian Communist Party, and other leading Czech Communists.

Slansky, a Jew, had been a political emigré in Moscow before the war and had lived in the Lux Hotel. He returned to Czechoslovakia after the Germans were driven out and played a leading part in Czechoslovakian politics as a staunch supporter of Stalin and his policies. He was active in the pursuit and persecution of "enemies of the people." As recently as July 1951, his fiftieth birthday had been celebrated with much fanfare and with congratulatory telegrams from Soviet leaders published in the Soviet press. Yet he still was arrested in November 1951. The trial, which opened in Prague in November 1952, was the last show trial of the Stalin period and it followed the pattern of the Moscow trials of 1936–1939 with preposterous charges of espionage, of plots to restore capitalism, of working for foreign intelligence, and abject confessions. But there was a frightening new element: Slansky was accused of being a Zionist agent.

The Czechoslovakian government had openly and officially opposed anti-Semitism. Slansky himself had organized the campaign to root out anti-Semitism. Now, he was being charged with having prevented the disclosure of the "true nature" of Zionism!

There were twelve defendants in the Slansky trial, ten of them Jewish, all of whom were found guilty and most of whom were put to death.

The next blow was not long in coming.

Early on the morning of January 13, 1953, Abram woke me. That day remains one of the most vivid in my memory. Abram always got up before I did and took in the morning papers. I grumbled, for I hated to be awakened unnecessarily, but he kept shaking me, telling me "Wake up, something terrible has happened!" He sat on the bed and read aloud a TASS report stating that the Soviet security organs had uncovered an organized conspiracy by doctors who plotted to kill Soviet leaders and other citizens by prescribing the wrong medical treatment for them. Abram read out the names of the conspirators—all but three of the nine were Jewish. The physicians named were among the most eminent in their fields and their patients were top Soviet leaders, including Stalin. The Jewish doctors were accused of being agents of "bourgeois nationalist Jewry," the non-Jewish doctors with being agents of British intelligence. According to the TASS statement, the "doctor-poisoners" had already caused the deaths of Zhdanov and another Soviet leader. An unsigned article on the front page of *Pravda* under the banner headline, "Contemptible Spies and Murderers under the Guise of Professors," presented the gory details. The plot had been uncovered due to the vigilance and patriotism of Dr. Lydia Timashuk, a radiologist in the Kremlin hospital who had observed the doctors' evil actions and written a letter to Stalin. The investigation would be completed in the near future.

Not for one moment did we believe the report.

"God only knows where this will lead," Abram said.

My editor that day was Aerova. She looked very solemn when I walked into the office.

"Have you seen today's papers, Mary?"

I said that I had.

"Isn't it terrible? The scum! They give all Jews a bad name! They ought to be shot!" She continued ranting and raving as I looked over my assignment and prepared to start work. I did not utter a word.

"Why don't you say something? Don't you have an opinion?" she demanded, interrupting her diatribe.

"I haven't absorbed it yet," was my reply, and she had to accept that.

Many of my coworkers were Jewish: my immediate boss, my closest colleagues, several of the Russian-language editors, the English translators, the German translator, one of the French translators, and two of the typists. Still, nobody said anything about the most sensational news of the day. All seemed to be stunned. There must have been a general TASS meeting that day or the next. Meetings were always called on such occasions so the masses could show their support and condemn whatever was slated for condemnation. I do not remember it. Most likely, I did not attend, either because I was working against a deadline or because I had gone home after my shift.

Shock waves went through the entire population, not just Jews. Whereas accusations of espionage, charges of lack of patriotism, and officially inspired mistrust of all persons of Jewish descent were serious and contributed to the anti-Semitic atmosphere of those years, they did not affect the majority of average citizens. The charges of deliberate medical mistreatment presented under huge headlines such as "Doctor-Poisoners" affected everyone who had ever used the services of a doctor, nurse, or pharmacist. "Incredible!" people said. Most incredible of all was that they believed it. The great majority of the people believed the unbelievable.[3]

Apparently, even many Jews, including some with a background similar to mine, believed it, too. I was at Ahsia's when a woman I knew casually, a former American, dropped in. She had come to share her distress and fears with Ahsia.

"How could they do what they did?" she said. "Jews! And doctors, the most humane of professions! To do such terrible things! What will happen to us now?"

She was a friend from back home whom Ahsia had known her for many years, so Ahsia was not afraid to speak out.

"Do you know what you are saying?" she said. "You are saying that you believe the report!"

"Don't you?" the woman asked in surprise.[4]

---

3. The poet Yevgeni Yevtushenko writes that he, too, believed the charges. See Yevtushenko, *A Precocious Autobiography* (New York: Dutton, 1963), p. 80.

4. Quite a few years later, when we were both back in the United States, I reminded the woman of that conversation. She denied it, asserting that she had never believed the report. She had completely forgotten. She was sincere then. She was sincere now.

"Ordinary" citizens seized upon the "disclosures" with a vengeance. Letters poured in by the thousands from persons claiming to have been improperly treated by Jewish medical personnel. Doctors were accused of deliberate misdiagnoses; surgeons were accused of bungling operations; pharmacists of mixing poisons into prescribed medicines. Hundreds of Jewish medical personnel were fired from hospitals, clinics, medical schools, and laboratories as "preventive" measures. Insulting Jews became a national pastime. Jews, especially the men, trod softly, trying to keep out of the way of hoodlums who were as likely as not to beat them up if they got the chance. For many Jewish families living in communal apartments with non-Jewish neighbors, each day was a nightmare. Jewish children were taunted by schoolmates, and they were picked on by playmates in the courtyard and the kindergarten. Could the pogrom atmosphere have been worse under the tsars when the "Black Hundreds" incited mobs with cries of "Kill the Jews, Save Russia!"?

Rumors that preparations were underway to deport all Jews to Siberia were widespread. I wondered aloud to Abram whether it might be possible to escape via Alaska (a fantasy of mine). I had suggested to Abram long before the "Doctors' Plot" that perhaps we or I should leave Moscow for a while and go off to some distant part of the country away from the center of the action where no one knew me, but he said that this was not a good idea at all. In Moscow, there were others like myself; in a provincial town, I'd stick out like a "white crow," fair game for local bureaucrats eager to distinguish themselves.

I did not believe the rumors of deportation plans and am still not convinced that they had any basis in fact, although memoirs that have appeared in the West say that they were true. The Soviet leaders must have been aware of the effect such a Nazi-like action would have internationally, especially on friends of the Soviet Union who persisted in denying that anti-Semitism was an official policy or the Soviet government.

As far as our neighbors and jobs were concerned, Abram and I had no trouble. Outdoors in the street, it was a different story. I was seldom bothered, but Abram was vulnerable. He looked like an easy mark. He wore glasses, which to Russians was the sign of a wimp; though of average height (about 5'8"), he was slightly built, and in spite of his light brown hair, hazel eyes and very white, freckled skin, he was always recognized as being Jewish. I still feel an ache, mostly for Abram, when I recall an ugly incident in which we were involved. We had gone into a riverside cafe one Sunday. A group of drunken men at a nearby table began to make anti-Semitic remarks, trying to provoke Abram. What could he do? Take on a gang of hoodlums? Complain to the management? We got up and walked out to the sound of jeers. We were both upset, but Abram was sick with humiliation.

328 / MY LIFE IN STALINIST RUSSIA

We found ourselves trying to foresee situations that might turn unpleasant and avoided them. But that was not always possible. One had to go about one's daily tasks. He became so sensitized to slurs that he avoided crowds, stores, and public transportation whenever he could.

In the midst of all this hysteria, I received a birthday present in the mail from my parents. The gift was so inappropriate that it was funny—a book of Jewish folklore accompanied by a letter saying that they wanted me to know more about my Jewish heritage. I remarked wryly to Abram that this book could be used against me as evidence of my ties to bourgeois national-ist American Jewry.

Jokingly, I kept among my official papers the cover of a package of Aunt Jemima pancake flour that had come in one of the yearly parcels my parents sent me. I said I would tell my interrogators that this was the picture of my grandmother, and that as a member of an oppressed race about which the Soviets were so concerned, they ought to let me go.

The relentless march towards an unknown fate was stopped in its tracks on March 5, 1953. Once again, Abram woke me early in the morning with momentous news: Stalin was dead.

We were not unprepared. It had been reported two days earlier that Stalin had suffered a cerebral hemorrhage. Nevertheless, the idea that Stalin was dead was overwhelming.

I was working the morning shift that week. People in the street were grim-faced. Many were weeping. As on the day the Doctors' Plot was an-nounced, Aerova was my editor. Tears streamed down her cheeks. Mournful music came from the public loudspeakers and over the indoor radios.

"What will happen to us now? What will happen to this country with-out Stalin to watch over it?"

For the next few weeks, I heard those words again and again.

To a certain extent, Abram and I felt the same way. Better the evil you know than the one you don't! We felt no grief at Stalin's demise, but neither did we expect any good to come of it. We were pessimistic and feared the worst.

Stalin's body lay in state in the Hall of Columns of the House of Trade Unions on the corner of Bolshaya Dimitrovka and Okhotnyi Ryad, a ten-minute walk from the TASS office building. The line to view the body stretched all the way to our corner at TASS and beyond. The crowds waited patiently to get a closer look in death of the leader most had only seen from afar as they marched past the Lenin mausoleum on national holidays. While most had come to pay their sincere respects, they were also curious about the other leaders who took turns standing on watch by the coffin—Georgi Malenkov, Lazar Kaganovich, Viacheslav Molotov, as well as other well-known personalities.

At the office, everyone not engaged in urgent work was permitted to leave early to go and stand in the line.

"Come, Mary, let's go," said Aerova when our work was done.

"No, I'll go with my husband," I replied.

I did not go the next day or any other day. Abram went with his organization. Along with friends and coworkers, he stood in line for several hours. Mounted militia kept the line orderly.

March 9th, the day of the funeral, was declared a national day of mourning. I was off that day and went to Liz's. Abram went to work, but expected his office would close early so that people could go to the funeral. He arrived at Liz's an hour or two after I did and told us that crowds were gathering in the streets. Little by little, from Liz's neighbors and our friends and acquaintances who stopped by in the course of the day, we heard the frightening story of what was happening on the streets leading to Red Square. The militia, mounted and otherwise, lost control of the huge crowds that thronged the streets. The surging mass crushed people underfoot, lifted them aloft, pushed them against lamp posts, and smashed them against trucks that were set as barriers. These barriers became instruments of death. Liz was worried. Her son, Donald, not quite fifteen, had gone to see what he could see. It was from him when he returned that we got the most graphic account. He had been in one of the worst spots—Trubnaya Square. He described the sheer terror of an amorphous body coming at him. He barely escaped with his life by climbing to the top of a pole.

For the next few days, the word *Khodynka* was on everybody's lips. This was a reference to the disaster of Khodynka Field outside Moscow at the celebration of the coronation of Nicholas II in 1896. The crowd got out of hand and it was estimated that two thousand people were crushed to death. There may have been as many killed at Stalin's funeral. Not a word about the disaster appeared in the Soviet press.

Thus did Stalin's reign end—in bloodshed and a massacre.

As was the custom in Russia when a tsar died, a general amnesty was declared. Announced two weeks after Stalin's death, it freed convicts who had less than five years to serve and reduced the sentences of others. It did not extend to prisoners convicted under Article Fifty-Eight—anti-Soviet agitation, espionage, treason. Those were political prisoners, although the Soviet judicial system, unlike the tsarist, did not recognize the political prisoner category. Muscovites were not overjoyed by the amnesty. Many remarked that hordes of common criminals would be released to prey upon the population. Indeed, there was an increase in street crime for a year or two after the amnesty.

The public was in a state of suspended animation, wondering what would come next. When the next event came, it was indeed cataclysmic. On April 4th, the doctors were declared innocent of all charges and freed. A TASS report said that a meticulous review of the preliminary investigation revealed that the charges against the doctors were false; their confessions had been obtained by "impermissible" methods of interrogation. All the doctors had been released and reinstated in their positions. Two had died under torture, but that was not mentioned. The report said that those responsible for the slander had been arrested and would stand trial. An article in *Pravda* on April 6th exonerated Mikhoels who (posthumously) had been linked to the "plot."

Such an admission was unprecedented in Soviet history. It was not only an admission of "mistakes"; it was an admission of fraud and torture. This lifted a tiny corner of the curtain, disclosing the methods used by the secret police.

For us, it was the first glimmer of hope.

\* \* \*

The events of the following months were anticlimactic: the arrests of major secret police figures, the exposé and execution of Beria (the first of the former leaders to fall and the only one to be executed), the announcement in September that the Soviet Union had the hydrogen bomb, musical chairs in the hierarchy. A struggle for power was going on in the upper reaches of power, but we knew very little about it. Events were reported after the fact, usually without explanation.

A heavy load was finally lifted from our shoulders. Maria was released from her connection with the secret police. Apparently, they lost interest in me. With the shake-up underway in their ministry, they had their own positions to worry about. By the summer of 1953, I felt secure enough to quit my job at TASS. For the next twelve years that I lived in the Soviet Union, I worked at home as a freelance translator and editor. Abram continued at his job. I even got to meet some of his colleagues.

Toward the end of 1955 and throughout 1956, prisoners returned from jails and labor camps, first at a trickle, then a river. Rose's husband George came home in 1956, gaunt and toothless. He rallied quickly, restored his health, got his old job back, and joined the Communist Party of the Soviet Union. He did not speak with us about the years of detention. Nadya, Aloysha, and Maya Ulanovsky returned. They, especially Nadya, spoke freely and in detail about their years of imprisonment. From them we got the most complete picture, beginning with their arrests, through the investigations, interrogations, convictions, and life in the camps. Incidentally, Nadya was questioned over and over about Ahsia. We surmised that those who did not return had been executed or had died. None of the Jewish writers and other cultural figures returned. It was not until I was back in the United States that I learned they had been shot in August 1952, just a few months before Stalin's death.

At first, the returnees were pardoned. Then the process of "rehabilitation" began (reversal of the conviction and restoration of rights). Families instituted rehabilitation proceedings for their loved ones who had not survived.

Jockeying for position in the Party and government leadership went on for about two years until Nikita Khrushchev came out on top. The events of 1953 to 1956 prepared the way for the most staggering event of all.

The twentieth congress of the CPSU opened in February 1956 in the usual manner, with the usual speeches. As First Secretary, Khrushchev delivered the keynote speech. His report was approved unanimously. Other Party officials spoke about various aspects of the economy, defense, foreign policy, and ideology. The newspapers carried all the speeches in full, accompanied by large portraits of the speakers. Then came a hiatus in the press with only scant information. Khrushchev gave another speech that was not printed in the press. This was the now-famous "secret speech" that revealed many of the unspeakable crimes of Stalin and his henchmen during the entire period of Stalin's undisputed power.

Rumors about the speech started up immediately, but it was several months before we found out more reliably what was in it. At first, copies of the speech marked "top secret" were distributed to selected organizations and read at closed Party meetings there. Then, the speech was circulated among wider audiences of Party membership. Later, it was read in offices, factories, universities, and institutes to selected non-Party members as well as to Party members. In the summer of 1956, we shared a *dacha* (country house) with Ahsia and had already moved there when Abram attended a reading of the speech for Party members only and we heard the details from him. The revelations were awesome, even for those of us who had suspected much and had heard first-hand accounts from ex-prisoners. Khrushchev had not minced words about the methods used to obtain confessions. The names of the victims he mentioned were known to everyone. We thought of the unmentioned little people, some of them friends, many acquaintances, and what they had endured.

Though much was said, much was left unsaid. The names of the rehabilitated victims did not include any of the leaders of the various oppositions in the struggle for power after Lenin's death. Another thirty years would pass before Bolsheviks such as Bukharin, Rykov, Zinoviev, Kamenev, and Trotsky would be permitted their places in history.

\* \* \*

This is not a fairy tale in which good triumphs over evil and everyone lives happily ever after. There were many ups and downs ahead. The pendulum swung between the comparatively liberal policies of the early sixties and the tightening of the screws that followed in the later sixties and seventies.

Anti-Semitism raised its ugly head time and again, sometimes with official encouragement. Of course, there can be no comparison with Stalin's reign of terror, but the wrongdoing of forty years could not be undone in a day or in a speech. The machinery of repression was not dismantled, and due process remained an incomprehensible concept in Soviet law.

However, it is the end of the story of my life in the Soviet Union. The next nine years can be divided into two periods—three years fighting for my husband's life and the next six years fighting to get out of the country. Abram fell ill with an incurable disease (pemphigus) at the end of 1956. The miracle we strove for and hoped for did not occur. He died in the autumn of 1959. With nothing left to hold me, I started my struggle for an exit visa, determined to fight to the end, even if the end turned out to be Siberia. I finally succeeded with the help of Elena Stasova, a one-time secretary to Lenin, a noted Old Bolshevik from an aristocratic Russian family, who in the last years of her life helped many individuals who had been wronged.

# SUGGESTIONS
## FOR FURTHER READING

On Birobidzhan, see Robert Weinberg, *Stalin's Forgotten Zion: Birobidzhan and the Making of a Soviet Jewish Homeland* (Berkeley: University of California Press, 1998).

On the factory where Mackler worked as an apprentice, see Kenneth M. Straus, *Factory and Community in Stalin's Russia: The Making of an Industrial Working Class* (Pittsburgh: University of Pittsburgh Press, 1997)

On state policies toward orphans and dependent children, see Alan M. Ball, *And Now My Soul Is Hardened: Abandoned Children in Soviet Russia, 1918–1930* (Berkeley: University of California Press, 1994).

On Magnitogorsk, see John Scott, *Behind the Urals: An American Worker in Russia's City of Steel* (Bloomington: Indiana University Press, 1989); Stephen Kotkin, *Magnetic Mountain* (Berkeley: University of California Press, 1995).

On Soviet marriage laws and policies toward women, see Wendy Z. Goldman, *Women, the State and Revolution: Soviet Family Policy and Social Life, 1917–1936* (Cambridge: Cambridge University Press, 1993).

On the purges, see Robert Conquest, *The Great Terror: Stalin's Purge of the Thirties* (New York: Macmillan, 1968).

On abortion, see Wendy Goldman, "Women, Abortion, and the State, 1917–1936," in *Russia's Women: Accommodation, Resistance, Transformation,* ed. Barbara Evans Clements, Barbara Alpern Engel, and Christine D. Worobec (Berkeley: University of California Press, 1991), pp. 243–266.

On Stalin's unpreparedness for World War II, see, for example, Harrison Salisbury, *The 900 Days: The Siege of Leningrad* (New York: Harper & Row, 1969); Robert C. Tucker, *Stalin in Power: The Revolution from Above, 1928–1941* (New York: W.W. Norton, 1990).

For a detailed description of the Babi Yar massacre, see Anatoly Kuznetsov, *Babi Yar* (New York: The Dial Press, 1967).

On the fate of Soviet Jews during World War II, see *Bitter Legacy: Confronting the Holocaust in the USSR,* edited by Zvi Gitelman (Bloomington: Indiana University Press, 1997).

On Elena Stasova and other female notables of the Communist Party, see Barbara Evans Clements, *Bolshevik Women* (Cambridge: Cambridge University Press, 1997).

# INDEX

⊱∞ᖇⓇᘯᘓ

Page numbers in *italics* indicate illustrations.

*Bicycle Thief, The* (film), 319
"Big Koenig" (Hungarian Communist), 218
biology, 99, 102, 103, 114
Birobidzhan, xi–xii, 9, 30, 48, 63; arrival in, 16–22; bedbugs in, 20–21, 219; departure from, 24–25, 26–29, 35, 69; Jewish immigration to, 43, 176; journey to, 10–11; life in, 22–24; washing facilities in, 105
birth control, 114
black market, 313
Blacks, 72–74
Bolsheviks, 31, 111, 331; marriage and, 150n6; origin of, 2, 53, 54n4; revolutionary morality and, 255. *See also* Old Bolsheviks
Borodin, Mikhail, 75, 92
bourgeoisie, 40
Bredel, Willi, 140
brigade system, 98–99
Britain, 130, 157, 161; air war with Germany (1940), 182; Communist Party of, 227; as "imperialist aggressor," 177; warnings about German attack on Russia, 183; World War II bombing of, 240
Brooks, Miriam, 8, *199, 211*
Budonny, Semyon, 290
Bukharin, Nikolai, 331
Bullitt, William, 97
Bund (Jewish Social-Democratic Party), 6
bureaucrats, xiii, 196, 280, 327; in Birobidzhan, 23; caricatures of, 33
Byelorussia, 18, 117, 162, 170; German occupation of, 259; Jews from, 176; partisans in, 187; Soviet annexations and, 182

Cantor, Harry, 91
*Capital* (Marx), 239
capitalism, 42, 255, 296, 325; caricatures of, 33; peasants and, 43
*Casablanca* (film), 319–20
Case, Albert, 148–50
Central Asia, 213, 217, 252, 259, 272
Chambers, Whittaker, 134
*Chapayev* (film), 107
Chaplin, Charlie, 267
Chernov (TASS official), 234, 254, 258, 282, 286; death of, 314; foreign press and, 233; as Old Bolshevik, 118; recommendation from, 251
Chicherin, Georgi, 90

children, 158, 169, 217; death of, 220–21; evacuation of, 235; flight from German army and, 186; unmarried mothers and, 256
China, 12, 75, 88, 90, 143
Chinese language, 83, 149
Chuvashia, 39, 53
*Circus* (film), 107
citizenship, 3, 76, 77, 85
*City Lights* (film), 267
civil rights, 40, 43
Civil War (Russian), 39, 42, 62, 140, 173; casualties of, 143; Crimean battles of, 247; fighting in Rostov, 178; Old Bolsheviks and, 190; population loss and, 120; White Guards in, 258
"claques," 145
class consciousness, 43
class struggle, 109, 112
clothing, 41, 48, 52, 170; bartering for, 218; loss of, 82; Soviet hospitals and, 221
Cold War, xi, xiii
*Collected Works* (Lenin), 57
collective farms, 22, 23n2, 46, 62; factories and, 88; Jewish, 77; private enterprise and, 313; in Soviet Georgia, 308, 311
Cominform (Communist Information Bureau), 288, 300
Comintern (Communist International), 87, 113, 123, 141, 158; arrests and, 306; foreign (non-Soviet) Communists in, 152, 315; Foreign Languages Publishing House and, 82, 83; purges in, 147; replacement of, 288; summer camp for children, 187; train reserved for, 196; World War II evacuation of, 213, 215, 220
Commissariat of Defense, 122–37, 146, 171, 235; closing of school, 246; Great Terror and, 278; interrupted education and, 258
communes, 44–45
Communist Party (Soviet/Russian), xi, xiv, 2, 72; American Communists and, 80; Central Committee, 113, 252, 284; expulsion from, 50, 53, 258, 283, 303; foreign language publishing and, 85; higher education and, 99–100; history of, 125; housing privileges and, 103, 104; loyalty to, 176; membership in, xiii, 22–23, 53, 88, 117, 154, 285; officials of, 15, 38–39;

conscription and, 268; outbreak of
World War II and, 182; propaganda
of, 254; Reichstag fire (1933) and,
97; Soviet propaganda efforts against,
241; Soviet reports of atrocities, 253;
Spanish Civil War and, 130. *See also*
fascism
*Neues Deutschland* (newspaper), 268, 269
*New Masses* (magazine), 84
New Year's holiday, 293–94
Nikolayev, Leonid, 110, 111, 112
NKVD (People's Commissariat of Internal
Affairs), 109, 125, 145, 152, 175,
176. *See also* secret police
*nomenklatura*, 285
*Not Without Laughter* (Hughes), 73
Nuremburg trials, 274

October Revolution (1917), 92
Odessa, 193, 321–22
Oken, Sophie, 84, 86, 141
Old Bolsheviks, 116, 118, 190, 251, 332.
*See also* Bolsheviks
Ordzhonikidze, Sergo, 126
Orlova, Lyubov, 107
Ostankino ("student town"), 104–105,
107, 113
OVIR (department of visas and
registration), 1, 2, 3
OZET (Organization for Agricultural
Resettlement of Jewish Working
People), 9, 77

Pale of Settlement, 32, 43, 114, 143
Palestine, 298
Pankratova, Anna, 116
paranoia, 290
Parodi, Tina, 290
Paryshev, Lucy, 218
passports, 63, 69, 323; OVIR and, 2, 3;
stolen, 70. *See also* internal passports
patriotism, 117, 172, 258, 288; anti-
Semitism and, 326; intelligence work
and, 125
Pavlich, Margo, 157–58, 257
Pavlovna, Vera, 93
peasants, 22, 26, 39, 151; capitalism and,
43; as city workers, 158; collective
farm markets and, 46; education
system and, 99; famine and, 62;
housing and, 178; Volga Germans
and, 188n1, 216; as working class, 42
People's Commissariat for Foreign Affairs,
77
permanent resident visa, 3

Peter the Great, 105
petty bourgeoisie, 43
plumbing facilities, 30, 38, 39, 105, 138;
in Birobidzhan, 17, 20; in student
dormitories, 113
pogroms, 5, 133, 194
Pokrovsky, Mikhail, 116
Poland, 117, 137, 162, 177, 299; Jews
from, 179; war with Russia (1612),
188
Politburo, 33, 153
Pollak, Betty, 84, 281–82
POUM (United Marxist Workers' Party),
130
*Pravda* (newspaper), 109, 260, 300; anti-
American campaign and, 296;
"Doctor's Plot" and, 325, 330
pregnancy, 180, 182, 184, 192; fear of,
114; regulations and, 185. *See also*
abortion
prison camps, 284, 289, 306, 330
privacy, 164
private enterprise, 169
private property, 313
*Professor Mamlock* (film), 161
Prokofiev, Sergei, 274
proletariat, 10, 22, 42–43, 99
prostitution, 265, 273–74
proverbs, 171
Provisional Government (1917), 105
Pulkka, Elvira, 164
punishment units, 146
purges, 2, 109, 131, 138–63
Pyatakov, Yuri, 125, 126

Radek, Karl, 125–26
radio committee, 261, 281, 284, 285
Raikin, Arkady, 268
ration cards, 35, 37, 40–41, 55; Red Army
demobilization and, 279; stolen, 62
Red Army, 125, 131, 162, 180, 184;
German invasion and, 185, 186; Jews
in, 259–60; retreat of, 185, 190;
soldiers' leave in, 236; World War II
battles of, 219, 247, 248–49
Red Squad (Los Angeles police), 8
refugees, 192, 193
registrar's bureau. *See* ZAGS (registrar's
bureau)
Reichstag fire (1933), 97
rest homes, 120
Ribbentrop, Joachim von, 161
Ricardo, David, 239

LAURIE BERNSTEIN
is Associate Professor of History at Rutgers University, Camden, and
author of *Sonia's Daughters: Prostitutes and
Their Regulation in Imperial Russia.*


ROBERT WEINBERG
is Associate Professor of History at Swarthmore College.
He is author of *The Revolution of 1905 in Odessa:
Blood on the Steps* (Indiana University Press) and
*Stalin's Forgotten Zion: Birobidzhan and the Making of a
Soviet Jewish Homeland: An Illustrated History, 1928–1996.*